Works of H... ...ton
available ... Methuen

A TRAVELLER IN ROME

A TRAVELLER IN ROME

BY

H. V. MORTON

METHUEN

First published in Great Britain in 1957 by Methuen
This edition published in 2001 by Methuen Publishing Ltd
215 Vauxhall Bridge Road, London SW1V 1EJ

Copyright © 1957, 1984, the Estate of H V Morton
The right of H V Morton to be identified
as the author of this work has been asserted in accordance with the
Copyright, Designs and Patents Act, 1988

Methuen Publishing Limited Reg. No. 3543167

A CIP catalogue record for this book
is available from the British Library

ISBN 0 413 75440 5

Printed and bound in Great Britain by
Cox & Wyman Ltd, Reading, Berkshire

1 3 5 7 9 10 8 6 4 2

CONTENTS

ACKNOWLEDGMENTS

My thanks are due to those who have faced the rigours of this subject and whose books I have mentioned, and also to the following for much help and kindness: Monsignor Hugh O'Flaherty, Father Anthony Kenny, of the English College, Father Alfred Wilson, of SS. Giovanni e Paolo, Major Dieter de Balthazar, of the Swiss Guard, Dr Angelini, of the Museum of Rome, Comm. Marcello Piermattei, OBE, Superintendent of the Non-Catholic Cemetery, Dr Guido Ricci and Dr Zaccardini Mario, of the *Commissariato per il Turismo*, Rome, and Dr Luciano Merlo, of the *Ente Provinciale per il Turismo*, Rome, Professor Ward Perkins, of the British School in Rome, and Messrs Longmans, Green for permission to quote from *The Shrine of St Peter*, Sir Alec Randall and Messrs William Heinemann, for permission to quote from *Vatican Assignment*, the Maryland Historical Society for the photograph of Elizabeth Patterson Bonaparte, Miss Margaret R. Scherer of the Metropolitan Museum of Art, New York, Messrs Glyn, Mills and Co, for the sketch of Charles Mills by the Count d'Orsay, and to their Archivist, Mr S. W. Shelton, without whose help I should have been unable to solve the enigma of Charles Andrew Mills. My thanks are due in full measure to Mr D. H. Varley, Chief Librarian of the South African Public Library, Cape Town, and to his skilled and obliging staff.

London, 1957   H.V.M.

[NOTE TO 2ND EDITION]

I am obliged to Mr E. C. Kennedy of Malvern College for pointing out the doubtful consolation that in the first edition of this book I erred with many distinguished authorities, including the *Encyclopaedia Britannica*, in repeating 'the Augustus legend' in connection with the Julian reformed calendar. This I have altered on page 117.

1958   H.V.M.

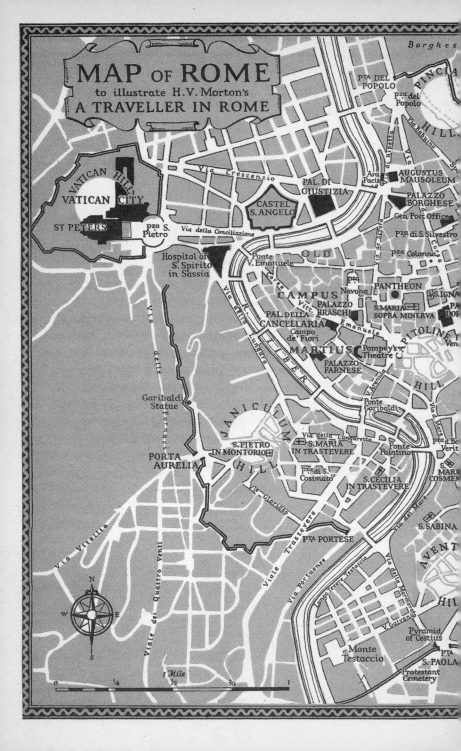

CHAPTER ONE

From a Roman balcony – the noise of Rome – walking about Rome – breakfast near St Peter's – the Fontana di Trevi – the growth of a superstition

§ 1

Those of us who had not fallen asleep glanced casually down at the Alps. They lay beneath our wings like a model in a geological museum, and though it was July, many a summit was still white.

There comes over one sometimes a sense of the wonder and fantasy of this age, and, as I adjusted my chair to a more comfortable angle, I thought how preposterous it was to be speeding through the sky to Rome, many of us unaware of the great barrier which awed and terrified our ancestors. While I looked down, trying in vain to identify the passes—the Mont Cenis, the St Gothard, the Great St Bernard and the Little, and the famous Brenner—a series of pictures flashed through my mind. . . . Hannibal and his hungry elephants, Charles the Bald dying in the Mont Cenis, the Emperor Henry IV hurrying through the blizzards of January, 1077, to make peace with the Pope, while the Empress and her ladies were strapped into ox-hides and let down over the frozen slopes like bundles of hay.

'Would you like a glucose sweet or a peppermint?' asked the air hostess, as we crossed the Alps.

The feelings of many centuries of Romeward bound travellers were expressed in a sentence by Lady Mary Wortley Montagu, when she wrote from Turin in 1720. 'I am now, thank God, happily past the Alps.' Even in her day, when the Grand Tour was beautifully organized, the passage of the Alps was full of danger or at least of apprehension. It was usual for the coaches to be unbolted and sent over on the backs of mules, while the travellers,

13

wrapped in bearskins and wearing beaver caps and mittens, sat in armchairs slung between two poles and were carried over the pass by nimble mountaineers. Montaigne, who went to Italy to forget his gall-stones, was carried up the Mont Cenis, but on the summit was transferred to a toboggan: and in the same pass Horace Walpole's lapdog, Tory, was seized and eaten by a wolf. Even while these random thoughts passed through my mind, we had left the Alps far behind us, and it was not long before we were fastening our belts for Rome.

The drive from the airport into Rome was long and dreary, but all the time I was thinking with pleasure of the 'room with balcony' to which I was speeding. For weeks I had lived with a mental picture of this balcony, though I had never seen it. There might not be bougainvillaea, I told myself, but no doubt there would be geraniums in pots; and I would stand there in the evening and watch the sun setting behind St Peter's, as so many had done before me, while the swifts—would there be swifts in July?—would cut the air with cries which every Roman child knows means 'Gesù . . . Gesù . . . Gesù!'

We saw the ruins of an aqueduct limping across the landscape, and though I recognized it from photographs I had seen, I could not give it a name. I was finding out in the first ten minutes that a visit to Rome is not a matter of discovery, but of remembrance. We dashed through the outer suburbs, where blocks of stark concrete flats, the modern descendants of the Roman *insulae*, but apparently a good deal more solid and upright, stood amongst piles of rubble; then we passed through the Aurelian Wall by way of a turreted gate and joined a great press of green tramcars and 'buses, while illustrations from books, the subjects of post-cards from friends, and the pictures upon the walls of old-fashioned vicarages, sprang into life all round us. Here and there we recognized an obelisk and here and there a fountain.

I transferred myself and my luggage to a taxi and sped downhill through a hot, golden afternoon towards my room and balcony. I caught a glimpse of a great number of people drinking coffee under blue umbrellas in the Via Vittorio Veneto, then we swerved into a side street and drew up before a rather severe archway.

§ 2

Could this be my balcony? Was this the place I had been dreaming about for weeks? I could see nothing but the building opposite, which had been carelessly splashed with brown limewash many years ago. From its windows faces looked at me with the hostile curiosity of those who observe a new boy. Men wearing odd little sculptors' caps made of newspaper were repairing the roof. I could see shops, restaurants, a barber's shop, and a quick lunch bar where food simmered in pans in the window, together with plates of peaches and jars of olives and artichokes. At the entrance to a subterranean vault a hunchback cobbler sat gnomelike, with his mouth full of nails, which he swiftly transferred to the sole of a shoe he was repairing. I turned away disappointed, another illusion gone, for this was not the balcony which more fortunate writers always seemed to find, with its romantic view of St Peter's.

My pensione was in a side street, within a few hundred yards of the Borghese Gardens. It was a rich and impressive address as long as friends used the post and did not call; then they would have seen a *cortile* in which waiters from the restaurant next door were always shelling prawns and shouting endearments to any maidservant who happened to appear at the upper windows. The caller also would have met the terrible lift, for Italy is a country of intransigent lifts. It is an invention that has not become properly acclimatized. It is often kept locked and is frequently in charge of a familiar, an old woman who lives in a basement and pops out with the key. Sometimes you have to pay to use it and on countless occasions you can go up, but have to walk down.

The pensione lift was possessed of a devil. I have never known a more evil-minded piece of machinery. It had good days and bad days. When angry, it would spit little blue sparks and stop on the wrong floor. Nearly every week someone had to be rescued between floors, and men in stained overalls would be hastily summoned to exorcize it. Sometimes, if you suddenly pressed the button on the ground floor, you would capture an aged woman on the top who would be delivered below like some angry Athena, flourishing a broom instead of a spear. On one occasion I trapped a dustman and two garbage bins.

For these reasons I often preferred to walk up the five flights of beautiful marble stairs. The exquisite steps of Rome are among my first memories: steps of marble and travertine, shallow Renaissance steps, so much kinder to the leg muscles than the steep steps of ancient Rome: steps curving left, right and centre from the Piazza di Spagna, as if to show you what steps can do if given a chance; noble steps up to S. Maria in Aracoeli; elegant steps to the Quirinal; majestic steps to St Peter's and to innumerable churches, fountains and palaces—the most wonderful steps in the world. Even the stairs in my pensione were poor relations of the Spanish Steps, and their marble treads and gentle gradient compensated me for those moments when the lift was cantankerous.

I have often envied those men who are unconscious of their surroundings. No doubt they miss a great deal of pleasure, but, on the other hand, they do not know the tyranny of inanimate objects and can move about the world like Kipling's cat. I have never been blessed with this indifference and have always been unhappy until I could make some kind of a retreat or haven for myself. It was easy to do so in the days when one travelled by train and boat, for it was possible to pack books and personal trifles; but now, when one descends by air with little except the clothes one is wearing, it takes some time to gather a few possessions together. However, in a week or so, with some books and maps and the furniture rearranged, my room began to lose its penitential air. I even began to like it. I looked forward to it at night, and to the moment when I would shut the door and think over the things I had seen that day.

Most of the flats opposite were permanently occupied, though a few were let to visitors, who stayed a night or two, then vanished from one's life. Among the permanent residents was a man who, the moment the sun struck his window-sill in the morning, put out a small cactus in a pot, and his first act on returning in the evening was to take it in. Above him was an old woman like some aged bird of prey, who sat peering for hours into the rooms of our building. We were evidently her recreation, her library of fiction. One morning, having slept later than usual, with the shutters open, I awakened to see her looking down at me, motionless, expressionless, like a peasant at a Connemara wake; horrified, I jumped up and closed the shutters. The transients over the way were usually hot, weary and sore-footed: young Americans with electric razors; earnest Germans; blond Danes; and American girls who gaily draped their windows with nylon garments. They were a fragment of Rome's mosaic of flitters, here today and off to-morrow: the modern world's equivalent of those sinners who in former days found grace in pilgrimage.

Much the same kind of visitors drifted through my pensione. They were nearly all young and earnest, and few ever stayed more than two days. I would often say good-morning to Swiss, Danes, Germans and French, and good-evening to English, Spanish, Swedes and Americans. The place was in constant movement and in a week or so I was the oldest inhabitant. There were two thin-legged girls in brown shorts, who appeared one day with Australian flags stuck into immense packs whose size and weight would have driven a guardsman to mutiny. Bent double, they were walking through Italy on those thin legs, their vision confined to the earth. In the evening they had changed, most surprisingly, into fresh cotton frocks, and the next morning they had vanished.

After a few days I would not have exchanged my balcony for the finest view in Rome. The little slice of street life below was a perpetual entertainment. It was a fragment of Martial's Rome. That great journalist anticipated the camera by many centuries: he was the photographer of imperial Rome. It came to me one day that his room on the Quirinal must have been similar to mine; and he had just as many steps to climb! He was horrified and dismayed by the noise of Rome; and so was I. He found it difficult to sleep in Rome; and so did I. I smiled to think what a fuss Martial made of the human noises of first century Rome: the hammering of the coppersmiths; the schoolmaster rebuking his class; the stray trumpet call; the masons chipping a new statue of Caesar; the money-changers chinking their gold; a delightful man-made symphony I should have thought. Yet Martial in ancient Rome, and also Hogarth in eighteenth century London, found such sounds intolerable. What would they have said to the mechanical pandemonium of modern Rome, a city where men judge a motor-car by its noise and the splendour of its backfires? What would Martial have thought of that absurd vehicle, the motor-scooter? The desire of every Italian to be mechanically propelled, and in the loudest possible way, has created a population of neatly dressed men sitting primly on these machines as if their office chairs had suddenly flown out into the streets with them. Lower in prestige than the Vespa and the Lambretta, but even noisier, is the ordinary bicycle fitted with a petrol engine. What it lacks in power, it makes up for in din. There is also the motorized tricycle-van, with a sound like a machine-gun range, in which tradesmen deliver their goods. It is extraordinary that a modern capital should allow itself to be turned into bedlam. London and Paris would not tolerate the noise of Rome for twenty-four hours. I have come to the conclusion, however, that the Italians do not hear the noise, or, if they do, they enjoy it. Like the Spaniard, I think the Italian is stimulated by tumult; it helps him to achieve that cerebral excitement in which he prefers to dwell.

The street life beneath my window would have been completely comprehensible to Juvenal or Martial, especially the food shops with their hot sausages and the barbers with their constant succession of near gilded youth with glossy locks. Disliking the necessary act of going to a barber, I am always fascinated by the great number of men in Latin countries who enjoy it. In Rome, as in Madrid, you see the same crowd of jolly, happy men with towels round their necks, gazing at themselves with approval in the mirrors and cracking jokes with the barber. Much the same scenes must have been witnessed during the clean-shaven period of ancient Rome, say from the time of Julius Caesar to the Antonines. This little segment of Rome had so regular a rhythm that I could tell what time it was merely by glancing out of the window. The waiters were always the first to arrive in the early morning, as they were the last to go. When, I wondered, do Continental waiters sleep? They would come along reading *Il Giornale d'Italia*, or, more likely, *Avanti!* or *L'Unità*, roll up the shutters and tackle the stacked chairs and tables. The men in the bar would put on white coats and get the Espresso machines ready for the first breakfasters. The early sun was already strong and the blinds would come down. The breakfasters would drink a cup of coffee standing and eat a bun. Again, that ancient memory. The old Romans were frugal breakfasters; a cup of wine or water and a piece of bread, and they were ready for the Forum or the rich man's levee. The fruit and flower barrows would then arrive. Carnations and gladioli would be refreshed at the tap at the street corner, whose stream ran perpetually to waste; then the peaches, the grapes, the wild strawberries, the oblong tomatoes, the lettuces, would be stacked on the barrows. The noise would become terrible. The street would be jammed with parked cars, scooters, bicycles and lorries. There would be outbursts of delirious hooting for the sheer joy of it. Once a week the most picturesque of our visitors would arrive. This was a Campanian wine cart loaded with barrels of *vino*, both *bianco* and *rosso*. These odd-looking carts are less frequent than I remember them years ago, when I recollect five or six of them in a line. They have two huge red wheels and the driver sits on one side, beneath a large semi-circular waterproof awning stretched on hoops. Two lengths of timber would be let down from the back to the road and upon these the little barrels would be neatly rolled into the wineshops.

I never knew what happened after eight or nine o'clock until dusk, when I would return to find the first neon lights glowing and the old lady over the way just a grey face against the gloom of her lonely flat.

Sometimes I would leave the pensione at six o'clock in the morning, which is the best time of all in the Roman summer. The air has been freshened during the night and seems to hold a faint scent of flowers. At such times—wonderful moment—the sound of Rome is the whisper and fall of her fountains.

§ 3

The best way to know a strange city is to walk everywhere. During my first three weeks I made it a moral issue with myself never to take a tramcar or a taxi, and I kept my word except on perhaps three occasions. Like all museums, Rome is hard on the feet, and the hills of Rome, though scarcely apparent to the motorist, are real enough, especially in the evening. On my way back, footsore and weary, I would sometimes think that the hills of Rome had been multiplied by ten or twenty. I would lie in bed at night and remember my day's walk, piazza by piazza, church by church, fountain by fountain, and palace by palace. I would set myself topographical examinations: you are in the Colosseum, I would say to myself, 'Now go to San Clemente and find your way to the Piazza dell' Esedra.' This piazza, incidentally, has been renamed the Piazza della Repubblica, but the old name persists. Or I would say, 'Find your way from the Mausoleum of Augustus to the Pantheon, then to the Piazza Navona and the Tiber, and cross the Ponte S. Angelo to St Peter's.' As I progressed, I was able to tell myself the names of the fountains and palaces I would encounter; and so, gradually, the map of Rome took shape in my head, and I realized that a city which had seemed so large at first was, in reality, so small that I could walk across it from the Pincian Gate to the Gate of St Paul in less than an hour.

The original Seven Hills of Rome have multiplied as the city has grown, and there are now nine east of the Tiber, and two, the Vatican Hill and the Janiculum, to the west. But the monument which astonished me, and of which one hears so little, was the Wall of Rome. It almost completely encircles the city and is pierced by about fifteen gates, which are still used every day. I walked all round the Wall at various times and the most spectacular stretch is to the south, between the Porta S. Giovanni and the Porta S. Paolo, a wonderful sector where one sees the mighty rampart with its machicolation stretching into the distance, with protruding towers and bastions. When the Wall was built, it was probably the mightiest fortification of its kind in the Roman Empire, and a thoughtful Roman, as he watched it being built in

A.D. 271, must have had much the same forebodings which some Londoners felt in the late nineteen-thirties as they read the Home Office pamphlets on ARP. The Emperor Aurelian built it at the first determined rumble of the coming barbarian storm, and so it is the father of all town walls. Europe was soon obliged to copy it, and Constantinople built a similar wall a couple of centuries later. Though patched, rebuilt and in places demolished, I thought the Aurelian Wall and its massive gates one of the noblest relics of Rome.

As I have said, I liked to be out before six in the morning, when the air is fresh and before Rome is properly awake. My favourite walk was down to the Tiber to have breakfast at a little café within sight of St Peter's. Sometimes I would walk down the hill, with the wall of the park of the Villa Medici to my right, to the terrace above the Spanish Steps; often I would go by way of the Fontana del Tritone for the pleasure of seeing Bernini's Triton un-obscured by taxi-cabs, a naked sea god larger than life, seated in the open hinge of a great shell. With both hands he lifts a conch shell to his lips and drinks with backward head from a stream of water that shoots into the air and falls back upon itself so precisely that his shoulders and body are always wet. In the course of three hundred years his shape has become blurred and worn by water, yet still he sits there with the air of an immortal among mortals.

In that early hour the sun is low, touching first the domes, towers and chimneys of Rome, then flooding downward over the walls until one half of the street is gold and the other in shadow. The old palaces are half in shade, half in sunlight, and the long shadows cast by their prison-like window grilles shorten and contract as the sun gets up. At this time in the morning I had some idea of what Rome must have looked like to the travellers of a hundred years ago, before it became the capital of Italy, and before the narrow streets of Renaissance Rome were choked with traffic and ruined by noise. The old palaces with their iron-bound lower windows, their walls of burnt sienna, yellow, and Roman red, the archways leading to courtyards where wall fountains dripped into moss-grown bowls, though triumphantly Renaissance, stood in dark and narrow lanes which recalled an older, mediaeval world. This moment of silence and dignity, which our ancestors knew, does not last long. Soon the first motors and scooters come hooting and exploding down the road.

One morning I walked to the top of the Spanish Steps and stood looking out towards the Tiber and St Peter's. This was the famous view of Rome I had hoped to see from my balcony. When Goethe was here in 1787, the Spanish Steps had been in existence for about sixty years, but the obelisk at the top had not yet been erected, and the ground was being prepared for the foundations. The excavators discovered that the earth was choked with the ruins of the Gardens of Lucullus, which in Roman times stretched back over the Pincian Hill. Goethe said that one morning his barber picked out of the ground a flat piece of burnt clay with figures on it. 'I eagerly secured the treasure,' he wrote. 'It is not quite a hand long and seems to have been part of a great key. Two old men stand before an altar; they are of the most beautiful workmanship; and I am uncommonly delighted with my new acquisition.'

As I looked down the long sweep of steps I could see the flower sellers at the bottom putting up their umbrellas, then walking over to that strangest of fountains, *La Barcaccia*, the work of Bernini's father, to refresh their carnations and maidenhair fern. I suppose the Spanish Steps have given as much pleasure as any of Rome's outdoor monuments. There can be few strangers who have not sat there on some sunny day, gathering strength for the ascent, and they remain in the memory, with that vivid splash of floral colour at their feet, as if they were one of Rome's finest palaces. Yet how odd and how unfair it is that they should be called the Spanish Steps; their only association with Spain is that their designer, Alessandro Specchi, also designed the façade of the nearby Spanish Embassy, the Palazzo di Spagna. They should really be the French Steps, for they owe their existence to the generosity of a French diplomat, M. Gouffier, and lead up to the French church, the Trinità dei Monti, and to the Villa Medici, now the Académie Nationale de France. I cannot look at them without remembering that they were the last earthly sight upon which the eyes of the dying Keats rested as he glanced from the windows of the sienna-brown house at the foot of the Steps.

Most of the travellers of the last century mention the models who once lounged there in picturesque costumes and attitudes, waiting to be hired by artists. Many were country people who came to Rome from the Campagna during the winter, the men in blue jackets and goatskin breeches and the women with linen headdresses and red or blue skirts. They were seen and humorously described by Dickens, who recognized 'one old gentleman with long white hair and an immense beard, who to my knowledge has gone half through the catalogue of the Royal Academy'. Lanciani is the only writer, so far as I know, who mentions the most interesting fact about these models: that some had Italianized Arabic names, such as Almansorre (El-Mansur), and came from the village of Saracinesco, high up in the Sabine Mountains. These people were believed to be the descendants of a Saracen foraging party cut off during the raid of A.D. 927, and who were permitted, upon renouncing their faith, to remain in the mountains.

La Barcaccia might be translated as 'the old tub', and this fountain is the last work of Pietro Bernini, the father of an even more famous and talented son. It is supposed that the idea of a sinking boat fountain was suggested by the great flood of Christmas Day, 1598, when a Tiber barge was washed up nearby, on the slopes of the Pincian Hill. The popular story that Bernini sunk the fountain and made the jet so low in order not to hide the Steps is incorrect, for the fountain was there nearly a century before the Steps. There are several late seventeenth century pictures in Rome which show what the Trinità dei Monti looked like before the Spanish Steps were built: I recall one in the Braschi Museum and another in the Keats Memorial House. The church at the top of the hill once stood on the brink of a steep ravine filled with trees, and there was just enough room for a couple of coaches to pass each other in front of the main entrance. It is extraordinary to see from these old pictures how casually the Renaissance and baroque artists dropped their pearls in the mud, so to speak, and many a famous fountain, as originally seen by contemporaries, stood surrounded by rough, unpaved roads,

23

dusty in summer and quagmires in winter. While I sat beside *La Barcaccia*, I noticed something which I was to see more than once at this place. A girl came from one of the nearby houses with a large jar which she filled from the fountain, from which one might reasonably conclude that some of the houses have no water supply: but this is not so. The water laid on is that of the Marcia Pia, while the fountain water is that of the celebrated Virgo, which any modern Roman will tell you, as an ancient Roman would have done, is the sweetest drinking-water in Rome. I glanced for a moment towards the window of the house where Keats had died, and I wondered if *La Barcaccia* had suggested that bitter epitaph: 'Here lies one whose name was writ in water.'

I sat there beside the fountain, thinking of the Piazza di Spagna and of the English milords of the eighteenth and nineteenth centuries who used to hire rooms and palaces hereabouts. Their travelling coaches were sometimes too high to pass under the archways into the courtyards and would stand in the centre of the square, side by side, as cars do today. An inquisitive herald could go round reading the crests on the polished doors and then tell his friends what wealthy peer or what society beauty had arrived in Rome.

I passed along the Via Condotti—the Conduit Street of Rome—which would soon be crowded, but was now empty and the shutters still down over the fashionable shop windows. The street leads across the Corso to wide, modern roads which run straight to the Tiber. In one of them I came to a little fruit and vegetable market tucked away behind the buildings and already in full swing. I bought two peaches and walked on until I came to the Tiber, still and pale blue in the morning sunlight, and, as a river, sadly unimpressive.

> *For once, upon a raw and gusty day,*
> *The troubled Tiber chafing with her shores,*
> *Caesar said to me 'Darest thou, Cassius, now*
> *Leap in with me into this angry flood,*
> *And swim to yonder point?'*

As a boy, playing the part of Cassius at school, a much better part I always thought than that of the priggish Brutus, I spoke those lines, thinking of the Tiber as a river even wider than the Thames at London Bridge; but in reality it is a disappointing river, and must have been so even before it was embanked. The magic of its name is potent, however, and I looked at it with respect and awe on this summer morning. I walked along the embankment and saw ahead of me, on the other side of the river, the great circular mulberry-red tomb of Hadrian, the Castel S. Angelo, with its baroque angel on the summit in the act of sheathing his sword. He is St Michael, who, the story goes, was seen by Gregory the Great in A.D. 590, when he was leading a procession of plague-stricken citizens to St Peter's. For three days the newly elected Pope, carrying a Cross, had led the citizens round Rome, chanting the *Kyrie Eleison* and begging God to stay the pestilence. As he crossed the bridge, St Gregory looked up to Hadrian's Tomb, where he saw the archangel sheathing a flaming sword and knew that the wrath of God had been appeased. I have read somewhere that the custom of saying 'God bless you' when anyone sneezes, which is general all over Europe, dates from that remote time. It is said that the plague would begin with attacks of sneezing, at the sight and sound of which horrified friends would say, 'God bless you', meaning, no doubt, 'God help you'.

Leading to this great monument is the Ponte S. Angelo, upon whose parapet stand St Peter and St Paul and ten vigorous angels known as the 'breezy maniacs' of Bernini, though they were fashioned by his pupils. Even on the stillest of mornings, when there is not a breath of wind and you can see every brick of the castle reflected in the glassy Tiber, these angels stand in some terrific seventeenth century gale.

Crossing the bridge, I looked up at the vast circle of eroded brickwork, gnawed by time and gashed by cannon balls, all that is left of the marble tomb which mighty Hadrian had built for himself and his family; the great Hadrian, who had presided over a golden age. At the thought of him and his sad, bearded face— they say he grew a beard to hide a scar—my mind went off to Hadrian's Wall, and I imagined him standing in our northern heather, gazing across the windy marches into Pictland, or in London, watching the galleys moored at Billingsgate. He was one of the greatest of all the imperial travellers. He visited every part of his dominions in a series of carefully planned royal tours, setting things to right, calling conferences, and preventing war by friendly discussion in a world which, by comparison with our own, seems to have been strangely reasonable.

I was now near St Peter's and in a few hundred yards I came to the broad processional approach made by the Fascist Government to commemorate the signing of the Lateran Treaty in 1929. That was the year in which I saw Rome for the first time. The broad Via della Conciliazione was then a delightful warren of old streets which withheld until the last moment the splendour of the church and its piazza. The basilica came suddenly into view with the impact of a glorious apparition. No one will ever again experience that thrill of surprise, for now St Peter's is visible a long way off, at the end of the unsatisfactory though well-meaning tribute of Mussolini's architects. The house in which Raphael's studio was still intact was among those pulled down to make this unfortunate avenue.

I noticed nearby, facing the river, a long building with a fine little Renaissance porch and an octagonal tower. To any Englishman this must be one of the supremely interesting places in Rome. It is the Hospital of S. Spirito, the living descendant of the old hospice built by the Anglo-Saxon kings in the eighth century and frequented by Saxon pilgrims for centuries. I walked across to the hospital to read the amazing street name written up on the wall—*Lungotevere in Sassia*. The word Sassia, or Saxia, commemorates the Saxon quarter which sprawled haphazardly over this part of Rome to the very doorstep of St Peter's. The English called their settlement by the name of the Saxon *burh* (not the Germanic *burgh*) and the word *borgo*, which is still to be seen written up in the street signs round the Vatican and St Peter's, is an Italianized version of the word. Everyone who crosses the Bridge of S. Angelo on his way to St Peter's must enter the territory of the old Saxon colony which linked Rome and England a hundred years before Charlemagne was born.

I approached St Peter's, which at that early hour of the morning was lit by the sun as it rose above the left arm of the colonnade. The Vatican stood in sunlight, and so did the church; the obelisk in the centre of the piazza cast a long, early morning shadow; the fountain on my right tossed its white head in the sun, but the one on the left was still in shadow. The vast piazza was empty save for a few hurrying figures, and there was not yet a single tourist coach. The only people ascending the great sweep of steps to the basilica were visiting priests who were going to say mass there. The sight of this church makes provincials of us all. We gape at it; at least I do every time I see it, as in imperial times the inhabitants of remote provinces must have gaped at the Temple of Jupiter or the Forum of Trajan.

The prosperous-looking shops at the end of the street, which sell either *Articoli Religiosi* or *Oggetti Sacri*, were not yet open, and I looked into their windows at the assortment of rosaries, medals, papal flags, models of St Peter's, bronze statuettes of the Apostles, white statuettes of St Cecilia, of the Santo Bambino, pictures of the Madonna del Sarto, of the Pope, and papal processions, and a hundred other little objects which link the pilgrim of today with the pilgrim of all ages. There is something ineffably touching about all such souvenirs, the love tokens of faith or piety; and I reflected that they would find their way to mantelpieces and walls all over the world to remind someone of Rome, and to prove that the owner had lived for a while in the odour of sanctity.

I went to a little café at the end of the street, where I was too early: but the waiter led me to an empty table on the pavement, pulled out a chair and said that the bread would arrive in a *momentino*, a word as charming as the Spanish *momentito*. What a place to wait for breakfast on a summer's morning! I could hear the fountains in the piazza. I could see one arm of the colonnade, crowned with its saints, and beyond, the Vatican. A projecting building concealed St Peter's itself, and I recalled that there used to be a delightful café on the opposite side of the road, on the very rim of the piazza, from which one could see the whole of St Peter's and could even read the inscription on the façade which says, in huge Roman letters, that it was completed during the pontificate of Paul V. That was in 1614. In England James I was on the throne, Walter Raleigh had not yet been released from the Tower to find El Dorado, and Shakespeare was still alive.

A boy bicycled up with the bread in a wicker basket. In a few moments the waiter had given me rolls, still warm from the bakehouse, jam, butter, coffee, and a plate for my two peaches. What could be more delightful than this moment in a just awakening Rome?

I remembered years ago, during my first visit to Rome, how I had put on evening dress in a February dawn and had gone down full of expectancy to wait in the chill morning light outside the Sacristry door of St Peter's. I had received a ticket for the Pontifical High Mass which Pius XI was to celebrate to mark the signing of the Lateran Treaty and the end of the 'Roman Question'. Sitting in a scented crush of mink and sable and gold braid in one of the rostra opposite the high altar, I saw the vast church fill with people. I watched with a feeling of enchantment as the gates of Time seemed to have been thrown wide to admit a procession from the halls of Karnak, or the Sacra Via. The Pope was borne into the church in the state palanquin, while trumpets sounded, peacock fans waved, and the packed church shouted its head off in welcome. For the first time in forty-eight years Rome was seeing a Pope who was no longer 'The Prisoner of the Vatican'. Within a few yards of the altar at which no priest save the Pope may officiate, I watched the intricacies of Pontifical High Mass. Hardly less interesting than the Pope himself was the figure of a prelate in a red soutane and a lace rochet, the Master of Ceremonies, who pulled a cardinal into place here and waved another there with a hasty wave of his hand. He was like the Spirit of Orthodoxy, a living and visible proof of the complexity of tradition; and the princes of the Church obeyed him as if they were erring choir-boys.

I finished my breakfast. These memories had kept me so long that now the piazza stood in the full blaze of the morning sun, and a guide was already standing with his charges, pointing here and there. I became aware of a dark little man, no doubt a guide, observing me with speculative interest. He approached and lifted his hat.

'Sir, you are English—yes?'

Although he had answered his own question, I nodded my head.

'Sir, do you know Major Jones of the War Office?' he asked.

Not to hurt his feelings, I said that the name did seem to ring a bell. This gratified him, and he brought from his pocket a frayed and dirty little notebook which he thumbed through and then, with an air of triumph, pointed to the signature of Major Jones.

'Ah!' he cried, 'such a nice gentleman, sir! So *simpatico*. Major Jones say my *trattoria* the best in Rome. Sir, you like *spaghetti, cannelloni, saltimbocca alla Romana*? I have!' Here he blew a kiss into the air. 'Good! Cheap! You will like too!'

With a bow, he gave me a card with the address of his restaurant. Six Vespas exploded past. Upon one, I noticed, sat a priest. Rome was awake again.

§ 4

They say that an Englishman, a Frenchman, a German, and an Italian were flung into prison, their arms pinioned, and, bound as they were, tortured in order to extract a confession from them. All spoke under the torture except the Italian. When this hero had regained his liberty, his friends asked how he had managed to endure his agony in silence. 'Well, you see,' he explained, 'I couldn't say anything because I was unable to use my hands!'

I fancy it must be almost impossible to speak Italian without gesticulation. It is a language that demands an accompaniment either of music or gesture; and in the national art of opera there are both. Rome is thus a city of gesticulation. There is gesticulation *pianissimo*; gesticulation *andante*; gesticulation *robusto*; gesticulation *fortissimo*; and it goes on around one all day long. When a motor car bumps into another in the street, the drivers leap out and address each other with gesticulation *furioso*, which is in the highest class of this art. No two Greeks who have cheated each other, or two Spaniards who have insulted each other, could better this performance: all the gestures reserved for emotional occasions are produced, such as crouching, placing the fingers bent against the forehead and suddenly extending them, hitting the breast and flinging the arms wide, turning swiftly away as if parting for ever, but whipping round suddenly with a pointing finger, bunching the fingers in front of the mouth; and the very insulting one, I imagine, of shrinking the neck into the shoulders and shrugging with extended arms, slowly and despairingly, as if one were addressing a hopeless and incomprehensible moron.

The landscape of Rome is itself declamatory. Upon the roof-line stand hundreds of gesticulating saints, their garments tossed about in a baroque breeze, their fingers admonishing, pointing and blessing. The undulating architecture with which the Church in the seventeenth century expressed its satisfaction with the Counter Reformation is itself a gay, inspiring background for gesticulation. It is a stage upon which a Puritan with modest, downcast eyes would be an impossibility: it is the Church flamboyant, the Church resurgent, the Church so sure of itself that it can be quite humorous at times. Even the dead inside the churches are in movement, at first leaning on their elbows, then, at a later time, standing up and waving their arms and gesticulating. Only against such a background could an English priest have said gaily to me, discussing a celebrated individual who had recently been received into the Roman Church, 'Yes, he's safely in the bag!' I realized the baroquerie of this comment. Afterwards, as I walked through the streets of Rome, the whirling saints on the roof-tops seemed to be saying, 'He's safely in the bag!', and the angels, the cherubs and the seraphim with trumpets to their bulging lips, seemed to be puffing into the air the joyful refrain, 'He's safely in the bag!'

The Rome that first prints itself upon the eye and the mind is not classical Rome, buried beneath the streets and covered with its shroud of Time, or mediaeval Rome, which now consists mainly of a stray and lovely campanile, or nineteenth century gigantism, or modern Rome, a mostly hideous mass of concrete, but this gay, declamatory Rome of the Popes, with its peachy, golden palaces, its once quiet piazze, its glorious fountains and its look of just having happened on some happy and fortunate day. You will find it in the curve of the Tiber, where the old Campus Martius used to be, and its eastern boundary is the Corso, which runs straight as a javelin from the Porta del Popolo to the Victor Emmanuel Monument, on the line of the old Flaminian Way.

Everything to the west of the Corso, in that bulge where the Tiber takes a sudden curve opposite St Peter's, is Renaissance Rome. It succeeded mediaeval Rome, which had been erected on the Field of Mars, hardly a good address in the time of the Caesars. Here the stocky legions were trained and the stirrupless cavalry put through its paces; here the people voted; here ambassadors, whom it was not considered politic to admit to Rome, were received and entertained outside the earlier walls; and here the emperors were cremated and a captive eagle released from their funeral pyres to wing their souls to Jupiter. No ancient Romans dwelt, however, in what is now the most crowded part of the city. For one thing, it was outside the walls until the time of Aurelian, and it was low-lying and was constantly flooded in the spring: but it was a great place for horse races, chariot races, and theatres. Julius Caesar was murdered there, in the portico of Pompey's Theatre, and not far away Domitian built an amphitheatre whose oblong shape is preserved in the Piazza Navona. Here, or perhaps on one of the other racecourses, a strange and horrible chariot race took place every October. As the winning chariot passed the post, the horse on the right was stabbed with a spear and its head was cut off and decorated with loaves of bread. Runners were waiting to race to the Forum with the bloody tail, which was given to the Pontifex Maximus, who handed it to the Vestal Virgins to be ceremonially burnt. This was probably an old and savage fertility rite to help on the harvest.

It must indeed have been a terrible time in the life of Rome, when during the barbarian invasions the population deserted the Seven Hills where they had lived for so long, and migrated to the low-lying Field of Mars. When the barborians cut the aqueducts and the copious and splendid water supply failed, the Romans were driven by lack of water to the Tiber and to wells in the marshy plain that eventually became mediaeval Rome.

I could never tire of the old streets near the Tiber, to the west of of the Corso. There is something worth looking at and thinking about every two yards. If this part of Rome were declared a zone of silence, as the Government will surely be obliged to make it, if it wishes visitors to continue to enjoy Rome, it would be perfect. One is willing to forgive the Renaissance Popes many of their sins for the sake of the beauty they created and the genius they nourished. A great deal of the haphazard charm of old Rome is that its ground plan is mediaeval. The palaces of the sixteenth century were erected in the narrow streets of the fourteenth. Many of the great palaces have elbowed their way in apparently by sheer strength of character, and stand like great galleasses towering above some little mediaeval harbour. To pass, for instance, from the Campo de' Fiori to the Farnese Palace is to traverse several centuries in a few yards.

Walking about the slums and palaces of Renaissance Rome, I sometimes had the strange idea that I was living in one of Shakespeare's plays; that perhaps I might meet Sir Toby Belch emerging from a *taverna*, or see Portia or Nerissa gazing into the window of a hat shop; or Touchstone on a Vespa, with Audrey on the pillion. Though the scene itself, the curved gingerbread gaiety of the baroque, never crossed the Channel to gambol through England as it did through Spain, the spirit that created these streets in Rome was that of Shakespeare's plays. After all, it is not so strange to link Shakespeare with Renaissance Rome, for Elizabethan England was soaked in Italian atmosphere and the returning fop with his 'little apeish hat couched faste to the pate, like an oyster', was already the *diavolo incarnato*. Thinking of Shakespeare, I reflected that he, and the men of his time, pronounced Rome to rhyme with room.

> '*Now is it Rome indeed and room enough,*
> *When there is in it but one only man,*'

says Cassius; and the same pun is repeated by Constance in *King John*. 'That I have room with Rome to curse awhile!' This pronunciation lasted until comparatively recent times, and there may be old people alive even now who can remember their grandparents speaking of going to 'Room'. When Kemble played the part of Cato, he spoke of 'Room', and Farington, in his *Diary* for 1811, says that the painter Lawrence had shown him a letter from Canning questioning Kemble's pronunciation, and arguing that Rome should rhyme with 'roam', as we pronounce it today.

So roaming about Room, or Rome, is the stranger's first joy and exasperation; for Rome has no centre. There is no part of the city which you can say at once is definitely the one and only heart of Rome. This seems strange in a country where every city is noted for its central piazza with its cathedral in which the life of the place is concentrated; stranger still when one reflects that ancient Rome, with its imperial fora, was practically all centre. The roads in the ancient world all led to this mighty heart of Rome, whose core was the Forum Romanum. It is eloquent of the death of ancient Rome and the end of her complicated life that the centre of the city should have been lost and forgotten and never rebuilt: it is as if in a thousand years the site of the Bank, the Royal Exchange and the Mansion House were lost, and the commercial heart of the London of A.D. 3000 were to be found in the Brompton Road.

Instead of one great forum, Rome has innumerable piazze scattered all over the city, and the stranger cannot decide which is the most important. There seems little to choose between the Piazza Colonna, the Piazza Barberini, the Piazza di Spagna, the Piazza dell' Esedra, and all the other piazze; and even the famous Piazza Venezia, with its adjacent monument to Victor Emanuel, is more a landmark and a beacon to the stranger than a civic centre.

The answer to the diffusion of modern Rome is to be found, of course, in history. Diocletian, finding the Empire too large to rule from one centre, divided it into an eastern and a western half, and Constantine built Constantinople, or New Rome, as the capital of the Eastern Empire. This part of the Empire lasted until the Turks captured Constantinople in 1453; but the line of the emperors of the West ended in 475, and the history of Rome then became that of successive barbarian invasions and the eventual abandonment of the old capital by the Eastern emperors. The Greek East went on its separate, prosperous way about 755, while the Latin West continued to fight on under the Popes. On Christmas Day, in the year 800, Leo III crowned his own Western Emperor, Charlemagne, in St Peter's; and the Middle Ages had begun. The structure of the ancient capital had by now completely changed. The centres of Rome were then St John Lateran and St Peter's, one church on the north-western boundary and the other across the Tiber. The whole town plan of ancient Rome disintegrated in confusion and decay. When Rome revived during the Renaissance, it was no ordinary city, but a priest state.

Its most important inhabitants were churchmen, monks and nuns. They did not need stock exchanges or market places, but churches and monasteries. This was the picturesque conglomeration which Garibaldi and Cavour inherited in 1870, when they made Rome the capital of newly united Italy.

When that happened, of course, two irreconcilable worlds came into conflict, and I think Augustus Hare was perhaps the first to see that the old Rome of the Popes, which he had known and loved, was to be swamped, and perhaps ruined, by the needs and ambitions of a modern capital. Writing only seventeen years after the unification of Italy, he deplored the changes that were taking place under what he contemptuously termed the 'Sardinian occupation'. Reading the literature inspired by Rome in the nineteenth century, and looking at the pictures of Rome at that time, one wishes that the patriots had chosen Milan and had left Rome in peace and quiet as a sanctuary of the spirit and of the arts. Imperial Rome is dead and turned to clay, but her ghost goes marching on. This spirit, so often visualized as a dethroned queen, was crowned again in spite of herself. 'What else is this city to me, a fervent lover of antiquity,' wrote Garibaldi, 'but the capital of the world? A dethroned queen! Yes; but from her ruins, immense, sublime, gigantic, there emerges a luminous spectre—

the memory of all that was great in the past . . . Rome, to me, the one and only symbol of Italian unity.'

It was obvious, from his choice of adjectives, that the Victor Emmanuel Monument was well on the way.

§ 5

The tourist coaches come rolling into Rome every day from all the countries of Europe. They are enormous glass houses in which the travellers sit in tired rows, insulated from the landscape and the people. At night these coaches stand in the side streets near the best hotels, and you may read the names of London, Berlin, Hamburg, Bergen, Vienna, Oslo, and many another place, on their dusty flanks. The next day you may meet the coaches in various parts of Rome, but on the following morning they vanish north to Florence or south to Naples. By the time the chamber-maids have made the beds, another consignment of travellers arrives, looking much like all the others: tired, a little bewildered, and glad to stretch their legs. It is all wonderfully organized. Never before in history have so many people seen Europe from behind plate glass. It is carefree travel at its best, and the wanderers return home in less time than it took our snail-like forebears to get as far as Boulogne. This coach traffic, which must surely owe something to mechanized warfare and the experience gained in transporting infantry by road, has ensured the existence of the great hotels of Europe. Currency restrictions and the extinction of the idle rich faced them with bankruptcy until along came the travel agencies with block bookings for the entire season. It is interesting to see how the hotels have trimmed their sails to this new wind of travel. The majestic and palatial establishments which formerly looked down upon conducted tours as the lowest form of human life, and even boasted that they never had anything to do with them, now fling wide their marble halls with joy; and the manager himself in his morning-coat sometimes waits on the steps to greet a particularly profitable tour, as he waited once for his lordship in his Rolls Royce.

Nothing surprised me more in Rome than the sweeping away

of the tradition of centuries. From the time of Cicero and Horace onwards, no one has ever visited Rome in summer unless he could go at no other time. In ancient days the wealthy Romans left the city for their villas by the sea or in the country the moment 'the first figs and the heat are furnishing the undertaker with his suite of black attendants', as Horace put it pessimistically to his rich friend; and this ancient migration still goes on. The Pope leads the way when he goes to his summer palace in the Alban Hills, and the well-to-do Romans follow, until by August Rome is a city in charge of seconds-in-command. For every Roman who leaves the city, however, at least a thousand visitors pile in; and they continue to do so throughout the hottest period of the year.

You know that the peak period has arrived when you meet girls dressed in jeans in the most fashionable streets of Rome, accompanied by young men attired for a fishing holiday on the Great Lakes or when a papal gendarme, in full dress with cocked hat and sword, waves an indignant white gloved hand and banishes a girl in shorts from the steps of St Peter's. The informal dress of the travelling tourist, which shocks and irritates the Spaniard, who looks upon it as an insult to his country, does not affect the Roman, who cannot be surprised by anything a visitor does. He has seen too many in the course of the centuries.

The hurried tourist is not, as one might imagine, a modern phenomenon. Dr John Moore, who was in Rome in 1792, mentions a go-ahead visitor who hired a guide, fast horses and a good carriage, and dashed around Rome methodically ticking off all the 'sights' as he passed them, and was able to say at the end of two days that he had seen everything. Sir Joshua Reynolds, who studied in Rome and caught a cold in the chilly galleries of the Vatican which made him deaf for the rest of his life, had something to say of tourists. 'Some Englishmen,' he wrote, 'while I was in the Vatican came there, and spent above six hours in writing down whatever the antiquary dictated to them. They scarcely ever looked at the paintings the whole time.'

One sees the same thing today, when droves of tourists are driven through endless galleries by inexorable guides, and the moment comes when even the hardiest do not pretend to be intelligent or interested any more, but plod on with downcast eyes beneath the painted ceilings. Many of these visitors appear to be impervious to heat. While Rome is prostrate in its siesta and the shops are shut until five o'clock, while the asphalt turns to moving black porridge underfoot and the taxi ranks present a view of drivers who have apparently died at the wheel, it sometimes falls to these travellers, who seem to be made of asbestos, to go out in the afternoon and find a deserted city.

In a class apart are the religious pilgrims, who are the original visitors to Rome. They are much the same as their predecessors down the long ages, and the things they wish to see are the same as those reverenced by the pilgrims of the Middle Ages. St Peter's and the chief basilicas are always full of them, and you can tell them at a glance from the other visitors. It is not only that they know how to genuflect without embarrassment and at the right moment, but, no matter where they come from, they are part of the Roman background. They may be strangers, but they are at home.

§ 6

In the side streets at the lower end of the Via del Tritone, you hear a steady sound of falling water. It is an arresting sound in a city, for it is not the polite whisper of a fountain, but the untamed roar of glen or mountain water. It is almost as though the Pass of Killiecrankie were visiting Rome. If you follow this sound through the narrow streets, it will lead you to the most spectacular fountain in Rome, and now its most popular sight, the Fontana di Trevi.

I remember years ago how quiet and deserted the Trevi used to be at night; how, if you took a *carrozzella* there, as I often did, you would discover it roaring away alone in the lamplight or the moonlight. Occasionally a couple would stroll up and toss a coin to the water-spirits to ensure their return to Rome. I did so myself the first time I was in Rome; and although I forgot to turn my back, I have found that the charm works. Even Sir George

Frazer of *The Golden Bough* tossed in his coin, as he admits in a note to his edition of Pausanias. 'In Rome itself,' he wrote, 'there is a fountain (the Fontana di Trevi) into the basin of which people still throw coins in the belief that by doing so they ensure their return to the Eternal City. The present writer did not scruple to comply with this custom.' It is pleasant to think of the great collector of superstitions standing there before the tumultuous fountain and—not scrupling to comply!

The Trevi had been worked into most of the nineteenth century romances written about Rome without any noticeable effect on the tourist traffic, but a little while ago a film, using Rome as a background for love stories, recalled the Trevi and its custom to the world, and this fountain is now the most visited in Rome. All daylong, and far into the night, a crowd fills the once quiet little piazza; tourist coaches draw up and pause just long enough to allow the passengers to throw in a coin and take a photograph; and coin-throwers are still there at half-past one in the morning, when the night is lit every few moments by the electronic flashes of photographers. I have seen the basin of the Trevi paved with nickel coins, and so many are thrown in the course of twenty-four hours that the local urchins are beginning to look quite affluent. They have invented many ingenious rakes and other implements, and two policemen are always on duty to restrain the *ragazzi* from stripping and diving in to this lake of El Dorado. At night the Trevi is floodlit, even when the moon is full!

This masque of water, though it is not my favourite Roman fountain, is one which constantly delights and surprises by its audacious fantasy. The idea of transposing a rocky landscape gushing with waterfalls, with Neptune and his steeds in violent action, upon the sedate and formal façade of a Renaissance palace is itself such a startling improbability that one stands amazed. It seems to me so characteristic of Rome that this romantic vision should be tucked away behind narrow streets, and in a piazza only just large enough to contain it. Where but in Rome would anyone have dreamed of erecting such a monument in such a place? In Paris it would have been isolated in a suitable square; in

London such a fantasy would perhaps never have been erected at all. It is the singular charm of Rome that, turning a corner, one comes suddenly face to face with something beautiful and unexpected which was placed there centuries ago, apparently in the most casual fashion. Rome is a city of magic round the corner, of masterpieces dumped, as it were, by the wayside, which lends to the shortest walk the excitement of a treasure hunt.

It is delightful to take strangers to the Trevi for the first time, and to enjoy their expressions of surprise and delight. I once took an American woman there whose comments would have delighted Bernini, who is said to have designed the fountain, and Niccolò Salvi, who killed himself building it a hundred years after.

'Why, it's a perfect little theatre!' she cried. 'Come along, let's go and sit in the stalls.'

I am sure this is just what Bernini and Salvi wished us to think as we descend the steps towards the basin of the fountain and separate ourselves from the everyday life of the streets. We are indeed in a baroque theatre, ready to surrender ourselves to the illusion; and there is nothing to take our attention from the rocky stage upon which Neptune stands so triumphantly while his sea-horses plunge and the tritons blow their horns. Sitting with one's back to the street, trying to follow the hundred little waterfalls that spout and gush from the rocks, one is temporarily lost to reality as during a good play.

The water that pours from the Trevi is the famous Aqua Virgo, which Romans say is the best and the sweetest of the waters. It comes from the Campagna, about fourteen miles away, and was first brought to Rome in 19 B.C. The Goths and Burgundians cut the supply in A.D. 537, and it was not fully restored until the fifteenth century. The Aqua Virgo enters Rome by way of the Pincian Gardens, and, after feeding *La Barcaccia*, at the foot of the Spanish Steps, supplies about fifteen large and forty smaller fountains, of which the Trevi is the most important. The first Trevi fountain was a plain and modest affair, and was round the corner in the Via dei Crociferi; but during the century and a half in which it served the district, Rome was becoming grander and more splendid, and Urban VIII, the Barberini Pope whose bees buzz all over Rome, decided to bring the Trevi up to date. Though he moved the fountain to its present position, Urban did not carry out Bernini's design. Ten Popes were to reign before the idea was revived by Clement XII, an amazing old man who was seventy-eight when he was elected, and reigned for ten years. Salvi, the architect, began his tremendous task about 1723, which was the year that another Roman landmark was begun, the Spanish Steps. These, however, took only three years to build, while the construction of the Trevi fountain occupied thirty-nine years, and was carried on during the pontificate of Benedict XIV and completed under that of Clement XIII, in 1762. By this time Salvi had died, his health ruined by the amount of time he had spent underground in the chilly damp of the aqueduct.

The visitors toss in their coins all day long, to laughter, cheers, and photographs. I wonder when the custom began, for it cannot be much older than the end of the nineteenth century. Mme de Staël's *Corinne* met her Oswald by moonlight at the Trevi in 1807, but there was no coin-throwing; neither did Charlotte Eaton throw a coin when she saw, and disliked, the fountain in 1817. The earliest reference I have been able to find is in *The Marble Faun*, which Nathaniel Hawthorne published in 1860. His mysterious character, Miriam, goes down to the Trevi at night and says: 'I shall sip as much of this water as the hollow of my hand will hold. . . . I am leaving Rome in a few days; and the tradition goes, that a parting draught at the Fountain of Trevi ensures the traveller's return, whatever obstacles and improbabilities may seem to beset him.' It looks as though a drink of Trevi water was the original tradition and that the casting of coins came later. At any rate by the time Baedeker published his eighth edition in 1883, the custom had been well established, and he gives the formula: to drink the water, (which no modern visitor does), and to cast in a coin. There is nothing said about turning one's back. By the time S. Russell Forbes wrote his *Rambles in Rome*, in 1892, the custom had developed into a ritual. 'If you wish to return to Rome,' he wrote, 'you should come here on the last day of your visit, take a drink out of the rim of the fountain with your left hand, then turn and throw into the water, over your left shoulder, a halfpenny.' Marion Crawford, writing six years later, has this to say. 'Whoever will go to the great fountain when the high moon rays dance upon the rippling water, and drink, and toss a coin far out into the middle in offering to the genius of the place, shall surely come back to Rome again, old or young, sooner or later.'

The Fontana di Trevi uses the same water over and again. It is stored in a tank in the building behind the fountain and is pumped under pressure through innumerable pipes. Once a week, on a Tuesday morning, the waterfalls are stopped while cleaners swarm over the rocks and wash down Neptune and his steeds before the week's supply of fresh water is pumped into the tank and put into circulation. I was attracted one morning by the ingenuity of a lad who was fishing among the votive offerings with a scoop on the end of a stick until police chased him away with a volley of angry '*vias!*' A priest of the water sprites, in the person of a sleek young street photographer, told me that in a good week during the height of the season as much as £50 to £60 worth of coins are taken out during the weekly cleaning of the fountain. I expressed surprise, but he assured me that it was so.

'What happens to it?' I asked.

'Well, most of it goes to the hospitals and the orphanages,' he replied, 'and the cleaners get a share of it.'

Facing the Trevi, at a corner of the little piazza, is a small church, SS Vicenzo ed Anastasio, which was built by the great Cardinal Mazarin, and the woman's head above the main entrance is said to represent his favourite niece, Maria Mancini. If any one believes that the self-made man had to wait for the age of Democracy, he should glance at the history of Cardinal Mazarin. His father was butler to the Colonna family and afterwards steward. He married an illegitimate daughter of the family and lived to see his son a cardinal, and the real ruler of France, and his granddaughter Maria married to Prince Colonna. When a widower, the retired butler married Porzia Orsini, and is the only man in history who married a member of each of these rival families. The church has a curious and macabre distinction. A bronze plate to the left of the altar records the names of twenty-two popes who bequeathed their hearts and viscera to this church, which is the parish church of the Quirinal Palace. Before 1870, when the Quirinal was a papal palace, Sixtus V, and all the popes who died after him in the Quirinal Palace, made this strange bequest. Their hearts are kept in marble urns, like the Canopic jars which contained the viscera of the Pharaohs.

§ 7

As you face the Spanish Steps you see the Keats House on the right, and the Babington Tea Rooms on the left. Between them lies that sinking boat which might, alas, be an ironic reference to the fortunes of the wealthy aristocracy whose members enlivened the Piazza di Spagna for two centuries. One day, when having tea in Babington's, the name struck me as interesting. The Babington Plot . . . Thomas Babington Macaulay. It is not a name you meet with every day. . . .

In the year 1893 an English spinster, aged about thirty, arrived in Rome with a capital of one hundred pounds to start a business suitable for a lady. She belonged to a branch of the Derbyshire Babingtons, a Catholic family whose most spectacular member was Anthony Babington, who was hanged, drawn and quartered in 1586 for leading a conspiracy against Queen Elizabeth. His death was horrible. His friend Ballard was hanged first, while Babington, instead of praying, stood by 'with his hat on his head as if he had been but a beholder of the execution'. He was executed next, with diabolical tortures, and cut down still alive. Elizabeth was so shocked by this that she commanded that the other conspirators, who were to die on the following day, should be properly and truly hanged before they were quartered. Babington's property went to Sir Walter Raleigh, and Elizabeth selected a fine clock for herself. Lord Macaulay was a connection of the family and was given the Christian name of Babington.

However, three hundred years after these happenings, Miss Anna Maria Babington arrived in Rome to make her fortune, accompanied by a friend. By a strange coincidence this friend also had an ancestor who had died at the hands of the public hangman.

She was Miss Isabel Cargill of Dunedin, New Zealand, whose grandfather was the founder of Otago and whose ancestor was Donald Cargill, the Covenanter. In a ringing Lowland accent Donald had denounced Charles II for treachery, tyranny and lechery, and went preaching about Scotland, as staunch a Protestant as Babington had been a Catholic, until he was caught and executed for high treason in 1681 at the Cross in Edinburgh. What an odd circumstance it was that these two women should have joined together to open a business in Rome.

The year 1893 was full of events which suggested to the two ladies what the English newspaper of the time described as 'a long felt want'. It was the episcopal jubilee of Pope Leo XIII, and Rome was full of visitors. In February the Holy Father blessed a crowd of fifty thousand; in March he made an Edison-Bell phonograph record for the President of the United States; in April he received the Princess of Wales, afterwards Queen Alexandra, and gave her a signed photograph. And as if this were not enough, April saw the silver wedding celebrations of King Humbert I and Queen Margherita of Savoy. The pilgrims had departed and Rome was now filled with royal visitors and society. Semi-state landaus drove up from the railway station to the Quirinal escorted by the tossing horsehair of the royal cuirassiers, and from them stepped the Kaiser, William II, and his consort, a bearded young Duke of York, afterwards King George V of England, then enjoying his last two months of bachelorhood, and many others in that regal age. Behind all the splendour and the gaiety there lurked a desire for a properly made cup of tea; and this the Misses Babington and Cargill proceeded to gratify.

Their first teashop was in the Via dei Due Macelli, and it was such a success that a branch was soon opened in the Piazza di San Pietro. In the following year the present building in the Piazza di Spagna fell vacant—it was originally the stables of the palazzo— and as this was in the heart of English Rome, there could have been no better place. Miss Babington and Miss Cargill decorated the rooms with a dado of Japanese matting and placed a palm in the centre of the front room. They installed gas lighting. The *Anglo-American* for December 10, 1894, reported that 'Miss Babington's tearooms are really worthy of a good and numerous clientèle. They are clean, comfortably furnished and well warmed and ventilated. There is a nice reading-room attached to the premises which are on the ground floor, hence no stairs to go up; and as to the food, both as regards the quality and the way it is served, and the modicity of the prices charged, I assure you Nice might very well take a leaf out of Miss B.'s book with very great advantage.'

The Babington venture had now taken its place in the colony which today is such a shadow of its former self. In 1903 Miss Cargill married Professor da Pozzo, a well-known painter, but she continued to work in the tearooms, taking turns at the cash desk with her partner. In 1928 Miss Babington, who was then a very old lady and nearly blind, retired from the business and went to live in Switzerland; and Signora da Pozzo carried on alone. The tearooms are now run by her daughter, the Contessa Dorotea Bedini.

'Perhaps the most remarkable thing about the business,' she told me, 'is that two members of the original staff are still with us, Giulia Nadoni, at the cash desk, and Anita de Santis, at the cake counter. During the last war I took my family to the Alps and was caught there by the 1943 Armistice and was unable to get back to Rome until the war was over. But, thanks to the loyalty of Giulia Nadoni, and indeed all the staff, the Rooms were kept open during the whole of the nine months of the German occupation, and were closed only for a few hours the day the Germans marched in. That also was the only time we had any war damage, for shrapnel smashed the windows. But throughout the war the name Babington was never taken down.'

So Babington's has been preserved to make tea in a world so different from that of 1893. It is doubtful whether Miss Babington would have approved of the modern tourists in their open-necked shirts and chromatic Miami beach jumpers who go there these days. Still there are others. You will often notice little groups of *contesse* and *marchesi* taking tea together and speaking the English taught them by those great ambassadors of England, the English governesses. The late King Alfonso of Spain liked tea and was a keen Babingtonite.

The English tearoom atmosphere is a curious thing. In order to see how strong it is you should cross the road into the Via Condotti and visit the Caffè Greco, which is older than Babington's and has hardly altered since Liszt, Byron and Wagner sat at the little marble tables. Among its more improbable habitués was Buffalo Bill.

Though they give you excellent tea, it would be more reasonable to order iced coffee. I overheard a curious scrap of conversation here. A young American was describing his rooms in an old palazzo.

'And bang in the middle of the courtyard is one of those marble well-heads,' he said. 'But I guess I'm very familiar with them. I was raised in a home where we sat on them.' His friends expressed some surprise. 'Well, my grandmother came to Rome,' he explained, 'and brought back two of them, which she had fitted up as lava-tories!'

§ 8

A line of red-wheeled *carrozze* stands at the top of the Via Veneto, waiting for clients from the expensive hotels. There is a bell on the harness of each horse, and the drivers are real Romans of the Romans from Trastevere. Italians tell me that their dialect and their irony are priceless: they must be to Rome what the now extinct gorblimey Cockney was to London. They are a survival of nineteenth century Rome, and no doubt great-grandfather, on his honeymoon, used to hold great-grandmama's hand in a *carrozza* as they drove through the silent streets to see the Trevi by moonlight: and today they are used chiefly by lovers, as of old, and by those who find it a novel experience to sit in a horse-drawn vehicle. The drivers, embittered perhaps by mechanical competition, have become avaricious.

Still, one night, thinking how delightful it must have been to drive through the streets in those happy days when there was no sound but the tinkle of the harness bell and the clop of the horse's hoofs on the stones, I approached one of the drivers, who leaned down from his seat and said:

'You wanna take a buggy ride?'

O Roma immortalis! So might some ancient Roman of the decline have addressed Goth or Vandal in the accents of the conquerors!

CHAPTER TWO

The Capitoline Hill – the tragedy of Rienzo – S. Maria in Aracoeli – the Santo Bambino – a diplomatic party – American Rome – the Borghese Gardens and the Pincio

§ 1

The Capitoline Hill is, I think, one of the most perfect spots in Rome. Lifted above the noise of the city and undisturbed by the conflict between old and new, one passes, as it were, through a gateway into the sixteenth century, where all the beauty of that age is frozen in three sides of a square of exquisite, peach-coloured buildings. In the centre Marcus Aurelius, his curly hair and beard newly scented and barbered, rides his bronze horse, still touched with gilt, as if he were riding on some sunny morning ages ago. In all cities there are certain places, a church or a garden, where one may go as to sanctuary in moments of happiness or sorrow; and in spite of its grand and stormy memories, this piazza on the Capitol is such a place to me. The centuries lap its feet and roll away in stormy vistas all round it, and the rock of the Capitol, where the philosopher rides his golden horse, is lifted like some ark above the flood of Time.

It is not a high hill, I believe about a hundred and sixty feet, and is a detached acropolis on whose summit the Romans built, six centuries before Christ, the greatest temple of the Roman world, the Temple of Jupiter Capitolinus. In his earliest semblance Jupiter was a primitive, Etruscan figure whose vermilion face was ceremonially painted once a year with a red pigment, *minium*. When the Roman Caesars and generals celebrated a triumph, they rode in a chariot, dressed as Jupiter, their faces painted red, and their horses white like the steeds of Jupiter; and the procession always ended on the Capitoline Hill, where the

47

victorious general would sacrifice to the god. In later imperial times the primitive red-faced god was replaced by a figure of gold. The temple roof tiles were gold, the doors were gold, and the threshold was bronze, and the building shone above the Forum, glittering in the sunlight.

At right angles to the Capitoline Hill, and separated from it in ancient times by a narrow marsh, is the long ridge of the Palatine Hill, where the Caesars built their palaces: and in the valley between these two hills was the ancient Forum. The main road of the Forum was the Sacra Via, which was sacred because it led, by way of the Temple of Vesta and the house of the High Priest, the Pontifex Maximus, to the Temple of Jupiter on the Capitol. So the Forum looked up to the Capitol, while the Capitol looked down over the heart of the Roman world, that centre of civilization to which all roads led and whence they began.

The legend is that when the first Temple of Jupiter was being excavated, a human head was found which was said to be that of a mythical hero called Tollius. The augurs interpreted the discovery as a sign that one day Rome would be the head (*caput*) of the world. So the hill was called Capitolium (a *capite Toli*), and so we get the word Capitol, which is used today in many states, notably in Washington, as the seat of parliament. The neighbouring ridge of the Palatine gave Europe the word 'palace'. Another word in everyday use was born on the Capitol, where the companion temple to that of Jupiter was the temple of his wife, Juno, in her form of Juno Moneta. As the Roman mint was in her temple, the word *Moneta* passed into the languages of Europe as 'money', 'monnaie', 'moneda', 'munt', and 'münze'. Though the temples have fallen and vanished from the earth, the words that originated on these hills of Rome are still upon the lips of men every day.

The Capitoline is also a symbolic hill. In the days of ancient Rome the approach to it was from the Forum, and the great temples of Jupiter and Juno, and all the other buildings, faced the Forum and had their backs to what is now modern Rome: but with the fall of Rome came centuries of decay. The Forum died and passed into ruins, and Jupiter himself was hardly a memory. His great temple fell to pieces and crashed down over the hillside. Life began to stir again when men of the early Middle Ages built a church dedicated to the Virgin Mary on the site of the Temple of Juno: while near the site of Jupiter's temple they built a fortified palace for the chief magistrate. These buildings did not face the old dead world, but the new; and in one of history's perfect gestures, they turned towards St Peter's.

Every time I went to the Capitol, I found something more to admire. First there are the twin stairways leading up the hill. It may be that the beauty and charm of the Roman fountains, so justly praised by all, have obscured the grace and ingenuity of the steps of Rome. Hardly a day passed with me when I did not pause to think how beautifully placed and designed was some often humble flight of steps worn thin by the feet of thousands who have always taken them for granted. Owing to the undulating ground, every opportunity for designing steps in all their variety was taken by the architects of the Renaissance: if the Spanish Steps could be called an exuberant flourish in the art of step-making, the two stairways leading to the summit of the Capitol are a supreme example of good manners in architecture. These two flights of steps stand side by side, with two centuries between them. The steep marble steps—there are a hundred and twenty-four—that lead to S. Maria in Aracoeli were built in the fourteenth century from offerings made to the Virgin during the Black Death. They were brought from the Quirinal Hill, and were the steps that once led to Aurelian's great Temple of the Sun. They were the only steps up to the Capitol until the Renaissance, and a glance at them, or better still a walk up them, will tell you that they were made for tough Roman leg muscles. Among one's first impressions of the ancient Romans, after walking about Rome, is that they were a race which scorned shallow, easily mounted steps. It is more tiring to climb this stairway to S. Maria in Aracoeli than to mount a hundred shallow Renaissance stairs. When the architects made the piazza of the Capitol, they were faced with the problem of designing an ascent which would be worthy of the already ancient flight and yet would not rival it. So they made, not a flight of steps, but a gentle ramp that, starting beside the older steps, inclines at a slight outward angle, and leads gracefully to the top. There is something in this gesture almost like the courtesy of a young man giving way to an older.

The tremendous sweep of Roman marble to the left is, as I say, a test of leg muscles, and I have seen an old engraving in which women are seen mounting them on their knees. They did so to petition the Virgin to straighten out their domestic difficulties, and to request the Queen of Heaven to give them a husband or a child. It is curious to reflect that, by a process of religious transference by no means uncommon, they were approaching the shrine once dedicated to the pagan Queen of Heaven, Juno, the goddess who looked after feminine affairs from birth to death. No doubt exactly the same problems were placed before Juno by women of the ancient world as those taken to-day to the Blessed Virgin.

Though I climbed the steps several times, I preferred the kinder Cordonata. Upon the balustrade at the top stand Castor and Pollux, not in harness but almost naked, and proclaiming the oddity of their parentage in two queerly shaped little caps which represent the half of a swan's egg, for their mother was Leda. Before me rode Marcus Aurelius, and behind him stood the Senator's Palace, the white statues upon its roof outlined against the Roman sky; to the Emperor's left stood the Capitoline Museum, and on his right the Palace of the Councillors, both now filled with many of the finest treasures of ancient Rome.

To anyone who has collected Roman coins this life-sized portrait of the curly-haired and bearded emperor is delightful. He is an old friend. An echo of his voice comes to one: 'Herein is the way of perfection,' he wrote, 'to live out each day as one's last, with no fever, no torpor and no acting a part.' And is there maybe a forecast of Christianity in this, another of his maxims: 'When anyone does you a wrong, set yourself at once to consider, what was his point of view, good or bad, that led him wrong. As soon as you perceive it, you will be sorry for him, not surprised or angry.' Yet it was not Marcus Aurelius, but, of all people, Trajan, who was the only Roman emperor to be made an honorary Christian, and the only unbaptized Christian in history. The story is that St Gregory the Great, touched by Trajan's compassion for the poor and for widows, asked God to open the gates of the Christian heaven to this good and compassionate pagan. And God, not too willingly, one gathers, answered St Gregory's prayer, but stipulated that the saint must not make too many such requests. The problem of an unbaptized Christian worried the Middle Ages until St Thomas Aquinas straightened the situation by explaining that Trajan appeared after death, just long enough to be baptized; so all was well. I thought, as I looked at the philosopher, that it might perhaps have been easier to have made a Christian of him than of Trajan. 'Whatever anyone else does or says,' wrote Marcus Aurelius, 'my duty is to be good.' And I always like to think of him going to the Colosseum with obvious reluctance, and annoying the audience, as he did, by reading or signing documents during the bloody games. By a stroke of irony he owes his preservation, the only mounted bronze statue of imperial days to ride the streets of Rome, to the delightful mistake of the early Christian world, which believed him to be Constantine the Great.

This perfect piazza was designed by Michelangelo, though it was completed by his successors. It was he who brought Marcus Aurelius from the Lateran, where he had stood for five hundred years, and mounted him upon a plinth made from one of the columns of the Temple of Castor and Pollux; and there he rides, the prototype of all the bronze horsemen who since that time have spurred forth into the public places of the world. From the hand of Michelangelo also are those beautiful steps that curve left and right up to the main entrance of the Senatorial Palace, which is now the Town Hall of Rome.

This building holds an unusual and happy memory for me. Years ago I attended a state ball there. It was the occasion of the marriage of ex-King Umberto to Princess Marie José of Belgium, in January, 1930. I remember travelling from Paris to Rome in the same railway coach as a young man whose coronation, as King George VI, I was to witness in Westminster Abbey seven years later. As Duke of York, he was attending the wedding as the representative of his father, George V.

Rome was in a condition of the utmost excitement and the streets were filled with roving groups of peasants from all parts of

Italy dressed in regional costumes, some accompanied by men beating drums and playing pipes, others, in sheepskin breeches, played melodious *pifferi*, rather like the Irish pipes, shepherds I was told, who had come from the Abruzzi.

As the correspondent of a foreign newspaper I was given a seat in the Chapel Royal of the Quirinal Palace where I watched the wedding party walk to the altar for the nuptial mass. It was the first time I had seen Mussolini. He strode forward grimly in the glittering procession wearing an air of calculated ferocity, and I remember thinking that he had the head of one of the later emperors, a Diocletian or a Jovian.

In the evening the Governor of Rome held a Ball on the Capitol to which much of the feminine beauty of Rome and, so it seemed, all the uniforms, orders and decorations in Europe, had been invited. As the guests flowed up the ancient stairways and filled the great reception rooms, which glowed with their tapestries and glittered with crystal chandeliers, I thought what a fantastic setting the Senator's Palace provided for this scintillating assembly.

As midnight struck we gathered at the windows overlooking the Forum to see, in the beams of searchlights, a Roman wedding procession slowly approaching in white togas along the Sacred Way. It was a pageant arranged in honour of the marriage, and it stole through the night to the sound of flutes, and vanished like a ghost into the darkness of the ruins.

A professor took me into cellars beneath the palace where the walls are massive blocks of peperino whose joints, so paper thin that a finger-nail scarcely detects them, were made by masons centuries before Christ. We talked of the earlier palace which Michelangelo pulled down to make way for the present one. Both palaces had been built on the tremendous remains of the Roman Tabularium, the Record Office, where the events of Rome were once preserved on bronze shields. I remember thinking it was rather like the last act of *Aïda*. The music from the palace above came faintly to us as we explored those tomb-like halls, and saw stone stairways leading down, it seemed, into the heart of the Capitoline Hill. As we discussed Rienzo, the most spectacular and fantastic figure in the story of the earlier palace, it never occurred to either of us—on his part indeed it would have been *lèse-majesté*—to reflect that the dictator around whom everything then revolved was himself a parallel to the famous Tribune. It seems to me that Rienzo and Mussolini are so alike, the same blend of admirable ideas and personal failings, the same operatic gestures, that the resemblance gives to the career of Rienzo a new interest.

Not long ago Mussolini seemed to be a modern phenomenon, but the truth is that he was a well-known historic type, and his terrible death proved that an Italian crowd, when angry, can be as savage as its predecessors of the fourteenth century.

§ 2

It is strange that Hollywood has not made one of its expensive historical *soufflés* of the life and times of Rienzo. The Papacy, so the world believed, had become a possession of France, and the Popes had deserted Rome for the pleasant 'prison' of Avignon. Rome became an endless riot of violent barons. It was a place of red brick towers clustered in the bend of the Tiber, a city of private armed bands, of clashes between Colonna and Orsini, of robbery, of murder and all manner of lawlessness; and it wore once again that air of tragic misery which had descended upon it ages before when, deserted by the Eastern emperors, it became a prey to the barbarians.

In this Rome of the early fourteenth century, Cola di Rienzo, who was born about 1313, grew up a poor lad, the son of a publican. He acquired Latin and wandered among the ruins spelling out the inscriptions and contemplating the past glories of Rome. How extraordinary it is that this dream of Rome was still able to fire men's hearts in a day when the population of the city could not have possessed a drop of ancient Roman blood. Rienzo, dreaming among the ruins, imagined himself a Caesar leading the ruined city into a new era of glory. He was handsome, fanatical, and had the gift of words.

It was the age of Petrarch. The Renaissance was dawning over Italy, and it may be that Rienzo was present when Petrarch was crowned with laurel on the Capitol. So began that odd alliance of art and literature with murder, arson, rape and pillage, which became so characteristic of a later time. How strange to think of the savage lords of Rome gathering on the Capitol to pay homage to the first modern scholar.

At the age of thirty Rienzo was sent on a mission to Avignon, to congratulate Pope Clement VI on his election and to beg him, on behalf of the innkeepers, who formed a great part of the Roman population, to return to Rome. The Pope liked this eloquent visitor so well that he detained him for a year. Upon returning to Rome, Rienzo saw his way clear. He had supreme faith in his star. The nobles laughed at him, and it became the fashion to ask him to dinner to hear him rant, declaim and threaten: but all the time he was organizing the citizens in secret, and bidding them work for the day when the power of the nobles should be overthrown and a 'new deal' established, the *Buono Stato*, as he called it, in which law, order and peace would rule. He looked even further, to a united Italy, a dream that was not realized until 1870.

He was a born propagandist. One of his methods was to arrange for artists to decorate the walls of Rome by night with allegorical pictures of Faith and Hope and of the widowed and weeping Rome, with angry Apostles, and even the ever new political symbol of the sinking ship. In the morning Rome would awaken and see these cartoons, and dream of the coming revolution. After two years of preparation Rienzo made his 'march on Rome'.

On the morning of May 20, 1347, the bell on the Capitol rang *a stormo* and the citizens went running there as they had been told to do. Rienzo and his followers had spent the night in a neighbouring church and now marched out, Rienzo in full armour, his head bare, and the banners of Liberty and Justice carried before him. He had chosen his moment well: the Colonna and the other nobles were not in Rome. In a scene of great enthusiasm his golden voice rang out, announcing the rules of the New Deal: murderers should be executed; all law cases should be heard within fifteen days; no house should be destroyed except by the authorities; every district of Rome should have its own home guard; a ship should be kept on the coast for the protection of merchants; bridges, castles, gates and fortresses should be held, not by barons, but by the people; the roads should be made safe and robbers put down; and many more such excellent rules. Without a hand raised against him, Rienzo was given supreme power and took the title of Tribune and Liberator of the Holy Roman Republic.

Those who remember Mussolini's march on Rome, and the years that followed, will recollect that nothing impressed the world more than the way he made the trains run to time and tidied up the streets. Rienzo's reforms had much the same effect on his contemporaries. Within a month he was writing to a surprised Pontiff to say that the roads were safe and that life in Rome was quiet at last. A contemporary wrote that 'the woods rejoiced, for there were no longer robbers in them. The oxen began to plough. The pilgrims began again to make their circuits of the Sanctuaries, the merchants come and go, to pursue their business. Fear and terror fell on the tyrants, and all good people, as if freed from bondage, were full of joy.' Old Stephen Colonna, who, at the news of Rienzo's triumph, had galloped back to Rome, threatening to 'throw this fool out of the window of the Capitol', had to fly for his life, and the nobles who had once laughed at Rienzo were forced to swear allegiance to him. So began his reign of seven months. Rienzo proved that he was a brilliant Senator, but a deplorable Caesar. Like his recent successor, when he gave up local matters for world affairs, he ruined himself by his own follies.

His vanity and his sense of the theatre were tremendous. He rode about Rome dressed in silk, half green and half yellow, furred with miniver, and a wand of steel in his hand on top of which was an apple of silver-gilt in which was a fragment of the Holy Cross. One day he decided to knight himself.

In the Baptistry of the Lateran is a basalt font in which it was once erroneously believed that Constantine the Great had been baptized. Rienzo spent the night in the Baptistry and took a bath of purification in the font. In the morning the crowds saw him stride out on the balcony of the Lateran Palace, clothed in scarlet, with the gold spurs of knighthood at his heels. The trumpets sounded and he addressed the crowd from the balcony; and the mind leaps forward six centuries to the balcony of the Palazzo Venezia. His voice was no longer that of the chief magistrate; it was the voice of an emperor. As he called upon the Pope to return to Rome, the startled protests of the Papal Vicar were silenced with a roll of drums. He claimed the right of choosing the German Emperor, a right, he said, invested in the people of Rome. He commanded all who disagreed with him to appear in Rome and give their reasons on pain of his sovereign displeasure. That night there was a great banquet. The nostrils of the horse of Marcus Aurelius spouted wine.

Rienzo's coronation was a ceremony devised by himself. High dignitaries of the Church placed a number of symbolic wreaths upon his head, of ivy, laurel, myrtle, of weeds gathered on the Arch of Constantine, and as each crown touched his head, a beggar, standing behind the throne, took it off and impaled it upon the point of a sword. Yet wrapped up in all this symbolism was an idea. He had invited envoys from the Italian cities to attend his coronation and he now married their cities to Rome with rings of gold. So the emperor of words and symbols was the first to visualize a united Italy. Yet what an exasperating mountebank he was! His life was a series of scenes and curtains. When he received a papal legate, sent to rebuke him and call him to order, he went to the vestry of St Peter's and donned the dalmatic worn by the Roman Emperors at their coronation.

His fall was hastened by a tactless drama in which, as usual, he had cast himself as hero. During a banquet he suddenly arrested all the nobility of Rome. He sent confessors with the Sacrament to them and in the morning they were led into a hall draped for an execution. As the nobles appeared before him, many on their knees begging for their lives, Rienzo descended from his tribunal and made a speech on the virtues of forgiveness and—invited them all to dinner! They left hating him and swearing to be revenged.

Open war soon broke out between the nobles and the citizens, and at the thought of wearing armour for anything but a procession, Rienzo grew pale and trembled. Nevertheless he went, shaking with fear, to battle. There was a fight in a pelting rain-storm at the Porta San Lorenzo in which many nobles were slain, and, more by luck than skill, the citizens won the day. Rienzo, who had not struck a blow, now believed himself a paladin. He solemnly dedicated his sword on the altar of S. Maria in Aracoeli. The Pope, offended by his arrogance, commanded the people to desert him, and after seven histrionic months they were willing to do so. Realizing that his play was over, he cried, 'Now in the seventh month am I driven from my dominion!', and fled for refuge to the Castel S. Angelo. The news of his abdication spread through the bewildered city, for there had been no rebellion. Through the puzzled crowds in front of the fortress pressed a slim young monk. It was his faithful wife finding her way to him in disguise.

Rienzo lived for another seven years, some say in the Abruzzi, among hermits and visionaries. Soothsayers promised him a new reign of glory and fame. One day he disappeared from the mountains and went to the Roman Emperor at Prague, who immediately handed him over to the Pope at Avignon. Clement VI had died and had been succeeded by Innocent VI, who saw in Rienzo a possible solution to the problem of the continued anarchy in Rome. Could he exert the old spell? The Pope thought it might be worth trying. So Rienzo, once again clothed in splendour, was sent to Rome with a papal force. The people remembered the brave shows of their old Tribune and swarmed out to meet him. They saw, however, not the romantic Rienzo of other days, but a gross, fat man. One who knew him wrote: 'He had a paunch like a tun, triumphant, like an Abbot Asinico. He was full of flesh, red, with a long beard. His countenance was changed, his eyes were as if they were inflamed—sometimes they were red as blood.' This was indeed the final drama. Could the old actor stage a come-back?

He was now a changed man. Fate had given him a second chance. 'He had no money to pay his soldiers,' says his biographer. 'He restricted himself in every expense; every penny was for the army. Such a man was never seen; alone he bore the cares of all the Romans. . . . He gave orders and settled everything, the times of attack, the taking of men and spies. It was never ending.' He had even become brave. Rienzo the actor had at last become a man of action; but, 'there is a tide in the affairs of men . . .' and Rienzo had neglected it. It was too late. The Romans wanted more theatricals. They did not like this strange, hard Rienzo who taxed them instead of making speeches. They wanted trumpets and pageantry; but instead they were getting new taxes on salt and wine, and conscription. In his youth Rienzo had often appeared to be drunk with power and glory; now in his middle age, when he was a tippler, he appeared most sober. The Romans shrank from his energy and his demand for sacrifice. At last, when he was capable of bringing about the *Buono Stato*, his followers would not have it. One morning, as he lay in bed in the Senator's Palace on the Capitol, having just 'washed his face in Greek wine,' as his biographer slyly described his breakfast, he heard a furious crowd shouting 'Death to the traitor!' In the old days he would have rung the *Patarina* and summoned the guard; but at last, it seems, he had become an ancient Roman. Dressed in armour and grasping the banner of Rome, he tried to speak to the crowd. They would not listen. He turned back to find himself alone in the palace, and soon he smelt burning and knew that the mob had fired the main gate. One chance remained to him: to die bravely. He threw it away. Knotting his bed sheets, he let himself down into a court-yard, having first cut off his beard and thrown a few rags over his grand clothes. He forced his way out into the crowd, joining in the shout of 'Death to the Traitor!', until someone, seeing the gold armlets under his rags, recognized him. The mob dragged him to the foot of the great flight of steps to S. Maria in Aracoeli, where in those days criminals were executed, and there he stood for an hour, no one having the courage to kill him. His face was 'black like an oven', he was clad in green silk, with the purple stockings of a baron. He stood with folded arms, until at last a man called Cecco del Vecchio took a sword and plunged it into his body. He was dragged by the feet to San Marcello, where for two days and nights he swung head down. On the third day the body was dragged to the Square in front of the Mausoleum of Augustus and was burnt on a pile of thistles.

If you look down from the Cordonata into the little hollow to the left as you go up to the Capitol, you will see an undersized statue of a man in a cowl. That is Rome's rather grudging tribute to one, who, in some ways, was born out of his time.

§ 3

From a point behind the Senator's Palace it is possible to see one of the greatest sights in Rome. The Forum lies below, stretching away from the Arch of Septimius Severus to the Arch of Titus, with the Colosseum beyond. It is terribly dead, like old bomb damage. The visitors peering about the ruins with maps remind one of people looking for a buried safe. A visitor today is, unhappily, unable to indulge in the romantic musings possible to his ancestors, for the decline of civilization is not, to us, a remote and romantic speculation. Secure in the belief that the world was getting better and even better, our forebears could afford the luxury of delicious and poetic moralizings amid the ruins: we have wept in them instead. Where the Victorians could feel a pleasant little shock from Macaulay's fantasy that a New Zealander would one day sketch the ruins of St Paul's, we merely wonder what kind of protective clothing he would be wearing. I looked down on Rome spread out beneath me: the Rome where Caesar had walked, where Cicero had spoken, where the Younger Pliny had bored his friends at literary luncheons, where Horace had strolled with Maecenas, where Claudius had pretended to be a soldier after his invasion of Britain, where Nero had neither fiddled nor sung, and where Vespasian had given a welcome touch of sanity and barrack-square discipline to the conduct of imperial affairs.

This vantage point behind the Senator's Palace is more or less where the Clivus Capitolinus came up from the Forum, and here the long-forgotten tourists of ancient Rome plodded, footsore as the moderns, to see the great temples and to look down upon the centre of the world, throbbing with its life, its sound and its colour. Before any great event the priests and augurs would ascend this road to take the auspices; and along this way would come the victorious general, a laurel wreath above his vermilion face, at the climax of his triumph. When his procession reached the foot of the Capitol, the prisoners would fall out to be killed, and at the precise moment when in the prison below they were strangled, or slain with an axe, the triumphant general, in the Temple of Jupiter above, would veil his head and sacrifice a snow-white bull that had been fattened on the pastures of the Clitumnus.

Anyone standing upon the Capitol eighteen centuries ago, upon a day when the games were being held in the Colosseum, would have heard the sudden roars of applause, the gasps of excitement and suspense from the throats of eighty-seven thousand people gathered in that now ruined amphitheatre beyond the Forum. They were a cruel and unimaginative people, yet, at their best, they had the three virtues of piety, gravity and simplicity. It is the preservation of those Roman virtues, to which Christ added the gift of compassion, which casts such beauty upon the Early Church.

I cannot join the chorus of those who deplore the excavation of the Forum. No doubt it looked romantic a century ago, when cows instead of tourists wandered about, while picturesque *contadini* leaned against fallen columns as great-grandmother produced her sketch-book, but the excavations have added enormously to our knowledge of ancient Rome and its people. Indeed a monumental work like Frazer's *The Fasti of Ovid* could not have been written in the time of Byron.

It is pleasant, as one looks down at the Forum, to think of the plump little figure of Edward Gibbon treading its stones 'with a lofty step', during his brief visit to Rome in 1764, when he first conceived the idea of writing *The Decline and Fall of the Roman Empire*. 'After a sleepless night,' he wrote, 'I trod with a lofty step the ruins of the Forum; each memorable spot, where Romulus stood, or Tully spoke, or Caesar fell (how strange that Gibbon of all men should have made this error!), was at once present to my eye.' I think that perhaps his step might have been even loftier could he have seen the excavated Forum as it is today.

Another name which comes to mind is that of Lady Elizabeth Foster, that 'bewitching animal', as Gibbon once called her, who became the second wife of the fifth Duke of Devonshire. She was one of several women before whom the great historian is said to have knelt and been unable to rise unaided; and it is true that Gibbon admired her greatly. Her allurement was such, he said, that if she had the mind to do so, she could call the Lord Chancellor from the Woolsack. Her last years were spent as a dowager in Rome, where she achieved the remarkable feat of linking the name of Devonshire with that of the tyrant Phocas. The column erected to that Byzantine despot, the last to be set up in the Forum, had been unidentified for centuries until the Duchess uncovered the base in 1813, during some excavations financed by her. This is still one of the most prominent objects in the Forum and was inaccurately apostrophized by Byron in 1817 as 'Thou nameless column with a buried base'.

'Oh Rome!' wrote Byron, 'my country! city of the soul!', from which one might suppose he was an old resident. Yet the truth is that he spent only twenty-three days in his 'country', but poets are unaccountable creatures, and are not dependent on time. During that brief visit, most of which was spent on horseback, Byron wrote a more lasting impression of Rome than many penned by those who have lived there all their lives. In Rome took place that amusing incident when the poet sat to Thorwaldsen, the sculptor. 'Will you not sit still?' asked Thorwaldsen. 'You need not assume that look!' 'That is my expression,' replied Byron. Thorwaldsen knew that he was trying to look like Childe Harold and paid no attention, portraying him as he saw him. When Byron was shown the finished work, he said it was not a bit like him. 'My expression is more unhappy,' he explained. So it is with his beautiful verses on Rome. They are 'more unhappy' than their writer was at the time. The reader thinks of some sensitive soul weeping in the Forum and choking back a sob on the Via Appia, while all the time Byron was leading a healthy, manly life in the saddle, hastily and inaccurately observing the scene, but nevertheless soaking up out of the air, as it were, the essence of Rome.

Turning back to the piazza of the Capitol, thoughts of Rienzo and Michelangelo are natural, but how strange it is to think that once the Union Jack was run up on the campanile! This happened in 1799, when Nelson was operating off the Italian coast and Napoleon's troops were retreating from Italy. A young naval officer, who later became Admiral Sir Thomas Louis, led a flotilla of boats up the Tiber and, landing in Rome, ran up the British flag on the Capitol. At the same time another Englishman, who afterwards became Sir Thomas Troubridge, captured several French ships loaded with Vatican art treasures, which the British Government returned to the Pope. I have read somewhere that in recognition for his part in the affair, Troubridge was given the right to incorporate the crossed Keys of St Peter on his arms. It is curious to see how unrelated events are often associated, for it was this act of justice on the part of the British Government which caused the Vatican, some years later, to grant permission for the establishment of the non-Catholic Cemetery in Rome, where Keats, and the ashes of Shelley, and a great number of English and other Protestants, are buried.

§ 4

A noble flight of steps leads from the Capitol to the church of S Maria in Aracoeli, which, as I have said, occupies the site of Juno's temple. Here the famous geese were kept, perhaps in a sacred goose-pen, or possibly they strolled pompously around as the 'Roman geese' do today in the precincts of Barcelona Cathedral. These birds may have been kept for the purpose of divination. It was the doctrine of the College of Augurs that any bird could give a *tripudium*, that is to say a sign given when eating, or refusing to eat, and though chickens were usually employed for augury, geese, with their wing-flapping, neck-stretching, head-nodding, sucking and guzzling, tail-wagging, to say nothing of the great range of their vocal accomplishments from the querulous quack to the hysterical cackle, must have been infinitely better prophets. Plutarch, who could never have kept geese, makes a point of explaining that when the Gauls tried to scale the Capitoline Hill, Juno's geese were on siege rations and were consequently abnormally lean and wakeful, and readily gave the alarm. It is my experience, however, that geese, even when gorged with food, are such excellent sentinels that they will cackle and flap their wings at night at any unusual sound. After they had saved the Capitol, nothing was too good for Juno's geese.

The Romans never forgot their patriotism. The censors, when they took office, recognized that the first charge on the exchequer was that of feeding the geese, and once a year a goose gorgeously arrayed in purple and gold was carried round the Forum in a splendid litter. This delightful spectacle was unfortunately marred by the usual touch of Roman cruelty, for a dog crucified on a cross of elderwood was also carried round, a reminder of the dogs which had failed to bark the night that the Gauls tried to scale the hill.

When I first entered the church of S. Maria in Aracoeli, I felt that I had stepped back into ancient Rome. Surely I was standing in the great columned hall of a law court or a public building. There were hundreds of such buildings in ancient Rome, of which the early churches are not only a reflection but also sometimes an actual survival. Under the open sky it is not always easy to imagine the ancient scene, but the old churches give one an immediate visual impression.

S. Maria in Aracoeli remains my favourite early Roman church. It is dim, and the marble pavement is vast. The twenty-two columns which support the roof were taken from all sorts of Roman halls and temples, for they are not uniform, and one has the words scratched on it '*a cubiculo Augustorum*', which proclaims its origin. No doubt these columns were drawn up the hill about 590, in the time of Gregory the Great, when the first church on this site was consecrated. While St Augustine was converting the people of Kent, Greek monks were saying mass here; four hundred years later it was served by Benedictines, but since 1280 the church has been tended by the Franciscans.

I wondered where Gibbon had sat, for it was in this church that he dedicated himself to his life's work. 'It was at Rome, on the 15th of October, 1764,' he wrote, 'as I sat musing amidst the ruins of the Capitol, while the barefooted friars were singing vespers in the Temple of Jupiter, that the idea of writing the decline and fall of the city first started to my mind.' In his time S. Maria in

Aracoeli was believed to be standing on the site of the Temple of Jupiter, and Gibbon would have been even more impressed by the sequence of events had he known that he was really on the site of Juno's Temple, listening to the priests as they sang hymns to the Virgin Mary on the spot where the Roman Queen of Heaven had been worshipped for two thousand years. I fancied him sitting there, a plump little man probably in a bag-wig, a snuff-brown coat, knee breeches and snowy ruffles. Boswell thought him an 'ugly, affected, disgusting fellow,' which is rather what other people thought of Boswell! Gibbon was twenty-seven when the idea came to him in the church, and he was fifty when the last volume of *The Decline and Fall of the Roman Empire* appeared. The last volumes were written in Lausanne, and he described 'the final hour of my deliverance'. It was the day, or rather night, of June 27, 1787, between the hours of eleven and twelve, that 'I wrote the last lines of the last page in a summerhouse of my garden. After laying down my pen, I took several turns in a *berceau*, or covered walk of acacias, which commands a prospect of the country, the lake, and the mountains. The air was temperate, the sky was serene, the silver orb of the moon was reflected from the waters, and all nature was silent. I will not dissemble the first emotions of joy on recovery of my freedom, and perhaps the establishment of my fame. But my pride was soon humbled, and a sober melancholy was spread over my mind, by the idea that I had taken leave of an old and agreeable companion. . . .'

Gibbon, like Byron, made no more than a tourist's visit to Rome, and it seems that he had no desire to return in his triumphant middle-age to visit the place where the idea first came to him that was to occupy his life and give him lasting fame.

In a corner of the church I found the gravestone of the man who found the Laocoön under his vineyard in 1506. So great was the sensation caused by this discovery that, as the tombstone puts it, the man, Felis de Fredis, had two claims to remembrance: that he had discovered the Laocoön, and—his own virtue. It is difficult for us, who have seen so many photographs of the Laocoön, to understand the excitement at the court of Pope Julius II when it was unearthed. The statue was well known from Pliny's description of it, but of course no one had ever seen it. Francesco, the son of Giuliano de Sangallo, who was a child at the time, has described how he, with his father and Michelangelo, went to the spot. 'We three set off,' he wrote, 'all three together; I on my father's shoulders. When we descended into the place where the statue lay, my father exclaimed at once, "That is the Laocoön of which Pliny speaks." The opening was enlarged so that it could be taken out; and after we had sufficiently admired it, we went home to breakfast.'

There must have been many such beautiful mornings in Renaissance Rome when old friends, known by references to them in classical literature, flung a white arm from a vineyard and were helped out into the sunlight.

While I was wandering round the church, I came to a closed door before which a group of women were silently waiting. A young Franciscan came up with a key and I followed the women into a chapel. The friar snapped on an electric light in a glass case above the altar, and the women dropped to their knees before a rosy-faced baroque statue, about two feet high, of the Infant Christ. It glittered with jewels from head to feet. The Franciscan began to tell us about the figure, which is the most famous miracle-working statue in Rome.

The Santo Bambino has appeared in nearly every book written about Rome since the seventeenth century, and I looked at him with the greatest interest. As a work of art he is not beautiful. Some say that he was carved by angels in olive wood from the Garden of Gethsemane; but others, who prefer to think that angelic woodworkers would be more highly skilled, say that the figure was carved by a monk in the seventeenth century.

Until quite recently Prince Torlonia kept a gilt coach ready day and night to take the Bambino to the bedsides of the sick in Rome, and many travellers have described the solemn procession through the streets, often after dark. So it was seen by Charles Dickens, who commented that the appearance of the Bambino at the bedside of weak and nervous people *in extremis*, accompanied by a numerous escort, 'not unfrequently frightened them to death'.

Sir Alec Randall, who was Secretary to the British Legation to the Holy See between the wars, has described in his book *Vatican Assignment* how the Bambino was brought to him when he was gravely ill.

'In 1927 I went down with a very serious attack of typhoid fever,' he writes. 'It seemed impossible for me to recover and I received the Last Sacraments. Then someone suggested that the celebrated "Bambino" from the church of Aracoeli should be brought to me. My devoted nurses, my wife and Sister Mary Campion, a "Blue Nun" (the English nursing order of the Little Company of Mary, distinguished by their blue hoods), agreed with some reluctance. Father Philip (Langdon), who was a daily visitor, offered to go in the Cardinal's car to bring the rather gaudy but revered statue of the Holy Child, together with the Franciscan friars who had the duty of carrying it to the dying. When they attempted to cross the Piazza Venezia a cordon of soldiers stopped them. In vain did Father Philip point to the Cardinal's arms and the privileged CD number on the car. The reply was that no one was to be allowed to pass until the Duce arrived and made his speech from the palace balcony. Father Philip returned to the charge; he was on his way, he said, to a dying man and he was taking the Bambino to him. At this the soldiers immediately saluted, broke the cordon and the Bambino duly arrived, was shown to me and the prescribed prayers were said. Sister Campion later rather grimly remarked that the excitement very nearly ended my life, but years after, when I was re-visiting Rome a number of people asked me whether I hadn't been an example of the Bambino's miracles. The most appropriate comment on this was made by Professor Giuseppe Bastianelli, who, in spite of being Mussolini's medical adviser, was no Fascist, but a sceptical scientist of the old liberal tradition. He said: "In a case like this the doctor can do nothing; the nurses can do a little, but only God can bring him round the corner." '

The Bambino is still the most famous doctor in Rome and goes out to hospitals, nursing-homes, and to the bedrooms of the sick; but nowadays, the friar told me, he travels in a taxi-cab.

'And when was the Bambino last taken out?' I asked.

'Yesterday, to a hospital very late at night,' replied the Franciscan.

'And how often does he go out?'

'Perhaps twice or three times a week, sometimes more.'

I stepped up to the altar and saw that, stacked in baskets and lying around, were hundreds of letters from all parts of the world: from Holland, Argentina, Germany, Sweden, Kenya (written by a child), the United States, England and Algeria. Those were the stamps I saw at a glance. Many of the letters were just addressed 'Il Bambino, Roma'. The letters come in a continuous stream. They are never opened. Each one contains a request from someone in trouble or pain. After a week the letters are removed and others take their place.

'What do you do with the old letters?' I asked.

'They are all burnt.'

'Unopened?'

'Of course. They have nothing to do with us. What is in the letters is between the Bambino and the writers.'

'Are any of the brothers stamp collectors?'

The young man smiled.

I commented on the astonishing collection of jewellery which shimmered on the statue. Hardly an inch of wood is visible. I was told a curious story. About four years ago, when the church was closed in the afternoon, a thief, who had concealed himself there, opened the chapel door and stripped the Santo Bambino of every jewel he possessed. The thief then hid again and when the church was opened at four o'clock, he quietly walked out. The sacrilege horrified Rome; but in just over a week the Santo Bambino was again completely covered with the jewels which I now saw—diamonds, emeralds, pearls, rubies, sapphires, pendants, necklaces, ear-rings and bracelets.

Once a year the Bambino is placed in a magnificent *presepio*, or crib, and is taken with stately ceremony to bless Rome from the head of the great flight of steps. This is the time, too, when hundreds of young Romans from the ages of four to ten appear in their best clothes and recite poems and make speeches which have been taught them by their parents and priests. I am told that most of them go through the ordeal like little Ciceros, which must be delightful to watch.

I wonder if the origin of the Christmas 'crib' is well known. It began with St Francis, who once asked Pope Honorius III for permission to celebrate Christmas with an unusual ceremony in the little village of Grecia, near Assisi. He explained that he did not wish to be charged with levity and therefore asked the Pope to judge whether his idea was right and proper. When the Holy Father learnt that all St Francis wished to do was to make a model of the manger to please the children and instruct the simple, he gladly gave his consent. St Francis then approached a grave and worthy man, and together they constructed a manger, an ox and an ass, with figures of the Blessed Virgin and the Child, which they placed in the church. St Francis was so pleased with his tableau that it is said he knelt by it all night long, sighing for joy and filled with an unspeakable happiness.

Before I left the church, I found one of the most unusual tombs in Rome in the chapel of the della Valle family. It is the grave of a Syrian girl named Gioreda Manni, and this is how she found her way to Rome. In the early seventeenth century, Pietro della Valle, an ardent young man, fell so deeply in love with a girl that when the affair came to grief he left the family palace and went on a pilgrimage to the East. While in Cairo it is recorded that he climbed the Great Pyramid and carved the name of his lady on the highest stone. But nothing cures an old love swifter than a new one, and it was not long before Pietro had fallen in love with a beautiful Syrian girl, a Nestorian Christian named Gioreda. They were married in Baghdad, but after a few years of great happiness Gioreda died in Persepolis. Pietro was frantic with grief and, like Joan the Mad of Spain, was unable to say farewell to the corpse of his beloved. He continued his travels accompanied by Gioreda in her coffin. He visited Shiraz, found his way to the coast, took ship to India, travelled to Muscat and across the desert to Aleppo and Alexandretta. After five years of wandering he arrived back in Italy and placed the body of his young wife in the family tomb on the Capitol. The story is not over, however. In the course of her travels, Gioreda had befriended a young Georgian girl with the unusual name of Maria Tinatin de Ziba, who joined the caravan as her companion. The sorrowing Pietro della Valle eventually married his deceased wife's companion and settled down with her in the family palace in Rome. They had fourteen children. So this romantic pilgrimage in search of consolation ended in a thriving nursery.

§ 5

After an energetic morning in and around the Via Appia I caught the usual catacomb chill and, having bought a thermometer, found that my temperature was a hundred and one. I suppose I should have gone to bed, but I had promised a friend in one of the embassies to attend an evening party in honour of a departing diplomat, and I felt it would be discourteous to cry off at the last moment. I told myself that the party would probably cure my chill and do me good. Therefore, with an enthusiasm for such occasions which I thought I had lost many years ago, I hailed a taxi at the top of the Via Veneto and enjoyed the night air of the Borghese Gardens as we swung down into that bowl of pine-scented dusk.

A costly lift with a keen sense of its duty purred obediently to the top floor of a block of fashionable modern flats. I stepped into a babel of charming, sophisticated people who were grouped against a romantic setting. A roof garden overlooked a great area of Rome. The million lights of the capital shone and glittered beneath us, and far off upon the sky was a long ridge where four sparks of fire marked the masts of the Vatican Radio. The sound of knives and forks, the laughter, a gay awning and a buffet loaded with everything one should not eat at night, the tinkle of glasses, and the well-dressed groups so picturesquely outlined against the stars, turned my mind to Lucullus and Petronius Arbiter, and, glancing at the darkened city, I thought it must indeed have looked much the same to Caesar's guests as they glanced down from a party on the Palatine.

Diplomatic Rome is one of the many Romes within Rome. It has twice the normal allowance of diplomats, for numerous countries accredit a representative to the Holy See as well as to the Quirinal. As the Vatican City is too small to house a diplomatic corps, the Vatican diplomats live in Rome and increase the diplomatically privileged palaces. This large population of foreigners exists in a chain reaction of social occasions; beneath crystal chandeliers cocktail parties, receptions and dinners follow each other throughout the season. If all diplomatic parties were as pleasant as this one, I reflected, the life of a young secretary or attaché must be ideal, indeed almost eighteenth century in its air of privilege and its charming triviality.

I remember talking a great deal about herbaceous borders to the wife of an ambassador and about ceramics to a trade commissioner, then I gravitated towards the most typical Englishman I had seen for years, who turned out to be a Spaniard. I led a celebrated film actress to the buffet and noticed her air of caution as she glanced round carefully, wondering what was on her diet sheet. She finally, with a charming air of surrender, selected *scampi*. Then there was the baroness. She was a determined little woman who had come to Rome about a ghost. There are many reasons for visiting Rome, but this was one that had not occurred to me. The spirit haunted a castle somewhere in Italy and threw stones and gravel at the baroness and disarranged her furniture. As she was a Protestant, the village priest, believing the spirit to be that of a heretic, would have nothing to do with it. She had come therefore to place the matter before the Vatican.

'And what do they say?'

'I am having luck,' she replied. 'I am making progress! Every day I see someone more important. Any day now I may meet a cardinal. Soon I shall convince them that the ghost is that of a monk—for my castle was once a monastery—and then they will be obliged to send someone to exorcize it.'

'And if you cannot convince them?'

'Then I shall wait until I can see the Holy Father himself.'

I wondered if the Vatican received many such visitors. One glance at the baroness proved that she would never leave Rome until the Vatican had promised that her ghost should be properly belled, booked and candled.

A clock was striking twelve as I found myself in a long, empty street. There were no taxis and I set off to walk. I had a headache and thought my heart was beating rather rapidly. My mood of careless gaiety had been replaced by one of sombre apprehension and alarm. I stood outside that great baroque welcome to Rome, the Porta del Popolo, through which the coaches of former generations entered the Eternal City. Passing beneath the arch, I saw the huge empty square in the lamplight, with the obelisk in the centre and four lions, one at each corner, from whose mouths water was gushing into marble basins. The night seemed airless and suffocating. I went up to one of the lions and placed my hand in the water, which was ice-cold. Unlike most of Rome's lions, which primly whistle a single spout of water into their basins, these lions in the Piazza del Popolo eject a thin blast, or wedge, like a curved sheet of glass. As I continued on my way up the Corso, I faced a possibility that always horrifies me: the prospect of being ill in a strange city and away from my own bed.

In the morning a dark young doctor said he would send a nurse to give me an injection. I was feeling too ill to ask why he could not do this himself. Much later the door was opened by an enormously fat old woman, an Italian Mrs Gamp. She stood breathing heavily and gazing short-sightedly round the room, trying to locate her victim. I watched her, fascinated, as she sat near the window, filling a hypodermic syringe, which she held two inches from the enormously thick lenses of her spectacles. It was fascinating to watch someone who suggested an alchemist's den, armed with such modern equipment. She gave me two more injections on the following day, and upon the third the young doctor came a second time, pronounced me well and presented his account. Then the nurse presented her bill, and the chemist his, for the penicillin. The total cost of my catacomb chill came to twenty-one thousand lire, or just over twelve pounds. It is expensive enough to be well in Rome, but to be ill is a luxury.

§ 6

At the top of the Via Vittoria Veneto a great number of red and blue sun umbrellas dot the wide pavements each side of the street. This is American Rome, just as the Piazza di Spagna was English

Rome a hundred years ago. Everything here is a little richer and more expensive than elsewhere: we are in the dollar area. Here you see the 'milords' of the new age, the film stars and the celluloid caesars, and those executives whose names occupy such a tedious crescendo of type before a film begins.

America's long and distinguished association with Rome seems to have begun when young Benjamin West arrived in 1760 as an art student from Pennsylvania, to the delight of Rome, which found him a novel visitor. Old Cardinal Albani, who was blind, and whose ideas of America evidently included coons and cotton, asked anxiously of those who introduced the young American whether he was white or black! When told that he was very fair, the old Cardinal, whose complexion was of the most southern sallow kind, asked, ' What! As fair as I am?', a saying which went the rounds of Rome; and 'as fair as the Cardinal' became a current phrase. Rome did not really begin to beckon Americans across the Atlantic until the mid-nineteenth century, the time when America's tradition of public statuary may be said to have been founded. The presence of unlimited quantities of marble, and a race of masons inspired by hereditary skill, made Rome the international capital of sculpture.

John Gibson, the son of a market gardener, and a pupil of Canova, represented England. Among his works is the statue of Queen Victoria enthroned between Justice and Mercy in the House of Lords, and there is a Gibson Gallery in Burlington House. He was an impractical, absent-minded man who posted unaddressed letters, lost his way, got out at wrong stations, and asked the Duke of Devonshire £500 for 'Mars and Cupid', now at Chatsworth, after it had cost him £520. 'He is a God in his studio, but God help him out of it!' said one of his American pupils. He tinted his statues, some suspected with tobacco juice, and his realistic Venuses shocked the New England susceptibilities of, among others, Nathaniel Hawthorne. One of these goddesses was known to the irreverent as 'Mrs Gibson'.

The Danish sculptor, Thorwaldsen, who designed the tomb of Pius VII in St Peter's, and whose colossal Christ and the Twelve Apostles are in Copenhagen, was the idol of the Scandinavians.

Then came a flood of Americans, women as well as men. There was the strangely named Moses Ezekiel, who had a studio in the Baths of Diocletian and a piano which Liszt often played; and William Wetmore Story, who helped Browning to look after Walter Savage Landor after his family had turned the poor old man out into the street at the age of eighty; Samuel Morse, of the 'Morse Code'; and Harriet Hosmer, the most distinguished of those American female sculptors who settled in Rome, as Henry James put it, 'in a white marmoreal flock'.

The American girl of 1850 was evidently quite a handful and must have interested the Romans, even more than her pony-tailed descendant of the present day. 'Hatty (Harriet Hosmer) takes a high hand here with Rome,' wrote Story to James Russell Lowell in 1853, 'and would have the Romans know that a Yankee girl can do what she pleases, walk alone, ride her horse alone, and laugh at their rules. The police interfered and countermanded the riding alone, on account of the row it made in the streets.'

These were the companions and friends of Nathaniel Hawthorne when he went to Rome, and their studios, seen through a rich romantic haze, are to be detected in his still charming but improbable novel, *The Marble Faun*. The book followed the popular recipe, first mixed by Mme de Staël in *Corinne*, and later by Hans Andersen, which was to write a travel book in the form of fiction. Our forefathers took *The Marble Faun* to Rome with them and solemnly went round identifying the places where Hawthorne's lay figures did this or that, just as, much earlier, they had visited the places consecrated to the musings of Corinne and Oswald. And how interesting to think that the old magic still works, and has been successfully applied by the cinema in *Three Coins in the Fountain*.

The most interesting of the American sculptors was William Story, who, with his wife and family, made Rome his home and died in Italy. The Storys and the Brownings were inseparable until Elizabeth Browning's death drove the poet back to England. Browning began to model in clay under Story's guidance, and Story took up the pen with admirable success; his book *Roba di*

Roma is a fascinating description of the Roman people during the last period of Papal Rome. Story cast a rather disparaging eye on the official American society of his day, which he described as 'very low, eaten up by jealousy and given shockingly to cabal and slander,' while he called the American Legation 'the jeer of the diplomatic circle'. But the international artistic set in which he and his wife moved seems to have enjoyed an Arcadian existence, working away happily, talking their heads off in the Caffè Greco, living for practically nothing in palaces, and selecting their models from Italians beautifully dressed in regional costumes, who daily draped themselves in picturesque attitudes on the Spanish Steps. It seems to have been a gentlemanly and predominantly Anglo-Saxon Montmartre; and everybody was sufficiently well-off to leave Rome in the summer and go into the hills.

Among those who were welcomed to this friendly American Story household was Hans Andersen, who, it may not be generally known, took his first upward step to fame in Rome. He arrived first in 1834, as a poor young man travelling on a meagre state grant, discouraged and very much at odds with life. Like many another Protestant visitor, he was delighted by Rome, yet at the same time vaguely disturbed by it. He was alarmed by the friars, suspicious of the nuns, and even the urbanity of the Jesuits seemed to him a bit satanic. It is recorded that during a great ceremony in St Peter's, while every one of the assembled thousands knelt as the Pope passed, the lonely figure of Hans Andersen remained as upright and rigid as a tin soldier.

Nevertheless he absorbed a great deal of the Roman atmosphere and went home to write the *Improvvisatore*, which is still well worth reading and a good deal less mannered than *The Marble Faun*. The book was an immediate success in Denmark, ran into various editions, and was translated; and Hans Andersen tasted his first success. He returned to Rome later as a distinguished writer, but seems to have had a miserable time there. It was winter, and he fell ill. There was a great deal of infection about and he was distressed, as indeed the whole of Rome was, by the tragic end of the twenty-two years old Princess Gwendolen Borghese, a daughter of the sixteenth Earl of Shrewsbury, who died suddenly from 'scarlatina', and was followed to the grave by her young children. Poor Hans Andersen spent Christmas alone in his lodgings, eating grapes; but his biographer does not explain where he found grapes in December!

About this time he attended a children's party given by William Story and his wife. Browning was also present. Hans Andersen read *The Ugly Duckling* to the children and Browning read *The Pied Piper*; then, with Story leading the way, playing a flute as the Pied Piper, they marched, laughing, through the Story apartments, which at that time were a series of vast rooms on the second floor of the Barberini Palace. Henry James, who edited Story's letters, says that Hans Andersen was often presented by small children with broken toy soldiers, fractured dolls, and other treasures, and these relics he never threw away but carried round with him in a bag. One can imagine the expressions at the Customs when the melancholy Dane arrived with his luggage!

An unusual story about Tennyson was told to Story by Browning. Having arrived at Florence on his way to Rome, Tennyson, who was an excessive smoker, was so upset when he was unable to buy a certain brand of tobacco, that he gave up his visit to Rome and returned to England!

It was in Rome that Thackeray began to draw the amusing little pictures for various children, including Edith Story, which he eventually expanded into *The Rose and The Ring*; and a delightful moment in the Barberini Palace, when Edith was recovering from an illness, was the arrival of Thackeray to sit on the side of her bed and show her the pictures and tell her the as yet unwritten story.

A more recent American arrival was Marion Crawford, the son of Thomas Crawford, the sculptor, a pupil of Thorwaldsen's. The father is remembered by a great number of statues and busts, including the equestrian statue of Washington at Richmond, Virginia, and the colossal 'Armed Liberty' at the Capitol, Washington; and the son for an equal number of popular novels with Rome and Italy as their background, of which perhaps *A Cigarette Maker's Romance* is the best remembered.

Sitting in the Via Veneto today among the film actors and

actresses, the business magnates, the officials of Economic Co-operation, the visiting senators and congressmen, the members of the United States Information Service, the United States Chambers of Commerce for Italy, and various other organizations, with a palatial American Embassy on the corner and the news-stands overflowing with American newspapers and magazines, one wonders what Story and Hawthorne would have made of it. Much of modern Rome would have surprised them, but I fancy no part more than that leading up to the Pincian Gate which their countrymen have made their own. It has a strong character which overflows into the side streets, where you find quick-lunch bars and American restaurants which specialize in club sandwiches, Chicken Maryland, apple pie, canned peaches, hamburgers and American coffee. These haters of colonialism have indeed created a barefaced colony where they feel safe and at home, and into which they can return, as into a fortress, after raids into foreign territory! There is something quite fascinating about the Americanism of this part of Rome. It is, in its way, imperial. *Civis Americanus sum*. . . .

I used often to wonder, while I sat under a blue sun umbrella in the Via Veneto, how many Romes there are. There is ecclesiastical Rome; diplomatic Rome; archaeological Rome; artistic Rome; business Rome; the tourists' Rome; and the everyday Rome in which the majority of the people earn a living. Even the stranger's Rome splits itself into a series of different Romes. For instance, I met a man who is writing a treatise on first century *terra sigillata*, and everything that had happened before Augustus, or after Trajan, did not exist for him. I thought he was to be envied in having his little sector of Rome so neatly and clearly defined. Then I met an elderly American priest fulfilling his life's ambition in treading the stones of Rome, who early every morning, armed with his priestly identification card, his 'celebret', went off to say mass in a different church. He was working his way slowly round the altars of Rome and was not interested in anything else. There was an architect for whom Rome was merely a series of elevations, doorways and window ledges. But the bewildered tourist who is flung into this whirlpool of history and association for two or three days and is expected to assimilate in that time the events of several thousands of years, how deeply he is to be pitied!

§ 7

Sometimes in the late afternoon, at the end of a hot day, I fancied that I could smell the sea in Rome. It was not a wind so much as a gentle freshness that fell over the city. It is called the *ponentino*—the little west wind—to distinguish it from the real thing, the *ponènte*. At such times I would decide to walk through the Borghese Gardens and see the sunset from the Pincio.

The Borghese Gardens have a pleasant, regular life of their own, whose chief characters are children, dogs and lovers. Every time I went there I would see the same man with an Alsatian dog and a red rubber ball, the same nuns in charge of tiny girls in pink print dresses, walking two by two, and sometimes even the same lovers, seated on the grass or eating ices under the stone pines. On Saturday afternoons there was a popular Punch and Judy show near the lake, and how amusing it was to study the circle of small upturned faces. On Sundays young men would take their girls out in rowing-boats on the lake and scull in the direction of the Temple of Aesculapius.

I would often come across lonely dells and shrubberies in these gardens; and I thought how sad the place was, and haunted, like everything in Rome, by its own population of ghosts. There are belts of stone pines which recall Respighi's symphonic poem, and great avenues of glossy magnolias, as high as oaks, and sombre belts of laurel and ilex. The Italian habit of placing a statue or a bust in some deserted spot gives to such old gardens a startling pagan significance. A timid Christian might well make the sign of the cross here, for the ear is prepared to hear strange music and the eye glances suspiciously at the dark bushes, expecting to see a lonely, discredited god.

You pass from the wildness of the Borghese Gardens into the formality of the adjoining gardens on the Pincian Hill, where there are geometrical flower-beds, avenues and vistas, and a

Who's Who of famous Romans (though Napoleon is surely an intruder!) ranged on marble plinths. The Roman nose was always a good target, and should you pass one day and notice that Agrippa or Virgil is noseless, it is good to find that in a day or two the missing organ has been swiftly replaced by the public works department, which is accustomed to these surgical operations and keeps a large stock of noses for the purpose. And here I would like to warn anyone rich enough to buy a bust or a statue from the dealers in the Via del Babuino that only about one in a hundred antique statues has come down with its nose intact. 'The five or six hundred heads discovered in my time,' wrote Lanciani, 'were all, except a dozen or two, without noses.'

No one tells you anything in Rome; you are either expected to know all about it, or to be intelligent enough to find out, and this applies particularly to the eccentric and capricious opening times of museums and galleries and other public places. Consequently, if you take the trouble to find out why Napoleon should be placed among the famous Romans, which seems at first so odd, you will discover that he is there, and rightly so, in an honorary capacity as the author of the Piazza del Popolo, which his architect, Valadier, redesigned, as he also designed the Pincian Gardens.

The Walls of Rome, which make a curious angle in order to include the Pincian Mount, are at this point known as the Muro Torto. It was the only portion not repaired and strengthened by Belisarius, on the assurance of the citizens that St Peter himself would look after this sector; and it is a fact that the barbarians never attacked there. Before I walked down to the famous terrace, I would often go to the garden gate of the Villa Medici to glance through the iron bars into a glorious picture of the sixteenth century sleeping happily among flower beds, cypress trees and long gravelled walks, where at any moment, it seemed, a cardinal might pass, in consultation with Velazquez, who stayed at the villa and painted this garden: but there was never a movement, except that of a languid butterfly hovering in the shrubberies or the flight of one of Rome's infrequent birds.

So I would come to the terrace, and the balustrade from which every visitor to Rome has watched the sun set behind St Peter's. Below me lay the Piazza del Popolo, where men and women were hurrying across a great arena of pale stone, while cars sped from the right through the Porta del Popolo—the old coaching entrance to Rome. In the centre of the piazza, remote and unconcerned, so old that nothing can matter to it any more, the obelisk stood, which was already an antique when Augustus brought it from Egypt and set it up in the shadow of the Palatine, in the Circus Maximus. All the chariots once passed this obelisk as it stood in the central *spina* of the course; and now it looks down upon Romans still speeding, still trying to beat each other to the post. There are three churches in the piazza, all dedicated to the Virgin, and the most interesting lay to my right, hidden by the trees of the terrace. This is S. Maria del Popolo, just inside the gate. The church was built in the twelfth century in order to exorcize the ghost of Nero, which was said to have wandered the slopes of the Pincio and to sit, accompanied by demon crows, under some old walnut trees. When the site was being cleared, Pope Paschal II cut down the trees with his own hands. The first church has disappeared, but the present one still covers the site of the tomb of the Domitii, where Nero's ashes were placed by two of his old nurses and his mistress, Acte.

I gazed at this splendid foreground, and then out across the roofs of Rome to the dome of St Peter's, now escorted by the four aerials of the Vatican Radio. It is one of the great views of the world, and as I stood with the declining sun in my eyes, the whole landscape, with the dome in the centre, the tomb of Hadrian with its Angel, and the long, dark ridge of the Janiculum to the left, took on the exquisite colours that are not the least of Rome's glories. It is not really the sunset, but the afterglow in summer that is so wonderful from the Pincio. The sun went down. A golden light hovered above the city, seeming to ascend from it. The dome grew sharper against the sky, and gradually an upsurge of dull red light spread in the west and moved up to blend and mingle with the still dark blue of a summer's day in Italy. This is the rich Homeric light that suggests the dust flung by galloping horses and the wheels of chariots, an epic colour which deepened and darkened as the blue sky turned paler, until there was a rusty glow all over the west, a promise that tomorrow would be as cloudless as the day just ended.

This is the perfect moment as night comes. The streets remain strangely luminous in the dusk, coloured pink as if the soft volcanic tufa had soaked up the sun and would store it until morning. The fading light glows from walls of saffron, rose-red and peach, and the pavements shine warmly, almost as though the lava remembered prehistoric fires. St Peter's dome was now black across the Tiber, standing against the last remaining bars of red. The chariots of the sun had gone, the dust of their wheels had settled; and the first stars burned over Rome. At this moment the heart is touched. First one and then another—one hardly knows where it starts—the bells of Rome are ringing the Angelus—the Ave Maria—and another day of life has gone. There is now the dark, and tomorrow.

§ 8

I always enjoyed my walk back through the cool night. The stone pines stood in a halo of reflected light, and the paths ran on into a belt of stealthy darkness ringed by the surrounding lights of Rome. Haunted by day, the Pincio and the Borghese Gardens are even more ghostly in the dark. Here is a part of Rome that has never been built upon since ancient times, the place where Lucullus had his fabulous palace and laid out gardens, and where he gave those feasts which have become even more famous in the long perspective of time than his victory over Mithradates.

The quickest way to a fortune in Roman times was to be governor of a province: and some of the most cultivated of Romans milked the Empire and returned, as Lucullus did, rich with the spoils of Asia, to settle down as millionaires and startle contemporaries by their extravagance. The Gardens of Lucullus stretched over the Pincian Hill, but the palace itself, with its porticoes, library, and a series of dining-halls, occupied the southern slopes, where the Spanish Steps are today. Plutarch says that once when Pompey was ill, his doctor ordered him a dish of thrushes—alas, still a Roman delicacy!—which could be found nowhere at that particular time of year except in the breeding pens of Lucullus on the Pincian Hill. Lucullus was the first to introduce cherries into Italy from Asia, and so to western Europe. Plutarch also tells the story of Cicero and Pompey, who, meeting Lucullus by chance in the Forum, decided to find out if the rumour were true that the famous epicure ate hardly anything when alone. As it was presumably near dinner time, and Lucullus was not giving a party, they asked if they might dine with him, and he, seeming rather confused, asked for a day's warning, to which they would not agree. Lucullus then sent a message to his steward, saying that he intended to dine in the Apollo Room; and when the three arrived they sat down to one of the stupendous feasts for which their host was famous. It appeared that each room had its own standard of expenditure, scale of entertainment and style of menu, and it was sufficient for the steward merely to know the name of the room in which his master would dine for him to put on the appropriate banquet.

But the ghost that comes stealing out of the shadows on the Pincian Hill is not that of Lucullus, securely resting beneath a mound of honeyed dormice and nightingales' tongues, but of the frightened Messalina, who was murdered in those same halls. This puzzling woman seized the Gardens a century after the death of Lucullus, when they belonged to her enemy, Valerius Asiaticus. Having hounded this wretched man to his death, she took possession of his property, and the gardens on the Pincian Hill became her favourite retreat. Here it was that she took refuge when at last her doting husband, the elderly Claudius, apparently the last man in Rome to hear of her escapades, was eventually roused against her. We shall never know whether Messalina was as bad as she had been portrayed. It is possible that a woman like Agrippina, her successor in the imperial palace, played a great part in her defamation. Messalina was only twenty-six at the time of her death, which seems an early age for her to have accomplished all the infamies attributed to her. However, the night poor Claudius was told that she was even worse than his former wives, Messalina, realizing that at last she had aroused the unpredictable cruelty of a weak man, fled to the Gardens of Lucullus, hoping that the storm would blow over. So it might have done had not Narcissus, the freedman, quickly despatched a tribune with a detachment of the guard with orders to execute the Empress. They found her on the Pincian Hill, seated on the floor of an apartment, weeping in her mother's arms: the mother who had remained in the background during the years of her prosperity and had now hastened to comfort her in her despair. As the garden gates were opened and the tramp of the approaching soldiers was heard, Lepida tried to persuade her daughter to leave the world like a Roman and to take her own life. The tribune and his guards entered the room. A dagger was handed to Messalina. She pointed it at her throat, then at her breast, but lacked the courage to press it in. The tribune then drew his sword and killed her at a blow.

Some time later the Emperor, noticing that she was not at the dinner table, asked where she was.

§ 9

Straining with every muscle tense in order not to embrace a nun, or to step back upon the bare toes of a Franciscan, one strap-hangs (in theory) in the fierce green buses of Rome, but in actuality clutching anything that will help to maintain equilibrium. At first sight nothing could be more forbidding than the public transport of Rome. As most Romans spend a great part of their lives rushing to work in the morning, rushing home to luncheon, rushing back to work after the siesta, and then rushing home in the evening, there are four rush hours when crowds, not queues, assemble at the 'bus stops. If swords and shields were to be served out to the waiting passengers, some wonderful battle scenes would be observed when a 'bus arrives.

A visitor who intends to stay for more than a few days in Rome, however, should learn how to use this admirable system, which will carry him into every corner of the city at a fraction of the cost of a taxi. The 'bus service is, in fact, the cheapest thing in Rome. It is worth mastering, not only for obvious reasons, but also for the sense of triumph such an achievement brings with it. Some little ribbon, or medal, should be given by the Municipality to those strangers who acquire the technique of 'bus travelling; some first step towards the coveted privilege of honorary citizenship.

When a 'bus stops in Rome, it hisses like an angry dragon and two little doors in the front fly open, apparently without human agency. They are actually controlled by the driver. The innocent stranger naturally thinks, as he waits for the dishevelled passengers to emerge and adjust their garments after their long fight down the crowded vehicle, that he is supposed to enter by these doors. When he tries to do so, they fold back with an angry snap, leaving him on the pavement with the impression of a great number of compassionate dark eyes gazing down at him with pity, before they are whirled off into the distance. No hero has probably ever succeeded in entering a Roman 'bus by these doors, and to do so would violate the principle of 'bus travel. The narrow back door, which is the only entrance, is guarded by an official who deserves a more impressive title than conductor. He is the imperator of the 'bus. He sits upon a little seat and issues the tickets, all the time commanding those who stand crushed and suffocated in the already full vehicle to pass forward. You hand him a fifty lire note as thin and worn as battle honours and he gives you a ticket and sufficient small coins to ensure your return to Rome for several centuries. You then struggle and insinuate your way to the front of the 'bus with determination. If you fail to do this, you will be carried on for a mile or two past your destination. The novice, of course, does not know when his destination is approaching and when he recognizes it, twenty Romans are standing wedged between him and the exit doors. The strategy of Roman 'bus travel is, therefore, to fight your way towards the doors from the minute you enter, so that at a moment's notice, with a muttered *scusi* or *permesso*, and a barked shin, you can reach the opened doors before they hiss themselves shut again. The fear that may afflict some beginners that they might reach the doors just before they close, and so become transfixed between them, and in this position be whirled on to the next *fermata*, need not worry anyone; for the drivers have no sense of humour.

The 'buses collect a wonderful cross-section of the Roman population, and standing wedged between priests, nuns, Franciscans, seminarists, and Italians of every description, one could not possibly be in any other city on earth. Those snorting green dragons are as characteristic of Rome as the red double-deckers are of London.

CHAPTER THREE

A ticket for the Forum – the Roman Toga – the Senate House – the Vestal Virgins – where Caesar was murdered – Cleopatra in Rome

§ 1

I bought a ticket for the Forum and walked down the long ramp to the pavements of ancient Rome. Fifty feet above me was a boundary wall upon which people would lean all day long, peering down into the ruins as if they expected something to happen; but nothing ever does, except perhaps a cat stalking a mouse through what once was the centre of the world.

As I walked, I began to think not of Romulus and Remus, or Caesar, or Augustus, but of ordinary Romans and the way they lived: and I thought first of all of the toga. I can think of nothing in modern life like the toga. It cannot be compared to the silk hat and morning clothes of Victorian respectability, because it was a national and not a class distinction. When you saw a man wearing a toga in ancient times, you knew that he was a properly attired citizen of Rome, a free-born Roman, with the Roman law behind him; he could not be crucified, flogged, or otherwise hurt or humiliated. St Paul was entitled to wear the toga; St Peter was not. If you were one of the lesser breeds, you probably looked at the man in a toga with envy and respect, as a member of the ruling race. To the provincial, a man in a toga was a man wearing the official dress of the governor and the magistrate. If a foreigner or a slave dressed himself in a toga, hoping to be taken for a true Roman, he could be prosecuted, and there was once a case of this kind over which the Emperor Claudius presided.

That solemn and formal attitude towards life, that *gravitas*, which distinguished the ancient Roman, could not have been

85

aided by a better garment. It is said that Cincinnatus was plough-
ing upon his farm on the *Ager Vaticanus* when messengers arrived
to tell him that the Senate had appointed him dictator. Catching
sight of them some way off, he sent his wife hurrying to fetch his
toga so that he could meet them with dignity. That was the act of
a true Roman. Once, it is said, the Emperor Augustus was
annoyed when he saw a group of citizens attending a meeting
improperly dressed and made a law that in future all citizens
entering the Forum, or attending the games, must wear the toga.
The Emperors were as particular about dress regulations as the
War Office used to be in the days of brass buttons, and, one after
the other, they issued edicts on the wearing of the national robe.
It was the most graceful and dignified dress ever devised, and the
fops and dandies, and the great lawyers, would spend hours on
their togas; and the Roman equivalent to a trouser press was an
arrangement of splints into which the folds of the toga were
pressed overnight.

The great advocate Hortensius spent much time dressing himself with the aid of a mirror, and he once sent a written protest to
a friend who had jostled him and disarranged the folds of his toga.
He had a special way of arranging the *umbo*, the bandlike fold that
crossed the chest, and when he entered the Forum he was such a
stately figure that the tragedians, Aesopus and Roscius, used to
follow him about and study his dress and deportment. The
exceptionally long togas affected by some dandies—the Emperor
Caligula once caught his foot in his toga and fell—were condemned by the moralists, and it was with the idea of linking
gravitas with *simplicitas* that Augustus affected a plain type of toga,
hand-woven at home by his wife Livia and her maids. It was
without doubt a frugal toga, for he was great enough to defy
fashion, but no doubt it was long enough to hide his built-up
sandals; for Augustus was only five feet seven inches in height.

There were several kinds of toga. The most splendid was the
toga picta, which was the purple mantle in which the statue of
Jupiter was clothed. In early times a victorious general celebrating
a triumph was allowed to wear the *toga picta*; this right was given
to Julius Caesar, who was the first Roman to wear the purple

whenever he wished. The Emperors from Augustus onward retained the privilege, but only on state occasions. The six hundred senators wore the *toga praetexta*, which was the ordinary white woollen toga bordered with a band, or hem, of purple, and this was worn on official occasions with red leather shoes of a pattern worn by no other Romans. Then there was the *trabea*, which was a toga with a red hem and was worn by certain priests and augurs, and possibly by the knights. Finally, there was the ordinary white toga of the plain citizen.

In spite of the distinction which the toga conferred upon the wearer, it was an unpopular garment, and Romans were always trying to avoid wearing it. It was heavy, it was inconvenient, for one could do nothing in it but walk about slowly or make a speech, and it was also expensive and had to be repeatedly sent to the fullers to be whitened. Both Juvenal and Martial were always grumbling about the necessity of wearing the toga if a man had to appear in polite society in Rome, and they both contrasted the tyranny of this garment with the freedom and informality of country clothes. Even such a man-about-town as the Younger Pliny mentioned, among the attractions of his rural villa, that it was not necessary to wear the toga there. So might a city clerk in the time of Dickens have disliked his silk hat, that inconvenient symbol which had continually to be ironed by the barber until it looked like a stray cat.

From Martial's references to the much-washed toga, it is clear that these garments did not stand up any too well to the frequent cleaning, and no doubt whenever the Emperor gave a show of gladiators, the upper seats, at least, where the general public sat, must have exhibited a wonderful collection of old and frayed togas.

So I thought as I strolled about the Forum Romanum on that brilliant morning of summer. What would it be like to find oneself back in imperial Rome, with the life of the Forum all round one? I thought how fascinated I should be by the hundreds of men in togas. I should be able to recognize by his red shoes the Senator hurrying to the Senate House; I should distinguish at a glance the augur in his red stripe, going off to feed the sacred pullets, the wealthy dandy in his costly toga, and the humble citizen in a threadbare toga, who had come to give evidence in a law case. And a fellow-feeling, no doubt, would have drawn me to some writer like Martial, as he pressed through the crowds, wearing a splendid but ancient toga, on his way to his publisher in the Argiletum. How interesting it would have been to have met a man who was really proud of his toga, perhaps some British princeling visiting Rome, who had been granted citizenship for political reasons, a dark, eager little Celt from the far-off Londinium beside the Thames, who had bought himself a Savile Row toga, one whose every fold and crease proclaimed the distinction of its wearer as he strolled about the Forum, trying to look more Roman than the Romans.

I smiled to myself as I walked up the Sacra Via, reflecting that it is only by human associations that the Forum can become understandable or even interesting. This wonderful graveyard, where the heart of the ancient world lies buried, can puzzle and repel many of its modern visitors: it can only become alive and understandable if one is able, in imagination, to restore the missing columns and regild the vanished roofs; to place the statues upon their plinths and to fill the narrow ways (and how surprisingly narrow they are) with a jostling, noisy crowd of human beings, smelling of pomade and garlic, each man pushing and shoving and living intensely in the moment, as still we do.

From the high ground near the Arch of Titus, where the Sacra Via begins, I paused and looked back along the full length of the Forum, and I tried to imagine what it must have been like in imperial days. Any piece of land which has been continuously occupied for thirteen or fourteen centuries must change with the times and can even alter so completely that its original inhabitants would not recognize it at all: but I do not think this happened with the Forum. There were alterations, reconstructions and rebuilding all the time, but, as most of the buildings were consecrated, the new ones occupied the same sites and were different only in their increasing splendour. It is true to say that though the Forum was always changing, it remained the same. A Roman of 100 B.C., had he been able to visit the Forum in A.D. 200, would have found the buildings different, but on the same sites as the places he knew. After recovering from his first surprise, he would soon have been able to make his way from the Senate House to the Temple of Vesta and to the other main buildings; he would certainly not have been as lost and bewildered as Shakespeare would have been in the London of Dr Johnson.

While I was standing on the Sacred Way, a young man and a girl with a *Blue Guide* passed by.

'Oh look,' cried the girl, pointing down to the black slabs of polygonal paving-stones. 'See the ruts made by the chariots! Isn't that too wonderful?'

People dislike to be corrected, or I should have told her that chariots were never allowed in the Forum except during a triumph, or when the Vestal Virgins drove out in the streets, and the wheel ruts were most likely those of the stonemasons' carts of Renaissance times, heavy with looted marble for new churches and papal palaces.

As I stood near the Arch of Titus, I thought what a wonderful glimpse of first century Rome the stranger must have enjoyed as he approached along the Appian Way. He would see the Sacred Way at this point, and the Forum lying ahead. On his left the Palatine Hill would have held to the sun the glittering palaces of the Caesars; and in the distance, rising above the clustered roofs of the temples and the law courts, would be the Capitoline Hill and the great Temple of Jupiter, with its golden doors and roof. I should choose the reign of Vespasian as the period when I should like to have seen the Forum in its pride and glory. I should like to have watched the Colosseum being constructed, and to have seen Nero's Golden House nearby, and the new Temple of Jupiter, which replaced the temple burnt down in the riots that preceded Vespasian's arrival in Rome. Above all, I should like to have caught a glimpse of that grand old soldier whose first steps to the purple were taken as a young officer during the Claudian invasion of Britain. It would have been interesting to have seen the old man, whose tough, firm face is so well-known to us, seated in the imperial litter, preceded by his lictors, and to reflect that when young he had forded the Medway and led the Second

Legion, the *Augusta*, along the coast of Hampshire into the West Country.

The Sacra Via led to the Temple of Vesta, where the Vestal Virgins tended the sacred flame. How surprising that such an immortal street should be so narrow and only about eight hundred yards in length. As we see it today, desolate and empty, with weeds growing on each side of it, it is hard to believe that this is really the famous Sacred Way, the road which was once crowded with people from morning until night.

It was at the top of the Sacra Via that Horace met his adhesive Bore—a gentleman we all know—who clung to him with volubility all the way down to the Forum. Cicero also has left a vivid memory of the Sacra Via as he saw it, packed with jostling crowds from end to end.

We must imagine this multitude of people crowding the roads, lining the steps of the temples and sitting on them, pouring in and out of the law courts, clustered round the offices of the financiers and the moneychangers: the white, formal figures of the Roman citizens, the slaves in their rough, belted tunics, and the foreign visitors gaping up at the temples, watching the curl of smoke from the circular shrine of Vesta, and pressing near to see a famous orator leave the law courts or a celebrated senator enter the House. The public water-clocks—the *clepsydrae*—would have interested and amused us. By the time of Vespasian they had replaced the old-fashioned sundials. It is extraordinary that a race as practical and businesslike as the Romans should have been so backward in horology. Long after the Greeks and Egyptians were telling the hours with mechanical inventions, time in the Forum was still announced by a herald stationed near the Senate House, who, when the sun reached its noon position, would call out, '*Meridies est!*'; and it is still stranger that this practical nation should for several years have used a Greek sundial calibrated for Catania in Sicily! Eventually accurate sundials were installed in public places and at last water-clocks were used everywhere. As the water dripped, a float descended, marking the twelve hours on a transparent cylinder. Some *clepsydrae* were more complicated. The water rotated a system of wheels which moved a pointer round a dial, not unlike a modern clock. Sometimes the pointer was a wand held in the hands of a figure which stood on the top of the *clepsydra*: and the finest of these water-clocks would toss up pebbles at the hour, or would whistle.

Had we pushed our way into the Basilica Julia, or any other law court, during the hearing of a case, we should have noticed that an official of the court would be carefully watching a water clock, which he would stop during the reading of documents and start again when the advocates began to plead. The Romans were almost as long-winded as the Greeks and it was necessary to allot so much time, or water, to the prosecution, the defence, and the judges. Every lawyer was obliged to finish speaking when the court official announced that the water allotted to him had run out. Pliny mentions that during an important case he was allowed ten large *clepsydrae*, but after speaking for nearly five hours, he had not finished. The case was so important, however, that he was granted four extra *clepsydrae*.

Martial addressed one of his epigrams to a longwinded lawyer. 'The judge has reluctantly allowed you seven water-clocks, Caecilianus,' he wrote, 'but you talk so long and so loud with your head thrown back, swilling tepid water all the time out of glasses. To satisfy your oratory and your thirst, we beg you, Caecilianus, drink out of the water-clock itself!'

It must have been a tremendous sight to have entered the Basilica Julia, that now desolate series of plinths and cracked pavements, when the *centumviri* were in session, while the water-clocks silently dripped away the hours and eighty judges in their spotless togas sat on their benches, and, on either side of them, the famous lawyers conducted a case. On the day of a great trial the huge basilica could never hold all those who crowded to hear the case; the upper galleries were also full, men on one side and women on the other. We know from Pliny that such events were as trying to the judges as they were to counsel and audience. The heat was terrible. The lawyers had to shout to make themselves heard. Sometimes the proceedings were interrupted by paid applauders—*laudiceni*—and the general impression is of a scene of noise, heat, and utter confusion, very different from one's idea of a Roman court of justice.

The most crowded buildings were the offices of the money-changers, the bankers, and the joint stock companies—the *publicani*. These were tucked away, as similar offices are in the City of London, in all sorts of buildings. The Roman Empire is probably the most fearful instance of heartless exploitation in history. Wherever the Eagles cast their grim shadows, there stood a tax-collector. The slave dealer, the commercial traveller, and the collector of taxes, moved with the Legions, and every successful campaign meant more tribute, more slaves, more loot, and a richer Rome.

It may seem strange to us that the Romans of the Republic and the early Empire controlled and policed the world without a civil service. The revenue was collected by companies and individuals on behalf of the State, and this profitable business was put out to tender. The successful bidder then signed a contract with the State to collect a stipulated sum, paid down a deposit and proceeded to collect as much as he could, all money over the sum agreed upon being profit. As these companies were concerned with the revenue of entire provinces, as well as with the proceeds of state quarries, salt works, mines, fisheries, forests, and a hundred other things, the investor had a wide choice. The system was bad and readers of Cicero's Verrine orations will recollect a gloomy picture of provinces suffering the extortions of venal governors and *publicani*: but the more money collected, the richer the shareholders. The Forum was the whispering-gallery of the world and a special corps of messengers was always speeding to Rome with news. Every whisper was interesting because it usually had some bearing upon the intricate investment situation. No wonder one gets the idea from Cicero, Horace and Martial that a Roman could not keep away from the Forum: it was the only place where he could find out what was happening to his money.

The bankers of Rome must have done a great business in the Forum, for they knew the exchange rates of the Empire and would take money on deposit and give you a draft on foreign bankers. When Cicero's son was sent to the University of Athens, he did not travel with a chest of money, as he would have had to do in the Middle Ages, but with a Letter of Credit to be payable in Athens. It is a pleasant insight into the affection which often existed between employer and employed, as well as into banking methods, that when Cicero's beloved secretary, Tiro, a freed slave, fell ill in Greece, it was a simple matter to arrange with a banker in Rome for him to receive all the money he needed and for the doctor's bills to be paid.

Yet how difficult it is, as you sit on a chunk of marble in the Forum, to imagine such bustle in this lonely place, to see in imagination the litters swaying above the heads in the narrow streets as a rich man comes along attended by his parasites, and perhaps by a slave called a *nomenclator*, whose business it was to know everyone's name and his occupation, and who skilfully whispered such information into his master's ear so that people should be flattered to think that he remembered them. The 'yes man' is a figure of great antiquity and was seen at his miserable best in Rome, clothed in a toga given to him by his patron, whispering compliments, perhaps loathing himself and his patron, but obliged to accept with gratitude invitations to dinner, knowing all the time that he would be put with other poor clients and served with inferior food and wine. He was not entirely a case of weak character: he was a social problem. He had nothing else to do. His pride prevented him from taking up a menial calling, and the state encouraged his penurious idleness. It was for him that the emperors built the wonderful, the incredible marble baths, circuses and amphitheatres. Though he might sleep in a garret, he could spend his waking hours in scenes of the utmost magnificence. Imperial Rome was composed of a few millionaires, a few hundred well-to-do people, and thousands of poor whites and innumerable slaves of all races and colours.

Whom would you choose to have met in the Forum? The Emperor! Yes, the sight of Caesar, of any Caesar, would well repay a visit to Rome. I should also like to have seen one of those wealthy freedmen, who had come to Rome from various parts of the world as slaves and sometimes became even more powerful than Caesar himself. And I should have been fascinated by the sight of an augur at work. That amazing hocus-pocus must have been the last word in solemn nonsense, and I imagine that few educated people in the time of Cicero could have believed that the flight of birds and other natural events had any real bearing upon human affairs.

§ 2

The most prominent object in the Forum is the Arch of Septimius Severus. The emperor who erected it was concerned with Britain throughout his reign; he also died there and was cremated at York.

Septimius Severus was a great soldier and a terrifying disciplinarian, who once disarmed and banished the Praetorian Guard. He was ruthless, unscrupulous, a fond parent and an indulgent husband; and, though there was nothing lovable about his character, one cannot help feeling sorry for a mighty ruler of the old Roman tradition whose two sons were unworthy of him.

Caracalla, the elder son, was given this nickname because of a hooded Gallic cloak which he adopted when he became emperor and introduced into the army. His name is perpetuated now only by the ruins of his Baths, where in summer Rome holds a season of outdoor opera. Like Nero and Henry VIII, he was apparently charming when young, and so tender-hearted, we are told, that 'if ever he saw condemned criminals pitted against wild beasts, he wept or turned away his eyes, and this was more than pleasing to the people'. What an unexpected glimpse this is of the Roman populace, whom one has always imagined howling for blood. However, Caracalla soon grew out of this and became a dissolute and horrible young man, while Geta, his junior by one year, whom he loathed, was not, one suspects, much better.

When Severus was sixty-two, racked with gout, and in the fifteenth year of his reign, great trouble broke out on the British border, where the Caledonians had begun raiding beyond Hadrian's Wall. Britain had been in an uproar since the beginning of the Emperor's reign, when its governor, a soldier named Clodius Albinus, had been declared a rival emperor by his troops, and, crossing into Gaul with the whole of the British forces, had been defeated by Severus outside Lyons, in the biggest action fought by Romans against Romans since Philippi. The defeat of the British legions disorganized life in the island, and the Caledonians became so threatening in their raids into the richer south that Severus, ill as he was, decided to go over himself to teach the barbarians a lesson. It is also said that he was glad of the opportunity to take Caracalla and Geta from the gay life of Rome and give them their first taste of discipline.

The Roman historians who describe what followed give the clearest glimpse of Britain since the days of Claudius, and for the first time we look into an incredibly far-off Caledonia, which was not yet Scotland. Arriving in the autumn of A.D. 208, with his sons and the Empress Julia, the Emperor organized a great army and made his headquarters at York. Caracalla and Geta were always quarrelling, therefore Geta was left in London to govern the south, while Caracalla accompanied his father. All winter the Roman engineers were busy felling timber and making bridges across rivers, marshes and tidal estuaries. The Caledonians were now greatly alarmed. They were, we are told, people who 'live in tents, naked and barefooted, having their wives in common, and they rear all the children which are born to them. The government of these tribes is democratical, and they delight above all things in pillage. They fight from chariots, which are drawn by small, swift horses; they fight also on foot, run with great speed, and are most resolute when compelled to stand. Their arms consist of a shield and a short spear, which has a brazen knob at the extremity of the shaft, that when shaken it may terrify the enemy by its noise. They use daggers also. They are capable of enduring hunger, thirst, and hardships of every description; for they will plunge into the marshes and remain there several days, with only their heads above the water. When they are in the woods they subsist on bark and roots; and they prepare for all emergencies a certain kind of food, of which if they eat only so much as the size of a bean, they neither hunger nor thirst.'

When spring came, Severus led his army into the wilds of Caledonia, travelling more often in his litter than on horseback. The Caledonians worried his rearguards and slaughtered his stragglers, decoying bodies of troops by putting out cattle as bait; though woods and glens were alive with the enemy, they melted away at the approach of the legions and it was impossible to bring them to battle. The Romans struggled through forests and across mountains and rivers in spate, fighting guerrilla actions everywhere. The ancient writers, who were never good at figures, give the Roman losses in the campaign as fifty thousand, which seems incredible.

Nevertheless the Romans pressed on northwards through Highland weather until they came 'to the extreme end of the isle of Britain', where Severus, feeling that he stood where no other Roman general had been, caused astronomical observations to be made, and satisfied himself that Britain was really an island. It seems likely, however, that he was no further north than the eastern shores of the Moray Firth.

Leaving the wretched legions, possibly to face a winter in Aberdeenshire, or at any rate in camps sufficiently far north to hold their territorial gains, he retired to York to wait until the fighting season should begin again. Here his health became worse, but his resolution remained unshaken. In the spring he returned to the front, directing the campaign. Either the hardships were intolerable, or Caracalla had been tampering with the loyalty of the troops, for a mutiny took place which the old man silenced by appearing in his litter, pointing to his swollen limbs and saying, 'Soldiers, remember it is the head that commands', and ordering them to fall in and obey him, which they instantly did.

The second campaign convinced the Caledonians that they could not hope to hold out against such a determined commander, and they sued for peace in the autumn, promising to be of good behaviour and to cede their land to the Emperor. He returned well pleased to York, where his health was not improved by the news that no sooner had his back been turned than the Caledonians had started a general offensive. Between his gout, his wrath and his determination to exterminate the Caledonians completely in the following spring, Severus became gravely ill. Added to his worries as a soldier was his grief as a parent; for it was clear that Caracalla was longing for him to die. When he did so, it was suspected that his end had been hastened by poison given by his doctors at the request of Caracalla; but this was a suspicion which usually hovered over the death-bed of an emperor. A funeral pyre was erected at York and Septimius Severus was cremated with all the pomp proper to the obsequies of a Caesar.

The Empress Julia and her sons took the ashes of the Emperor back to Rome in an alabaster urn. Caracalla and Geta were now joint heirs of the Empire. Their hatred of each other was undisguised. They themselves contemplated separating as far as possible from each other, one ruling the west, the other the east; but this did not really suit Caracalla, who wished to rule alone. The Empress arranged a meeting between her sons in the private rooms of her palace. Caracalla went to it accompanied by centurions who had orders to slay Geta. The young man rushed into his mother's arms, where he was stabbed to death, his brother an onlooker, if not an assistant.

All this time the triumphal arch of Septimius Severus, which had been built in A.D. 203, five years before the Caledonian campaigns, was standing in the Forum. It bore the names not only of the Emperor, but of Caracalla and Geta. As soon as he had murdered his brother, Caracalla gave orders for Geta's name to be erased from every monument upon which it appeared in Rome. You may see on this arch the space of the deletion. The words taken out were *et Getae nobilissimo caesari*, and they can be reconstructed from the holes left by the clamps of the bronze letters which were removed.

Caracalla reigned only seven years, a time filled with his atrocious mass murders. It is said that he was haunted by the ghosts of his father and brother, who pointed their swords at his breast, and nothing would drive them away, though he spent his life making pilgrimages to strange gods and shrines. He tried to exorcize them by sending hundreds of his contemporaries to be companions to them in the shades, and it is highly probable that he was now mad. He was killed in his thirtieth year by an equerry who, while helping him to mount his horse, plunged a dagger in his side.

The thousands of British visitors who gaze at this arch every year may perhaps reflect, as I did, that it was placed there by one of the first explorers of Scotland.

§ 3

I had been inspecting the Arch of Septimius Severus, and thinking of the old Emperor swaying through Scotland in his litter, when I noticed a few paces away a flight of steps leading to a battered building entered by two tall bronze doors. I mounted the steps and found that I was standing in the Senate House—the Curia—of ancient Rome, the most famous building in the annals of law and, politically, the most important place in the Roman world.

It was revealed in 1937, when the ancient church of S. Adriano was demolished. As the church came down the Senate House emerged, apparently little the worse for its entombment of thirteen centuries. Beneath the floor was found the original pavement of Diocletian's time, on which the Senate used to meet in those fateful ages before the fall of Rome.

I was astonished by the faces of those around me as they gazed impassively about them, apparently unconscious that the ground on which they stood was historically sacred. Here was indeed the venerable great-grandmother of parliaments. I felt the need to share my delight with someone. I spoke to a man standing beside me, but he replied in some language I could not understand. I remembered Gibbon treading the Forum with a lofty step, and thought how he would have stood in wonder at this sight.

The hall is by no means magnificent and is not large. Three tiers of marble seats face each other along its length and at the end, facing the assembly, the presiding magistrates had their curule chairs. At the far end of the hall there is a mass of brickwork which once held the altar and the famous statue of the golden Victory brought by Augustus from Tarentum.

There were various peculiarities about the Curia. It was a consecrated building and had the status of a temple. The Senate could not meet before sunrise or after sunset, therefore the all-night sittings of Parliament, so familiar to us, were unknown in ancient

Rome. The first act of a Senator when he entered the House was to approach the Altar of Victory and cast a few grains of incense on the brazier which glowed before it. As in our own House of Commons, there was no tribune and speakers addressed the assembly from their seats; when a division was taken, those in favour of the motion moved over to one side and those in opposition to the other.

The building we now see is as it was during the late Empire, at the time of Diocletian. In its long history it has been enlarged, restored, and twice burnt to the ground, but it is believed to occupy the site of the earliest assembly hall of Rome's third king, in 670 B.C., where the elders used to meet in their rough sheepskin coats. In successive buildings on the same site the affairs of the Republic and the Empire were discussed for centuries; from this place the Roman world was ruled; every great man in Roman history had lifted his voice there and its floor has known the tread of every Roman orator and emperor. There was a time in Republican days when the habits of the Senate were so austere and frugal that heating the House in winter was an unthinkable luxury. I remembered a letter written by Cicero to his brother in 62 B.C., in which he said that an important meeting had to be adjourned because of the cold; and members of the public were highly amused by the sight of the revered elders emerging from the icy hall wrapped in their purple-striped togas.

I suppose my interest must have been so marked that the attendant, who guards a barrier to prevent visitors from walking on the old marble, waited until we were alone and then, with a charming and understanding Italian smile, quickly moved the barrier and waved me on to the floor of the Senate. I examined every detail and was interested most of all by the brickwork at the end of the hall, which had held the Altar of Victory that stood in front of the lovely statue from Tarentum. Every theological student will remember the debate in the fourth century about this statue, but who could imagine that its plinth can still be seen? The correspondence which has come down to us, the protests of Symmachus and the reply of St Ambrose, introduces us to one of the strange problems which arose at a time when Rome was not yet entirely converted to Christianity and the old gods were still defended by a few aristocratic diehards.

A time had arrived when the Senate was composed of a mixed gathering of Christian and pagan members. The Christians objected to the ancient rite of paying homage to the golden goddess, which had been observed in the House since the time of Augustus. Not to observe this act was to the pagans much worse than the refusal of a British Member of Parliament who, for some reason, might decline to bow to the Speaker. The Christians, however, persuaded the Emperor Constans to remove the statue. Their victory was not for long. Back it came with Julian the Apostate, and it remained in the Senate House for about twenty years, during the reigns of Jovian and Valentinian I. When Gratian became emperor, the Christians persuaded him to have the statue removed once again, and this was done in A.D. 382. The leader of the pagan party was an upright and sincere aristocrat named Symmachus, who revered the gods of his ancestors. He petitioned the Emperor to restore the statue, but was exiled from Rome for his pains. When, in the following year, Gratian died, Symmachus returned to Rome and immediately made the same petition to the new Emperor, Valentinian II, a boy of thirteen. The petition is a fascinating document, a queer blend of superstition, patriotism and traditionalism, written by a sincere man during the fast fading twilight of the gods. It is pathetic, too, in the picture it gives of the writer, an old man facing a new world which he distrusts and dislikes.

St Ambrose, the Bishop of Milan, and one of the most energetic of the Early Fathers, heard of the petition and asked to see a copy of it. He sent a reply to the Emperor, answering it point by point in a clear and commonsense way. One feels in the petition the weight of an old, tired-out religion, and in the reply of St Ambrose the confidence and vigour of the new faith. Among the arguments of Symmachus was an appeal to the past splendour of Rome and to her great history, to prove that the old gods had defended the state. Replying, St Ambrose cited various moments in Roman history when it seemed to him that the old gods had been asleep. He wished to know, for instance, what they were doing on the night when the Gauls scaled the Capitol. 'Where was Jupiter at that moment?' he asked. 'Was he speaking in the goose?'

This highly entertaining correspondence ended, of course, in a victory for the Christian party, and the statue of Victory never again entered the Senate House. What happened to it nobody knows.

§ 4

Men of all nations climb about the House of the Vestal Virgins, where for eleven centuries the presence of a male would have been punished with death. It is the only place in the ruins where you do not have to think of Horace or Juvenal to evoke the shades of the past, and here, no matter how Christian you may be, you cannot be unaware of the nobler, gentler side of paganism, almost as though one of those beautiful little fauns in the Capitoline Museum had frisked in from the sunlight and was nestling his head against you, asking to be scratched.

I like to imagine that the Early Fathers felt that way too, otherwise surely they would not have allowed this *atrium* to become, as it did, the architectural prototype of the Christian nunnery: neither, I imagine, would they have married their daughters to the Church with much the same rites which admitted a novice to the sacred order.

The House of the Vestals is in ruins and all the hasty visitor sees is a confusing mass of brick walls and a wide, grass-grown space in the centre where a number of goldfish live in two oblong pools. Some are enormous and all loved the bread I sometimes remembered to take for them. Along one side of the vanished colonnade stands a row of white statues. These were found in the ruins, and represent some of the chief Vestals, the *Vestales Maximae*. Upon the head of one is the purple-edged head veil, the *suffibulum*, the only representation of this vestment, I believe, ever known. It was worn only when salt cakes and other offerings were made to Vesta.

That is all you can see; but in imagination you can reconstruct a two-storied cloister of the utmost magnificence, where everything was of marble. Fragments of the columns that upheld the first storey have been found: they were of *cipollino*, and the smaller ones above were of the rare and precious *breccia corallina*. The bedrooms of the Vestals were on the upper floor and the walls of these rooms, encrusted with marble, collapsed in time into the ground floor. Here a sad tale is revealed. The marble palace was an ice chest in cold weather. It was surrounded by tall temples and built against the side of the Palatine Hill. If you go there in the afternoon, you will see that it is one of the first places to fall into shadow as the sun passes behind the hill; and it must have done so even earlier when the Palatine was covered with tall palaces. In an attempt to fight the cold and damp, the Vestals put in double walls on the side of the hill and raised the floors everywhere, sometimes very oddly on sawn-off *amphorae*, and between these rows of halved wine-jars the hot air was made to circulate from a central furnace. It is melancholy to reflect that honour and sanctity must have been accompanied by rheumatism and arthritis.

And who were the Vestals and what did they do?

In primitive times fire was a magic element which could be created by rubbing together two dry sticks. In such communities a hut was sensibly set apart where a fire was always burning from which the people could take this precious element. While the men were at war, or hunting, and the married women were looking after their homes and children, the care of the fire naturally fell to the charge of young maidens with no other responsibilities. As the Romans became civilized, what had in tribal days been a matter of commonsense became a religious cult and the care of the fire was a symbolic rite which involved the safety and welfare of the state. In the days of Rome's greatness the thought that the sacred fire might be extinguished was horrifying, and the curl of smoke from the top of the Temple of Vesta was a daily sign to Rome that all was well with the Empire.

In the earliest days the huts of the primitive Latins and Etruscans were circular and made of reeds. When men began to build in stone, they still built the Temple of Vesta in circular form; and so it remained until the fall of Rome, a marble memory of a primitive straw hut. Everything connected with Vesta and her worship, and the function of the Vestal Virgins, was charged with this same religious antiquarianism. At first there were only four Vestals, then six, and at a much later time, seven; but six was the number throughout the greater period of Roman history. They were sacred and above the common law; they enjoyed great privileges and wealth. The Chief Vestal had the right of audience with the Emperor at any time; she and her priestesses were preceded by a lictor when they went out, and if by chance they met anyone being led to execution, they had the privilege of pardoning him, no matter what his crime. Another privilege, remarkable in a city like Rome, where all wheeled traffic was forbidden in daylight, was the right to drive out in the streets at any time. They had two vehicles, one a high, antique state tumbril, and the other a light, daily carriage. Even a consul was obliged to give way deferentially if he met them when they were out driving.

The Vestals were under the paternal care of the Chief Priest, the Pontifex Maximus, who was the only man who had any influence over them and the only one allowed to enter the Atrium Vestae. It is also likely that he filled their house with maidservants who spied on them, for their slightest words and deeds were watched and noted.

Vacancies in the sisterhood occurred only when a Vestal died, or retired after thirty years of service. Her place was then filled by one of a number of young girls who were offered by their parents. They had to be physically perfect and with no peculiarities or deformities. A novice had to be over six years old and under ten, and her parents had to be irreproachable. There is evidence that a girl was once rejected as unsuitable because of domestic difficulties between her father and mother; such a novice, it was believed, would have been unwelcome to the goddess of the hearth. Having been chosen, the young Vestal said farewell to her parents and was delivered to the Pontifex Maximus. He led her to the now grass-grown court of the House of the Vestal Virgins and addressed her in solemn words, giving her the title of *Amata*, perhaps a reference to the gentle worship of the hearth to which she was now dedicated. The ceremony ended when her hair was cut off and offered on the sacred tree, after which she was clothed in the white garments of a Vestal Virgin. During this ceremony she took a vow of chastity for thirty years. After that time she was free, if she wished, to leave the order, and even marry. It is said that remarkably few Vestals ever availed themselves of this freedom, preferring to remain Vestals and enjoy their extraordinary privileges until they died in a sanctified old age.

There must have been a great deal for a Vestal to learn, for she spent her first ten years in learning, the next ten years in practising what she had learnt, and the last ten in instructing novices. Their constant care, day and night, was, of course, the fire in the centre of the exquisite little Temple of Vesta, which stood, and whose ruins now stand, a few paces from the Atrium. It was the prettiest little temple in Rome, a gay, delightful circle of marble with white columns around it connected with lattice work. From the centre of its conical roof an opening released the smoke of the sacred fire. There must have been a comforting red glow at night from this opening; and it must indeed have been pleasant, when going home through the Forum after dark, to glance up and see it, knowing that the Vestal on duty was fire-watching and that all was well.

If the fire went out accidentally, and sometimes it did during the eleven centuries, it was the most terrible of all *prodigia*, and I suppose damp wood, a tropical shower of rain or a somnolent Vestal, might cause this disaster. If the Vestal Virgin on duty were to blame, a savage punishment was in store for her. She was stripped, and in the dark the Pontifex Maximus flogged her, no doubt a memory of the beating the girls received in prehistoric times if they were careless. Then together they rekindled the flame, probably by drilling a hole in a board of sacred wood. That was the method employed by the Pontifex Maximus once a year in March when, the fire having been allowed to go out, the New Year Fire was created—a pagan version of the ceremony of the Holy Fire that is still observed every Easter by the Orthodox Greeks in Jerusalem.

No priest learning to say mass has to be more exact than had the Vestal Virgin in the observance of her ritual. They were forbidden to use water from pipes, and all the water in the House of the Vestals had to be carried from a sacred spring some distance away.

In early times the Vestals had to perform this task on foot, carrying the water in earthenware vessels on their heads, but later on servants did this drudgery for them. The pottery used by the Vestals was of the most antique kind, clay dishes and cups that had gone out of fashion centuries before. At the annual baking of the sacrificial bread, made from ears of the first corn, the Vestals used methods employed in prehistoric days, before the grindstone was invented. It is amazing to think how in the course of time archaism can become charged with religious significance.

In addition to the temple services, the Vestals had custody of certain mysterious objects with whose preservation the existence of the Roman state was believed to be bound up. Naturally, when the Forum caught fire, as it did frequently, the Vestals deserted the sacred flame and their one anxiety was then to preserve the relics. One of these was the Palladium, which was believed to have been a statue rescued from the flames of Troy by Aeneas. The ultimate fate of these objects is one of the mysteries of Rome, and when the Atrium Vestae was excavated in the last century, it was hoped that some light might have been cast upon this: but the excavators came to the conclusion that the last Vestals carried their secret with them to the grave.

Every Vestal wore a peculiar headdress known as a fillet. This was a diadem-like band of wool and was the symbol of her virginity. When a Virgin forgot her vow, she was said to have sullied her fillet. This did not often happen; indeed, in the course of eleven centuries there are barely a score of instances. There was, however, one terrible year, 114 B.C., when there must have been a very bad influence in the school, for an unprecedented scandal occurred when no fewer than three Vestal Virgins sullied their fillets, and paid for their sins by the hideous death of burial alive, which was the penalty for incest under Roman law. The offending Vestal, having been charged and found guilty, was stripped of her insignia and scourged. Plutarch has left the best account of what followed.

'The Vestal convicted of incest is buried alive in the neighbourhood of the Porta Collina, under the Agger of Servius Tullius. Here is a crypt, small in size, with an opening in the vault, through which a ladder is lowered; it is furnished with a bed, an oil lamp and a few scanty provisions, such as bread, water, milk and oil. These provisions [in fact, a refinement of cruelty] are prepared because it would appear a sacrilege to condemn to starvation women formerly consecrated to the gods. The unfortunate culprit is brought here in a covered hearse, to which she is tied with leather straps, so that it is impossible that her sighs and lamentations should be heard by the attendant mourners. The crowd opens silently for the passage of the hearse; not a word is pronounced, not a murmur is heard. Tears stream from the eyes of every spectator. It is impossible to imagine a more horrible sight; the whole city is shaken with terror and sorrow. The hearse being brought to the edge of the opening, the executioner cuts the bands, and the high-priest utters an inaudible prayer, and lifts up his arms towards the gods, before bidding the culprit good-bye. He follows and assists her to the top of the ladder, and turns back at the fatal moment of her disappearance. As soon as she reaches the bottom, the ladder is removed, the opening is sealed, and a large mass of earth is heaped upon the stone that seals it, until the top of the embankment is reached, and every trace of the execution made to disappear.'

The site of this terrible entombment has been known since 1872, when Professor Lanciani worked out its situation. He placed the burial crypt below the present Via Goito, about fifty yards from the east door of the Ministry of Finance and not far from the main railway station. There, in all probability, those Vestals betrayed by Venus still lie in their horrible vaults, with the traffic of modern Rome passing above them.

The last glimpse of the Vestals is a sublime one. When the temples were secularized in A.D. 394, the order of the Vestals was abolished. About this time Serena, the beautiful wife of the Vandal general, Stilicho, was in Rome, and visited the Temple of the Great Mother on the Palatine. There she saw the statue of the goddess standing above her cold altar, still robed and jewelled. She mounted the steps towards the statue and unclasped the necklace of the goddess, placing it round her own neck. An aged Vestal Virgin, perhaps the last of her order, who had accompanied Serena to the temple, cried out aloud at the sacrilege and was removed, cursing Serena for her impiety. A few years later Serena was strangled by order of the Senate on the suspicion that she was intriguing with the Goths, and the last pagans in Rome felt that the old gods had spoken when the neck that had worn the jewels of the goddess felt the cord of the executioner.

So it seemed to me that the very dust of the House of the Vestal Virgins was compounded of memories. No religious order in the world has probably departed into the shades with fewer stains on its character. I seemed to see the priestesses of the sacred fire passing in their snow-white robes, century after century, mysterious and hieratic in all they did, and also in their sacred tasks symbolic of all women, no matter of what race or religion, who may also be said to be priestesses of the hearth.

From behind a mass of masonry the voice of a tourist cried out: 'What's there? Anything to see?'

Another voice, whose owner was evidently consulting a map, read out, ' "House of the Vestal Virgins"! No, nothing to see. Just a lot of junk. . . .'

And two young visitors emerged, climbed over a wall and passed on into the ruins.

§ 5

One day when I was walking up the Sacra Via I came to the small, round temple which guide-books call the Temple of Romulus. It was built in memory of a prince who was given that name in a moment of antiquarian enthusiasm by his father, the Emperor Maxentius. The boy died and three years later the fond parent, weighed down by his armour, plunged to his death in the Tiber. It was the battle of Sacra Rubra, when the victorious Constantine the Great came into Rome with the symbol of Christ on his standards.

It was not Romulus I was thinking about, however, as I looked at the round temple. I was thinking of the absence of doors in the Forum, and here was a beautiful pair in bronze, the exquisite green colour of a patinated mirror or a coin. As I admired them, one began slowly to open. It was eerie, in that silent and deserted place, to see a sign of human life in the little temple. While I wondered who or what might emerge, there came into view an elderly little Italian, one of those mysterious custodians of the ruins, the plain-clothes men who have little locked huts here and there, full of beautiful egg and tongue moulding.

I mounted the steps and told him how much I admired the doors. He said they are the only Roman doors still swinging on their original hinges. I found this hard to believe, but he was quite certain, and he ought to know. His name was Giuseppe Protti and he told me he had worked in the Forum for thirty-five years, under many archaeologists. He was holding in his hand a bronze Roman key of a type you may see very much corroded in the British Museum. I asked him if I might have the experience of opening a door that, according to him, has been swinging on its hinges for so long. He showed me how to put the key in the keyhole, then to press hard with the palm of the hand, and after several unsuccessful attempts the great bronze leaf, at least eighteen feet high, slowly opened inward. Alas, the temple is now a store-room for marble columns and fragments of masonry, for picks and shovels. A splendid door has never opened on a more commonplace scene.

I went on up the Sacra Via, past the place where I am sure Horace met the Bore, and to the magnificent Arch of Titus. If you wish to see how architecture can slide downhill, compare this splendid work, built in the first century, with the heavy and lifeless figures on the Arch of Septimius Severus, at the other end of the Forum, made two and a half centuries later.

Titus, the son of Vespasian, concluded the Jewish War and destroyed the Temple of Herod, as Josephus describes with much vigour. Inside the Arch, in high relief, you may see Titus riding in his triumph through Rome with the spoils of his campaign, which included the Tabernacle and the Seven-Branched Candlestick of gold. These are the only contemporary sculptured representations of these objects in existence, and their ultimate fate is even now a mystery.

It is known that until the barbarians sacked Rome, they were kept in the Temple of Peace, which was Rome's finest museum, and they were among the few articles to survive the fire of A.D. 191. It is believed that part of the Jewish spoils disappeared during the Gothic sack of Rome in A.D. 410, and they have never been heard of since. Procopius, writing in the sixth century, says that when Genseric and his Vandals, Berbers and Bedouin, sacked Rome in 455, what was left of the treasure was piled into boats and shipped safely to Carthage. There, it would seem, Belisarius discovered it and sent it to Constantinople.

This is contradicted by the strange legend that when Alaric died in the south of Italy, his followers turned aside the river Busento and constructed a great tomb in which they piled his trophies round his dead body, including the Jewish spoils from Rome; then, turning the river back into its bed, they slew the workmen so that no one would know where Alaric had been buried. The Jews, however, believe neither of these stories. Writers in the *Talmud* say that the spoils of the Temple were simply flung into the Tiber, where they remain to this day. I believe that at some time in the eighteenth century the Jews of Rome petitioned the Pope to be allowed to dredge the Tiber, but this was never done.

There is an ancient superstition among the Jews that it is not right, or lucky, to pass beneath the Arch of Titus, and many a time, while watching groups of visitors passing through the Forum, I have tried to discover whether this superstition were still observed: but so many who appeared to be Jews passed fearlessly under, and so many who looked equally Jewish seemed to avoid the Arch, that I was unable to come to any conclusion about it. When I mentioned this to a guide, he replied that there was no doubt about it, and that he had repeatedly noticed that Jewish members of his groups invariably gave the Arch of Titus a wide berth. There is however no prejudice against visiting the Colosseum, which was built at the same time by enormous gangs of Jewish captives.

§ 6

As you look at the marble faces of the Caesars in the museums of Rome, it may occur to you that even the bad ones had redeeming features. Who can believe, as he looks at the sad, dignified face of Tiberius, that he was the aged reprobate who retired to pursue his excesses in Capri at the age of seventy? Who can imagine that the calm, sensitive Claudius was quite the utter ass and poltroon he has been pictured, or that even Nero was entirely without brains and dignity? What are we to make of it? Do these statues lie, or is *The Lives of the Caesars* just a collection of malicious political gossip? Suetonius, the author, was a queer character of whom little is known except that he was probably born in the reign of Nero, and was a retiring and superstitious individual who did not quite fit into his environment. He tried practising law and gave it up, he tried the army and resigned, and eventually became Hadrian's secretary until he was dismissed for behaving disrespectfully to the Empress. He seems to have found his greatest happiness in libraries and in the chaste delights of research. As he had access to the royal archives, he would have had every opportunity of finding out intimate details of the lives of exalted personages, but their vices rather than their virtues seem to have attracted him. Like many another quiet, retiring character, he had an ever-willing ear for scandal. He was also a first-rate political journalist and knew the subtle art of omission.

I believe scholars would agree with me that the reading of moral infamies into innocent habits and eccentricities was typical of Roman political propaganda. A criminal libel seems to have been the Roman equivalent of a modern cartoon, and hardly any great character was immune. Perhaps the Romans just laughed it off as we laugh at a cartoon. And this malicious sniping continued in Rome right down to the age of Pasquino.

The Caesars were nearly all frightened men. The new Caesar often climbed to power upon the murdered corpse of his predecessor, and it was common policy to defame the dead Caesar. The most terrible feature of the system, though we who have lived through the age of Hitler and Mussolini should have little difficulty in understanding how it happened, was the impotence of the once all-powerful Senate. Even so, it seems strange that for centuries a band of toughs like the Praetorian Guard should have been allowed to elect the Emperor; and then, when they felt like it, to murder him and choose someone else. Had the Senate been strong enough to discipline the Praetorians when they murdered Caligula and flippantly elected Claudius, whom they found hiding behind a curtain, history might have been different: but they lost control of the situation at the beginning and ever after were in the humiliating position of having to make their congratulations to a candidate elected by the palace guards.

In a situation in which any general in the army might become a rival to the reigning emperor, it is not surprising that many a man was suddenly struck down and that many an emperor decided to live a short life and a gay one. The nervous tension was well illustrated by Domitian, who was so afraid of assassination that he had the walls of his palace lined with sheets of mica so that he could see what was happening behind him; and the degrading formula for remaining in power was expressed on his death-bed by Septimius Severus, when he said to his sons: 'Enrich the soldiers: trouble about nothing else.'

Of the fifty-five emperors who reigned from the time of Augustus to that of Jovian, a period of some four centuries, twenty-eight were murdered and three committed suicide; only seven men succeeded their fathers. Between 235 and 285 only one of twenty-six emperors died a natural death. The fearful cruelties and assassinations, the feminine intrigues and the rule of favourites popularly associated with Byzantium, or the courts of the Caliphs, were well established on the Palatine; and one marvels that any men could be found who were willing to be Caesar. Yet there was never a lack of candidates, indeed men murdered, bribed and intrigued century after century to wear the mantle that so often, and so swiftly, became a shroud.

In contemplating the bloody history of the Caesars, one thinks inevitably of the first, Julius Caesar, who has been called the greatest man of antiquity. He died because a band of idealistic republicans and disaffected senators believed that he wished to establish an hereditary monarchy. Some of the busts made of him in his last years show a sad, lined face, the cheeks hollow, and the mouth drawn down, the face of a disillusioned man of seventy; yet Caesar was only fifty-eight at the time of his death.

Contemporaries noted the change that had come over him: his bouts of bad health, the frequency of his epileptic fits, his forgetfulness, his ill-temper, and his looks of fatigue and overwork.

Caesar was not murdered on the Capitol, as Shakespeare says, nor in the Forum, but half a mile away, in the splendid new theatre which Pompey had built in the Campus Martius. The reason why the Senate was meeting so far from its historic home in the Forum was because the Senate House was being reconstructed and could not be used.

It is interesting to trace, as I did one morning, the movements of Caesar on the last day of his life. At the time he was living with his wife, Calpurnia, in the official residence of the Pontifex Maximus in the Forum, a building next to the House of the Vestal Virgins. Caesar was the last Pontifex Maximus to live there; when Augustus succeeded, he lived on the Palatine and incorporated the old *Domus Publica* with the House of the Vestals.

It was to this house, and to the solitude of the Forum at night, that Caesar returned on March 14, 44 B.C. He had been dining with his friend, Lepidus, and after dinner he had read through some state papers, with one ear tuned in to the conversation around him. Someone began a discussion on 'Which is the best death to die?' Caesar glanced up from his papers and said briefly, 'A sudden one,' and continued with his reading. Arriving home, he found it difficult to sleep; and so did Calpurnia. She had a dream in which she held his dead body, and was so upset that she tried to persuade him to cancel his attendance at the Senate.

Women often possess a sixth sense which wise men do not underrate, and Caesar was at first disposed to take her advice. At least sixty men had been admitted into the plot to murder him and no doubt Calpurnia was aware of the atmosphere of foreboding. Caesar at the age of fifty-eight, a cynic whose gallantries were a joke in the army, was apparently still loved by his wife, whose fears for his safety, and whose desire to protect him, were not influenced by the fact that her notorious rival, Cleopatra, was at that moment established in Caesar's villa on the west bank of the Tiber. However, when the time came Caesar brushed aside Calpurnia's fears and went off to the meeting with a young man who had been sent to escort him; for the conspirators were trembling with anxiety to get their bloody deed over and done with before the plot leaked out.

It took me fifteen minutes, walking slowly from the ruins of the *Domus Publica* in the Forum, to reach the scene of Caesar's death. It is not possible to say which road he took, but it is probable that on his way he would have glanced up at the scaffolding round the new Senate House as he left the Forum, and it may be that work had stopped there, as the Ides of March was a public holiday. Every year on March 15 the population of Rome streamed out to celebrate a festival associated with a mysterious deity called Anna Perenna, who was visualized as a drunken old hag. The crowds picnicked under the trees, or beneath arbours of boughs, drinking a great deal; and Ovid says that people flocked to the Campus Martius to revel and to pray that they might live as many years as they drained cups of wine. Such a scene of bank holiday jollity was Caesar's last glimpse of Rome.

Pompey's Theatre, in the Campus Martius, was the most magnificent building of its kind in Rome, and is said to have resembled the Greek theatre at Mitylene. An enormous semi-circle of marble seats, open to the air, could seat an audience of seventeen thousand, and behind the stage were covered colonnades and gardens planted with sycamore trees, where the audience could stroll during an interval. Adjoining these gardens was the Curia of Pompey, where a semi-circle of seats rose in tiers, facing an apse in which stood the famous statue of Pompey. This was the hall in which the Senate was to meet. At the foot of Pompey's statue Caesar fell, stabbed by twenty-three wounds, and it is recorded that his last action was to see that his toga covered him decently before he fell to the marble floor. Brutus, an ostentatious prig and not an entirely honest one, 'inflicted perhaps the greatest mischief any one man ever inflicted upon his generation', as Professor J. F. Mahaffy has said.

The site of the splendid building lies somewhere beneath the crowded streets near the Largo Argentina. Ranks of taxis and lines of tramcars today congest what was once the approach to Pompey's Theatre, and not a vestige of the building remains above ground: but if you explore the picturesque little streets at the back of the Teatro Argentina you will come to a shabby piazza where a large block of flats, workshops and office buildings clearly follows part of the curve of the auditorium, and this place is called the Piazza Grottapinta. A dark little archway leads to the diminutive Piazza del Biscione, where a modest restaurant, Da Pancrazio, has an underground dining-room in the foundations of the ancient theatre. Here you can sit surrounded by blocks of Travertine and walls of *opus reticulatum* and lift your glass to the memory of the great man who was so foully murdered not far away.

Like so many parts of Rome, these streets appear to slip back several centuries with the coming of darkness. I thought I knew them fairly well until I tried to find my way about at night. The scene had changed completely, and I was wandering lost in the Rome of the Renaissance. The shops and offices were closed, and from the flats and underground dens swarmed a great crowd of men, women and children, the resident population, who, in the light of the street lamps, seemed to me to have the faces and the gestures of long ago. When I came to the little archway, intending to cut through to the Piazza del Biscione, I found it closed at both ends with locked iron gates. In the darkness of the archway I could see a lamp burning beneath a picture of the Madonna. I asked a man why the archway was locked. He said that once a girl had been murdered there and ever since it had been locked up after dark.

If the Piazza Grottapinta represents the curve of Pompey's Theatre, the colonnade must lie somewhere beneath the Via di Chiavari, and the Curia must have stretched towards the Largo Argentina. Therefore, if you wish to find the spot in Rome nearest to the place where Caesar fell, you would, curiously enough, find it on the steps of the Teatro Argentina. This theatre has existed since the eighteenth century, though it has been rebuilt. It was here that the first performance of Rossini's *The Barber of Seville* was hissed in 1816. The unhappy composer fled from the theatre in despair and took refuge in his lodgings in the Via de 'Leutari: but in twenty-four hours he was to pass from despair to fame, when the audience on the second night acclaimed the opera as a masterpiece. Rossini was still prudently in hiding and the delighted crowd marched to his lodgings with torches and bore him in triumph to a banquet.

§ 7

For some hours Caesar's body lay where it had fallen. Then three of the four slaves who had carried his litter entered the Curia and, gathering up the bloodstained corpse, took it home. As they were a man short, the litter was tilted and one of Caesar's arms was hanging down. This was the sight that met the eyes of Calpurnia as the slaves brought their master home to the *Domus Publica*.

Most English people, with memories of Shakespeare, look for the place in the Forum where Mark Antony made his speech and where the sorrowing mob, dragging out the chairs of the magistrates and anything that would ignite, burnt the corpse there and then, refusing to allow the funeral cortège to go on to the Campus Martius. And this place is quite easy to find. It is almost in line with, and to the north of, the three remaining white columns of the Temple of Castor and Pollux, which are one of the landmarks in the Forum. Nothing remains now but a semi-circular recess of massive brickwork and tufa, which is the foundation of the altar that was afterwards erected on the spot. The *Domus Publica* lies only a few yards away, so that the funeral procession could hardly have started before the mob took control.

Among the many problems created by the murder of Julius Caesar not the least interesting was that of Cleopatra. From the Janiculum Hill I looked down on the English-looking park of the Villa Doria Pamphili, where Cleopatra once lived in Caesar's villa. She was detested by a section of Roman society and probably also by the common people. Though she was a Macedonian Greek without a drop of Egyptian blood, the Romans liked to think of her as an oriental harpy who boded no good to Rome. 'I detest the Queen,' wrote Cicero to Atticus, though whether she had snubbed him or whether the old republican hated her because he believed her to be the main cause of Caesar's regal ambitions, it is impossible to say: but he was not the only one who disliked her. Rome had been shocked and affronted when Caesar placed her statue, with two large British pearls in its ears, in his new Temple of Venus Genetrix, a sign, so some thought, that he expected the Roman people to regard his mistress as a goddess.

She was twenty-four years old at the time of Caesar's death. The son she had borne him, Caesarion, was then an infant of three. As the child grew up, his looks and his walk reminded people of Caesar, and it is strange that Caesar should have made no mention of this child in his will. In the confusion that followed the murder Mark Antony rose in the Senate and put forward the claim of Caesarion to be Caesar's heir, but this was challenged and nothing came of it.

Cleopatra had now lost the love and protection of the greatest man in the world, and also her dream of the future. The talk in Rome before the murder was that Caesar had intended to marry her and to move his capital to Alexandria, where, like a Pharaoh, he intended to reign with her over a united Roman and Hellenistic world. With Caesar as her husband, and her child legitimized, Cleopatra saw herself the mistress of the world, while her son, whose blood united the Macedonian blood of the Ptolemys with the Roman blood of the *gens Julia*, would inherit an empire the like of which even Alexander the Great had never contemplated.

A letter written by Cicero in April mentions the departure of Cleopatra. She had bravely remained in Rome for a month, waiting to see which way the tide would turn; and when it turned against her child, an Egyptian fleet took her home to Alexandria.

It was, however, during the visit of Cleopatra to Rome that an event of the greatest importance took place, in which she was associated, an event which has influenced the lives of men ever since. This was the reform of the calendar. The year had fallen into confusion and Caesar decided to start it afresh with the Julian

Calendar, which remains the basis of our present system. Some of Egypt's court astronomers were invited to Rome to help to devise a new calendar based on the Egyptian calendar of Eudoxus. Among these astronomers was Sosigenes, the most celebrated astronomer in Egypt; and it was with him that Caesar collaborated.

The year before the new calendar came into operation must have seemed endless: it contained an additional ninety days! Then the first Julian year began, with its days distributed between months of either thirty or thirty-one days, excepting February, which originally had twenty-nine days and thirty every fourth year. The month Quintilis was named July in honour of Julius Caesar, and a generation later Sextilis was named after Augustus, though the story that he stole a day from February to make his August as long as Caesar's July is merely an old and vigorous legend. It has been repeated for centuries and is to be found even in some editions of the *Encyclopaedia Britannica*. It originated apparently in *De Anni Ratione*, by a Yorkshireman, John Holywood, or Sacro Bosco, who lived in Paris about AD 1230, and drew on his imagination to explain the shortness of February. But the ancient authorities prove that Sextilis had thirty-one days many years before it became the month of Augustus.

It is fascinating to stand on the Janiculum and, glancing down into the lovely park of the Villa Doria Pamphili, to reflect that the Julian Calendar was devised there in Cleopatra's villa over nineteen centuries ago.

Cleopatra was not really good-looking if the statue in the Vatican Gallery is the one from the Temple of Venus Genetrix. We see a young woman standing in a graceful attitude, wearing a Greek dress. There are no traces of the devastating charm and sparkling brilliance which ancient writers say were among her attractions. The statue might be that of any aristocratic young woman of the period, and indeed were it not labelled 'Cleopatra', no one would give it a second glance.

After Caesar's death the remaining thirteen years of her life were spent in an attempt to rebuild her dream of a world empire. She married Mark Antony, and if proof were needed that

Caesarion was truly Caesar's child, we have it in the splendid ceremony at Alexandria when Antony named the thirteen-year-old boy co-regent with his mother and gave him the mighty title of King of Kings. After the Battle of Actium, when Antony and Cleopatra were defeated by Augustus, the young Caesarion, then a youth of seventeen, was sent to India in the hope that he would be safe there; but while still on his way, he was decoyed back to Alexandria and put to death by Augustus.

Some scholars have seen in Cleopatra a female Alexander, who dreamt of uniting East and West, and no doubt she was more interested in power than in men. When she married Antony, he was nearly fifty and she was in the late thirties and putting on weight. Plutarch says, 'she feigned to be dying of love for Antony, bringing her body down by slender diet'. When Augustus saw her in her tragic defeat, a short time before her suicide, he found her on a small pallet-bed 'having nothing on but the one garment next her body'. Her hair and face were wild and disfigured, her voice trembling, and her eyes sunken and dark. She had surrounded herself with pictures of Julius Caesar and had with her the letters he had written to her. Augustus sat beside her and tried to calm her, telling her that she had nothing to fear: but she managed to cheat him.

Augustus must have been told almost immediately of Cleopatra's suicide, for in an attempt to save her life he rushed members of a North African tribe, the Psylli, to her. In Rome they had a great reputation as snake charmers and were supposed to be immune from snakebite and able to extract venom from the bodies of those bitten by snakes. But the poison of the *Echis carinata*, known in India as the krait, which was most likely the cause of Cleopatra's death, can kill in twenty minutes; and when the experts arrived, it was too late.

Her death deprived Rome of a great sight—the Queen of Egypt in golden fetters. Augustus was obliged to make a wax figure of Cleopatra for his victory through the capital.

§ 8

'Can you tell me why Rome fell?'

The question was put to a guide by a spectacled Englishman who looked to me like a science master. He was standing with a group of tourists upon the road above the Forum, while the guide pointed down to the chief ruins. The poor guide brushed aside the interruption and continued with his patter: but again came that question, and the guide, casting a glance of dislike at the man, hastily led his flock back to the coach, and off they sped to the Colosseum. I felt sorry for the guide. It was an unfair question so early in the day, with the Colosseum and the Vatican Museum to be worked in before luncheon!

I walked up the Palatine Hill later that morning and ordered a bottle of iced beer at the little hut which stands above the palaces where many an early emperor had gloried and drunk deep. And the young man's question haunted me. It could be argued that Rome did not fall, but was transformed into a spiritual empire by the Church. That, however, was not what the young man meant. He was asking why the western half of the greatest military state in antiquity was conquered by the barbarian tribes, for the Eastern Roman Empire did not disintegrate until the Turks captured Constantinople in 1453.

It is perhaps strange that while no one is surprised that Babylon, Egypt, Persia and Greece should have fallen, the collapse of Rome in the West continues to interest the world and is the subject of a post mortem still in progress. No modern historian believes that the barbarians were the cause of the fall of the Western Empire. The old oak was rotten inside long before the barbarians pushed it over.

Had I been the guide, I should have suggested to the young man that the key to the fall of the Western provinces was the anarchy and civil war of the third century. After the death of Septimius Severus in 211, there were twenty-three emperors in seventy-three years, two of whom reigned for a month, three for one year, six for two years, while the reign of Alexander Severus for thirteen years was phenomenal. Sometimes the news of an emperor's election in the provinces reached Rome together with the news of his assassination. Seventy odd years of civil war and military anarchy, of requisitioning, depopulation, taxation, disrupted commerce, inflation, scarcity and terror, ended in the reforms of Diocletian, which were an attempt to hold the state together.

It is difficult to imagine the Roman of Diocletian's time, in his embroidered dalmatic, as a descendant of the Romans of the age of Cicero, neither is it easy to recognize in the oriental despot, who expected courtiers to kiss the hem of his garment, a resemblance to the Augustan Caesars, who walked about the Forum, laughing and joking with their friends.

Most extraordinary of all was the wealth and the thoughtless gaiety of Rome. A population brought up to sleep in slums and spend the day in marble palaces continued to think of nothing but games and races, and more than one observer noted that Rome was rushing, laughing, to her doom. The immense ruins of Diocletian's Baths date from this time of inflation and scarcity, and one looks at them trying to reconcile them with reality.

Every expedient was tried by Diocletian to stave off the crash. He froze wages and prices in 301, and created a bureaucracy animated by the spirit of a century of extortion. The tax collector became the terror of the countryside. Men fled their homes rather than meet him and revenged themselves on the state by becoming brigands. Wealthy landowners, developing a technique of tax evasion, managed to exist on their estates, surrounded by serfs and armed men—a forecast of the Middle Ages—defying and bribing the Treasury.

Perhaps the worst aspect of state control was the decision to freeze men as well as prices and wages. It became illegal for a man to change his employment, and a son was obliged to follow his father's calling. All trades, occupations and professions became hereditary. A man who fled from a baker's shop, wishing to become a silversmith, would be hunted down and brought back like an escaped criminal. The Roman-born were no longer soldiers. The armies were chiefly barbarian mercenaries commanded by Romanized barbarians, for the emperors preferred their troops to be led by officers who would not dare to aspire to the purple. That was to come.

In this grim caricature of Plato's Republic, the only place where a man ceased to be a tax-producing unit, and became a human being with an immortal soul, was the Church. The bishops were truly the shepherds of their flocks and had the courage to stand up to authority. St Basil once offended a Praetorian Prefect by his plain words and was told that no one had ever dared to speak in such terms to him. 'No doubt,' replied St Basil, 'you have never met a bishop.' In addition to taxation and state control, Rome never recovered from Constantine's removal of the capital to the Bosphorus. Great numbers of the wealthy and the notable, as well as the most enterprising of the artisans, followed the Emperor and helped him to found his new city.

Modern historians, philosophers and economists, carrying on the enquiry begun by Gibbon, have attempted to isolate the germ of national decay and to find out why nations once famous for their energy lose heart and decline, while others, hitherto undistinguished, are inspired by enthusiasm. Rostovtzeff mentions the 'disenchantment' which afflicts civilization, and the feeling that the future is not worth while. 'Wherever we observe this process,' he says, 'we note also the psychological change in those classes of society which had been up till then the creators of culture. Their creative power and creative energy dry up; men grow weary and lose interest in creation and cease to value it; they are disenchanted; their effort is no longer an effort towards a creative ideal for the benefit of humanity, their minds are occupied either with material interests, or with ideals unconnected with life on earth and realized elsewhere.' In the western provinces of Rome he says the development of this state of mind—'apathy in the rich and discontent among the poor'—was slow and secret, but when the Empire, after centuries of peace and tranquillity, was forced to defend itself, the necessary enthusiasm was lacking. 'In order to save the Empire the state began to crush and ruin the population, lowering the proud but not raising the humble. Hence arose the social and political conflict of the third century, in which the state, relying upon the army, or, in other words, the lower classes, defeated the upper classes and left them humiliated and beggared.'

Tenney Frank mentions the race dilution that occurred by marriage with inferior strains; Seeck writes of the 'extermination of the best' in war; Jules Toutain cites the tyranny of state control, which meant that 'nowhere could one find initiative or free labour'; and all these accumulated symptoms meant paralysis, so that when the barbarians, who had a fifth column everywhere in the state, poured across the weakened frontiers, there was not sufficient left of the old Roman pride, energy and enthusiasm to drive them back. The energy and enthusiasm now belonged to the barbarians who poured in, to settle and to loot, awed by the great stone cities in which they found themselves.

The first glimpse of our early European ancestors is not particularly pleasing. Apollinaris Sidonius was a Roman aristocrat with a keen eye who had an estate in what is now France, and he saw the successive hordes passing on towards the Alps. Maybe as a boy he had seen the flat-nosed Huns with their thin beards, sitting their horses like centaurs; he certainly saw, and smelt, the Burgundians, who dressed their hair with rancid butter and, he says, offended the sensibilities by their table manners and the unsavoury messes which they loved. He saw the Goths in kilts of wild beasts' skins, and the blue-eyed Saxons who sailed the sea in cockle-shells of hide and slew their prisoners to gratify their gods. The Franks emerge from his account as perhaps the most presentable of them all: people with blue-grey eyes and yellow hair, who went clean-shaven, like the people of old Rome, and wore belted tunics.

Many of the tribes settled down in Gaul and took over the Roman towns, sometimes with the approval of the inhabitants, who preferred the easy rule of the barbarians to the extortions of the imperial officials. There were many Roman refugees to the barbarians, and even the worst of the barbarians, Attila, employed a Roman secretary. With the exception of the Huns, the tribes were not complete savages animated by a hatred for civilization; on the contrary, most of them admired Rome and some of their leaders, like Alaric and his brother-in-law Athawulf, or Adolf (a name which means 'father wolf' and until recently was still a popular name in Germany), asked nothing more than to be Roman generals and bear a Roman title.

Reading of these stormy days, or thinking of them on the Palatine Hill, it seems unbelievable that the world should have been so staggered when that huge, defenceless, self-indulgent city, Rome, which the Western Emperor had already deserted as too dangerous, should have been sacked by her admirer, Alaric, in 410: but the world was appalled, for the majesty of Rome had been humbled and the world that men had known until then had, it seemed, come to an end. Even as we read of it, and know it to have been inevitable, as the heirs of Rome we feel a sense of horror, as of some crime we are compelled to witness, as we think of the host of Goths assembled round the Aurelian Wall towards the end of August, in the year 410.

There are times in history, when an epoch is about to end, when a woman sometimes appears who has a great influence upon her age, and in her strange and often tragic destiny we see a reflection of the moral climate of the time. Such a woman was Galla Placidia, the daughter of Theodosius the Great, and the half sister of the feeble Emperor of the West, Honorius. 'Her extraordinary career is coincident with the downfall of Imperial Rome,' wrote Gregorovius, 'as Cleopatra's had been with that of Republican Rome.'

One could fill many pages with descriptions of the sacks of Rome by the Goths and Vandals, yet perhaps convey a better idea of the atmosphere of the time and the general background by the story of that young and beautiful member of the Imperial House. Galla Placidia was living in Rome in the summer of 410 when Alaric the Goth camped outside the walls for the third time in two years. The Senate and the people were terrified. Rome, the beautiful Rome still untouched by the hand of Goth, glittering with its palaces, its imperial fora, its amphitheatres and baths, its temple roofs still gleaming with golden tiles, and the streets still lined with statues hung with gold and silver, was unprepared for a siege.

On his first visit Alaric had been bought off with gold and silver,

with scarlet-dyed skins and with five thousand pounds of pepper·
In August, 410, he was an angry man and in no mood to make
bargains: he wanted to teach Rome a lesson and to humiliate her,
for he was a man with a grievance. For years he had led irregular
armies on behalf of Rome, but failing to achieve his ambition,
which was to become a Roman general and bear a Roman title,
he turned against the civilization which he admired and led a great
army here and there, looting and slaying.

We shall never know why Placidia did not escape from Rome
as so many did, rich and poor, before Alaric and his Goths
arrived. The poor fled into the country, the rich went off to their
estates in Sicily and elsewhere, or sailed to North Africa, taking
jewellery and any portable wealth they could carry. These
refugees reached even Palestine, where St Jerome welcomed them
with tears and sympathy to his retreat at Bethlehem, but St
Augustine in Africa was enraged by them. Having escaped the
terrors of the siege, their first desire upontheir arrival in Carthage
was to find out what was to be seen at the theatres. St Augustine
stored up that indication of the feckless Roman mentality for use
in *The City of God*.

Placidia may have thought it beneath her dignity to fly, for it
would surely not have been difficult for the sister of the Emperor
to have joined her brother in Ravenna, where he and his court
were safe in a fortress in the marshes. It may be that no one
believed that Alaric would dare to pillage Rome, and that he
would, as usual, agree to a price.

Having blockaded the city until it was hungry, the barbarians
swarmed in through the Salarian Gate on the night of August 24.
Thousands of slaves had deserted to the Goths, and these were only
too anxious to be guides and to show the invaders where the safe
was kept. The scene as the Goths filled every region of Rome,
driving before them a terrified crowd, was the most disgraceful
in the history of the city. Not one heroic action on the part of a
Roman was recorded. The demoralized citizens, dragged from
their hiding-places, gave the barbarians whatever they asked.
Alaric had given his troops leave to plunder for three days, and
three days only, but he had commanded them not to kill unless

necessary, and to respect the churches. He was an Arian Christian and so were many of his followers. The Pope, Innocent I, was not present. He had gone with an embassy to Ravenna, to beg the miserable Emperor to save the city.

For three days the terror continued, but no damage was done to the buildings of Rome. The Goths were interested not in painfully knocking down statues and obelisks, but in cramming valuables into their pockets. The Aventine, with its hundred and thirty aristocratic palaces, was the worst hit region. The greatest violence was shown there, as the Goths suspected the trembling owners of having concealed their treasures. It was there that St Jerome's pious friend Marcella was beaten by the looters, as she clung to their knees and begged them to respect the virtue of her adopted daughter, Principia. Strangely enough, some Goths behaved less like barbarians than many later, and so-called Christian, looters of Rome. Touched by Marcella's appeal (says St Jerome, in a letter describing the details of the sack, as it was reported to him in Bethlehem), the soldiers took Marcella and Principia to the safety of St. Paul's Without.

A similar incident was recorded. A Goth burst into a room where a young nun stood guard over a hoard of gold and silver goblets and plates. As the robber was about to fling himself upon the treasure, the girl said that he might do as he liked, but, as the objects belonged to St Peter, the Apostle would no doubt punish the sacrilege. The terrified Goth immediately left and reported the incident to Alaric. Then, by the orders of the leader, a procession was formed and the Goths, reverently carrying chalices, lamps and jewelled crosses, solemnly marched to St Peter's through the tumult of the streets, and deposited the treasure at the tomb of the Apostle.

It is not known what happened to Placidia during the three days, but no doubt she was well protected by Alaric and his brother-in-law Adolf. When the Goths withdrew, carrying with them an immense booty, they took with them, politically their most valuable acquisition, Galla Placidia, half sister of the Emperor of the West and aunt of the Emperor of the East.

Fugitives from Rome, hiding in the mountains and the woods,

must have been appalled as they watched the Gothic host moving south with its wagons piled with the treasures of the ancient capital of the world, and in the centre, protected by barbarian spears, the lovely and aristocratic captive, the Emperor's step-sister, then in her early twenties. The thoughts of this aristocratic young woman, who had been brought up to believe that her family was sacred, are not known, but her future conduct suggests that perhaps she was not a reluctant captive.

Alaric's plan was to cross into Africa and cut off Rome's corn ships, but he was fated never to put it into action. While in the south of Italy, at a town now called Cosenza, in Calabria, he died suddenly, and Placidia must have been a witness to his strange funeral, which I have already mentioned, when the river Busento was diverted and then turned back to cover the tomb in which the Gothic king lay surrounded by his treasures. For two years the princess wandered with the barbarians, now commanded by Adolf, while Honorius and his commander, Constantius, who had been in love with Placidia for years, did their best to obtain her release.

In the year 414 the imperial courts at Ravenna and Constantinople were shocked by the news that Placidia had married Adolf and was Queen of the Goths. This event took place at Narbonne, in the house of a leading citizen. Dressed as a Roman princess, with the Gothic King at her side, also in Roman dress, Placidia watched, surely with mixed feelings, as fifty handsome Gothic boys wearing silk garments appeared, each bearing two gold plates, one in either hand. Fifty of the plates were laden with the looted gold of Rome, while fifty contained the jewellery stolen from the palaces of the Aventine. Such was the wedding present of the Roman princess. The wedding was a gay one. There was dancing, in which Goths and captive Romans mixed cheerfully on the happy occasion.

The marriage lasted only a year. Placidia bore Adolf a child which died, and soon afterwards the Gothic king was murdered by a groom. Renewed attempts were then made by Honorius and Constantius to obtain possession of Placidia, and eventually she was exchanged for 600,000 measures of corn. She returned to

Italy after having lived with the Goths for five years, and was almost immediately married—and apparently against her will— to her devoted lover, Constantius. She was then about twenty-seven. In the following year she gave birth to a daughter, Honoria, who was to play a part in history almost as strange as that of her mother, and, the year after, to a son, who became the Western Emperor, Valentinian III.

Constantius was soon raised to the dignity of co-ruler with Honorius and was crowned Augustus, while the ex-queen of the Goths became a Roman Augusta. When this news was received in Constantinople, Placidia's nephew, the Eastern Emperor, Theodosius II, refused to recognize her new dignity, possibly because he had never forgiven her marriage with the Gothic king. This so insulted Constantius that with some difficulty he was prevented from making war upon Constantinople: but his days were numbered. After a reign of only seven months he died, and Placidia was again a widow.

Now began a strange and unpleasant period of her life, when her miserable half brother conceived a passion for her and made his affection so obvious that a scandal occurred which led to riots in the streets of Ravenna. Placidia was much embarrassed by the situation, and court intrigues led to her departure, with her two children, for the imperial court at Constantinople. Her reception would undoubtedly have been chilly had not Honorius conveniently died of dropsy, and immediately Placidia's future became a brilliant one. Her son, Valentinian, now six years old, was proclaimed Western Emperor, and she returned to Italy as his regent and Empress of the West. For ten years she ruled the dying Western Empire, and for another fifteen was the power behind the throne. She died aged about sixty-two, and her superb mausoleum, gleaming with mosaics, is still among the great sights of Ravenna. For many centuries the embalmed body of Placidia, wearing royal vestments and seated upon a throne of cypress wood, is said to have been visible through a hole in the wall: but in 1577 some children, playing with fire, destroyed both Empress and throne.

It is common knowledge that daughters often resemble their

fathers, and in the character of Placidia, and also in that of her daughter Honoria, there was a strain of energy and a capacity to rule which were absent in the male descendants of Theodosius the Great. Honoria was a spirited girl whose unhappy fate it was to watch her inept brother misgovern his Empire while she was prevented from marriage with any man who might have had designs on the purple. She was still a spinster at thirty. At that time she fell in love with her steward, a man named Eugenius, and it was believed that with his help she intended to murder Valentinian III, or drive him from the throne. Their intrigue was discovered, however, and Eugenius was put to death. Honoria was then betrothed to a simple, wealthy man who, it was hoped, would keep her out of politics. In this extremity she did an astonishing thing: this gentle, well-bred Roman lady sent her ring secretly to Attila, King of the Huns, begging him to come and help her. In this we can surely see the influence of her mother's life, and may assume that perhaps Placidia, in telling her daughter stories of her life as Queen of the Goths, did not inspire her with any horror of the barbarians.

Attila was, however, a vastly different person from the pro-Roman Goth. He was a short, swarthy, broad-shouldered man with a flat Mongolian nose, deep-set eyes, and a few thin hairs instead of a beard: he was a bully, arrogant and incapable of pity. A brilliant description of him was written by Priscus, the historian, who went with an embassy to the Huns. He described the rough huts of the encampment and the royal hall in which he attended a banquet. While the savage warriors were served on silver plate, Attila sat in the place of honour, eating lumps of meat from a wooden trencher. His followers drank from golden goblets, but 'the Scourge of God' drank from a common wooden bowl. When the torches were lit in the hall, and jesters and half-wits came in to tumble and make jokes, the Huns rocked in their seats, but Attila never relaxed a muscle of his face.

The Hun was delighted to receive Honoria's appeal and decided to look upon it as a proposal of marriage. Perhaps he smiled to himself to think of marriage with a Roman woman of thirty, but it was nevertheless as good an excuse as any to bully

Ravenna and Constantinople.

For two years, 451–452, he led an immense army of Huns, Franks and Vandals against the Western Empire in order to claim his 'bride', and it was during this campaign that the citizens of Aquileia, deserting their city, took refuge among the Adriatic lagoons, and so the wonderful city of Venice was founded. As Attila approached Rome in 452, the panic of 410 was repeated, and an embassy which included the majestic figure of Pope Leo I went out to meet the Hunnish king. Entering his tent, they found that his advisers were divided on the wisdom of sacking Rome. In one of history's brighter moments, the Hun stayed his hand and turned away. Christian tradition has it that he had seen the figures of the Apostles threatening him; and there seems no doubt that the fate of Alaric, who died so soon after the sack of 410, influenced his decision. The next year Attila lay dead in bed, while the girl he had married the night before sat beside his corpse in tears. Some said he had burst an artery; others that the girl had slain him in his sleep.

What happened to Honoria we do not know. She makes her brief, extraordinary appearance in the twilight of civilization, summoning to her aid, out of the frustration of her life, the wild forces that were tearing the western world apart. Mother and daughter are curiously symbolic of that marriage between barbarian and Rome from which Europe was to be born in the distant future.

Two years after Attila's death, in 455, Rome was sacked by the Vandals under Gaiseric. These people had crossed over to North Africa and had become a sea power. They were fated to die out eventually, under the influence of the climate and an easy life. A Roman poet has described fat Vandals lying on their ships, lazily watching while their African slaves looted for them.

Gaiseric, whose mother had been a slave, had an uncontrollable temper and was lame from a fall from his horse. He led a great force of Vandals and Moors to Rome, and while their ships were tied up to the quays in the Tiber, they looted and murdered for fourteen days, until their vessels were piled with treasure. The Goths were gentlemen compared with the Vandals. They spared neither churches, women nor children; and the word 'vandalism' has ever since perpetuated the memory of their fortnight of savagery.

They stole the gilded bronze tiles from the roof of the Temple of Jupiter and took even the copper cooking-pots from the kitchens of the Palatine. As they had artistic and architectural tastes, they removed works of art from the palaces to decorate their African villas. Some stories say that Alaric had already taken the Jewish treasures from the temple of Peace in the Forum, others that the Vandals stole them, or at any rate what was left of them. They withdrew in their heavy ships, taking with them the Empress Eudoxia and her two daughters. Rome was paralysed.

Famine, looting, massacre, fire and plague continued, and in the year 476 the Western Emperors came to an end and barbarian kings ruled Italy. Among them was an unusual barbarian, Theodoric the Ostrogoth, who, though he never learnt to read or write, had a profound respect for civilization. For thirty-three years, from 493-526, Rome enjoyed a strange golden age. Her conqueror fell in love with her; her enemy became her knight errant. Dressed as a Caesar, Theodoric held court at Ravenna, and when he visited Rome he stayed on the now deserted Palatine. He addressed the Senate in Babu Latin and formed a police force to protect the hundreds of statues which still stood in the streets and fora. Under cover of darkness the degraded Romans of the time were always hacking off bronze limbs to melt down, and a contemporary historian notes that these statues were not entirely dumb, but gave a bell-like warning to the watchmen when attacked by the picks of Roman robbers. That a Goth should have protected the great generals, consuls and poets of the past from Roman thieves is a terrible glimpse into the decline of Rome.

When Theodoric died in 526, the unreal afterglow of his kingdom faded at once and the Byzantine Emperor decided to win back the western provinces. In 536 Rome was recovered for the Eastern Emperor, Justinian, by his great general Belisarius. Ten years later the stage was taken by a remarkable character, Totila the Goth.

He laid siege to the city until the population was dying of starvation in the streets. Nettle soup, rats and dogs were luxuries. When the civilian population was given permission to leave, a procession of ghosts staggered out, some to die by the way, many to be cut down by the waiting Goths. Still the great Aurelian Wall was impregnable, and while the remaining population pulled up and ate the grass and weeds that grew in the streets, there was a grandeur and nobility in their resistance which redeemed Rome's cowardice in the days of Alaric. At last four Greek sentries deserted to the Goths and offered to open the Asinarian Gate, near St John Lateran; then they slipped back at night to their posts. The Gate was opened, and in the first light of December 17, 546, Totila and his army swept into a dead city. There was nothing on which to vent their fury. Incredible as it seems, there were only five hundred civilians to be found in the whole of Rome, and they were hiding in the churches. The palaces stood empty; the house doors were open; the famous streets and the imperial fora were silent and deserted; here and there a statue from the great days stood surveying Rome's tragedy. So the Goths carried out a bloodless sack, like burglars who enter a house while the family is away.

It was the policy of Totila to level the walls of every city he captured, and this he decided to do with Rome. He removed all the gates and began to level the wall. The last inhabitants were expelled from the city, and in the empty streets the Goths continued their destruction. When they had pulled down a third of the wall, a message arrived from Belisarius bidding Totila to think twice, and ending with the warning that to destroy Rome would ruin his reputation in the eyes of the world. Totila was a strange man, swept suddenly by moods of pity or kindness, certainly of magnanimity, and he decided to leave Rome to its fate. For forty days Rome did not contain a single human being. Animals hunted about, and wolves came down in the winter's cold to tear at the thousands of shallow graves.

Belisarius then marched on Rome and repaired the wall. He

lured back a few inhabitants with food, and life began in the city once again. In two years' time Totila again besieged Rome, and history was repeated. Sentries betrayed the city and the Goths took it: but their strange leader was no longer anxious to destroy Rome; he now wished to restore it. Great spaces within the walls had been sown with corn and the population was that of a small country town. Totila attracted new inhabitants from near and far, and before he left, he organized a macabre occasion.

The Circus Maximus, which could hold two hundred thousand spectators, was still intact, and upon its marble tiers, at the invitation of the Gothic king, the miserable population of the tragic city assembled to witness games. These chariot races of 549 were the last to be held in Rome, and the ghosts of the old Romans must have wept and wrung their hands at this parody of the past. The games over, Totila went off to punish Sicily. Four years went by, and he was then obliged to defend Rome against a Byzantine army. He was slain in battle and buried secretly, but a Gothic woman revealed his grave to the Greeks, who dug up the body and sent it to Constantinople where it was placed at the feet of Justinian.

The history of Rome for the next hundred and seventy years was that of a dependency of Constantinople. A Greek exarch at Ravenna represented the Byzantine Emperor. A Greek official lived in a corner of the mouldering palaces of the Caesars on the Palatine, and was the nominal ruler of Rome, though the real ruler was the Pope. Greek monks filled the monasteries and served the churches; Greek Popes succeeded each other on the throne of St Peter, and the churches of Rome were covered with beautiful mosaics, some of which still survive. Not a drop of old Roman blood could have survived in a population, which, now that the aqueducts had been cut and the hills were without water, was huddled near the Tiber, on the Campus Martius. This was the Rome seen by the first Saxon pilgrims from England.

In 731 Gregory II cast off allegiance to Constantinople and the reign of the viceroys ended. The Rome of the Caesars was now to become the Rome of the Popes. In that great moment the Papacy finally turned its back upon the Greek East and its face towards the Latin West, which under its guidance was to become Europe. Armed with spiritual authority and moral power, and wise with the knowledge of the past, the Papacy was not a military state and needed a champion. On Christmas Day in the year 800 Pope Leo III placed a crown upon the head of Charlemagne, King of the Franks, and the crowd in St Peter's hailed him as *basileus* in the form of words used at the coronation of the Emperors of Byzantium. Dr Delisle Burns wrote: 'The shout that greeted Charles the Great as Emperor of the Romans was the infant's cry at the birth of the First Europe.'

CHAPTER FOUR

The Pope at a window – the Papal Farm – a day on the Palatine Hill – Caesarian palaces – the writer in Ancient Rome – Nero's Golden House – The Colosseum

§ 1

As the heat of summer increases, more Romans continue to leave Rome while more visitors arrive, and there comes a moment when a black saloon car glides from the Vatican. In the back, a frail white figure traces the sign of the cross to left and right. The crowds kneel, then stand and wave towards a white skull-cap in the vanishing rear window. The Pope has moved to his summer palace at Castel Gandolfo.

Anyone at all sensitive to historical atmosphere now begins to feel that Rome is empty; and since the departure of the monarchy this sensation is singularly strong, for kings may come and go, but the Pope remains for ever. There probably has never been a Pope who is more certain to be canonized than Pius XII, and the stories I had heard about him made me anxious to see a man who will one day be numbered among the saints. I was therefore delighted to be given a ticket for one of the public audiences which the Pope holds twice a week in summer, and I thought the occasion justified a hired car.

The driver of this car was a mild looking Italian until he settled himself behind the wheel, when he became aggressive, if not actually homicidal. We shot round the Piazza Barberini, weaving our way in and out at great speed, missing by an inch or so a man on a bicycle loaded with carnations, braking violently to avoid another car, shooting ahead to overtake it, for he was one of those drivers who consider it dishonourable to be passed, and darting up narrow Renaissance streets hooting insanely until the passers-by dashed for shelter.

'In one year,' he said, turning to me and accelerating, 'I have nine accidents. . . .'

As if this had not sunk into my mind, he took both hands off the wheel and shouted, 'Nine!'

'But,' he continued, leaning towards me jocosely and flicking one hand up and down gaily, 'I am in the right each time and—I getta the money!'

We careered on our way. The old woman in black, who in every Italian street steps straight off the pavement and walks towards what seems to be certain death, appeared before us. He missed her. I looked back and saw her continuing her journey as if nothing had happened. The cars around us, which were travelling just as fast as we were, swerved aside by one of those instinctive Italian motoring movements not unlike birds in formation who part and form again, and we saw right in our path a blind man being led across the street by a small boy.

In any other city in the world we should have hit another car and the list of dead and injured would have been considerable; but with the instinctive sensitiveness of the Italian driver for the problems of other Italian drivers, the cars just gave us enough room to avoid the blind man. Then we cheerfully crashed some of Rome's few traffic lights and nearly shaved a man's fiancée from the pillion of a Vespa, and, passing outside the walls, found ourselves on the Albano road, where we speeded up.

'How does it happen that you speak such good English?' I asked.

'I was your prisoner,' he replied simply, with an air of humility.

This was intended to be a whimsical reference to the fortunes of war, but I thought it unfair that he should have made it a personal matter. All I could think of in reply was, 'Well, I hope I treated you well.'

We raced along the road out of Rome, past the place where the trams end, past the stark blocks of flats that stand in mounds of rubble where Italian film companies site their dramas, along the road where a ruined aqueduct gropes across the Campagna, and past the airport; then we climbed towards the green hills.

The driver was really a nice, kindly fellow, a genuine Roman from Trastevere, with something about him that reminded me of the old-time Cockney's ironic and philosophic acceptance of the harder facts of life. Like all Italians, he knew somebody who knew somebody who knew somebody else, the Jacob's Ladder ascending slowly towards the godhead of influence; and with so many cousins, nephews and uncles scattered about Rome, I gathered that there was practically nothing he could not do with diplomacy, family piety and time.

We speeded across the plain and were soon climbing into the cool Alban Hills. When the Pope goes to Castel Gandolfo, the district bristles with police posts. We saw sentry boxes beside the road every five hundred yards, where the sentries stood leaning on their rifles, watching us go past. As we approached one post the driver hooted continuously and waved out of the window to an angry-looking policeman.

'Who was that?' I asked.

'The cousin of my wife,' he replied.

We shot up a steep and narrow street and came to rest in a sunny piazza with a central fountain. At the far side of the piazza stood the enormous entrance gate of the papal palace, where two handsome young Swiss Guards in their slashed red, yellow and blue uniforms were smiling into the cameras of about a hundred girl guides from Belgium. The driver said he would go and look up his grandfather and meet me after lunch. As the audience did not begin until six, I had the afternoon to spare.

I spent a pleasant hour at a pavement café, watching the crowds drawn by the papal audience to this hot little hill town. There were families in touring cars, groups of tourists, bands of pilgrims with their priests, girl guides from Holland and Belgium, boy scouts from England, Spaniards, Danes, Americans, and even a number of little yellow priests who might have been Siamese. The waiter told me that this was only the advance guard: the real crowd would not arrive until the coaches came from Rome in the late afternoon.

Christians in their best moments have always impressed observers by their cheerfulness, I reflected, and it was this characteristic that I chiefly noted in these crowds. Speaking many different languages, they were united in their Church and in the Esperanto of its liturgy, and were at that particular moment over-joyed and excited at the thought that later that afternoon they would stand in the presence of the successor to St Peter and receive his blessing. A tall American of the pink, well-shaven kind who reminds one of advertisements for inter-office telephones, stood before me and, with the air of an eighteenth century marquis, asked if he and his wife might sit at my table.

They had crossed the Atlantic to visit the cemetery at Nettuno where their son lies, a young man who was killed on his twentieth birthday upon the beaches of Anzio.

'He was a fine boy,' said his father.

'He was a good boy,' said his mother quietly, as she sipped her coffee.

'We were honoured with a private audience with the Holy Father some weeks ago,' said the man, 'but we wanted to come and see him again before we go back home, even if we just get a glimpse of him from the edge of the crowd.'

I walked over to the tall brown gates of the palace, where the two Swiss Guards were still standing, halberds in hand, while cameras whirred and clicked. The Pope's summer home, which he loves and in which he stays as long as possible, is a huge, late Renaissance palace built by Maderna, the architect of the façade of St Peter's, and in order to build it, he had to pull down an old castle of the Gandolfi which had stood for centuries on this wonderful site overlooking the Lake of Albano.

The strange thing about Castel Gandolfo is that you cannot see this superb lake lying far below until you seek it out, for it is concealed by the streets of the town. I saw the lake unexpectedly when, looking for somewhere to eat, I turned down a lane and came to a terrace built on a ledge of rock, and there, four hundred feet below, I saw the crater of an old volcano, now a circle of blue water cupped in surrounding hills. It was a beautiful scene; that enormous circle once devoted to fire and now quenched by heavenly blue. On the rocky ledge was the romantic little restau-rant that you find more often in a novel than in real life. A dozen tables were set beneath a vine trellis where small grapes were already forming, and beyond the shade was the sunlight, the crystal air and the distant lake below.

The only other people were two old Italian priests in dusty soutanes and broad, heavy shoes, their lined and uncomplicated faces shining from the immense mound of spaghetti they had consumed, not to mention a flagon of local wine. I ordered *stracciatelle alla Romana*, an egg soup with the tang of the sixteenth century in it, *scaloppine al Marsala*, and some Gorgonzola cheese. With an air of pride the waiter placed on the table a carafe of local wine, which, he said, came from the padrone's own vineyards and had been blended with the wine of Nemi. He waited until I had tasted it, and retired a happy man when I told him that it was better than any of the wines of the *Castelli*. I was just finishing my meal when the driver stood before me. He had had luncheon, but was pleased to finish the wine.

'Would you like to see the Pope's farm?' he asked.

I thought this an admirable idea, for I did not know that the Pope kept a farm, and we returned to the car and drove through the gateway of an imposing villa where a man lifted his hat to me and bowed as if I were royalty. It passed through my mind that a relative of the driver's must have been involved in this welcome. We swept on down a magnificent avenue of ancient trees and came to a wide terrace with a stupendous view of Rome across the Campagna. Steps from the terrace led down to a geometrical Renaissance garden planted with box, red and pink begonias, and heliotrope. There were fountains, mazes and hedges. The vista ended in a group of black cypresses, never long absent from the Roman scene, which seemed to advance like a band of sombre monks, as if to tell us that there is something more serious in life than mazes and waterfalls.

The Pope walks for an hour or so on the terrace, admiring the gardens, which are those of the Villa Barberini. He arrives by car along a special road built to link the palace with the villa, and I was told that he usually leaves his car on the terrace and walks about, sometimes never lifting his eyes from a book. We entered a little *giardino secreto* enclosed by hedges, where a statue of the Blessed Virgin stands beside a fishpond.

'You notice the Virgin is holding a little bunch of flowers,' said the driver. 'The Holy Father picks them for her.'

She was holding four or five small yellow flowers of a kind that I had noticed growing on the banks round about, and they were fresh and had been recently picked. What a beautiful moment this must have been: the old pontiff all alone in the garden in his white caped soutane and his red velvet shoes, looking about among the hedge banks on a quiet sunny morning for wild flowers to give the Madonna.

We drove through a gate into a busy agricultural scene, where men and women were reaping several acres of maize, and on we went past fields of potatoes, cabbages and leeks and through orchards of apple trees almost ready with a heavy rosy harvest. Everything had that beautiful air of neatness seen only in exhibition farms, where behind neatly concealed dung-hills one seems to sense the presence of a sergeant-major who insists on burnished spades. We passed a number of henhouses, each one delightfully decorated with a mosaic above the door depicting some incident in hen life. A great number of White Leghorns and Rhode Island Reds picked delicately among maize leaves in front of their palaces, rather as if the courtiers of Louis XIV were enjoying a *fête champêtre*. I should like to have stopped to examine the hen mosaics, but the driver dashed on towards the dairy. There, in a cowshed lined with blue tiles, we saw forty fine Friesland cows being fed in the most modern surroundings. The names, milk yields and maternal particulars were recorded above the mild faces. I was at last able to make the pun that had to be made, and must be made by everyone who visits the Pope's farm.

'Where is the papal bull?'

I was led to an adjoining paddock, where an immense, low-slung black and white animal named Christy, the gift of an American to the Holy Father, paused with his mouth full, and gazed at us angrily. He had the bloodshot eyes of an assassin and the lashes of a film star.

My driver now let out a cry of dismay and said we must hasten back to the town for the audience. I made him promise not to hurry too much, but in a few minutes he had left me at the bottom of the hill, for the crowds were now so great that he could not attempt to take the car to the piazza.

I walked up in a great procession of people, all making for the palace. It was really exciting: I could feel it in the air. Everyone was anxious to be in time. The ordinary visitors were reinforced by a number of seminarists from their summer schools round the lake; I noticed several Englishmen in their black cassocks, a few Scots in violet cassocks with red girdles, and a couple of Germans whose cardinal-red cassocks give such colour to the streets of Rome before the summer migration begins. There was a young Franciscan friar who might have stepped out of a fresco by Fra Angelico; he had a thin golden beard and curious pale eyes, eyes which might see a vision. And, of course, among the striding throng were those foot-sloggers of the Church, the sturdy Italian village priests in their broad, thick boots.

Our fears were well founded. The courtyard was full. A great mass of people pressed up, pleading to be let in, but papal police despairingly pointed with white-gloved hands to the throng inside, while the Swiss Guard stood picturesquely with crossed halberds. I pushed my way to the gate and was somehow drawn inside, where I found myself ascending the marble stairs of the palace. The sound of the crowd in the courtyard below was like bees swarming. Then several thousand voices began to sing a hymn. A Swiss Guard pointed to an open window and told me I could stand there. About twenty people were already in position and I could see nothing. I walked out of the room and up a flight of stone stairs that led to the roof. Here I expected to be alone, but there must have been a thousand people leaning over the parapet, sitting on wooden stands, and even perched dangerously on the tiles. At last I found a place against the parapet from which I had a splendid view of the packed courtyard below and the central balcony of the palace, where a red banner was suspended. While I was watching this scene, a man who was standing next to me said: 'Perhaps you don't remember me, but the last time we met was in Bulawayo!'

In the crowds below was a curious white patch which turned out to be the caps of hundreds of American sailors from a visiting cruiser; there were innumerable shrill young girls with banners, in the charge of nuns, and noisy young boys with their village priests, and friars, nuns, and every kind of visitor. Suddenly the crowd gave a triumphant shout, louder than anything it had so far uttered and, glancing down towards the balcony, I saw that a frail, upright figure in white had appeared in the black oblong of the window, and was standing smiling to left and right and making a motion for silence. With an expiring *'Viva il Papa!'* the voice of the crowd died away.

Pius XII then seated himself on a red and gold chair, adjusted a loudspeaker, and began to address the members of his enormous family. One's first thoughts on seeing the Pope must be historical. It is with awe that one looks at a man whose sacred office extends back to the days of imperial Rome. There is no other such link on earth. The temporal aspect of his office has accumulated round his person the ceremonies of the Caesars; but he is not only Caesar, but the Pope, the Father, and this side of him we now saw as he talked quietly to us in a conversational tone from the balcony of his country home. It was, in a sense, even more impressive, I thought, than when I had last seen him, borne aloft in the *sedia gestatoria*, with the trumpets sounding and the peacock fans waving; for this is how the first Popes spoke to the first Christians, as fathers to their children.

It may be a strange thing to say of a small figure in white on a distant balcony, but I was aware that this man was radiating to us all an extraordinary sense of peace and tranquillity; of holiness, for there is no other word. Even had I been unaware of his ascetic life and his saintliness, I should have felt this. He is a thin aristocrat, whose hands are of the thin and attenuated kind that El Greco loved to give his saints. His face is thin and sallow, his eyes dark and deep set. He is so upright and precise in his movements that it is difficult to believe he is eighty years old.

He was once known as the Polyglot Cardinal, and has addressed audiences in eight languages. He is the first Pope to have flown, to descend into a mine, and to visit a submarine. In 1917 he carried to the Kaiser the offer of Benedict XV to mediate in the first world war. He knew Hitler before the last war, and he was elected in 1939, on his birthday, when he was sixty-three years oɪ age.

These thoughts ran in my mind as I listened to his voice. The crowd cheered from time to time. He waved it into silence. He spoke in Italian; then in Spanish, to a group of Latin-American pilgrims; then in French; then in German. Each group, addressed in its own language, made the courtyard ring. The Pope then asked: 'Are there any English here?' There was a roar from the sailors: 'America!'

The Pope smiled, turned to them and spoke in English. When he had finished, they lifted the palace roof with a 'God bless the Pope!'

Then he turned to the children and said in Italian, 'Children, I am speaking to you.'

'*Viva il Papa!*' came in a shrill cry as every child waved a little flag at the balcony.

'Are you good children?' asked the Pope. There was a roar of delighted laughter.

'*Si, Santo Padre, si, si, si!*'

'Do you always say your prayers?'

'*Si, Papa, si, sempre, sempre. . . .*'

'Do you eat well; do you sleep well?'

Then the Pope gave them a simple talk on living a good and truthful life. When he had finished, half the women near me had their handkerchiefs to their eyes, and it was indeed what the Spaniards call *emocionante*. The Pope then rose and with uplifted arms blessed the crowd. He bowed his head a moment in prayer, turned and went into the palace.

I drove thoughtfully back to Rome. Some days later I was telling an official in the Vatican my impressions of the audience and, passing to lighter things, said how glad I was to have seen a papal bull. He asked me to explain. An expression of the utmost dismay crossed his face as I told him about the farm.

'But how did you get in?' he asked. 'Permission is never given!'

So, you see, in Italy it is important to know someone who knows someone who knows someone!

§ 2

When the traveller in ancient times approached Rome along the Appian Way, his first glimpse of the splendour of the capital would be the group of imperial palaces lifted in sunlight on the Palatine Hill. The Caesars had lived there in increasing grandeur since the establishment of the Empire, and no more splendid palaces existed in the world. Here they administered their mighty inheritance, here they lived, often in a world of flatterers and slaves, and here they sometimes fell miserably to the dagger of an assassin.

The crowded palaces were already ancient when in the fourth century Constantine the Great decided to move the capital of the Empire to Constantinople. Gradually another Palatinate, with many a dome instead of a column, was reflected in the waters of the Bosphorus. The splendour of the Byzantine palaces became a legend. Vikings talked about them in the long northern winter; savage Balkan chiefs and nomads of the Steppes knew of their splendour and spoke round their camp-fires of the imperial throne flanked by golden lions, and of the tree of gold with enamelled singing-birds which stood behind the throne. As the palaces of Rome mouldered on the Palatine, the royal halls of Byzantium became more and more splendid until, in 1453, the Turks captured Constantinople and the Sultan walked wonderingly into the palaces of the emperors. Those who today explore the curious ramifications of the Sultan's Palace at Istanbul may fancy, not without reason, that they see the only reflection left on earth of the once crowded Roman Palatine.

The Palatine was not, however, always a royal hill. During the Republic, from 509 to 31 B.C., it was the dwelling-place of the aristocratic and the wealthy. The 'new men', the successful orators and financiers, felt they had arrived when they set up house there. It was what Park Lane was in the reign of Edward VII. Augustus had been born on the Palatine and decided that he would like to live there. A suitable house was available and it was granted to him by the Senate when he was twenty-seven. It had belonged to the famous orator and rival of Cicero, Quintus

Hortensius, who had a great love for animals. Hortensius lived quietly in Rome and reserved a display of his wealth for his country villas, of which he had several. In his splendid estate at Tarentum he had a cellar of ten thousand *amphorae* of Chian wine and a collection of wild animals which he had tamed. It is said that during his banquets the guests, hearing the sound of pipes, would glance up and see a slave dressed as Orpheus advancing from the trees, followed by all kinds of animals gambolling round him to the sound of his flute. He had tamed the sea-fish in his salt-water ponds at Bauli and used to feed them by hand, and on one occasion he was reduced to tears by the death of one of his favourites. He was also fond of trees and gave them chemical fertilizer in the form of wine; once he asked Cicero to speak in his place in order that he might return to the country and fertilize a favourite plane-tree at the proper time.

The house of this agreeable character was a simple dwelling on the Palatine, and just what Augustus was looking for. He was too adroit to assume the air of grandeur adopted by the lesser men who succeeded him and, though in time he bought the house next door and enlarged his home, it is said that for years he always slept in the same little bedroom. Thus the house of Hortensius became the nucleus of the cluster of palaces which eventually covered the Palatine.

One of the chief builders was Tiberius, the Caesar of the Crucifixion, who built himself a palace on the north-west side of the hill, which his successor, the crazy Caligula, extended to the edge of the hill overlooking the Forum and directly above the Atrium Vestae. Here Caligula was murdered and here the trembling Claudius was elevated to the purple by a couple of passing soldiers. Nero considered the palaces of his predecessors unworthy of him and deserted the Palatine for his fabulous Golden House. Neither Vespasian nor his son Titus built palaces, but Domitian, Vespasian's younger son, transformed the centre of the hill and the southern side of it, building a stadium and a wonderful palace where he lived a haunted, terrified life, to die at last in one of his marble halls with a dagger in his stomach. Then came an interval of about a century during which nothing was added to the hill.

This period included the great reigns of Trajan, Hadrian, and Marcus Aurelius. Then, with Septimius Severus, whose arch still stands in the Forum and whose adventures in Scotland I have mentioned, the south-western side of the hill became covered with new and splendid buildings. By this time, however, the Palatine was so crowded that the emperor, in order to find room, had to build a great platform on the enormous arches which can still be seen from the Via del Circo Massimo and which form the most striking feature of the Hill today.

With the exception of Augustus, the palaces were built by the least worthy of the Caesars. Tiberius was not an attractive person; Caligula was mad; Nero, though he did not add to the Palatine, was the most lavish builder of them all; and Domitian developed into a cruel tyrant. The good emperors are not represented at all: Claudius, who, though a neurotic, was not a bad man, left nothing, neither did Trajan, Hadrian, Antoninus Pius, nor Marcus Aurelius. Thus the palaces on the Palatine represent the *malaise de pierre* of a number of extremely odd and ill-adjusted Caesars: and that is its simple history.

§ 3

It was one of those summer days that pounces on Rome like a lion. The sun was already hot at nine o'clock and would be intolerable at noon. I thought that it would be a perfect day to solve, to my own satisfaction at any rate, the mysteries of the Palatine; there are shady stone pines there, grassy banks, and on a former visit I had noted a place overhung with oleanders and ilex trees where a little spring trickled into a stone sarcophagus. It was the perfect spot for a picnic.

In one of those superb grocers' shops in the back streets of Rome I bought some Parma ham and Bel Paese cheese, at the baker's next door, some *grissini*, and at the fruitstall a couple of peaches. I evidently had not made myself understood at the grocer's, for I had enough ham for ten people, which was just as well as it turned out.

On my way to the Palatine I was walking down a narrow lane beside the still half-buried Forum of Julius Caesar, when a ginger tomcat of sly and battered appearance, a perfect Nym or Bardolph of a cat, approached me with tattered tail erect. Most animals are transformed by human kindness and cats as much as any. Some of these half-wild creatures that live on their wits in the ruins of Rome have retained an ancestral memory of the fireside, and though ready to fly to their holes and dens at any sudden movement, are often anxious to hear a human voice. Nym had evidently known better days and stood whirring like a small dynamo in my path. As I bent down to say a few words of comfort and to stroke him, quick as a flash a paw struck out at my bag of ham. I was as surprised as if a stranger had stopped to ask for a match and had picked my pocket. Retiring to the shade of a wall, I gave him a slice upon which he pounced ravenously. This act, so much against the nature of a cat, which will suspiciously sniff roast chicken as if it were poison, revealed the kind of life he led. Meanwhile, as if in answer to a whistle, expectant whiskers appeared from every corner of the ruins, and soon cats, grey, black, tabby, white, ginger, and every combination of these colours, some of them lean females with kittens just able to totter, were gazing at me in an apprehensive circle. Nym was furious. Having found the ham (and myself), he was anxious to reserve us for his own use, and he flattened his ears, growled in his throat, and made threatening gestures with an uplifted paw. He was evidently the King of the Gipsies.

For many centuries the stray cats of Rome have inhabited the halls where Jamshyd gloried and drank deep They were noticed by travellers in the eighteenth century; our forebears fed them in the nineteenth; and there are just as many as ever. I should like a biologist to explain to me why, in such conditions of unrestricted breeding, white has persisted with such vigour. I should have thought that the reversionary colour would have been grey or tabby. The end of this story is that in five minutes about fifty cats had finished sufficient ham for ten people, and I left them returning to their dens among the ruins, amazed by this astonishing windfall.

I climbed the Palatine Hill and found myself in the loneliest and most ghostly place in Rome. Stone pine and ilex cast their shade upon uneasy mounds where the skeleton of a palace thrusts a marble bone into the light; steps lead into grassy cellars; long, dank passages which once linked hall to marble hall stand like the gaunt remains of an underground station; and the sun has cracked and split pavements of coloured marble that once had known the footsteps of the Caesars. From one side of the hill I looked down into the Forum and saw it from end to end, gleaming in the hot morning: from the other side I gazed down at the astonishing spectre of the Circus Maximus, an immense oblong traced in brown dust, once a racecourse of glittering marble which had held two hundred thousand spectators and now a vast, eloquent space.

The solitude of the Palatine Hill, which gave the word 'palace' to the languages of Europe, is uncanny. You eagerly scan the face of another explorer as he approaches you, then you are alone again in foundations that speak of shining walls and towering columned porticoes, of storey mounting upon marble storey, of roof above roof, culminating in the golden statues of gods and men, and gilded four-horse chariots like the quadriga of Lysias, whose milk-white steeds 'blew the breath of morning from their nostrils'.

One of the most interesting ruins on the Palatine is the so-called House of Livia, which is now believed to have been the House of Augustus. A few steps took me down into a series of small rooms festooned with medallions which are still sharp and fresh: Polyphemus is still pursuing Galatea into the sea and Hermes is still rescuing Io. It was with a sense of awe that I thought perhaps the eyes of Augustus may have rested on these walls nearly two thousand years ago. The attendant was chiefly determined that I should not miss the lead water main that runs towards the bath-room.

If this is really the House of Augustus, it is even smaller than I should have imagined, though it is well known that he lived in the greatest simplicity. He even made his haughty consort, Livia, weave his togas. Once a year, because of a dream, he would sit at the door of his house like a beggar and receive alms from passers-by. He was frugal in his diet and often ate bread soaked in water and a handful of raisins; he drank little wine. He suffered from insomnia and once when a man reputed to be a millionaire died in debt, he sent to the auction to buy the pillow which had enabled such a man to sleep. Augustus was not tall, but he was so well built that this was unnoticed until he was standing among a group of men. His hair was light brown and his face is as well known to us as that of any man who lived so long ago. It is an intellectual, almost ascetic face, perhaps a little cold and inscrutable. His lips are never seen in a smile, yet he is believed to have had a sense of humour. He once described a nervous man who tremblingly placed a petition in his hand as one who appeared to be offering a penny to an elephant. Only one of his epigrams, a highly improper one, has been preserved by Martial. He was probably the first collector of fossils and palaeolithic implements, which he used to find in the sea caves of Capri, and he was the proud possessor of a whale's skeleton.

In extraordinary contrast to the megalomaniacs who succeeded him, Augustus permitted the utmost freedom of speech, and even allowed the humblest individuals to say the rudest things to him. Tiberius once criticised his stepfather for this, considering such tolerance unworthy of the most powerful man on earth, but Augustus replied: 'My dear Tiberius, don't give way to youthful excitement, or be so very indignant at some one being found to speak harm of me. It is quite enough if we can prevent them *doing* us any harm.' Yet with his many attractive qualities, he could be cruel and heartless. His first wife, Scribonia, was some twelve years his senior and he had married her for political reasons. Nevertheless one feels that he might have chosen a kinder moment to divorce her than the day she presented him with a daughter. He then insisted on marrying Livia, the young wife of Tiberius Nero, who, upon her divorce, came to him with her two small sons. Augustus adored her all his life, though scandal associated his name with that of many other women. He died at the age of seventy-six, with his arms around her, and his last words are said to have been: 'Livia, remember our life together; and now, farewell!'

Livia was once asked, says Dion Cassius, how she had managed to keep the affections of Augustus, and she replied, 'My secret is very simple: I have made it a study of my life to please him, and I have never manifested any indiscreet curiosity with regard to his public or private affairs.' They were childless and, death having removed the heirs of Augustus's own family in circumstances which seemed to contemporaries highly suspicious, Livia's son by her first husband, Tiberius, succeeded to the Empire jointly with Livia. She was the mother of the Caesar of the Crucifixion.

Her statues show a tall, graceful, haughty woman, who could have sat to an artist as a typical Roman matron of Republican days. One looks into her features in vain for some sign of an ambition that would not shrink from murder, but the fact remains that the heirs whom Augustus would have selected perished, while Livia and her son succeeded. During the first years of the new reign she tried to dominate her son, but he hated her, and when she died at an age well over eighty, Tiberius made no pretence at sorrow and did not attend her funeral.

A short walk took me to the edge of the Palatine overlooking the Circus Maximus. Here a huge platform on several levels, scattered with the stumps of many columns, is all that remains of the Temple of Apollo. Before the Battle of Actium, when the fate of Augustus was uncertain, he vowed a temple to the god, and when Antony and Cleopatra had been vanquished and the young man found himself master of the world, he hastened to fulfil his vow. Those who saw this temple describe its grandeur and its beauty, the rarity of its marbles, and the inner shrine where a Greek statue, which at first sight resembled a musical maiden, represented Apollo with his lyre: and in its base was concealed a safe in which Augustus deposited the Sibylline books. What happened to the oracles is one of the mysteries of ancient Rome. Lanciani says that they were still there as late as A.D. 363 and were, indeed, the only objects saved when, in that year, the prefect of police, Apronianus, and the fire brigades, were helpless to prevent the destruction of the temple: but after this they are never heard of again.

Even more wonderful than the temple seem to have been the two libraries, a Greek and a Latin, which were included in the same architectural plan. This was evidently an act of piety on the part of Augustus, who carried out the scheme which Julius Caesar had contemplated. The reading-room of this library, which was large enough to accommodate a meeting of the Senate, was decorated with medallions in gold, silver and bronze of famous writers and orators.

Those who have been amused by Pliny's description of the 'readings' given from time to time by authors and would-be authors may imagine such events in progress here. It was the custom of the time for writers to read their books to a select audience of friends before they were published, and it was fashionable to be seen attending such occasions. Juvenal says that he was goaded into writing poetry in order to revenge himself on those whose epics he had been obliged to endure in silence. Among the terrors of Rome he mentions fires, the collapse of badly built houses, and 'spouting poets in August'. Of course only a famous writer could expect to give a reading in the Library of Augustus; the average literary man had to be content with an empty room hired for him by his patron, where the chairs and benches had to be rented as well, and sometimes also the audience.

Pliny was describing a fashionable occasion, possibly in the Augustan Library, when he wrote of the reluctant guests approaching the hall as if compelled by main force, some lingering outside and sending in messengers to find out how many pages were still to come; then 'when they hear the moment of deliverance is not far off, they come in slowly, sit on the edge of their chairs'. Pliny himself was an indomitable reader and took a poor view of such conduct. On one dreadful occasion, during wet weather, he treated his friends to a two days' reading, and says that when he offered to conclude, his audience begged him to continue for a third day. How well we can imagine the insincere applause! And we can see Pliny, suddenly appalled by the sound of his own voice, pausing with some such words as, 'Well, I really think I ought to stop now!'; and the cry of the sufferers, 'No, my dear fellow, please continue! We mustn't miss a word.' On another occasion he invited friends to dinner and read poems to them on two successive nights. At last they rebelled and told him that he was not a good reader. This dismayed him. He wrote to a friend asking for advice. Should he get one of his freedmen to read for him? If so, how should he behave while the reading was in progress? 'Shall I sit in a fixed and indolent posture, or follow him as he pronounces, with my eyes, hands and voice; a manner which some you know practise?' Poor Pliny, through the irony of his remarks one can sense his injured vanity.

Contemporary writers tell us a great deal about an author's life, how his works were published and how many copies went to an edition. After having read his new work in public, the writer would take it to a publisher, who employed a number of copyists. While a reader dictated the book, scribes wrote it down in black ink on sheets of papyrus, which were afterwards pasted together into a roll. Twenty scribes working several hours a day could no doubt produce a thousand copies, which was considered a fair edition, in a fraction of the time it takes now to publish even the smallest book. When completed, the roll of papyrus was attached to a spindle called the *umbilicus*; and the book collector could spend as much as he liked on having the ends of the *umbilicus*, known as the *cornua*, beautifully decorated, coloured, or fitted with gold or silver knobs. He could also have the edges of the papyrus coloured, much as we now have gilt-edged leaves, and he could have the title, which hung from the manuscript rather like the seal of an old document, embellished, and the whole work enclosed in a costly case or *membrana*.

I have rarely seen an actor read an ancient manuscript on the stage in the right way, which is to take the roll in the left hand and withdraw the first few inches with the right, then to continue to ease the roll with the left hand, and to wind up with the right, until the end is reached. In order to rewind tightly, it was often convenient to tuck the first page under the chin to have both hands free to roll the *umbilicus*, which explains a remark of Martial's that may have puzzled some modern readers: he refers to an unread book as one that 'has not been worn and scrubbed by bushy chins'.

The author usually sold his book outright to the publishers, though, of course, he was free, if he liked, to issue it himself by employing his own scribes; but this was rarely done, and no wonder. Copyright did not exist and anyone could bring out a pirated edition. The experience of quarrelling with one's publishers and being welcomed by another was a pleasure denied to the ancient writer, because it was pointless. The angry publisher could always get his own back. Horace was published by the Sosii Brothers, Martial by Atrectus and Secundus, Quintilian by Tryphon, and Seneca by Dorus. Cicero's rich friend Atticus sometimes published him in what it is pleasant to imagine were sumptuous private press editions. No author could live on the proceeds of his work, and Martial is full of the woes of a literary life, and says that he was no richer because his epigrams were read in Britain, Spain and Gaul, a reference to foreign editions which will find an echo in many a modern heart.

The 'Booksellers' Row' of ancient Rome was, in Martial's day, the Argiletum, near the Forum, where the publishers had their shops. Some of these were richly furnished as lounges in which the buyer could sit and inspect the works advertised on each side of the door. The manuscripts were kept upon shelves, stacked no doubt one upon another like bales of cloth, and it is possible that a Roman bookshop might have looked more like a draper's to modern eyes. I do not know whether any lending-libraries existed in Rome, but there were reference libraries, not only in Rome, but also in the country towns. Aulus Gellius says that once, when staying with a distinguished man at his villa near Tivoli, an argument rose among the guests on the danger of drinking iced water in hot weather. Those who considered the habit harmless doubted certain quotations made by a fellow guest, who, to prove his point, ran out to the public library and returned with a quotation from Aristotle strongly denouncing iced water as dangerous to health. Gellius adds that the guests were so much impressed by the quotation that they all decided to give up iced water in future. What interests me is not their decision, but whether the man who ran to the library was allowed to return with a copy of Aristotle, or whether he just wrote out the quotation; and this Gellius leaves in doubt.

I passed on from ruin to ruin and came to the welcome and

unexpected sign, 'Bar', with an arm pointing into the dark shades of the Farnese Gardens, where beneath tall trees and dark hedges cardinals once whispered their worldly secrets while the hooded cypresses bent to listen. The spectral old trees seemed filled with intelligence as if they were sucking something out of the storied soil. Though not a soul was there, I turned round quickly in the old garden to make sure I was not being followed in this haunted place.

In the centre of the decayed avenues stood a reassuring wooden hut, which was the bar. The attendant told me, nodding to a Vespa parked against a tree, that he motored up every day in summer and kept open until he heard the Ave Maria bell. I retired with my drink to a seat beneath a hedge, entirely taken up with the thought that the Farnese Gardens are planted on the ruins of the palace of Tiberius and Caligula. They have never been thoroughly excavated, though in the last century a guardroom was found upon whose walls members of the Praetorian Guard had scribbled words which prove that the habit is timeless. One soldier had written in Greek, 'Many have written many things on this wall, I nothing,' to which a comrade had added the word 'Bravo!' Tiberius was living in this palace when no doubt someone from the Foreign Office kept him in touch with the Jewish agitation in Jerusalem, and told him that Pontius Pilate 'had the situation well in hand'. Here, later, his successor, the mad Caligula, led his fantastic life, if we can believe all that was recorded of him.

Caligula's behaviour disgusted the Senate and the people and, at last, the army. It was decided to murder him in the fourth year of his reign. The conspiracy was really republican in spirit and the man selected to cut him down was the tribune of a Praetorian cohort whom he had insulted. The moment chosen was during the annual Palatine games and theatrical performances, when Caligula, leaving the theatre, was on his way back to the palace to bathe and dine during an interval. Learning that a choir of Greek boys had arrived to take part in the performances, he turned aside to speak to them in a passage where they were drawn up. At that moment the tribune drew his sword and aimed a blow which felled the Emperor to the ground, but did not kill him. He was able to scream 'I am still alive!', when soldiers standing near plunged their swords into his body. The fullest account of his death is by the Jewish historian Josephus. He doubtless obtained the details from Herod Agrippa I, the grandson of Herod the Great, who was in Rome at the time. Herod had been educated there and he knew the royal family intimately. He was fated to play an important role in the important events that followed the murder.

While the palace was in an uproar, Claudius, the uncle of the dead Emperor, then a man of fifty-one, concealed himself behind a curtain. He was a clever, pedantic don who has been compared with our own James I. He had been treated in youth as the fool of the family and he suffered from nervous peculiarities, such as a stammer, a twitch of the head, and a stumbling gait, which seemed amusing to his contemporaries. Hearing the soldiers tramping through the palace, Claudius, trembling behind the curtain, forgot that his feet were not hidden. The soldiers dragged him out, but instead of slaying him as he fully expected, recognized him as a member of the royal family and hailed him as Emperor! So began that fearful system of election by the army which lasted until the fall of the Empire.

At this point Herod Agrippa I took a hand in events. The news that Claudius (with whom he had been at school) had been proclaimed Emperor suited him well, but at the same time he knew that the Senate was in favour of a republic. Hastening to the Curia, he met on the way the unhappy Claudius being borne in a litter to the Praetorian barracks, and managed to give him a few words of advice and encouragement. Arriving at the Senate, he expressed loyalty to the republic, but pointed out how impossible it was to fight the Praetorian Guard with urban cohorts. He reduced the Senate to a calmer frame of mind and suggested that perhaps the most sensible thing would be to request Claudius to stand down, and he, as an old friend, offered to be one of the emissaries: but while he was pretending to be a republican, he was sending secret messages to Claudius, telling him to hold fast. His clever Jewish brain played a part in weakening the resolution of the Senate and in strengthening the unfortunate Claudius; and what a singular thought it is that the Emperor who invaded and subdued Britain in A.D. 43 owed his elevation to the purple, in some measure, to the grandson of Herod the Great.

Leaving the haunted gardens, I came to the site of the Palace of Domitian: but instead of the marble corridors which these words suggest—the soldiers on guard, the silent slaves passing across floors of inlaid silver, the fountains in courtyards, and vistas of onyx and porphyry—all I could see were many acres of rubble. Yet here had lived and died that strange emperor whose sombre reign was filled with spies. The son of the homely, democratic Vespasian and brother of the excellent Titus, Domitian was not, by all accounts, a credit to the family. The fear of assassination unnerved him to such an extent that his terror became infectious and everyone walked in dread. His spies and informers were everywhere and his prisons were full of suspected persons.

The Emperor's sense of humour was sinister and macabre. He once invited a number of the most important people in Rome to a feast at the palace. Upon arrival they were conducted to a chamber draped in black from floor to ceiling. The horrified guests then saw that beside each couch stood a tombstone upon which a name was written. They took their places as indicated and waited for the arrival of an executioner. Instead a number of naked little boys, painted black, entered and slowly performed a solemn dance. Then funeral cakes were served with the food offered to the spirits of the departed. While the guests tried to eat, the silence was broken only by the voice of Domitian recounting gruesome stories of murder and massacre. Perhaps even the Palatine Hill had never witnessed a stranger scene. When the banquet was over, the guests were astonished to be told that they could leave, and no sooner had they arrived home than a messenger came from the palace. Instead of the death sentence which everyone expected, each guest was given a valuable present.

His fears of assassination increasing, Domitian ordered the walls of a portico in which he used to stroll to be lined with a shining stone from Cappadocia called phengites, probably thin sheets of the mica which was used for window-panes. He could then see what was happening behind him. This Hall of Mirrors did not save him, however, for he was killed in his bedroom in the thirteenth year of his reign, when he was forty-three years old.

The last occupant of Domitian's palace was a Scot named Charles Mills, who built himself a Gothic villa in the ruins to which the society of nineteenth century Rome was always welcome. The Villa Mills, which appears in all the nineteenth century travel diaries, was pulled down only recently. In its gardens one spring day in 1827, Lady Blessington met an old lady, tall, dignified and graceful, dressed in a robe of rich, dark grey Levantine silk, and a bonnet of the same material, worn over a lace cap. A superb Cashmere shawl, which looked to Lady Blessington like a tribute from some barbaric sovereign, fell gracefully over her bent shoulders. The old lady mentioned her son, who had died a few years before, and said: 'I shall soon join him in that better world where no tears are shed.' She was escorted to her carriage; and the mother of Napoleon drove away from the ruins of the palaces of the Caesars.

§ 4

The sun beat down upon the ruins and crickets chirped in the scorched grass. The heat by this time was intense, and I began to seek out my shady picnic place.

Round the south-western shoulder of the Palatine a tall, overgrown bank conceals the little Franciscan church of S. Bonaventura, and here a jet of water pours from a lion's mouth into an old stone sarcophagus. It was lined with moss like green plush, and the water was clear and sweet. I drank, then twice or three times plunged my head into the icy depths. In the hedges round about blackberries were growing, and wild roses and mint. There were dwarf oaks, red and white oleanders and bay trees. Here I sat in the shade, enjoying the cool sound of the water, and ate my lunch, the only stranger, I thought, on the Palatine Hill.

When I had finished, I took a path that led down round the extreme flank of the hill and soon I saw below me the Colosseum and the Arch of Constantine. What a view this was of Rome's hideous yet wonderful Colosseum. It stood there, every arch and scar clearly visible, and so close that it seemed I could have tossed a penny into its centre. It is a battered, undying monster, with a great gash in its side whence came the Farnese Palace and many others.

I found a place in the shade and must have fallen asleep, for when I opened my eyes I saw a neat young Chinaman kneeling in the long grass about twenty paces away. He was beautifully dressed in a suit of tussore silk. He knelt and bowed his head several times towards the Colosseum, then, rising, moved an inch this way and that, and eventually framed the monument in the viewfinder of his camera. I wondered what he thought of Rome, the matrix of the West, and if he felt as alien as I should feel among the tilted roofs and dragon tiles of Pekin. To be alone with a Chinaman on the Palatine Hill cannot often happen, I thought, yet I let this unique moment pass without speaking to him. He closed his camera and, with a farewell glance at the Colosseum, disappeared round the bend of the hill.

I began to understand what Rome must have been like a hundred, two hundred, years ago, when there was grass everywhere, flowers, and peace. I recalled a pretty watercolour by Samuel Prout in the Victoria and Albert Museum, which shows a Franciscan and a few peasants loitering in a lane from which springs up, half buried, the Arch of Constantine. I glanced down at the Arch and saw it isolated now in a great expanse of roadway and encircled by motor cars, coaches, vans, Vespas and cyclists, which came swirling round the Colosseum.

§ 5

Men sit all day at the ticket-office, only too glad to admit you to Nero's Golden House, for this is one of the less visited places in Rome. From the evidence of these buried rooms it is almost impossible for any casual visitor to imagine what the Golden House must have been like except that it was gigantic. The guide led me into a dark chamber with a curved ceiling, where painted festoons and flying cupids were still upon the walls, and he pointed to a hole in the roof which he said had been made by Raphael and his contemporaries when they climbed down to copy the frescoes. Approaching the ruins from the top, the artists of the Renaissance naturally thought of them as caves or grottoes, and consequently they called the Roman wall paintings *pittura grottesca*, whence comes the word 'grotesque'. Their enthusiasm for these bright and cheerful little 'grotesques' was immediate, and they appeared to offer a perfect solution to the problem of covering the great number of walls which had to be decorated during the Renaissance.

The Roman interior decorators of the first century, who put so many birds and winged cupids on their walls, would have been astonished could they have known what long flights their little creatures were destined to take, first to the Vatican and then to walls all over Europe. Oddly enough, it seems that the heavy William Kent, the builder of the Horse Guards, was the first to introduce these delicate fancies to England—rather like an elephant bearing a butterfly—but his work in Kensington Palace was soon exceeded when the Adam brothers introduced veritable migrations of birds and whole flights of cupids, to say nothing of urns, sphinxes and griffins, to walls from Syon to Harewood House and back again.

Although Lanciani described the Golden House as 'a fairy-like establishment', it must have been more like one of those international exhibitions which were a feature of life between the wars. The palace covered a square mile of land seized by Nero after the fire of A.D. 64, and was built and laid out most sumptuously by the best architects of the day. Its vestibule contained a statue of the owner a hundred and twenty feet high, which, in the reign of Hadrian, was moved to another site by a team of twenty-four elephants. It was a versatile statue. Later emperors were in the habit either of altering its face, or of removing the head altogether and replacing it by their own, so that it might be recognized as Titus at one period and as Commodus at another. What happened to this colossus is not known, and indeed the disappearance of such massive objects is a mystery of later Roman history.

The grounds of the Golden House contained farms and vine-yards, and woods full of game; a zoo; botanical gardens; sulphur baths, supplied from the *aquae Albulae* twelve miles away, and salt-water baths, fed by water from the Mediterranean sixteen miles away; and thousands of superb statues from Greece and Asia Minor. Some of the halls of the palace were encrusted with gems and mother-of-pearl. One of the state dining-rooms had a sliding ceiling which parted to shower flowers and scents upon the assembled guests, and another was a planetarium moved by machinery where guests could watch the rising and setting of stars and the movements of the planets across an ivory firmament. Suetonius tells us that when Nero took possession of his new house he glanced round and remarked, 'At last I am lodged like a man'. His tenancy was, however, a short one; indeed I was shown a room in the ruins, plastered but still unpainted and un-finished, left apparently in that state at Nero's death.

The only other visitors in the ruins were a French couple who kept asking the guide a hundred questions, which irritated him almost beyond endurance, for he was one of those guides who disliked to be decoyed from the main line of his patter. One of their questions, which he never answered clearly, was, 'But, please, will you tell us what happened to the Golden House after Nero died?'

Much of the popular hatred for Nero had centred round this extravagant piece of self-indulgence, and it became a policy with Vespasian and his son Titus to return this territory to the populace, and how gladly they must have done so. A bluff old soldier like Vespasian, who was simple and frugal, who loved to visit the farmhouse where he had been brought up by his grandmother and to drink a toast from the silver goblet she had used, must have found the Golden House an embarrassing piece of extravagance. He gave Nero's ornamental lake as a site for the Colosseum, and Titus followed later by pulling down a portion of the Golden House itself and erecting his Baths there. So the Roman people, who had once hated the sight of the House, were now invited to enjoy it.

'Do you think Nero burned Rome?' asked the French couple.

The guide had his revenge.

'I was not there,' he replied with a wicked smile.

'I do not believe he did,' I put in, just for the sake of argument, 'and neither do I think he sang, or danced, or played any musical instrument while it was burning.'

'But surely,' said the Frenchman, his spectacles shining with the light of battle, 'Tacitus says that when people tried to put the fire out they met others, who prevented them and even fed the flames?'

'Sir,' I asked, hedging, 'have you ever been in a big fire?'

'No, sir,' he admitted.

'Well, sir,' I continued, 'I can tell you that at such moments people imagine they see all sorts of things.'

The woman then came firmly to the rescue of her husband.

'I am sure Nero burned Rome!' she said.

'Then, Madam,' I remarked, 'a wise man accepts a woman's instinct as infallible evidence. It would be ridiculous for us to think any more about it.'

We walked across the street and had coffee together at the little café opposite the Colosseum tram stop. I had thought the Frenchman a professor: but I was wrong. He was a wine merchant from Bordeaux.

§ 6

The first sight of the Colosseum is highly gratifying. It reassures the most bewildered visitor. No one could mistake it for anything but a large shambles designed with the utmost skill to focus the attention of many thousands of people upon a small field of action, then to disperse them with the greatest possible efficiency.

The amazing thing about the Colosseum is the fact that it is built in a marsh, and that its stupendous weight has been resting for all these centuries upon artificial foundations set in water. This part of Rome is still waterlogged with springs which trickle down from the Esquiline Hill, as you can see today in the underground churches beneath S. Clemente. How the Colosseum was built on such a soil is a wonder of engineering, and I can well imagine that any architect might forsake all else in Rome to study the problems of this triumphant mass. In the year 1864 one of the periodic stories about buried treasure in the Colosseum was revived with success by a certain Signor Testa. He claimed to have a clue to 'the Frangipani treasure', believed to have been concealed there in the Middle Ages when that family turned the amphitheatre into a fortress. Pope Pius IX became interested and gave permission for the excavations, which were followed with breathless interest by everyone in Rome. Nothing of intrinsic value was found, though the effort was not wasted as it gave Lanciani his only chance to examine the foundations of the Colosseum. He wrote that he saw 'the upper belt of the substructures, arched like those of the ambulacra above ground; and underneath them a bed of concrete which must descend to a considerable depth'. So beneath the visible arches of the Colosseum are others, carrying the weight of the building on cores of the indestructible Roman concrete sunk into the water.

It was the Venerable Bede, writing in his monastery at Jarrow somewhere about A.D. 700, who first addressed the building as the Colosseum in the famous proverb that Byron translated as:

> While stands the Colosseum, Rome shall stand;
> When falls the Colosseum, Rome shall fall;
> And when Rome falls—the world.

Bede had never been to Rome, but no doubt he had heard of the Colosseum from Saxon pilgrims and may even have preserved a saying current in Rome in those days.

I climbed all over the mighty monument, thinking that it is the most comprehensible ruin in Rome. It demands little imagination to rebuild it in its splendour and fill it with eighty thousand spectators, with Caesar in the royal box, the senators in their privileged seats near the rails, the aristocracy, and the Vestal Virgins; then, ascending, to the mob in the highest seats of all, for the audience in the Colosseum was seated in strict social rotation. There was an official called a *designator* who saw to it that people kept in their proper places. There were at various times dress regulations which had to be obeyed. Roman citizens were obliged to attend the games in the toga, and the magistrates and senators came in their official dress. This enormous gathering, rising in tiers and mostly clothed in white, must have presented a mighty spectacle, with the Senators in their striped togas and red sandals, the Consuls in their purple tunics, the ambassadors and members of the diplomatic corps in the dress of their various countries, the Praetorian Guard in full dress, and the Emperor in his royal robes. High above the gallery protruded stout masts where sailors from the fleet at Misenum, who had been trained in the manipulation of a vast awning, swarmed among the ropes and pulleys as in some gigantic galley. Even with a slight wind the sound of this *velarium* was like thunder, and on gusty days it could not be used at all. One can imagine what it must have been like to walk through the deserted Forum on a day of the games and to hear the flapping of this great awning, then to be pulled up by a savage roar of sound from eighty thousand voices.

Such a gathering of people assembled to enjoy suffering and death must have been a fearful sight, and I remembered the story of St Augustine's friend, Alypius, who was taken to the games against his will by a number of fellow-students. At first Alypius shut his eyes and refused to look, but, hearing a sudden savage shout, he opened his eyes to see a gladiator beaten to his knees. His heart filled with pity for the man, then as the death blow was delivered he 'drank down a kind of savageness' and sat there, open-eyed and initiated. With the exception of Seneca, not one of the writers of antiquity, not even the kindly Horace and the gentle Pliny, condemned the degradation of the amphitheatre, and the world had to wait for Christianity before men had the courage and the decency to close such places.

As I climbed about the broken tiers and ledges, I thought of the organization which fed this monstrous circle of savagery. All over the Empire officials trapped and bought wild animals for the arena, and in the course of centuries the number of noble beasts which died to please the mob is said to have almost exterminated certain species from the Roman world. It is said that the elephant disappeared from North Africa, the hippopotamus from Nubia, and the lion from Mesopotamia. Long before the Colosseum was built this slaughter of animals used to be the popular prelude to the combat of gladiators; one display occupied the morning and the other the afternoon. Sulla once exhibited a hundred lions in the arena and this, Cicero says, was the first time these animals were allowed to roam about instead of being tethered to stakes. In 58 B.C. several crocodiles and the first hippopotamus to be seen in Rome were exhibited in a trench of water in the arena, and during a *venatio* attended by Cicero in 55 B.C., six hundred lions were slain and eighteen elephants tried to break down the barriers in an attempt to escape. The only animal which roused any compassion in the heartless Roman mob was the elephant. Cicero says that this was due to a notion that it had something in common with Mankind; and the elder Pliny says that these animals, which had been procured by Pompey, 'implored the compassion of the multitude by attitudes which surpass all description, and with a kind of lamentation bewailed their unhappy fate,' until 'the whole assembly rose up in tears and showered curses on Pompey'. Unfortunately such pity did not go very deep, and for centuries to come the mob continued to watch the slaughter of elephants and every other kind of animal; indeed, as the Empire declined these fearful shows became even more extravagant.

There were schools in Rome where men were trained to fight animals and to devise tricks to amuse and thrill the mob. Such men, known as *bestiarii* or *venatores*, were lower in rank than the gladiators. Criminals could be sentenced to join such establishments and to be trained in an arena with the animals. After the Colosseum was built, the animals destined for the amphitheatre were kept in a zoo known as the Vivarium, on the neighbouring Caelian Hill. On the day of the games they were placed in cages and drawn down to the Colosseum. An underground passage can still be seen in which the beasts were taken under the amphitheatre and placed in lifts, worked by pulleys and windlasses, which pulled the cages up to the arena.

The death of animals merely stimulated the palate for the afternoon combat of men. In imperial times there were four state schools in which gladiators lived under strict discipline. They were fed on a special diet and trained in every kind of weapon from the sword and the lance to the net and lassoo. The professional gladiator, like the modern film actor, was the idol of the crowd and, of course, of some women. There is a wall-scribble in Pompeii which describes a certain gladiator as 'the maiden's sigh'. With good fortune their popularity lasted longer than that of a film star today, for we hear of old warriors, the heroes of a hundred fights, winning the 'wooden sword', which was handed to them in the arena as a badge of honourable retirement. And strange as it may seem, some of these old gladiators were unable to keep away from the bloodstained sand; the popularity, the applause and the excitement sometimes drew them back from retirement. There was also a great deal of money to be made.

In addition to the state schools, there were numerous private *Ludi*, where gladiators were maintained at the expense of rich amateurs or businessmen, who hired them out to fulfil engagements all over the country, as the promotors of bullfights today engage *matadores* with their *cuadrilla*. The Colosseum could also be rented. A rich man, or a politician anxious to curry favour, could organize games to take place in the Colosseum, and while they were in progress he occupied a place of honour, the *editoris tribunal*, a special seat which has now disappeared.

The Vestal Virgins were the only women allowed in the official seats, and if the Empress attended the games, she sat with them. Women were not encouraged, however, to attend the amphitheatre and could sit only in the upper tiers with the *plebs*. In later times they were allowed to fight and were sometimes pitted against each other as gladiators; but this, like the woman *matador* of today, was not usual.

How the Vestal Virgins, who were so carefully protected against the harder facts of life, were expected to endure the games, I do not know, and I have read that it was sometimes necessary to move them to the higher parts of the Colosseum where they could not see so much. From the first moment until the last, when a ghastly figure dressed as Charon, or a denizen of the underworld, appeared and tapped with a wooden mallet the heads of those not yet dead, the 'entertainment' can hardly have been one fit for their eyes, and that these cloistered women were required to be officially present indicates one of the great differences between the pagan and the Christian world.

The gladiators paraded in carriages on a day of the games, just as modern bullfighters do. Arriving at the Colosseum, they lined up and took part in the *paseo* to the sound of music, and marched around the arena, with attendants following, bearing their weapons. When they reached a point opposite the royal box, they would fling up their right hands and give their famous cry: 'Hail Caesar, we about to die salute you!'

The weapons were then inspected, and any which had been tampered with were thrown out. Sometimes the duellists were selected by lot; sometimes experts in the use of different weapons would be matched against each other, a swordsman against a man with a net and a trident, and so forth. At a signal from the Emperor a series of life and death duels began, while the band of trumpets, horns, flutes, and a hydraulic organ, struck up and added to the noise of excited thousands, and the shouts of the instructors, who urged on the fighters with bloodthirsty incitements and, if they were not really trying, used a whip on them.

The most merciful combats were those in which the beaten gladiator had the right to appeal for his life. If he had fought well, the crowd might save him from death, as they leaned forward with their thumbs up, a sign meaning *Mitte!* ('Let him go'), but if they wished to see him die, the thumbs would be turned down— *Jugula!* ('Kill him!'); and the master of the world, glancing around to interpret the wishes of the multitude, would give the signal of life or death.

No mercy, however, was possible in the combats known as the fight to the death, in which a company of gladiators fought until only one survived; and even more horrible than this were the noon interludes, before the serious contests began, when a crowd of miserable robbers, highwaymen, murderers, and others condemned to death, were driven into the arena and given weapons with which they were compelled to kill each other. The deaths of Christians in the arena in Nero's time, and later, were of this character, but as the Christians could not be expected to slay one another, wild beasts were let loose to do the killing. It is extraordinary to contrast the gravity and dignity of Roman life at its best with the hideous degradation of mind exhibited in the public amusements of Rome.

One of the most vivid impressions of the Colosseum is the account by Dion Cassius of an occasion when the crazy young Emperor Commodus, who wanted to be worshipped as the royal Hercules, appeared as a *bestiarius* in the arena. Dion Cassius was present in his official capacity as a Senator, dressed in his robes and wearing a laurel wreath. He describes the young Emperor, dressed as Mercury, shooting a hundred bears with his bow and arrow as he darted about the galleries of the amphitheatre. Then, descending into the arena, Commodus slew a tiger, a sea-lion, and an elephant. At intervals during these exploits the senators, ashamed to see the son of Marcus Aurelius lowering the imperial dignity, were nevertheless obliged to give certain ritual shouts. or acclamations: 'You are the master!'; 'You are always victorious!' Then, says Dion Cassius, the Emperor advanced towards the senatorial benches holding up the head of an animal he had just killed, and, with his dripping sword held aloft, 'he shook his head without saying one word, as if by that action he intended to threaten us in the same manner as he had served the beast'. Many of the senators were convulsed with laughter, but, as this might have cost them their lives, Dion Cassius says he quietly pulled some of the laurel leaves from his crown and chewed them and 'advised those sitting near me to do the same'.

Reading these ancient authors I had an idea that many of them disliked the games, but accepted them as a national institution and one that had the blessing of the head of the state. The Emperor Tiberius disliked them and made no secret of it, and so did Marcus Aurelius, who caused great offence by talking and dictating letters while he was seated in the royal box: but it was not until Christian times that opposition could make any real headway and the games gradually fell into disuse. The last games were probably a mere memory of the past, for Cassiodorus says that the wild beasts imported by Theodoric in 519 were a novelty to his contemporaries. The games held by Anicius Maximus in 523 are the last to be recorded. If the bones of horses and bulls discovered by professors in the Colosseum in 1878 belong to this occasion, it would appear that in later times it had become a bullring.

And so it became in the Middle Ages, with occasional plays and pageants. Then, with trees and weeds gaining upon it, robbers and hermits took up residence there, while witches and sorcerers made it the headquarters of the Black Art. It was here on a dark night that Benvenuto Cellini experienced his celebrated encounter with devils. With a Sicilian priest and a young boy from his studio, he went to the Colosseum to hold a séance. A magic circle was drawn, the proper incantations were made and perfumes burnt; then, visible to the priest and the terrified boy, but not apparently to Cellini, the amphitheatre became filled with demons. A million warlike men surrounded them, said the frightened lad, and his terror was shared by the priest, who trembled like a reed. Cellini says that he also was afraid, but told them that all they saw was smoke and shadows. The boy shouted 'The whole Colosseum is on fire, and the fire is upon us!', and refused to look again. Eventually they left as Matin bells were ringing, and on the way home the boy reported that a couple of the demons were still following them, sometimes frisking ahead or capering on the rooftops.

Centuries later the Georgians and Victorians claimed this same site to be the most romantic ruin in Rome. Upon the ancient stage stained with the blood of innumerable men and beasts our great-grandmothers put up their easels and sketched a shepherd and his goats near a broken marble pedestal. By that time trees and shrubs were growing where senators had once sat in official dignity, and hermits in the upper circles now added a touch of romance.

A botanist wrote a book on the flora of the Colosseum, noting two hundred and sixty species, which investigators later increased to four hundred and twenty. It became the fashion to see the Colosseum by moonlight. Leaving the candlelight and the card tables, the ices and the after dinner sweetmeats, satin and velvet would crowd into *carrozze* and go by the light of a full moon to the fallen giant.

'It is not possible to express the solemn grandeur of it,' wrote

Lady Knight in 1795. 'The moon entered the broken part and struck full upon that which is most perfect, and as by that light no small parts were seen, you could almost believe that it was whole and filled with spectators.'

Here, later, Byron heard 'the owl's long cry'. Dickens and Dr Arnold, and a hundred more, added their tributes to a scene of melancholy that had no equal in the world. Then, as soon as Rome became the capital of Italy, the Colosseum was weeded by archaeologists and the four hundred and twenty varieties were heartlessly torn from their crevices. So it stands today, still arousing wonder and incredulity: a colossus in stone with a gash in its side from which thousands of tons of travertine crashed in the Middle Ages. If all the stones which once filled that gigantic gap could fly back to their original positions, the Palazzo Venezia, the Palazzo Farnese and the Palazzo della Cancellaria, and many more, would suddenly disintegrate and vanish.

CHAPTER FIVE

*A visit to the Catacombs – on the Via Appia – Early Christians
and the Sacrament – St John Lateran – a hermit Pope – Westminster Abbey's link with the Forum – S. Clemente – a Mithraic
temple below a church*

§ I

A 'bus that leaves the Colosseum for the Via Appia every
half-hour would have delighted John Leech when he was
illustrating A'Beckett's *Comic History of Rome*. Such
conflicts of the ages are numerous. What, for instance, could be
stranger than to glance down and see the letters SPQR, which
once terrified the world, now embossed by the municipality of
Rome upon every drain-cover and manhole? Also, how incon-
gruous to hear a friend say: 'When you're near the Via Appia, do
drop in for a drink; we live quite close to the tomb of Cecilia
Metella.'

To the Romans this is the most ordinary thing in the world.
They see nothing odd in it. When you sit at the little café near
the 'bus stop and gaze with interest at the Colosseum a few paces
away, you may notice perhaps that not one Roman as he waits
for a tram or a 'bus, ever gives it a glance. They know it is there
and would miss it if it collapsed, but it has stood for such
a long time and they have all seen it since they were born. To live
in a permanent state of historical or archaeological awareness in
Rome would be to go mad. Gibbon was a wise man to write his
book in Switzerland, and I should not be surprised to hear that
Gregorovius was considered to be a little peculiar after twenty
years of historical writing in Rome.

The Via Appia 'bus is usually half empty. It runs out along
the road between the Caelian Hill and the Palatine. The flat
summit of the Caelian once held a reservoir for the naval battles of

169

the Colosseum, and lower down the hill a fine sweep of steps leads to the church of St Gregory, once a Benedictine monastery where St Augustine and his companions were living when they were sent to convert the English.

The 'bus leaves the walls by the old Porta Appia, which is now the Gate of St Sebastian, and in a few moments shoots under a railway arch and crosses a miserable trickle of a stream. It is difficult to believe that this is the romantic Almone, where once a year the high priest of Cybele and his revolting dervishes bathed the Mother of the Gods, which was merely a black stone like the Aphrodite of Paphos, and celebrated their sterile rites to the sound of drum and tambourine.

There is a pleasanter memory a little further on, where the small baroque church of Domine Quo Vadis stands by itself on the side of the road. This is the traditional meeting-place of our Lord with St Peter, so charmingly told in the apocryphal *Acts of Peter*. A number of patrician ladies, attracted by St Peter's preaching, decided to forsake their husbands and live in chastity. The angry husbands were determined to put Peter to death as 'a dealer in curious arts', but a certain woman 'which was exceedingly beautiful', named Xantippe, warned the saint of his danger and advised him to fly from Rome. Peter at first objected, but his fellow Christians persuaded him to preserve his life for the sake of the infant Church.

'And he obeyed the brethren's voice and went forth alone, saying: Let none of you come forth with me, but I will go forth alone, having changed the fashion of my apparel. And as he went forth of the city, he saw the Lord entering into Rome. And when he saw him, he said: Lord, whither goest thou? And the Lord said unto him: I go into Rome to be crucified. And Peter said unto him: Lord, art thou being crucified again? He said unto him: Yes, Peter, I am being crucified again. And Peter came to himself: and having beheld the Lord ascending up into Heaven, he returned to Rome, rejoicing, and glorifying the Lord, for that he said: I am being crucified: the which was about to befall Peter.'

The *Acts* then describe Peter's crucifixion, head down, and say that when Nero heard of his death, he was enraged, 'for he desired to punish him more severely and with greater torment'. The writer of this document, probably a Greek of Asia Minor, who wrote about A.D. 200, evidently knew little of Rome, and had certainly never read Tacitus, for he claims that Nero, alarmed by a vision, refrained from persecuting the Christians.

The Via Ardeatina lies close to the church of Domine Quo Vadis, and it holds memories of a more recent martyrdom. In March, 1944, men of the Italian Resistance Movement threw a bomb in the narrow street opposite the main gates of the Barberini Palace, the Via Rasella, and killed thirty-two German soldiers. In reprisal the Germans rounded up at random three hundred and thirty-five Italians, none of whom had had anything to do with the explosion—a group which included businessmen, priests, a few foreigners, and a boy of fourteen—and drove them to the deserted sandpits of the Via Ardeatina. Machine-guns were then turned on them, and the dead bodies were hidden beneath an avalanche of sand caused by touching off mines in the neighbourhood. Immediately the Germans had left Rome the dead were dug out and identified, and a dignified memorial, some think the most touching memorial to the savagery of war they have ever seen, was set up in the sandpit. When I visited the grim place I turned to say something to a man who was standing next to me, and he replied in German. I wondered if it were a case of a murderer returning to the scene of his crime.

The 'bus then continues along a narrow stretch of the Via Appia which has the appearance of a country lane. The walls of villas, and garden gates which give a view of shady paths leading to sienna-brown houses covered with creepers and bougainvillaea, succeed one another; and you think that this road cannot have altered since our ancestors of the nineteenth century drove out here in their carriages. The 'bus finally draws up with a dragonish hiss—a small dragon and rather out of condition—not far from the tomb of Cecilia Metella. Stretching ahead is the Appian Way, straight as a Roman javelin, lined on each side by funereal cypress and stone pine. The old pavement of polygonal blocks of basalt still exists in stretches of fifty or a hundred feet. The thick stones are scarred and grooved with the traffic of twenty centuries.

Within a short distance are four of Rome's most interesting catacombs.

§ 2

About fifty catacombs are grouped in a circle round Rome, and new ones continue to be discovered. There is little doubt that many an early Christian is still securely sleeping beneath the pavements of modern Rome. Father Marchi estimated that six million Christinas must have been buried in the catacombs and that if all the galleries were placed end to end, they would stretch for six hundred miles.

Two circumstances influenced the making of a catacomb. It was against the Roman law for burials to take place within the walls, therefore the catacomb had to be outside Rome. The most suitable ground was the soft volcanic rock known as *tufa granulare*, and the site had to be free from underground springs and high enough not to be flooded in wet weather. The old idea that the catacombs were disused quarries and sandpits was dismissed long ago: they were all carefully mined by a guild of Christian grave-diggers known as *fossores*, and it is a realistic insight into human nature that when the first beauty of the primitive church had passed, Gregory the Great had to forbid certain of these men from taking bribes to dig graves near that of a popular martyr.

The catacombs were never secret hiding-places where the Christians lived. The references in the lives of the saints to one 'who lived in the catacombs' meant that he lived in one of the buildings on the ground above; and even if the mounds of excavated tufa could have been concealed, there was no reason why the catacombs should have been secret. The Roman law relating to the dead and to burial was precise and compassionate. The body, even of an executed criminal, was generally handed over to friends and relatives. That was why Joseph of Arimathea had no hesitation in approaching Pilate for the body of our Lord, and why Pilate immediately assented to his request. Under the same law, except in times of the bitterest persecution, the bodies of martyrs were handed to the faithful for burial.

Like all other tombs, the catacombs were sacred places. 'Every person makes the place that belongs to him a religious place,' ran the law, 'by the carrying of his dead into it.' The catacombs were all known to the magistrates and to the police, and had to be constructed to certain rules. The surface area of the ground was not to be exceeded by the excavations underneath. Therefore when a catacomb was full, the *fossores* cut steps to a lower level and started a series of galleries below the first. Some are on six levels, and the earliest tombs are, of course, the nearest to the surface.

Five catacombs date from Apostolic times, but the greater number date from the second to the fourth centuries. With the triumph of the Church in the fourth century, burial in the catacombs became a rare event, and when St Jerome was a schoolboy in Rome in 365, the tombs werealready becoming a curiosity that struck awe into the minds of those who visited them.

'When I was a boy in Rome being instructed in the liberal studies,' wrote St Jerome, 'on Sundays, with others of my own age, I used to wander about the sepulchres of the Apostles and martyrs; and I often went into crypts dug out of the depths of the earth, which have along the walls, on each side as you enter, bodies of the dead; and everything is so dark that the words of the prophet are most fulfilled: "They descend alive into hell." Now and then a light from above modified the horror of the darkness, but it seems rather a hole pierced to let down the light than a window, and as you advance step by step, and are immersed in the blackness of night, you are reminded of the words of Virgil: "The very silence fills the soul with dread." '

There are two strange things about the catacombs. One is that had we used the word to an early Christian, he would either not have known what we meant, or he would have directed us to the burial place called *Ad catacumbas* on the Appian Way. The name means 'in the hollow', a reference to the lie of the land, and this place was particularly revered as the traditional resting-place of the bones of St Peter and St Paul, which were placed there to save them from certain eastern Christians who had come to Rome to steal them. A church which was built there in the fourth century has remained one of the seven pilgrimage churches of Rome, and its name came to be applied to all the underground burial places. The word used by the early Christians to describe a catacomb was cemetery, from the Greek word for dormitory or sleeping-place.

The second strange thing is that, with the exception of *Ad catacumbas*, every cemetery in Rome was lost and forgotten for six hundred years. It seems almost impossible that the burial places of six million people could have been lost; and the explanation lies in the history of Rome.

From the fourth to the sixth centuries the catacombs were the most famous places in Rome, and pilgrims came from far to visit the tombs of the Apostles and the martyrs. Guide books were written to help them, and when they had seen the churches built above the tombs of St Peter and St Paul, they went on a round of the catacombs. The old Roman horror of *violatio sepulchri* persisted and developed into the fear that to disturb the bones of a martyr would be to invite disaster. So strong was the prejudice against moving the dead that Constantine built St Peter's on the slope of a hill at great cost and labour, and St Paul's Without on a cramped site near a main road, in order that the tombs should remain untouched. What a complete change of mind was to occur!

When the barbarians invaded Rome in the fifth century the catacombs, all outside the walls, were ransacked for valuables, and in order to save the bones of the martyrs from desecration the Popes decided to remove them into the churches. They were brought into the city by the cart-load. It is recorded that when the Pantheon became a church in 609, twenty-eight wagon-loads of bones were placed in the crypt, and in 817 two thousand, three hundred bodies were placed in S. Prassede. This naturally changed the pattern of pilgrimage. Visitors now found the tombs of the martyrs in the churches, and gradually the rifled catacombs fell into disrepair and eventually were abandoned and forgotten. The entrances became blocked and overgrown. The only one known to the pilgrims of the Middle Ages was *Ad catacumbas*.

On May 31, 1578, a man digging for *pozzolana* in a vineyard near the Via Salaria broke into a tunnel and found himself in a world of the dead. He saw a narrow, rock-hewn passage lined on each side with tomb niches, and as he ventured inside he found the gallery to be intersected by others leading on into a labyrinth. His discovery amazed Rome. The men of that time were more excited by the thought that a city of the dead existed unsuspected beneath their feet than by the fresh and beautiful world of early Christianity which had emerged after its long entombment: the funeral lamps, the glass chalices with portraits of St Peter and St Paul, the pictures of the Good Shepherd, the touching epitaphs. Much was to be destroyed, scattered and lost for ever before men valued the wonderful resurrection of the innocent childhood of the Christian faith.

§ 3

The Via Appia has not become vulgarized or noisy, and though it might be an exaggeration to say that you expect to see the legions marching home laden with the spoils of Asia, you do feel that the bushes might part to reveal the mocking features of Horace Walpole, or the earnest face of Nathaniel Hawthorne; possibly even Mr and Mrs Robert Browning. Here is the desolate Campagna one has read about, the once malarial flatness, the lonely tombs, the odd chips of marble, the distant view of Roman domes, and the tomb of Cecilia Metella, which roused such inquisitive queries in the mind of Byron.

> But who was she, the lady of the dead,
> Tomb'd in a palace? Was she chaste and fair?
> Worthy a king's—or more—a Roman's bed?

Here, too, is the church of St Sebastian—*Ad catacumbas*—a low façade upheld on antique columns, but inside, alas, of baroque reconstruction, with a statue of the saint stuck full of arrows like a porcupine. A little French monk who has invented a wonderful kind of esperanto composed of a number of English, French, German and other European words, took me down under the church.

'Good . . . magnifique, hein?' he asked, as we stood in the cool darkness of the catacomb, which is on four levels. There are perhaps many more impressive catacombs, but none more historically interesting than this one. When a Latin poet—perhaps it was St Ambrose—saw one day in the fourth century three groups of Christians setting off in three different directions in Rome, it was almost certain that one group was going to the Vatican Hill, another to the Via Ostiensis, where St Paul was buried, and the third to this catacomb, which at that time was covered by a church dedicated to the Apostles.

We descended to a lower level and saw the tombs of men who had lived in Apostolic days, and we returned to the site which was revered all through the Middle Ages as that where the bones of St Peter and St Paul were deposited. This is a curious story. It is referred to in one of the metrical inscriptions of Pope Damasus, who tidied up the catacombs in 366, but a better account is given by Gregory the Great, two and a half centuries later.

This Pope was embarrassed to receive a letter from the Byzantine Empress, Constantia, a lady who was accustomed to having her own way, asking that the head of St Paul, or some other part of his body, might be sent to her. Gregory's letter of refusal, a masterpiece of courtly tact, told 'my most tranquil lady' that it was not the Roman custom to dig up, or dismember, saints, but to send cloth which had been in close proximity to the martyr's tomb. He then told her that in years gone by certain believers from the East, who had come to Rome, had managed to steal the bones of the Apostles from their tombs. They carried them as far as the second milestone from Rome, depositing them in a place called Catacumbas: but when they attempted to remove them in the morning, they fled in terror from violent thunder and lightning, and the Romans came and recovered the bodies. To soften the blow, St Gregory said he would send his 'most serene lady' some filings from the chain which had bound St Peter.

Some believe that the bones of the two Apostles were hidden

in the same place again, during a period of persecution. At any rate the tradition was so strong in the early centuries that every pilgrim who came to Rome went to the Via Appia to offer his prayers. When the site was excavated in 1915, wonderful evidence of the cult was discovered. The walls were covered with those scribblings, so regrettable in modern times but so valuable if sufficiently ancient, when they are dignified by the word *graffiti*. Both the Apostles are mentioned in the prayers. 'Peter and Paul, remember us,' wrote one pilgrim; another wrote, 'Paul and Peter, pray for Victor'. Some pilgrims wrote in Latin, some in Greek. 'I, Tomius Coelius,' wrote one, 'partook of a refreshment-meal for Peter and Paul', a curious glimpse into a world where thought was Christian but habit was still pagan.

§ 4

A short walk brought me to the impressive Catacomb of St Domitilla. Three tourist coaches were drawn up outside and in the ticket-office spectacled monks were selling guide-books and post-cards while one intoned: 'How many English?', 'How many French?', 'Germans this way, please'; and we sorted ourselves into the language groups created by the fall of Rome.

Grasping a taper, I followed an English group which descended on the heels of a French group; and no sooner had we left the daylight behind than the chill of the catacomb came up and gripped us like a bony hand. Even the humorist of the party, who had been lively enough at the ticket-office, fell silent after a half-hearted attempt at facetiousness and we walked in single file into a darkness lit only by the flickering of our tapers. Like bunks in a ship the burial niches rose one above the other in the rough walls. Every few yards or so we came to an intersecting tunnel, when we bunched together, determined not to stray.

The monk patiently told a questioner, as I suppose he does many times a day, that people are sometimes lost in the catacombs and search parties have to be organized to find them. The best thing to do if lost is to sit down and wait; the most dangerous thing is to descend steps and find yourself in another series of galleries where you may not be able to hear the shouts of those trying to locate you. Recently two tourists were lost for forty-eight hours.

With the same patience, as if saying something expected of him, the monk told another questioner that the Christians never lived in the catacombs, but came there only to worship at the graves of the martyrs and to celebrate the Eucharist, often at dawn. In times of persecution, however, a hunted Christian could always take refuge there, confident that he was not likely to be found.

It was in this catacomb that Antonio Bosio, the 'Columbus of the Catacombs', was lost in 1593 and wandered without light trying to find his way out, his only fear the thought that he 'might contaminate with his wretched body the sepulchres of the Martyrs'.

The monk would pause now and again to explain something, and we would draw near to listen, our faces lit by the tapers; and echoing in the darkness ahead we could hear a voice explaining in French, another in German, and yet another in Italian. It was impressive to be a part of this European microcosm, standing solemn and awed at the gaunt cradle of our faith and civilization.

With what loving care the early Christians decorated the rough volcanic walls. One fancies them leaving Rome on some holiday, or when work was over, with brushes and little pots of colour, and maybe a stepladder. Perhaps they would sometimes hear mass at a martyr's tomb before taking their lamps to the grave they wished to decorate with those touching little pictures, some of which have become so faint that you need the eye of faith to see them, though others are almost as fresh as the day they were painted so long ago. We saw what must be one of the earliest paintings of the Madonna and Child with the Magi. There was a painting which showed our Lord enthroned with the Apostles, and another of six martyrs approaching the Saviour to receive their crowns like athletes of God. Someone, perhaps a docker, had painted a little scene of a grain market, with warehouses and workmen unloading barges on the Tiber.

One's first feeling of dismay at finding oneself in this dusty maze of death is soon replaced by an affectionate fellow feeling for those who had lived so long before us and had trodden out the first paths of faith. They must have been much like ourselves. Who can see without emotion the words they wrote when they closed the eyes of those they loved, the words we still use: not the hopeless pagan *Vale*, but *Vivas in Deo* and *In pace Christi*.

As we went on, we heard the sound of a hymn, so faint at first and lost in the intricate galleries that it might have been a ghostly echo of the past: as we proceeded the sound became louder, until we came to a place where, looking down upon an open space in the catacomb, we saw fifty pilgrims kneeling before an altar. The priest in charge had just finished mass and was packing his vestments in a little case. It was one of the most beautiful appointments with the past that one could imagine. Our guide told us that twenty or thirty masses are said in the catacomb every morning; sometimes a priest comes alone, sometimes with a band of pilgrims.

In 1881 a remarkable discovery was made here. A crypt was entered which looked like a room in a Pompeian house, yet it was an early Christian tomb, and the excavators were astonished to find the name 'Ampliati' engraved in beautiful early Roman letters. 'Salute Ampliatus my beloved in the Lord,' wrote St Paul in his *Epistle to the Romans*. This may have been his tomb.

We came up willingly enough into the sunlight, and I walked on under the stone pines to the Catacomb of St Calixtus, who was Pope from 221 to 227.

In this catacomb are buried close together several early popes whose names are written in Greek, a reminder that for at least two centuries the language of the Church was Greek, as so many essential Christian words are to this day: catechism, chrism, Eucharist, presbyter, diocese, cope, hymn, psalm, and homily. But the Latin Church soon became bilingual. Converts were asked in which of the two languages they would prefer to profess their faith; but Greek gradually died out and by the time Athanasius visited Rome in the fourth century he had to learn Latin in order to speak to the clergy.

In this catacomb too is to be seen the tomb of that gentle and sweet patron saint of music, St Cecilia, who, says legend, heard such heavenly sounds that in order to express them, and the devotion in her heart, she invented the organ. She was a rich patrician, with a palatial house on the site of which St Cecilia's Church in Trastevere now stands—one of the loveliest churches in Rome—and it is said that she was martyred in the vapour bath whose foundations still exist. The story is that she was locked in with the heat full on, but in the morning was found unharmed, kneeling in prayer. Orders were then given for her to be executed, but the executioner could not sever her head.

Over five hundred years later, in 817, Pope Paschal I commanded a search to be made for her body in the Catacomb of St Calixtus, but he was unable to discover it. One early morning during Matins, which were sung soon after midnight, the Pope fell asleep in St Peter's, and St Cecilia appeared to him in a vision, telling him that he had been so near her when he was seeking her tomb that she could have spoken to him. He searched again and found the tomb. Opening the coffin of cypress wood, he saw the incorrupt body of the saint lying as if she had just fallen asleep.

The body of St Cecilia was seen again much later, in 1599, when Cardinal Sfondrati opened the coffin and was amazed to see the Saint 'not lying on her back like a body in a tomb, but upon the right side like a virgin in her bed, with her knees modestly drawn together, and seemingly asleep'. Stephen Maderna, the sculptor, was sent for and asked to make an exact copy of the body in marble. His work is to be seen today in the Church of St Cecilia, and a replica has been placed in the catacomb. This figure of a young girl apparently asleep, her head turned away, showing the marks of the sword, her fingers making the sign of the Cross, is sold in miniature in all the pious shops of Rome; and it must find its way to every part of the world. The sculptor added these words to his work: 'Behold the body of the most holy Virgin Cecilia, whom I myself saw lying incorrupt in her tomb. In this marble I have made for you the image of that saint in the very posture in which I saw her.'

The Salesian Father who took me over this cemetery had made a study of the *agape*, or love-feast, and every time we came to one of the tomb alcoves where such meetings were held, or to a fresco picturing such an event, he had something to say about it. He called it the first expression of Christian brotherhood and charity. It was observed by Christians before the Gospels were written, and must have been handed down to the first converts by those who had been present with the Saviour at the Last Supper in the upper room. I asked him when he thought the Eucharist became separated from the *agape*.

'I think it always was separate,' he replied. 'Imagine a band of Christians like those who gathered to hear Paul talk far into the night at Troas. They would eat together and at a certain moment, when the meal was over, the table would be cleared, prayers would be said over some of the bread and the wine, and they would all solemnly partake.... "Do this in memory of Me".

'But,' he continued, 'the pagan convert was always liable to confuse the *agape* with the tomb feasts with which he was familiar, and St Paul, you remember, had trouble with the Corinthians on this very matter. In later times, when thousands of pagans were admitted into the Church, the *agape* became frankly a pagan festival, as St Paulinus of Nola saw when his parishioners arrived with baskets of food and wine for the *agape* of St Felix and sat up all night, passing round the bottle! Such scenes made St Augustine furious. Having seen so-called Christians revelling round a martyr's tomb, he cried, "The Martyrs hear your bottles, the Martyrs hear your frying-pans, the Martyrs hear your drunken revels!" But by this time, of course, the Blessed Sacrament had long been separated from the *agape*.'

'Do you think it probable,' I asked, 'that during the persecutions the Christians of Rome came down into the catacombs, ostensibly to hold a tomb feast, but really to celebrate the Eucharist?'

'Yes, I do think that is exactly what used to happen,' he replied. 'It would have been unsafe for them to have said mass above ground, but down here in the catacombs they had a legal right, as a burial society, to hold anniversary feasts in the tombs. Naturally they would use this opportunity to say mass.'

He pointed out a hundred things I should have missed. He

explained that for sanitary reasons the bodies in the catacombs were generally enclosed in plaster and hermetically sealed in the tombs; even so, perfumes or deodorants were kept burning. Glasses were often firmly embedded in the plaster with which the bodies were covered. When early explorers found them, they noticed a hard, dark deposit which they took to be dried blood, and believed that every tomb in which such glasses were found was that of a martyr. What the glasses really held was the Sacrament, which was not only buried with the dead but was also sent to the sick and even carried by the living round their necks in a little box.

'The custom of burying the Sacrament was not forbidden until 393,' added the Father, 'and nowadays no one may carry it on his person except the Holy Father. Two recent Popes did so. When Pius VII was taken from Rome at Napoleon's orders, he wore the Blessed Sacrament in a little vessel made for the purpose; and again when Pius IX fled from Rome during the nationalist rising of 1848, he also carried it round his neck in the same receptacle.'

'You spend a great deal of time in the catacomb,' I said. 'What impresses you most?'

'Well,' he replied, 'though I am asked a hundred questions every day, no one has ever asked me that! I can tell you without pausing to think: it is the atmosphere of utter faith and complete trust.'

We walked up into the daylight.

'I sometimes think,' he said, as if to himself, 'that the world today, with its materialism, is much like the Roman world of centuries ago. When I go down into the catacomb, I am in touch with a faith that could move mountains.'

We shook hands, and he hurried over to a group of tourists who were impatiently awaiting him.

On the way back to the Colosseum in the 'bus one feature of the catacombs lingered in my mind. In all the hundreds of miles of tunnels not once is Christ pictured on the Cross. The Christ of the catacombs is the Good Shepherd: a youthful, beardless figure in Greek dress, who at a first glance might be Apollo or Orpheus. The early Christians never knew the bearded, crucified Christ of the Middle Ages, a conception which originated with the Byzantine Greeks and has dominated art ever since. The emblems of the Passion, which occupy such a great place in later art, are also never seen in the catacombs.

The atmosphere, as the Father had said, is one of faith and trust. The epitaphs carved on the tombs are happy and confident, as if the dead were waving goodbye and smiling as they left for a journey. The words 'rest' and 'sleep' are everywhere. I could not remember having once seen that word 'farewell' which sighs its hopeless way through all pagan cemeteries. As I remembered the dark galleries, the image came into my mind of a troopship in the dark, with its rows of bunks, their occupants sleeping, confidently awaiting the light of a new day.

Here only are to be heard the humble voices of the first Christians, and the message they give is one of faith, hope and charity. What affection, love and kindness are buried away in the dark. A girl is called by her parents, 'sweet as honey'; husbands and wives describe each other in terms of affectionate gratitude. 'To Aurelian Felix,' is one epitaph, 'who lived with his wife eighteen years in sweetest wedlock, of good memory. He lived fifty-five years. Snatched home eternally on the twelfth day before the kalends of January.' We read, 'Alexander is not dead, but lives above the stars, and his body rests in this tomb.' Other epitaphs were: 'Gemella sleeps in peace'; 'the dormitory of Elpis'; 'Victorina sleeps'; and a year-old child was described as 'recently illuminated', which was the ancient term for baptism.

One echoes the words of a mediaeval pilgrim who wrote on the walls: 'There is light in this darkness; there is music in these tombs.'

One of the marvels of Rome is that the traditional portraits of St Peter and St Paul have been preserved in the catacombs, and every artist who has painted the two Apostles owes something to this tradition. The portraits were engraved in gold leaf on the bases of the glasses or chalices which, as the Salesian Father had told me, were embedded in the plaster round the bodies. There are hundreds of these glasses to be seen in the Vatican Museum, and the type of portrait never varied. Both Apostles are shown as men of middle-age and both are bearded, but while St Peter has a fine head of curly hair, St Paul is almost bald. Those who have studied the portraits believe that they embody a tradition which goes back possibly to the days of Nero and to those who knew the Apostles by sight.

I was reminded of a story which the late Monsignor Stapylton Barnes was fond of telling to illustrate the length of human memory. His mother, who died in 1927 at a great age, could clearly remember, as a small girl, hearing Victoria proclaimed queen in 1837. When a child she was often taken to see a very old lady who remembered the French Revolution and the execution of Marie Antoinette in 1793. This old lady had spent her childhood in Philadelphia and had known Benjamin Franklin, who was born in 1706. Thus it would have been possible for Franklin to have described some event of his early childhood—perhaps the great fire in Boston of 1711—to the little girl, who could have told it in her old age to another little girl, Mrs Barnes, who could have passed on the story to her son in the twentieth century.

In his book *The Martyrdom of St Peter and St Paul*, Monsignor Barnes refers to the great sweep of human events commanded by such lives, and says 'it would have been possible for a Christian child in Rome in the year 67 to have been actually present at St Peter's martyrdom and to have seen him nailed to the cross, and still to have been alive and able to tell the tale in 150. And the child to whom he told it then could have told the story again in his extreme old age to one who lived to see the peace of the Church in 312 under Constantine.'

§ 5

The gay young men of imperial Rome drove fast chariots, cultivated low companions, kept late hours, drank too much, and sometimes became amateur gladiators. The pattern of high spirits in Juvenal's eighth satire is much the same as that in Pierce Egan's *Life in London*, and characters like Corinthian Tom and Jerry Hawthorne would have been as much at home in the Rome of Nero as in the London of the Regent. The equivalent of a night club in ancient Rome was an 'all-night tavern' where, says

Juvenal, the visitor was greeted on the doorstep by a cringing Syro-Phoenician, 'permanently scented', and welcomed by Cyane, the hostess, 'her dress tucked up, carrying a flagon of wine for sale'.

Among the rakes castigated by Juvenal was Lateranus. 'The bloated Lateranus,' he says, 'whirls past the bones and ashes of his ancestors in a swift car,' a sentence which Alberto Moravia might write today about a modern Roman and his Ferrari.

Juvenal was thinking of Plautius Lateranus, the notorious playboy, evidently one of those big, good-natured men who never meet trouble half-way, but go out and bring it home with them. An entanglement with Messalina, which did not prove to be a dangerous matter for many of his contemporaries, would have proved fatal to him had he not been the nephew of the Emperor's favourite general, Aulus Plautius, the conqueror of Britain. In the next reign he joined the Piso conspiracy and agreed to be the one who was to hold Nero down while others slipped their daggers into him. A plot is in danger of discovery in direct proportion to the number of people in it, and this one contained so many conspirators that it was doomed to discovery; and Lateranus, among others, was executed. Like so many men of his type, he absolved his follies by a courageous death.

Nero confiscated the Lateran property, but it was restored to the family in later times. It eventually became part of the dowry of Fausta, the wife of Constantine the Great, and as soon as Constantine had given freedom to the Church, he made a gift of the Lateran Palace to the Pope. He thus ensured one of Fate's most unlikely associations: that the name of one of Messalina's lovers and that of St John the Baptist should go down the ages together as St John in Lateran, the mother church of Christendom.

The fame and splendour of St Peter's and the Vatican have overshadowed the older home of the Papacy, and it is difficult to imagine that for a thousand years the 'Lateran' created much the same mental image in the European mind as the word 'Vatican' does today. At the end of the Via Merulana, the great church and its attendant palace come into view upon a hilltop, with a stretch of the machicolated Aurelian Wall running at a lower evel, and a view towards the Alban Hills which must have been superb before the modern builder arrived. And how much finer the Lateran site is than that of St Peter's. St Peter's was man-made; the Lateran must always have been magnificent.

The destruction of the old Patriarchate and the ancient church of St John is one of the tragedies of Rome. Though little of the original structure had been left by fire, earthquake and riot when Sixtus V pulled it down, its survival would have preserved a miracle of the Middle Ages. Sixtus, however, was an old man in a hurry, and had no sentiment; he swept away the huddle and cluster of Byzantine and mediaeval buildings in one of his great architectural transformations. We have a faint idea of what it must have been like from the Baptistry with its singing doors—the most eerie sound in Rome—and from the dark, archaic little papal chapel at the top of the Scala Santa.

Like St Peter's and all the Constantinian foundations and, incidentally, pagan temples, St John Lateran faces the rising sun. The giant statues on the roof, of the Saviour, St John the Baptist, and the doctors of the Church, seen white against the sky early on a summer's morning, are as memorable as the dome of St Peter's. As you approach the church, two tall bronze doors as green as a patinated coin catch the eye. They are noble and heroic-looking doors which might have swung on brazen pivots in the palace of Priam. There is such venerable grandeur about them that I was not surprised to be told that they came from the Senate House. This is something to think about. They stood in the Forum all through the Christian-Pagan debates of the fifth century and they opened, perhaps sadly, as the golden Victory of Tarentum was expelled. They were no doubt locked and barred when Alaric's Goths swept into the Forum—I searched the green bronze for traces of hammers and axes—and they were still there when the Vandals came to Rome. I have seen only two other such doors in Rome: those of the Pantheon and of the Temple of Romulus in the Forum. They are among the most eloquent and impressive of relics. There must have been many such splendid doors, as there were hundreds of bronze statues, but bronze can be melted down into coin, and all have now vanished except these three, the statue of Marcus Aurelius, and a few others in museums.

The Church of St John Lateran is disappointing, in spite of its magnificence and size, its shining coloured pavements, its purple and golden roof, and its papal altar gleaming like a jewel box, where the heads of St Peter and St Paul are kept behind a gilt grille. It is disappointing because, knowing its story, this vast baroque temple seems to have nothing to do with it. How gladly we would give all this grandeur for one glimpse of the old church and the Patriarchium.

There cannot have been a more bewildered Pope in history than Miltiades, of whom little is known except that he reigned only from 311 to 314 and that he received from Constantine the gift of the Lateran Palace. What an astonishing transformation it was! Christians had lived through the worst persecution the Church had known. They had seen Pope after Pope slain or dragged into exile. The sacred books had been sought out and burnt, the clergy had been imprisoned, Christian property had been confiscated; then suddenly the reign of terror ended with the victory of Constantine, a young man of twenty-four who eight years previously had been proclaimed Augustus by the British legions at York. The families of countless martyrs must have felt that the voices of those who had perished in Diocletian's inquisition had prevailed in heaven.

The Lateran basilica was the first great Christian church ever built, and its mosaic of the Saviour was the first picture of Christ to be seen in a public place. Constantine filled the church with gold and silver, and a few years afterwards built St Peter's, St Paul's-Without-the-Walls, the Church of the Holy Sepulchre in Jerusalem, and other churches on the sites of the chief shrines of Christendom.

It was from the Lateran that Leo I went out with all the pomp and majesty of the Church to turn Attila from Rome; St Gregory the Great was living there when he sent St Augustine to convert the English; and all the Popes of the Middle Ages lived in the Patriarchium until the riots and violence of Rome drove the Papacy to Avignon in 1303.

When Gregory XI returned to Rome in 1377, he saw a ruined

city where a population of perhaps seventeen thousand huddled in squalor and misery. From his lodgings near the Vatican, Adam of Usk said he used to watch wolves and dogs fighting each other near St Peter's. The Lateran was uninhabitable, and so the Pope went to live at the Vatican.

Twenty-eight mediaeval Popes are known to have been buried in the Lateran, though few of their tombs have survived. I did, however, see one, that of the first Frenchman to occupy the chair of St Peter, Sylvester II, who reigned from 999 to 1003. His contemporaries believed him to be a magician who had sold his soul to the devil, such was the effect of a little science and scholarship on that dark age. Having studied with the Arabs and Jews of Córdoba, in Spain, Sylvester introduced Arabic numerals into Italy, and he possessed two satanic inventions, a steam organ and a mechanical clock! The Romans who saw the aged pontiff scanning the heavens at night from a tower in the Lateran, or making cabalistic signs on parchment, whispered that there was something uncanny about him, and the monks, who were the novelists of the Middle Ages, told stories about him for centuries. It is a strange city we see in these stories, a Rome translated by the mediaeval imagination to the borders of fairyland. It was a place of mysterious ruins where statues guarded vaults full of gold.

Such was the statue mentioned by William of Malmesbury, which stood with outstretched hand and pointing finger, perhaps an emperor or an orator, and upon its head the words 'Strike here'. Ignorant men had battered the statue with hammers, hoping to discover gold inside it, but it was said that the Pope, with his superior knowledge, marked where the shadow of the pointing finger fell at noon and returned at night with a lantern, accompanied by one servant. At Sylvester's magic words the earth opened at the marked spot, and he and his servant entered a passage which led into the scene that every mediaeval treasure-hunter longed to see.

They stood in a palace of shining gold. Golden soldiers were playing with golden dice; a golden king and queen sat at a golden table, with golden delicacies before them. A huge carbuncle hung in the golden room, shining like a star, while a golden archer stood with his arrow drawn to the head, aimed at the carbuncle. The moment Sylvester or the the servant stretched out a hand to touch anything, the golden figures sprang into life and appeared to rush forward. This alarmed Sylvester, but not his servant, who snatched a golden knife, whereupon the golden archer shot his arrow at the carbuncle and the room was plunged in darkness. The servant flung back the knife and, terrified, the invaders ran back through the passage and out into the safety of the night.

When this enlightened Pope died, stories were spread about his tomb in the Lateran: that his bones rattled when a Pope was about to die, and so forth. When his tomb was opened in 1648, his body was seen for a moment, lying in pontifical vestments, his hands folded on his breast. At a touch the body shivered into dust, out of which were picked a silver cross and a signet ring.

Of all the horrors of which the old Patriarchium was the scene, perhaps the most ghastly was the Corpse Synod of 896. Pope Stephen VII, who seems to have been driven insane by political hatred, dug up the body of his predecessor, Formosus, and placing the dead Pope on a throne, clothed in his vestments, went through the mockery of a trial. A trembling deacon stood beside the corpse as an advocate, but was too shocked and terrified to utter a word. The corpse was condemned, every act of his reign was annulled, and the body was flung into the Tiber, from which some fishermen recovered it and gave it decent burial. The author of this macabre scene was himself smothered with a cushion in the following year.

It is a temptation when in the Lateran to dwell on the melodramatic memories of the mediaeval Papacy, but it must not be forgotten that the period produced more saints than sinners. Neither should one forget that the blood and thunder of a savage age underlines the extraordinary ability of the Papacy to ride out storms and miseries which would have ended any other institution. Boccaccio wittily expressed this idea in his story of the Jew who went to Rome and was horrified to discover a squalid little city in which the throne of St Peter was occupied apparently by Anti-Christ: but he became a Christian at once, his argument being that a religion which could exist in spite of the Papacy must have a divine origin!

The most touching of all the Popes, Celestine V, belongs to the Lateran period. He was elected in 1294, in a moment of revulsion against the crimes and follies of the time, after the Papacy had been vacant for two years because of rivalries among the Cardinals. One day a pious Cardinal happened to mention the name of Peter, a hermit who was living in the mountains above Sulmona, where Ovid had been born. It was decided to make him Pope. Three bishops bearing vestments and the decree of election set off to find the hermit, and were led by a shepherd's path to a remote cave where the old man lived. He was eighty years of age. Bewildered and terrified, he tried to run away, but was at last persuaded that it was God's will he should be Pope. His shabby hermit's gown was taken from him, he was robed in pontifical vestments and, mounted upon an ass, was led down from the mountain, while choirs sang and knights jingled ahead on their chargers.

The poor old man lived for five months in a bare cell constructed for him in the papal palace. He signed everything that was put before him and did all that he was told. Unlike so many saints, who have been able to detect a dishonest man a mile off, poor Celestine V was so ignorant of the world that he was unable to understand the men or the motives which surrounded him. He prayed perpetually, longing for the peace of his mountain and the stars. The usual malicious Roman story said that the wily Cardinal Gaetani—who became the next Pope, Boniface VIII—had rigged up a speaking-tube to the Pope's cell, and in the silence of the night would whisper—as if a voice from heaven were calling—urging Celestine to renounce his crown. He did so, and became one of the six Popes who abdicated.

The old man happily took off the purple and put on his hermit's robe; but he was not allowed to remain for long in his cave. Everywhere the people fell on their knees before him and begged him to be Pope again. There is something infinitely pathetic in this longing for a saint in high places to drive the moneychangers from the temple. It was obvious that a consecrated Pope who was hailed everywhere as a saint could not be left at large. He meekly surrendered himself to the papal officers and when he was told that, having renounced the tiara he must also renounce his freedom, he bowed his head and consented to end his days in a gloomy fortress on the top of a hill. It must be part of the mysterious processes of God that many a good deed has been achieved by a bad Pope, while the election as supreme pontiff of a simple early Christian, who might have come from the catacombs, had no effect whatsoever upon the times. But the Church, for all its sins, did not forget him, and ten years after his death, Celestine was made a saint.

In another part of the church I saw the tomb of that great Pope, Innocent III, who has been called the Augustus of the Papacy, a man remarkable not only for his learning, his wisdom, his iron will and his triumphant career, but also for having attained the sacred chair at the age of thirty-seven. He was the Pope who excommunicated King John and placed England under an interdict.

A young Pope was always the rarest of phenomena, and from the Renaissance onwards was almost an impossibility. Thus the Papacy presents the most remarkable spectacle in history of old age in action. Most of the pontiffs were elected at an age when a king would have been considered fit only for abdication, yet the invigorating effect of St Peter's Chair is well known. Many a tottering old man became rejuvenated the moment the tiara touched his brow. A good instance was Paul III, who, as sixty-eight year old Cardinal Farnese, bent double and walking with a stick, appeared to have one foot in the grave, but upon election straightened up and reigned for fifteen years!

In the old days the candidate who was considered a *creatura papabile*, or a possible Pope, was usually over sixty years of age, a man of kindly character with few family ties, and one who was acceptable to the European powers. A mean man with enemies in the Sacred College did not stand a chance. His spiritual qualities did not matter: the Church could attend to that.

No ordinary state could have survived the series of short reigns which the Papacy regards as normal, for even to this day the death of a Pope may mean the resignation of all government officials, as well as Nuncios and Ambassadors in foreign countries, and the Sacred College rules the Church until the next Pope is elected. Centuries ago the interregnum was a time of terror in Rome. The prisons were opened, law and security lapsed, the nobles placed chains across the streets and their men-at-arms fought battles and worked off old scores, and Rome was turned upside down.

'Not a day passed,' wrote Girolamo Gigli, 'without quarrels, homicides, and ambuscades. Many men and women were found killed in various parts of the city; many headless bodies were found, many, also headless, which had been thrown into the Tiber; many houses were broken into by night and sacked; doors were broken open; women were done violence to, some killed, and others carried off by violence; many young girls were dishonoured, forced and taken away.'

Today, as of old, the College of Cardinals put away their red robes and wear purple when the Pope is dead, and his death is still surrounded by observances that go back into distant ages. As soon as he dies, the Cardinal Chamberlain is summoned to identify the body. Kneeling down, he performs the ancient Roman *conclamatio*, which is to call the dead man by name, not his name as Pope, but by his baptismal name. In the old days it was customary to tap the dead Pope three times on the forehead with a silver hammer. The Ring of the Fisherman is removed from his finger and broken up. The bells of Rome are then ordered to toll, which is the first official intimation that the Pope is dead.

When the elaborate ceremony of the funeral is over, Rome thinks of nothing but the election of the new Pope. It is perhaps not widely known that every adult Catholic male, even though a layman, is eligible to become Pope, though since the end of the fourteenth century only Cardinals have been elected, and since the beginning of the sixteenth century, only Italians. In those rare instances in the past when a lay Cardinal was chosen, he was immediately consecrated Bishop of Rome. Many more Popes have been elected from the Lateran than from the Vatican for the Patriarchium was occupied by the Popes for ten centuries, whereas the Vatican has been their home for only a little more than half that time.

§ 6

When I had passed from St John Lateran into its cloister, I stepped back many centuries. It seemed that I was no longer in Rome, but in England or France in the thirteenth century. I found myself in a comprehensible Benedictine cloister, but with a difference. It glittered as if in some tinted Byzantine afterglow. The twisted columns and arches were covered with cubes of red, green, and gold mosaic. It was immensely effective in the Roman sunlight, though it might have looked a little gaudy in Yorkshire. It belonged to the encrusted eastern world of jewels and damasks.

The cloister dates from the thirteenth century, when several families of marble-cutters, the most famous of whom were the Cosmati and the Vasselletti, searched among the ruins of Rome for attractive coloured marbles, especially the rare red and green porphyry. They cut them into cubes, squares and circles from which they composed a great number of geometrical patterns, and so originated a style of church architecture which became popular in Rome for about a hundred years. The Church of S. Clemente is the best example of their work, and the cloisters of the Lateran and St Paul's-Without-the-Walls show what they could do out of doors.

When these marble-cutters were the fashionable church decorators in Rome, Henry III was rebuilding Westminster Abbey. In 1258 the new Abbot of Westminster, Richard of Ware, travelled to Rome to receive the Pope's confirmation of his election and he remained there for two years. He was evidently attracted by the Cosmatic work which he saw everywhere, for when he returned to England he persuaded the King to have the tomb of Edward the Confessor decorated in this style. Abbot Ware went to Rome again and returned with two of the best marble cutters, Peter and Odoricus, and a quantity of coloured marble.

The result of this strange and fascinating architectural link with mediaeval Rome may be seen in the Saracenic-looking tomb of the Confessor. I have often thought that it might have been made for Saladin, and it is, I think, the most unusual of all London's ancient monuments. The niches round the tomb, quite oriental in shape, were for pilgrims who wished to kneel and pray at the tomb, as near as possible to the body of the saint. The twisted columns, the mosaics, the general atmosphere, all recall the few mediaeval churches of Rome, and upon the pavement of the tomb the artist has signed himself 'Peter, a Roman citizen'.

His companion, Odoricus, was the designer of the splendid but now badly damaged pavement in the Presbytery. He also signed his work, but his name can no longer be made out. The pavement is of porphyry, serpentine, palombino, and other Roman marbles, and the design, by some complicated mediaeval computation, is intended to symbolize the duration of the world. It is curious that Holbein should have been interested in this, for it is undoubtedly upon this pavement that the Ambassadors are standing in his famous picture in the National Gallery.

What a strange thought it is that in the heart of London a Saxon king is lying surrounded by marbles from the ruins of ancient Rome. I wonder if Henry III, whose passionate reverence for the Confessor found expression in the rebuilding of the Abbey, remembered that Edward had once vowed to go on pilgrimage to Rome, but was unable to do so, and had to ask the Pope to release him from his vow? If so, it would not perhaps have seemed inappropriate to bring Rome to the tomb of the Saint who was unable to go there.

§ 7

The old octagonal Baptistry is dark, and the so-called musical doors lead into a chapel. They are tall and heavy, and, I was told, made of gold, silver and bronze. They came from the Baths of Caracalla. As the guardian slowly moves one, it grates rather badly on its metal groove. Then the grate becomes a groan, and as the man continues to move the door a high note separates itself from the groan and goes singing and vibrating through the air. The sound completely fills the little building and I thought of a trumpet calling the pagan world to its altars. It is an imprisoned sound, a pagan sound, captive in this Christian building.

The basalt font in the chapel is interesting, and the old legend that Constantine the Great was baptized there is still current: but he was not baptized until he was on his death-bed, like many another sinner in those days.

I crossed the road to the building which faces the Lateran Palace and contains the Scala Santa. Twenty-eight steps of Tyrian marble, now covered with protective wooden boards, are said to have been brought by St Helena from Jerusalem, and to have been those which the Saviour descended after His trial by Pilate. Pilgrims ascend them on their knees, and having reached the top, they walk down by one of two corresponding staircases on either side of the Scala Santa. Facing them when they reach the top of the stairs is the glorious old papal chapel, the Sancta Sanctorum of the old Patriarchium, the Sixtine Chapel of the Middle Ages, which is not open to the public.

There is never a day without its kneeling figures slowly ascending the steps, telling their beads. In Passion Week the Scala Santa is crowded from morning until night. It was upon this staircase that Martin Luther, when half way up, suddenly stood upright and walked down, the first man ever known to have done so. The night before the famous 'twentieth of September', in 1870, Pius IX was driven to the Lateran and ascended the Scala Santa on his knees. Arriving at the top, he prayed in a loud voice, broken by emotion. He left by a side door and saw his troops encamped upon the wide space between the Lateran and the walls. The commanding officer begged for his blessing, which Pius gave, while the troops presented arms.

Afterwards the Pope drove, not to his old home at the Quirinal, but to the Vatican, which he never again left.

§ 8

Tradition says that St Paul was beheaded two miles from the Ostian Gate, at a place called *Ad Aquas Salvias*, and known now as Tre Fontane. The three springs which are said to have leapt up where St Paul's head touched the ground, and over which now stand three churches, once formed swamps and made this site the most malarial near Rome. In the last century, when *mal aria* was believed to be a mysterious poison distilled from the earth, the Trappist monks were seen creeping about, pale and shivering. Now the springs have dried up, possibly assisted by the great numbers of eucalyptus trees, whose bare, plane-like trunks and trembling leaves are today a feature of the scene. The Trappists distil a liqueur from the leaves which has a strong pharmaceutical tang, but is nevertheless popular with many of the visitors, who buy it at the gatehouse. One of the monks has designed a delightful label in red and blue for the bottles, so that the words *Liquore Eucaliptina* resemble the initial letter of an illuminated Gospel.

The most interesting victim of the mosquitoes of Tre Fontane was Rahere, the jester of Henry II, who, during a pilgrimage to Rome in the twelfth century, caught malaria there and vowed that should he recover he would found a church in London. This was the origin of St Bartholomew the Great, and attached to it was a hospital, the first charitable institution in the city. It is strange to wander about the still gloomy surroundings of Tre Fontane and to think that 'Bart's' was also in the air at that moment so long ago when an *anopheles* mosquito was winging its way to the English pilgrim.

After his martyrdom, St Paul's body was claimed by a Roman matron named Lucina, who gave it burial in her family tomb, near a vineyard on the road to Ostia, about a mile and a quarter from Rome. She was one of the leading members of the first Christian community, and a discovery in the Catacombs some years ago inspired an attractive theory that she was Pomponia Graecina, the wife of Aulus Plautius, the conqueror of Britain.

I walked to St Paul's, now standing in a squalid district of factories, gas-works, and tramlines, and I thought of the early pilgrims, who approached the church protected from rain or sun beneath a magnificent colonnade a mile and a quarter long, which was upheld by eight hundred columns of marble. The total disappearance of this enormous construction is a mystery of Rome, and Lanciani calls it 'an instance of wholesale destruction which is without a parallel in the history of the destruction of Rome'.

Constantine built the first church around the grave of St Paul, as he had done around that of St Peter, but it was a much smaller church than St Peter's. This had nothing to do with the Emperor's veneration for the Apostle. It was the rule of Constantine's architects, at a time when a Christian church was an architectural novelty, that the building must enshrine an untouched tomb, which must occupy the chord of the apse, and that the main doors should face the rising sun, like the doors of pagan temples. St Paul was buried so close beside the main road to Ostia that it was impossible to build a large church on the cramped site, and it was not until 386 that the building was reconstructed, which involved its total destruction and the erection of a new church on a different axis, with its apse to the east. St Paul's was therefore the first great basilica to be orientated in a manner which became usual in later times, and is, of course, the rule today, while St Peter's still faces the rising sun.

This glorious basilica, infinitely more beautiful and impressive than St Peter's, is, strange to say, a modern reconstruction and only a little more than a century old. The church which had been standing above the tomb of the Apostle since the fourth century was burnt down one July night in 1823, when a workman on the roof threw a pan of blazing charcoal at his companion. One of the red-hot coals must have found a crevice in the tinder-dry roof, where it lay and smouldered. About two o'clock on the following morning a monk, who happened to glance from the window of the nearby monastery, was startled to witness a great sheet of flame suddenly ascend into the sky as the roof of the church collapsed into the nave. Nothing was left except a portion of the walls, some calcined columns, and the arch of the nave, which remains the only memorial in Rome to the reign of Placidia, once Queen of the Goths.

Rome was stunned. The only person who was not aware of the calamity was Pius VII, who lay dying in the Vatican. He was eighty-three years old and in the eyes of his subjects almost a martyr. He was the Pope who had been forcibly taken to France by Napoleon, and Stendhal reports the curious fact that, as he lay dying, the thought kept worrying him that a disaster threatened the church. He continued to ask whether anything had happened, but that St Paul's, where he had spent his youth as a young monk, no longer existed, was mercifully kept from him; and the day after the fire he died in ignorance of the disaster.

Many must think, as I do, that no other building gives one a better idea of the majesty of Rome than St Paul's Without, and if one did not know that it was a reconstruction one would, at a first glance, accept it as a stupendous survival from the past. It lacks the authentic antiquity of such basilicas as S. Maria Maggiore and S. Maria in Aracoeli, but it faithfully reproduces the grand old church of St Paul; and it must have been a proud moment in 1854, thirty-one years after the fire, when Pius IX consecrated the basilica in the presence of prelates from every part of the world. It is a pity that the exterior is so tasteless, but that is forgotten as you look down the nave and see eighty tall columns of granite reflected on a floor of polished marble, like trees at the edge of a lake. The eye moves onward to the triumphal arch, which is a relic of the old basilica and was likened by Cardinal Wiseman to the title-deeds of the new church, linking it with its immense antiquity and with the far distant Rome of Galla Placidia.

The Czar, Nicholas I of Russia, contributed altars of malachite, and the six huge columns of Egyptian alabaster near the doors were given by the Khedive, Mohammed Ali: but it is the great arch and its mosaics which catch the eye, and beneath it stands a canopy which covers the grave of St Paul. The tomb retains the position in which it was found in the time of Constantine, and the privileged visitor who ascends the steps of the altar and looks through the iron grille, can shine a torch on a venerable stone upon which are carved the words: PAVLO APOSTOLO MART. . . . In the centre of the stone is a round hole into which the early pilgrims let down rosaries and articles of clothing to be sanctified by contact with the Apostle's relics. It is not, however, likely that they are still there, for in 846 the church was sacked by the Saracens, who robbed it of the bronze sarcophagus in which Constantine had buried St Paul.

The tomb was not scientifically investigated when the church was rebuilt, but the men who sank the foundations for the canopy had the same experience as those who, during the rebuilding of St

Peter's in the sixteenth century, made the foundations for the heavy bronze columns of Bernini's baldacchino: they found the space around the Apostle's tomb crowded with ancient burials. The bodies were lying several layers deep, all with their heads turned towards the tomb, clothed in long robes darkened with age, and bound like mummies with bands of linen.

It must have been a strange experience for Christians of the fourth century, when the enlarged basilica had been completed, with its apse facing east, to see the priest officiating at the altar with his back to them, now, of course, the normal position, but then to be seen only in St Paul's. St Peter's has never been re-orientated, and when the Pope celebrates mass at the high altar, he stands facing the congregation and looks east, in the earliest tradition of Christian public worship. I have seen the same thing in humble little Coptic churches in Egypt, where the priest still faces the congregation, as the Pope does.

I stepped through a door and found myself in Benedictine cloisters glittering with green, red and gold Cosmatic work. They are perhaps even finer than the cloisters of St. John Lateran. In a few yards one steps from the gravity of Rome into the gay, coloured world of the Middle Ages. The cloisters are crowded with stones and inscriptions recovered from the church after the fire of 1823. I noticed above the gate the arms of an abbot of St Paul's, surrounded by the ribbon of the Order of the Garter. This is a relic of pre-Reformation times, when the Kings of England were the patrons and protectors of St Paul's, as the Kings of France were of the Lateran, and the Kings of Spain of S. Maria Maggiore.

In those days the monarchs of Europe were always addressed by the Vatican with certain formal titles: the King of England was 'Most Religious', the King of France, 'Most Christian', the King of Spain, 'Most Catholic', and the King of Portugal, 'Most Faithful'.

§ 9

I was sitting in the cool shade in S. Clemente one afternoon, with a white blaze of afternoon heat outside, waiting for Brother Paschal, an Irishman, to take me down to the churches and the temple of Mithras which lie beneath the present building. There was no one else in the church, except the young lay brother whom I could hear shuffling the postcards outside the vestry and preparing the bookstall for the post-siesta visitors.

S. Clemente is the most beautiful of the mediaeval churches of Rome, but it appears centuries older than it is. It looks like a perfectly preserved basilica of the fourth century, complete in every detail. You step from the Via di San Giovanni in Laterano, not far from the Colosseum, into an atrium open to the sky, with a fountain in the centre; in front of you is the exquisite church of cool white and coloured marble, with its altar standing beneath a semi-dome gleaming with mosaics. It is Old St Peter's in miniature, and, indeed, like all ancient basilicas of the fourth century.

No one questioned that it was not the first church of S. Clemente, which was known to have existed as early as 350, until in recent times the earlier building was discovered beneath it, its walls choked with the rubble of the Norman sack of Rome in 1084. Guiscard and his Normans had been called in to rescue Gregory VII, who was besieged in S. Angelo by the Emperor Henry IV, and the price of his release was a smoking ruin, with Rome deep in the débris of churches and houses. Three days of fire and carnage had raised the street level of whole districts by many feet.

When the Normans departed, S. Clemente lay in ashes, but the builders picked from the ruins the columns of the nave, and whatever else they could salvage, and so perfectly was the church recreated on the ruins of its predecessor that it was accepted as a work not of the eleventh century, but of the fourth.

As I sat glancing around this beautiful church, a poor old woman like a little black ghost, her head covered with a ragged shawl, came shuffling along in carpet slippers and approached a life-sized crucifix in one of the aisles. She was like a bundle of old, dry leaves wrapped round with cobweb. First she knelt and told her beads, then she approached the crucifix and, bending forward, kissed the feet and placed her cheek against them, whispering all the time. I watched her lift a corner of her shawl and wipe the feet, as if wiping away the blood. She then looked up into the face of Christ, and, with her arms held out in the earliest attitude of prayer, an attitude one still sees on the walls of the catacombs, began to speak to Him; then again went forward and kissed His feet. She seemed to be holding a conversation with the crucifix, pausing as if for a reply and then speaking again, sometimes blowing up a kiss. Then she touched the feet again, and stood there as if she were standing on Calvary, waiting for Christ to be taken from the cross.

I fancied from her manner that she was in the habit of talking to Christ like this, perhaps telling Him her anxieties, and maybe the events in the tenement where she lived. 'The infinite pathos of Human trust,' I thought, then I seemed to hear St Paul, 'We walk by faith, not by sight'; and these lines came into my mind:

And Wisdom cries 'I know not anything';
And only Faith beholds that all is well. . . .

After all, I thought, is there much difference between this poor old creature and the great mystics? St Teresa, who was on the same easy terms with God, and even on one occasion became angry with Him, would have understood this old woman. I remembered that a great scientist, now dead, once said to me: 'We know nothing. Science leads us to a sunny mountain, but from the top, where we expect to see everything, there is nothing but an impenetrable mist.'

I rose and went towards the sacristy to see what had happened to Brother Paschal. In doing so, I had to pass the old woman who, now aware of me, held out a bony hand for alms as I approached. I gave her a miserable fifty lire note. The effect was embarrassing. She seized my hand and kissed it repeatedly, placing her cheek, which was wet with tears, upon it, talking swiftly all the time and nodding up to the figure on the cross. Startled by her gratitude and ashamed of my miserly gift, I gave her a note which I thought would perhaps keep her for a week, and now I could not escape, for she held both my hands and led me up to the crucifix. I then understood that she was thanking Christ for having answered her prayers. Feeling disturbed and almost an imposter, I disengaged her hands and went quickly into the little room near the sacristy where the young lay brother was arranging the postcards.

'Who is that old woman?' I asked.

'I don't know,' he answered in a good Irish brogue, 'but maybe the poor old soul's a bit daft.'

So, I thought, many have felt about the saints.

When I returned with Brother Paschal, she had gone. He switched on the lights in the dome, and there sprang into view one of the most exquisite mosaics in Rome. Here is a Christian version of the meticulous little grotesques I had seen in Nero's Golden House, but the birds and the animals are not just creatures, but symbols. The central feature is a great cross stretching down from heaven to earth. Where it touches the earth everything bursts into leaf and flower, and there are rivers of life-giving water. A little hart is feeding at the foot of the cross, a symbol of the baptised, and four stags are drinking from the rivers that gush from the foot of the cross—'as the hart panteth after the fountains of water; so my soul panteth after thee, O God.'

In 1645 S. Clemente was given to the Dominican Order by Innocent X, and was handed over *in perpetuum* to the Irish Dominicans in 1667. It is built on the site of the paternal mansion of St Clement, who is said by many writers to have been the third successor to St Peter in the Apostolic See. He may have been the fellow worker mentioned by St Paul in the *Epistle to the Philippians*, and is said to have been the author of the *Epistle to the Church of Corinth*.

The name Clement seems to have been as popular in first century Rome as Robinson is in modern London, and the great number of stories which have clustered round this saint suggest that even though he may have been given a composite personality, the essential Clement was an influential member of the early church.

Brother Paschal led the way to the lower church, and told me how in 1857 Father Joseph Mulhooly, then Rector of the Irish Dominican College, became convinced that the present church was not that mentioned by early writers. Making some exploratory tunnels, he found that his surmise was correct, and that the church was built upon a mass of burnt and charred rubble packed into the walls of an earlier building.

The expensive and difficult task of clearing out the rubble and underpinning the present church occupied half a century, and there is still more to be found. Pius IX generously supported the excavations and contributions were received from every part of the world. Father Mulhooly lived to see the fourth century church revealed with its frescoed walls, many of which bore traces of the Norman sack of 1084. The problem of disposing of hundreds of tons of earth and rubble was itself a difficult one. The pretty little garden of S. Clemente, which looks down towards the Colosseum, was raised several feet in height, and the present apple trees, vegetables and flowers, are growing lustily on the débris of the Norman sack of Rome.

The underground church was lit by electricity and was chillier than a catacomb. We could hear the tinkle of water from the numerous springs which filter down from the Esquiline Hill, and as we descended, the sound of the water became louder and the dark eyes of Byzantine saints gazed at us through a film of dampness. All these frescoes should be photographed in colour before they disintegrate.

At the lowest excavated level we passed into a surprising scene, a vaulted Mithraic temple, with its altar standing in the centre, showing a sculptured Mithras slaying a bull. There are stone seats on each side of the temple on which the initiates reclined, and a neighbouring room was a school for novices. Separated only by a corridor from this pagan temple, we entered the remains of what is believed to have been the first century house of St Clement. It was a large and ancient palace whose masonry suggests Republican rather than Imperial Rome. This is one of the buildings with which it is almost certain that St Peter and St Paul were familiar.

We left this astonishing scene—I think one of the most unexpected in Rome—and went up to the College, where the Prior received me in a hall hung with portraits. Among them I noticed Charles Edward in late life when, alas, he was no longer 'bonnie'. The Dominicans were closely associated with the exiled court of England: Prince Charlie's confessor was a Dominican, and the Prior of S. Clemente was deposed from his office in 1766 for entertaining the prince with royal honours against the instructions of the Vatican.

The church was also connected with the beginings of the diocese of New York in the early years of the last century. I was shown a portrait of Father Richard Luke Concanen, who was consecrated first Roman Catholic Bishop of New York in 1808; but as Napoleon's troops were holding all the ports, he spent two years trying to find a ship to take him across the Atlantic. On the day fixed for his departure from Naples, he died, aged seventy-two. Eventually another Irishman, Father John Conolly, arrived in New York in November, 1815, after a voyage from Dublin which lasted sixty-seven days. Though he was the second bishop, he was the first to take possession of the See. There is an interesting letter which shows how primitive the New York Catholic diocese was at the time. When the bishop arrived, he found only four priests, three churches, and thirteen thousand Catholics, of whom eleven thousand were Irish, or born of Irish parents.

§ 10

As I was mounting the noble flight of steps which leads to the church of S. Gregory the Great on the Caelian Hill, there was a sudden surge of people coming down; then, after a moment, stepping slowly all in white, came a pretty little bride on the arm of a young man in a blue suit.

The old custom of throwing confetti is still observed at Roman weddings, or of giving it to the guests in boxes. This is not the coloured paper which gets down the bridegroom's neck and hangs for months about the upholstery of hired cars, but sugared almonds. It is a survival of the pagan custom of nut-throwing at a wedding, and I remember, when ex-King Umberto was married to his Belgian bride many years ago, how the marble stairs of the Quirinal Palace were lined by footmen who held silver bowls full of sugared almonds which they spooned into the hands of the guests. There are rare occasions, I believe, when these nuts are thrown, or strewn, as in ancient times, but today, when they cost eight shillings a pound, it is more usual to give them to the guests in little caskets.

To ascend the steps to S. Gregory's church, and to look around, is a tremendous experience for any Englishman. Here in the very heart of Rome, with the palaces of the Caesars a few steps away, and the Forum, in which Gregory noticed the fair-haired Angles, just around the corner, St Augustine departed in the spring of 596 to convert the English. Upon these steps Rome, Thanet and Canterbury run together in the mind. One looks down upon the road, the Via Triumphalis, upon which so many legions set out to subdue the world, and upon that same road in later times the legions of the Church passed to their spiritual conquests.

St Gregory lived in an age when men, seeing no hope on earth, believed the world was soon to end. It was like another Flood. The monasteries were the Ark in which what was left of civilization took shelter from the approaching storm. Rich and learned men retired to monasteries with their libraries, and members of the greatest families in Rome, men and women, gave away their wealth and were to be found living in caves and cells. There were three thousand female nuns and recluses in Rome in Gregory's time, sending out a perpetual shield of prayer over the dying city, which was threatened by the Lombards. Rome was hungry and was swept by disease and malaria which spread from swamps caused by the severed aqueducts. Yet life went on. We learn the strange fact that poets still recited in the Forum of Trajan.

When he was young, Gregory had worn jewels and silk, for even in the darkest days, rich Romans seem to have been well dressed; but as soon as he inherited his fortune, he turned the family mansion into a Benedictine monastery, and his widowed mother went to live in a cell nearby. She grew vegetables which she sent up daily to her son. When he was not fasting, he ate them raw in the great house which had once been full of servants, and so destroyed his digestion. In his last years as Pope, writhing with pain, St Gregory would rise from his bed only with difficulty for three hours at a time, yet this invalid took with him into the Church the genius of the Roman ruling class and became a spiritual Caesar and the founder of the mediaeval Papacy.

He was living as a monk in his old home on the Caelian when he took his walk through the Forum and saw the fair-haired English slave boys. It could not have been their fair hair which attracted him, for no one could have been more familiar with blond barbarians than a Roman of the sixth century. Even in the days of the first Caesars there had been a brisk trade in German tresses, which fashionable Roman women wore over pads, and in more recent times Rome had been sacked and threatened for centuries by blond savages. It must have been something else about these boys which attracted Gregory's notice and roused his compassion.

Shortly after seeing these boys, he left for England himself, with a few monks, but was recalled to Rome. Had he not been recalled, the great pontiff might have been the first Archbishop of Canterbury. When he reluctantly became Pope, the first monk to do so, and, as he put it, the pilot of a sinking ship, he planned his conversion of England. It had never been absent from his mind. The leader chosen by him was Augustine, the prior of the monastery on the Caelian. He set off in the spring of 596 with about forty monks, but the party became faint-hearted and Augustine returned to Rome, begging to be relieved of the mission. Gregory would not hear of this, and sent him back with encouragement and advice.

The well-known story of Augustine's arrival in Kent, and his conversion of King Ethelbert and ten thousand of his people, takes on a new interest on the Caelian Hill, where the walls of the monastery in which Augustine lived are still standing, beneath the present church. There is probably no other site in Rome which would more richly repay excavation, and in 1890 a committee under the presidency of Cardinal Manning made a search through the cellars of the adjoining monastery, and found 'that the house of the great pontiff and the monastic establishment from which

Augustine started to preach the Gospel in Great Britain are in a marvellous state of preservation, and could easily be excavated without impairing in the least the stability of the modern church above'. That was the verdict of Lanciani, also a member of the committee, but for some reason or other the scheme failed and nothing has been done since. Perhaps the excavation of St Gregory's home will be made someday. It is one of the marvels that still lie beneath this storied soil.

There is not much of interest in the church, which is modern, but nearby is a little garden where there are three chapels which an old monk unlocked for me. They are disused, dusty, and some of the frescoes are flaking from the walls. One chapel is dedicated to St Silvia, the mother of St Gregory, a second to St Andrew, where the condition of a fresco by Domenichino and another by Guido Reni are in a sad state. In the third chapel of St Barbara I was shown the long Roman table at which it is said St Gregory served twelve beggars every day with his own hands, and legend has it that one day he entertained an unexpected thirteenth guest, who was an angel. A fresco here shows St Gregory talking to the English boys in the Forum.

I was passing through the courtyard on my way out when two English names caught my eye on memorial tablets let into the wall. One was Robert Pecham, who died in Rome in 1569, and the other was Edward Carne, who died there in 1561. Both were English Catholics who preferred to die in Rome rather than to return to a Protestant England. Sir Edward Carne had estates in Glamorganshire and was well known at the Vatican. He first appeared in 1530, representing Henry VIII, who had been cited to attend personally, or by proxy, before the Pope, in connection with his divorce from Catherine of Aragon. Carne was in Rome again twenty-five years later as ambassador from Philip and Mary, who had restored Catholic worship in England. He was still there in Elizabeth's reign, when he requested permission to return home on account of his old age, and because he wished to see his wife and family again The Queen agreed, but the Pope refused to let him go, because of Elizabeth's hostile attitude to Rome. Carne received a great deal of sympathy on his 'imprisonment', and Paul IV was harshly criticized for his treatment of a poor old man. When the Pope died and was succeeded by Pius IV, renewed attempts were made to obtain Carne's release, but Pius IV also refused to allow the old man to leave Rome. Many years afterwards it became known that the crafty old knight had himself arranged his detention with both pontiffs, having decided to live and die a Catholic. He feared that if he returned home, his estates would have been confiscated and his family persecuted.

I descended the noble steps to the road. Every day of his life, I reflected, St Gregory while in Rome, and before he went to live at the Lateran Palace as Pope, must have seen the Colosseum; a few paces would take him past the Circus Maximus, already weed-grown and deserted, above which rose the imperial palaces, unoccupied for centuries, but still capable of housing a stray Exarch from Ravenna. The last time they received an emperor was twenty-five years after Gregory's death, in 629, when Heraclius visited Rome and was invested with the diadem in the throne room on the Palatine. What a ghostly moment that must have been; for the Middle Ages were ready to be born.

I walked back to the Colosseum, then through the Forum and the Arch of Titus to the Victor Emmanuel Monument, where I found a taxi. I was thinking that it is easier to reconstruct the Rome of the Caesars than the ruined Rome which Gregory knew.

§ 11

The path of the Roman Catholic pilgrim to Rome has been made smooth for him for many centuries. It leads him to the four great patriarchal basilicas; the mother church of St John Lateran, St Peter's, St Paul's-Without-the-Walls, and S. Maria Maggiore. Having said the prayers prescribed in each church, he may also visit S. Lorenzo, S. Croce in Gerusalemme, and S. Sebastian, thus completing his round, famous since the Middle Ages, of the 'Seven Churches of Rome'.

This, of course, takes time, and it often happens that the most devout visitors are obliged to leave Rome without having seen those unique little churches which were built on the site of private houses centuries before St Peter's. It was in the upper chamber of a private house that Jesus gathered His disciples for the Last Supper, and it was in private houses in Rome and elsewhere that the Gospel was first preached and the Eucharist celebrated before special buildings were erected for this purpose.

'Salute Prisca and Aquila,' wrote St Paul, 'and the church that is in their house.' He used the word 'church' meaning not the building, but the people who met in it. 'Salute Nymphias,' he wrote again, 'and the church that is in her house.' To the early Christians the place where they met to worship and pray, to be baptized, and to celebrate the Eucharist when the bishop attended for this purpose, was known by the title, or name of the owner— *titulus Pudentis*, *titulus Lucinae*, and so on: and when the organization of the Church had advanced sufficiently, certain of these *tituli* were placed in charge of a permanent priest. He was known as a Cardinal, from *cardo*, the hinge, or pivot, on which everything turns. These *tituli* became the parish churches of Rome, and to this day every Cardinal is the titular priest of one of them. His first act upon becoming a member of the Sacred College is to take possession of his church. He arrives dressed in his scarlet robes, to be met at the door by the parish priest, who offers him holy water. As he walks up the nave he genuflects three times, then, seated upon his throne, he receives addresses, after which he replies, and the ceremony ends as the clergy come up, one after the other, to receive his embrace or kiss his ring.

All over Rome one recognizes these titular churches by the shield of arms, those of the Cardinal, which are hung up over the porch. His portrait in oils will be seen inside, framed and hung in a conspicuous place, and from the roof of a chapel hangs the dusty old red hat of some former titular Cardinal, which will remain until it disintegrates, or until the existing titular dies and bequeaths his hat to the church.

These wonderful churches have all been rebuilt at various periods, and the oldest bear a strong resemblance to each other. A bell-tower of fine red brick frequently rises beside them and the porch is formed by a row of antique marble columns supporting a flat architrave that carries a tiled roof sloping back to the main face of the building. The nave is generally supported by columns taken from ancient temples, and behind the altar is an apse and a semi-dome covered with mosaics. You are reminded of the houses seen at Herculaneum, which, if the central atrium were roofed in, would look much as these churches do. Most interesting of all, you may be taken into a crypt where you may see the foundations of the original Roman *titulus*: the very walls which, tradition says, sheltered the Apostles.

These ancient churches fall into groups which can easily be visited by anyone on foot. S. Pudenziana and S. Prassede lie on either side of S. Maria Maggiore and are only a short walk from each other; S. Clemente and SS. Quattro Coronati are near each other in the gridiron of streets to the east of the Colosseum; St Gregory the Great and SS. John and Paul are close together on the Caelian Hill; then near the Tiber, at Ponte Palatino, is S. Maria in Cosmedin, and about three hundred yards away is S. Sabina, and another three hundred yards takes you to S. Prisca. There are many more, but these happen to be my favourites; and I think that anyone who sees them will have a good idea of the Byzantine-mediaeval churches which developed from the *tituli*, or church-houses, of ancient Rome.

Twenty-four steps lead down to the church of S. Pudenziana. From the bottom I looked back at Time rising in feet and yards like geological strata to the modern street level. The church is not impressive, neither is it beautiful compared with many of the other early churches, but it is the cradle of Western Christianity. Beneath it are the ruins of a first century house in which tradition says St Peter lived and celebrated the sacred mysteries, and presided over meetings of the faithful. This tradition goes back to the time of Pius I, and the year 145, when old people were still living who had received firsthand accounts of the Apostles from those who had known them, or whose elders had known them, seventy-eight years previously. St Paul is said to have lived here too, and it is claimed that St Mark may have written his Gospel here.

The house belonged to a man of wealth and position, Cornelius Pudens, who is believed to have been a member of the Roman

Senate. Some think he was the friend referred to by St Paul in his *Second Epistle to Timothy.* 'Eubulus greeteth thee, and Pudens, and Linus, and Claudia, and all the brethren.'

Two relics associated with St Peter were treasured here for centuries. One was an ancient chair, said to be the senatorial chair of Pudens, used by St Peter as his episcopal throne. This is now one of the treasures of St Peter's and is locked away in a recess in the Tribune; and the other relic was a venerable wooden table on which it was believed St Peter had celebrated the Eucharist. This has been enclosed for centuries within the high altar of St John Lateran, save for a portion which has remained in S. Pudenziana.

When Cardinal Wiseman was titular Cardinal of S. Pudenziana, he became interested in this altar and had the wood in St John Lateran examined scientifically and compared with that in S. Pudenziana. He proved that both were of Roman date and belonged to the same table. You can see the wood behind a sheet of plate glass let into a side altar in S. Pudenziana, where Cardinal Wiseman enclosed it after the examination.

The most beautiful feature of this church is the mosaic in the dome, the oldest in Rome. This marvellous glowing picture looks as fresh as it must have done to the eyes of the earliest pilgrims. We see our Lord seated and surrounded by His disciples. All are dressed in the toga, like Roman senators. On either side of Jesus sit St Peter and St Paul; and behind them stand two women in draperies of green and gold, the two daughters of Pudens, Pudentiana and Praxedes, who hold wreaths above their heads. Behind the group is a street scene, which may be the Rome of the time, about 390—or perhaps Jerusalem. Immediately behind the Saviour rises a mound, which may represent Golgotha, from which springs a huge jewelled Byzantine cross. The clouds in the sky part to reveal the symbols of the four Evangelists.

When the church was restored in the sixteenth century, workmen exposed ancient Roman foundations in which they discovered a splendid marble statue of the Laocoön, larger, it was said, than that in the Vatican, but as they were working *a cottimo,* on contract, and fearing they would not receive extra pay for digging out the statue, they covered it up. And there it still lies.

I walked along to S. Prassede, which I often visited to see the most glorious little Byzantine chapel in Rome, a small vaulted chamber covered with gold and coloured mosaics, and built by Pope Paschal I about 800, as a tomb for his mother, Theodora. She is seen among the stiff figures, wearing a square nimbus which indicated that she was still living at the time the mosaic was completed. There are few other places in Rome so Byzantine as this little chapel, shining and fresh, where nothing seems to have changed since that distant day when Rome was full of Greek monks and the Pope was still under the jurisdiction of the Emperor at Constantinople. St Praxedes was the sister of St Pudentiana, and both were the saintly daughters of Pudens. They were so overwhelmed by the horrors of the first persecutions that they prayed for martyrdom. A flight of steps goes down beneath the altar, where you can see their sarcophagi lying in a vault to which Paschal I moved them from the Catacombs more than a thousand years ago.

A perfect idea of what a titular church looked like in early times is S. Maria in Cosmedin, which was built from part of a grain hall where free corn was doled out to the populace in ancient times. This gift was known as *panis gradilis*, or 'step-bread', from the law that it was not to be given out at the bakeries, but from the steps of some recognized public building. This must have been a busy distribution centre, near the docks and the grain warehouses.

Some people think that restorers have done too much to this church, but the less critical visitor will be grateful to them. They have brought back a great deal of its queer half-oriental beauty. While I was there the church echoed to the cries of a party of Italian schoolgirls who were putting their hands into the 'Mouth of Truth', which stands in the porch of the church. This is a big circular stone from some ancient Roman drain or manhole, in the form of a fierce-looking face with the eyes, nostrils and mouth represented by holes in the marble. It was a famous sight to pilgrims in the Middle Ages, who believed it to be the work of the magician, Virgil, and that whoever swore falsely with his hand in the mouth would have his fingers bitten off. There was a German story, known to all in those days, of an adulterous woman who had placed her hand in the opening and swore innocence, to find herself without one of her fingers! I watched with amusement the alarm of the girls as they dared each other to thrust their hands into the dark gash, and the dismay of the little nun in charge as she cried, 'Silenzio! Silenzio!', and waved an umbrella in a vain attempt to keep order.

There is no view more charming in Rome than that from the porch of this church. Opposite is the circular temple with the fluted columns, wearing its low-pitched Tanagra hat, known for ages as the Temple of Vesta, though perhaps it was dedicated to the god of harbours, and nearby is the fine temple known of old as Fortuna Virilis, though it is now believed to have been a temple to Matuta, the goddess of dawn. Just round the corner is the Arch of Janus, framing in its curve another wonderful old church, St George in Velabro, with a campanile and a pillared porch. I always climbed the steep road at the back of the round temple and walked to the Tiber embankment and the Ponte Palatino, which leads across to Trastevere. If you take a few paces along this bridge and turn to look back at the river bank, you will see the outlet of the famous Cloaca Maxima, the main drain of ancient Rome.

St Sabina, whose church is to be found nearby on the Aventine, was a Roman matron who was converted to Christianity by her Greek slave, a woman named Seraphia. They both suffered martyrdom in the time of Hadrian, and a church was built over Sabina's palace which I think is one of the most beautiful of all the early churches, and might be compared even with S. Clemente. I can understand a friend of mine who spends a night in Rome twice a year, and always visits this church while he waits for an air connection. Though it has been stripped of most of its decoration, it has not lost its beauty; indeed it seems to have gained in purity of line. The twenty-four fluted white columns of the nave came from the building, probably a temple of Juno, which had stood on the same site, and there is nothing to distract the mind from the simplicity and Roman dignity of the ancient scene. A young Dominican brother, who was arranging flowers for the altar against a dark archway, might have been posed by

Zurbaran in that sharp contrast of light. He took me to a peephole in the wall of the church and asked what I saw. It was an orange tree in a garden, a descendant of an orange tree, he said, planted by St Dominic seven hundred years ago, and he also pointed out a marble slab upon which the saint often lay prostrate in prayer.

St Francis and St Dominic were in Rome at the same time and there is a story that they met. Two men less like each other, except for their humility and their passionate faith, can scarcely be imagined. St Francis was a visionary, a Christian Orpheus singing to the birds and the trees, and pointing up towards heaven: St Dominic, a Spaniard, was practical and fanatical, perhaps with something of the intellectual vigour of Moslem Spain in him, horrified by the sins of Mankind, and pointing down to hell. The church of S. Sabina was given to him by the Pope and it is still the address of the General of the Order.

I asked if there were any memorials of St Dominic, and was told of a chapel in the priory which was once his cell, but as I thought all signs of him would now be effaced by the trappings of piety, I did not ask to see it. I went on up the road thinking that there are still parts of Rome like this stretch of the Aventine which remind one of the tranquillity of the Roman scene as described by writers of the last century. Today such places have to be sought out, or are encountered unexpectedly. The road to the Via Appia is one as it narrows between old garden walls and vine trellises; and another is the lane that winds up to the little church of S. Bonaventura behind the Forum. It is a cul-de-sac and ends at a locked gate, on the other side of which is the Palatine: but if there is any place in Rome where you might expect to meet St Francis, it is in this lane. And when you reach the top, venerable Franciscans are sitting in the sun, reading with their spectacles on the ends of their noses.

I now added to these lovely bits of Rome the little piazza, designed by Piranesi, into which I stepped. It was a scene Shakespeare might have had in mind when he wrote the stage direction: 'Scene I. Outside Olivia's House.' Old walls rise round, soaked in the sunlight of countless Roman summers, and through a brass-bound peephole in the garden door of the Knights of Malta you see, far off upon the other side of the Tiber and framed in an avenue of tall, dark trees, the dome of St Peter's. As I put my eye to the hole, expecting Malvolio at any moment to step out into the avenue, there was a mighty noise, and I was swept aside by a crowd of excited people who had arrived in a coach. They filled the little square with their chatter, and when the last person had placed his eye to the hole, they trooped back to their coach and were whirled away. I continued my walk downhill to the Circus Maximus and decided to call on Father Alfred at the Church of St John and St Paul on the Caelian Hill.

The Passionist monastery on top of the Caelian, and its enormous garden, are known only to cardinals and monks, and it was therefore a privilege to be able to see them. They are Vatican property, and as the rule of *Clausura* is strictly observed, this unchanged corner of Rome is familiar only to the inhabitants of the monastery and to those of the Order who go there in retreat.

Side by side with the monastery is a glorious mediaeval bell tower erected upon the titanic arches of the temple of Claudius, there is also a church whose porch was built by the only English Pope, Hadrian IV, eight centuries ago, and the façade has been restored recently by Cardinal Spellman of New York, who is the titular Cardinal. Inside the church are the bones of Paul Francis Danei, known as St Paul of the Cross, who founded the Passionist Order at the beginning of the eighteenth century. Underneath the church is a Roman palace of the third century, with twenty rooms, including a steam bath, a library and a wine cellar, revealed seventy years ago by a monk, Father Germano, who was convinced that something wonderful was to be found there. Burrowing like a mole under the church, the father discovered the original house and the scene of the martyrdom of St John and St Paul, whose very existence had until then been doubted.

In strange contrast to church and monastery, I noticed, on the other side of a lane, a huge galvanized iron roof. I asked Father Alfred, a Passionist from Lancashire, what it was.

'Oh, that's the roof of a film studio!' he replied.

Where, I thought, could one have a more characteristic expression of Rome? Within a few yards, side by side, are the arches of the Claudian temple, the graves of two martyrs, an ancient Roman palace, a mediaeval campanile, the bones of St Paul of the Cross, the restorations of an American Cardinal, and— a film studio!

I went beneath the church with Father Alfred and prowled through the rooms of a double storey Roman palace. The Christians, who had made an oratory in the building which was known to all the early pilgrims, did not think the pagan frescoes in the dining-room entirely suitable and had plastered them over with imitation marble. This has fallen away to expose graceful gods and goddesses, while fat cupids sail in little boats and portly dolphins frisk and gambol beneath them in the water. The house was at the corner of a street. As if we had stepped out of the back door, we found ourselves in an old, buried road of ancient Rome. We looked up at the high brick wall of the house and at windows from which many a Roman housemaid must have exchanged a smile and a word with those who passed below. Now the darkness of a tomb enclosed house and road. An electric light shone from above, casting its eerie shadows; and it was almost unbelievable to think that Christian piety had preserved this bit of third century Rome as securely as the lava has preserved Pompeii.

We went up to the monastery. A long corridor is lined with the portraits of distinguished Passionists. Father Alfred paused in front of one.

'Does he remind you of anyone?' he asked.

'Yes,' I replied. 'Father Winston Churchill!'

'Absolutely correct,' said Father Alfred. 'He is Father Ignatius Spencer, a Passionist, and a great-uncle of Winston Churchill.'

We went out into the garden, which is one of the unknown glories of Rome, not as a garden, for the Passionists have more reflective occupations, but as a foreground for the most unusual view of Rome that I know. The large stretch of land had been flattened for Passionist beans and artichokes by Agrippina when she built the temple of Claudius; and Vespasian, when he constructed reservoirs for sea battles in the Colosseum, laid the foundations of Rome's last farm, where the monks keep four cows, a few pigs and hens: and it is a pleasant reflection that cows now graze on the site of the *vivarium*, or menagerie, in which wild beasts from every part of the world were kept until they were required in the Colosseum.

Who would have dreamt that cows are still milked within sight of the Colosseum: one might say within sight of the Campo Vaccino, for the Forum is only just out of view at the back of the Palatine? A hen passed proudly with her chicks.

'The cats from the Forum and Trajan's Market come prowling round at night,' said Father Alfred. 'We have to lock the hen houses!'

Here, I thought, the last of Pio Nono's Rome, which was also the Rome of the Middle Ages, has been casually preserved on the Caelian. Time has stood still here for centuries, and by the strangest of illusions one looks down over Rome, at the Colosseum, the dark fretwork of the ruined Palatine, and the distant dome of St Peter's, seeing it as if it were an etching by Piranesi.

'When I go back to my noisy lodgings among the neon lights,' I told Father Alfred, 'I shall think of you here in the peace of the Caelian, with the hen houses locked for the night, the cows in the byres, and the angry faces of Trajan's cats peering out of the shrubberies. It is a bit of Rome left over from another age.'

CHAPTER SIX

A visit to the Lake of Nemi – an audience at Castel Gandolfo –
Cats of Trajan's Market – Roman palaces – the English in Rome –
Fountains of the Villa d'Este – Hadrian's Villa

§ 1

The Italians sometimes use the word *accidente*, accompanied by charming and ingratiating smiles, to cover up a personal fault, or carelessness, and to disclaim responsibility for something which might have been avoided. One is reminded of Gibbon's description of the man who was always talking about his faults, which he called his misfortunes.

When the slapdash, but charming, proprietor of the pensione came to me with a tale of *accidenti*, and handed me a letter with a Vatican seal dated five days before, I knew that some careless person, probably himself, had put it in the wrong division of the letter rack. The wonder was that it had been discovered at all. I must admit that I was annoyed when, having opened it, I found that the Maestro di Camera had courteously given me five days' notice for an audience with the Pope at Castel Gandolfo; and now it was the day. However, as in Ireland, there was no point whatsoever in showing irritation; the only thing to do was to make a joke of it.

There was no time to be lost, so I telephoned for a car, changed into a dark suit, put on a solemn tie, and was soon driving out or Rome towards Castel Gandolfo. The lovely summer morning blew away the last traces of my resentment as I mounted the road to this glorious little mountain fastness. It was about eleven o'clock when I arrived. The Swiss Guards were still standing on each side of the palace gates, the fountain was still singing in the square. Having tucked the car away in the shade, I examined my card and discovered that my audience was not, as in my haste I had imagined, for the morning, but for the afternoon.

I had therefore many hours to spare in this exquisite place, which I think is the most beautiful of all the Alban hill towns. I walked to the little restaurant beneath the vine trellis, built on the edge of the mountain, that looks down for four hundred feet into the huge, circular blue crater of the Alban Lake. The grapes, which had been hard little peas when I was there before, had now plumped up and were almost ready for the table. The waiter brought me a glass of the local wine and told me, as he had done on my first visit, that it was a mixture of Alban grapes with those of Nemi. I sat happily looking at the stupendous panorama, noting how the water changed from sky blue at the edges to navy blue in the deep, unruffled centre of the lake, and thinking how delightful it must be to own one of the white villas that shine among the woodlands and crown the heights all round, repeating, I thought, the appearance of this landscape in antiquity.

Nemi—I was drinking the wine of Nemi, that sinister spot where once murderers had lived, sword in hand, waiting to be slain. It was that tragic lake which had inspired Frazer's *Golden Bough*. Nemi was only a few miles away, and I decided to go there.

The road led up and down the mountains, now in the shade of oaks and elms and now in sunlight, and I remembered with what interest I had collected, during the nineteen-thirties, references to the draining of the lake and the recovery of the two Roman galleys which had sunk at their moorings centuries ago. They were used in the time of Caligula for lake festivals and to ferry crowds across to the temple of Diana. A few miles and I was in the little town of Genzano, famous for its strawberries and for the carpeting of its main street with flowers every year during the feast of Corpus Christi; and there I stopped a moment to stand upon a terrace and look down at the distant Lake of Nemi.

It is much smaller than Albano, and even more obviously a volcanic crater. But while Albano is gay and cheerful, Nemi is dark and gloomy and the immense sides of the volcano, now covered with woodlands, lead down to the arena of some prehistoric cataclysm. The lake shores are not dotted, as at Albano, with happy little villas, but rise up black and threatening, splashed with dark woodlands and streaked with vineyards. I thought of its awful story and of the restless murderers who once prowled its banks. In a few minutes I had descended the mountain road and was running beside the edge of the lake. The sides of the crater are so high that wind does not often ruffle the lake, and on this morning the water was motionless, wrapped in its memories.

In primitive times, and even until well into the second century after Christ, Diana was worshipped here with strange and barbarous rites which had survived from the childhood of the human race. Her high priest had to be a runaway slave who had murdered the previous high priest. Having committed the murder and taken the title of the King of the Wood, he was liable to be murdered in his turn by another runaway slave; and he spent his life, sword in hand, guarding a certain tree which grew in the wood. He watched it day and night, for the first act of his would-be murderer was to break off a branch of this tree, which represented the Golden Bough that Aeneas plucked before he took his perilous journey into the other world. Having broken it, the newcomer had the right to kill the King of the Wood and reign in his place. That is why the lakeside of Nemi was haunted for centuries by a sinister figure watching the Golden Bough, peering into the shadows of the wood, always waiting for his murderer to appear.

It is almost unbelievable that this savage rite could have survived into the days of imperial Rome, but it undoubtedly did. The mad Caligula, thinking that the King of the Wood had lived too long, sent a younger and more powerful slave to slay him. Not the least curious thing about Nemi is that relics of this worship of Diana can be seen in Nottingham! The relics were found during excavations made on the site of the temple at the end of the last century by Sir John Savile Lumley, afterwards Lord Savile, who at that time was English ambassador in Rome. Nottingham, Naples, and Copenhagen, are, I believe, the three places where relics of Nemi have been wafted by the winds of chance.

Sir James Frazer said of Nemi that 'no one who has seen that calm water, lapped in a green hollow of the Alban hills, can ever forget it'; and I thought it looked particularly impressive that morning, with no breath of wind to liven the surface. The tall lips of the old crater enclosed it and excluded the sun for the greater part of the day. There cannot have been a more solemn sanctuary in the whole of Italy, and the two big pleasure boats upon the lake, with their beautiful bronze ornaments, must have been a striking contrast to the gloomy shores to which they plied.

There is a museum on the lakeside into which the galleys were taken after their recovery from the ooze of the lake, and I went to it full of expectation, remembering the photographs in the *Illustrated London News* of the time, which showed their vast skeletons, one of which was two hundred and forty feet long, with a beam of seventy-nine feet. When I entered the museum, I saw a scene of chaos and destruction. Walls and roof bore signs of fire, and there was nothing to see except a mass of twisted girders upon which the galleys had once rested. They had been burnt to a cinder. The caretaker told me that in 1944, when the Germans were retreating, the major in charge of a detachment of troops at Nemi destroyed the galleys just before he marched away. It was an act of spite and hatred. Perhaps only Attila could have understood the satisfaction he enjoyed as he turned and saw the smoke rising from those wonderful relics, the only examples of their kind in the world. All that was saved were a few gilded copper plates, some bronze nails and an anchor.

Curiously enough, four little water colours and sketches of the lake survived the destruction: one is by Edward Lear, another by Turner, a third by Lieutenant Middleton, and a fourth by Corot. They hang upon the wall amid this scene of savage destruction, evocative of a more civilized century than ours.

§ 2

Back at Castel Gandolfo, a papal chamberlain led me through a number of rooms whose windows looked down to the blue oval of the lake. We came to a corridor where five people were waiting and there he left me. One glance was enough to show that, like myself, they had been summoned to a special audience. There was a door at the end of the corridor, and we whispered together uneasily, rather like boys outside the headmaster's study.

There was a dark young man in evening dress, a Christian Arab, whose pockets bulged with rosaries and other objects which he had brought for the Holy Father to bless; there was a slim, blonde American wife with her husband, and I thought she would never look more charming than she did that afternoon in her black lace mantilla and her long black dress; and two elderly Frenchmen.

The door of the Pope's study at the end of the corridor opened, and we all turned expectantly. There came out, however, not the Pope but a prelate in purple, who arranged us a few paces apart on either side of the corridor, and told us that the Pope would say a few words to each of us as he passed. It was correct, he told us, to go down on one knee and kiss the papal ring. Having worked us into a condition of pleasant anxiety, he departed, and there followed twenty minutes during which we were occupied with our thoughts.

My own were of a day many years ago in Istanbul when a friend took me to meet the Œcumenical Patriarch of New Rome in the Phanar. We dived down some mean streets and came to what looked like the usual Greek monastery. Some bearded Greek priests took us to a room in which there was a wall safe full of books and manuscripts, which we examined, and, while we were doing so, various sable and bearded dignitaries entered and we were introduced to the last ghosts of the Byzantine world, the Great Logothete, the Didaskalos, the Protekdikos. Finally the Patriarch himself entered, a fierce old man wearing a violet *kalemaukion* above the square beard of an Assyrian king. He was referred to in a fulsome and almost blasphemous Byzantine manner as 'your most divine All-Holiness'. He made a gesture with a ringed hand, and the priests carried round little cups of Turkish coffee and green figs in syrup. As usual on these occasions, no one had anything to say, but it was enough for me to have seen the Patriarch of New Rome seated upon his throne, with his serpent-headed crozier at hand.

Now I was waiting to be received by the Patriarch of the

West, which is one of the Pope's many titles. How differently, I
thought, history has dealt with the Vatican and the Phanar, and
how regrettable, though how inevitable, was the separation of
the Latin West from the Greek East. Who could have imagined,
in the fifth century, when the East was powerful and the West
overrun by barbarians, that the Papacy would tame its invaders
and out of them form a new empire? Who would have believed
that the Eastern Emperors would go down before the armies of
Mohammed and that the Orthodox patriarchs would see the
banners of the Prophet hanging in S. Sophia?

The door at the end of the corridor opened. The Pope walked
out, accompanied by a Monsignor, who had our names upon
a slip of paper. There were no Swiss Guards and none of the
ceremony which surrounds such occasions in the Vatican. The
simplicity was immensely impressive. The Pope approached us
in turn, a spare, erect, cool and remote figure in spotless white,
and gave to each of us for a few moments something like the
kindly, watchful interest of a great surgeon visiting his con-
valescents. The Arab was so overcome that he went down on
both knees and spilled out his rosaries, which the Pope patiently
and solemnly blessed, tracing the sign of the cross above them so
precisely and exactly that I felt I could see a cross suspended in the
air where his fingers had drawn it.

When my turn came, I made my reverence and found myself
looking with interest at the most beautifully made red velvet shoes
I have ever seen. There was a small gold cross embroidered on the
toe. The shoes looked comfortable, and the Pope's foot was small,
narrow and aristocratic. I rose and found myself gazing into a
pair of dark eyes behind gold-rimmed glasses. I felt I was in the
presence of a beautifully dressed hermit. Pio Nono, I have read,
scattered snuff on his white cassock, which had to be changed
several times a day, but this Pope was a credit to his valet. Everything about him was fastidious. He had spoken in French to the
Arab, now he spoke in English with a strong accent, and when I
answered his questions, he drew a beautiful cross in the air and
passed on. And I knew that I had spoken to a holy man.

On the way back to Rome I reflected that I had just spoken to the only living link with the Apostolic age. Describing my experience to an English Monsignor who works at the Vatican—we were walking across the Piazza of St Peter's at the time—I said how odd it is that at such moments the mind often focuses itself upon some irrelevant detail. I should never forget the Pope's elegant red velvet shoes.

'How very strange,' said the Monsignor. 'Only this afternoon I was in a shoemaker's shop just round the corner, in the Via Mascherino, and the cobbler told me that he had made shoes for the Pope!'

As it was not out of our way, we called there. It was a small one-room shop littered with scraps of leather from which uppers had been cut, with plenty of old shoes on shelves waiting to be mended, the kind of shop you would find in any city. A young man sat on a stool, hammering away at a shoe. Yes, he had made shoes for the Pope. He got up and sought among a number of wooden lasts which were festooned in a corner. He detached a pair and handed them to us. 'Pius XII' was written in pencil on the sole. A pair of red velvet shoes made to the Pope's measurements would cost £12, he told me, and such presents were often given to the Holy Father by nuns and wealthy Americans.

§ 3

Every visitor will have noticed how enormously cats outnumber dogs in Rome. Dogs, of course, are difficult to keep in flats and the price of a dog licence is high. Only perhaps an Italian official could have divided the canine species into two parts: watch and de luxe! A licence for a watch-dog costs two thousand lire, about twenty-three shillings, while a licence for a de luxe dog is five thousand lire, or nearly three pounds. The most aggressive and watchful Pekinese can never get out of the de luxe class, and neither can the most affable mongrel ever enter it. This odd but admirable arrangement has abolished the stray and unwanted dog from the streets of Rome.

Stray cats, on the other hand, have always been a feature of the ruins. Aquatints of the last century show women in crinolines and men in stove-pipe hats and blue frockcoats gazing down at the cats in the Forum of Trajan, which was then the chief cattery. This no longer exists. The cats have migrated to the Market of Trajan not far away, which is secluded and in a desirable central position, within easy striking distance of the voles and mice of the Palatine and the hen roosts of the Passionist Fathers on the Caelian.

I went there to see the second century shopping centre, and re-turned several times to feed the cats. They live in the basements of what was once a splendid and massive market. The shops and offices were in three storeys, with arcaded fronts, and stood in a wide half-circle, facing an open space, with a similar half-circle on the opposite side that has now vanished, or which may lie beneath the pavements of modern Rome. The shops were mostly large single rooms which were closed by wooden doors running in grooves in the stone, and, like many booths in the East today, their size probably bore no relationship to their resources. They reminded me of the shops to be seen in the old parts of Istanbul and Aleppo.

The cats of Trajan's Market may number two or three hundred. They form the largest of all the cat colonies in Rome. The animals are of every age, size and colour and, on the whole, are sus-picious and wild, though here and there a cat is still close enough to a hearth to be talked to and perhaps even stroked. The number of kittens proves that family life is safe, and the old embattled toms tell of the fierce fights which take place there. You will see nothing but lean vanishing bodies and baleful little faces gazing suspiciously from holes and corners until you produce a paper bag, when from every corner of the ruins cats will come and surround you. Kittens hardly able to walk will totter up and sit expectantly on the edge of the gathering. They are a pathetic collection and an unnatural one. Cats are individualists and it is painful to see them obliged to live in these distasteful packs. The herd instinct is, of course, absent and even in a crowd cats manage to remain detached.

At ten-thirty every morning the animals become unusually

alert and sit facing one way, towards the entrance to Trajan's Market. Two women appear with bags, whereupon every cat emerges and makes its way towards them. The women are extraordinarily methodical. One woman feeds the kittens and the other takes the adult cats and the blind toms, for in the fighting they sometimes tear out each other's eyes. The food produced is the usual cold spaghetti and tomato sauce, which no cat I have ever known would deign to touch: but these poor creatures are ready to fight for it. After they have been fed, out comes boracic and sulphur powder and the injured animals are doctored.

I assumed that the women were members of an animal welfare society, but when I spoke to them, I found that they were two ordinary humble housewives who loved cats and could ill afford the time and the money spent on looking after the colony.

One of the women told me that her association with the colony began with a cat called Mimi. Four years ago her landlord threatened to turn her out of her flat unless she got rid of her pet. She brought Mimi to Trajan's Forum and left her. In the morning she returned to feed her, but found so many hungry cats that she has been coming every day for the last four years. Mimi is still there and greets her mistress every morning.

The women know every cat in the colony. There are, of course, outstanding personalities. There are Bello Primo and Bello Secondo; there is a huge black tom known as the Charcoal Man, and a little grey cat called the Mouse. I noticed the arrival of a lordly cat with a red ribbon round his neck. He never touched the food, but sat on a wall, sleek, well-fed and spoilt, watching the proceedings. This, I was told, was Bello Primo. Once he had belonged to the colony, but a woman who lives nearby, impressed by his air of potential magnificence, had adopted him and taken him away. He had ceased to be a lean and hungry animal and had rapidly assumed the airs and graces of a normal cat: but every day at feeding time habit asserts itself, and Bello Primo appears, not to eat the cold spaghetti and the more desirable strips of cold tripe, but to sit and watch.

One day I arrived to find the women in great distress. '*Poveretta Piccolina!*' they cried as they held out to me the corpse of a tabby kitten which they had been nursing. 'We must bury her,' they said. 'Let me do it,' I offered in a moment of unguarded generosity; but how to dig a grave in Trajan's Market without a spade or even a penknife! The earth was like iron. At last, finding a potsherd, I managed to scrape out a little hollow and into this I placed the body. It is not every visitor to Rome, I thought, who can say he has buried a body in Trajan's Market.

§ 4

The Victor Emmanuel II Monument is the eighth hill of Rome. It is criticized for its glaring whiteness, for its size, for the innumerable statues on it, and for the arrogant way it shoulders the Forum of Trajan and hides the Forum Romanum and the Capitoline Hill. In fact there seems to be nothing right about it. It remains, however, one of the few places in Rome where you cannot be run over; it is a Mappin Terrace of comparative solitude upon whose slopes you may wander undisturbed, except for the attentions of young men with ingratiating manners and American accents who wish to sell you guide books and fountain pens.

The Monument would have shocked Augustans as much as it would have distressed Victor Emmanuel, who was by all accounts a modest man. The Brescian marble of which it is built can never be mellowed by Time. The story in Rome—a typical Pasquinade, by the way—is that when the Monument was built, the Prime Minister was deputy for Brescia, and that the contract for marble kept his seat safe for over a quarter of a century!

If you go to the dome of St Peter's, or to the Janiculum, and look towards the Capitol, it is extraordinary how this snowfield detaches itself from Rome and how clearly the gilded figure of the King, who abolished the Papal States and drove the Pope out of the Quirinal, stands out from the background. Can it be, I have asked myself, that the men of 1885, who conceived this monument, wished the imprisoned Pope to have this symbol of United Italy always before his eyes from his windows in the Vatican? If so, it is good to think that Time, which takes the sting out of most things, has made this gesture pointless.

As I climbed among the tons of assorted allegory, I was stupefied by the amount of national emotion put into it. It is one of those over-statements which shock but fascinate the Anglo-Saxon mind. It is as if the march from *Aïda* had been carried out in marble. And what an appropriate thought. One of the passwords of the *Risorgimento* was '*Viva* Verdi!', the letters of the composer's name standing for 'Vittorio Emanuele Re D'Italia'.

I found the Monument peopled mainly by nuns and boy scouts. The scouts raced to the top with the energy of youth, as if anxious to shout 'Excelsior' from the highest pinnacle; the nuns walked sedately to the southern terrace, where they turned their kind, mild faces towards the dome of St Peter's. From the northern platform there is just as fine a view across the Forum to the Colosseum. I climbed until I was level with Victor Emmanuel II, with his huge moustache, his plumed helmet and his sword, sitting his war horse with the triumphant air of a permanent Caesar.

There is a *Risorgimento* museum in the great pile, where I found a young Englishman earnestly studying relics of that time and making notes in a book. We were the only people there. The young man was a history teacher, his subject was the nineteenth century, and he knew his Trevelyan by heart. We went out and sat on the steps, and discussed what I have always considered a fascinating subject: the curious psychological drama of those two men, Pius IX and Victor Emmanuel.

The Pope was seventy-eight years of age when the Papal States were threatened by the armies of United Italy. He was spectacularly handsome and in his youth had tried to enlist in the Noble Guard, but had been rejected because of a tendency to epilepsy. It was the kindly Pius VII who turned his thoughts to the Church, and young Giovanni Mastai-Ferretti became a devout priest and a dramatic and unexpected preacher. Sometimes he would speak in a dark church with a skull beside him on the pulpit; once he covered a thigh bone with spirits and set fire to it to illustrate the terrors of hell. He was said never to have read a book, but his piety was without limit. He devoted himself to the poor and was well acquainted with the slums of Rome. He was Pope at fifty-four, and a handsomer Pope was never seen when he came out in his white cassock on the balcony of the Quirinal to bless the crowd for the first time. Revolution was rumbling over Europe and at first Pius IX was adored as the liberal Pope who wished to reform the ramshackle Papal States, to introduce the railway and even to permit newspapers. He became, also, a papal Haroun al Raschid, slipping out in disguise to the slums and the prisons, and there are innumerable stories about him: how once he stopped his coach and took an injured Jew to the Quirinal, how he wrote a letter to himself on behalf of a felon in prison. The crowd loved their 'Pio Nono' for two years, then revolution struck Rome, the Secretary of State was murdered, and the bewildered and distressed Pope fled from the city.

He returned, protected by a French army of occupation, a changed and saddened man, but still kind, still a model of piety, still desiring popular approval. His popularity, however, had now gone: it was even whispered that he had the evil eye. He left the temporal care of his states to others and devoted himself entirely to spiritual matters. In 1870 the French army was called from Rome to fight the Prussians, and the army of Victor Emmanuel, with the whole country in sympathy, was ready to march in and make Rome the capital of Young Italy. Other capitals had been proposed in an attempt to avoid a clash with the Pope, but Rome was thought to be the inevitable choice. Even to the last Pius could not believe that the Blessed Virgin, whose Immaculate Conception he had propounded, would allow his throne to be taken from him. But the day came when he left the Quirinal for ever; and the Italian army marched in without bloodshed.

Poor Victor Emmanuel, a bluff soldier of fifty, and the last European king to charge the enemy, as he had charged the Austrians, with his sons beside him, was a devout Catholic. He once said to Cavour that he would go with him to the gates of Rome, but not a step beyond. To his last day he never allowed a thing to be touched in the Pope's room in the Quirinal, which remained full of crucifixes and other devotional objects, just as Pius IX had left it when he went as 'prisoner' to the Vatican. What wounded the feelings of the religious monarch more than anything was to be compared to Anti-Christ, and to be obliged to bow his head under the anathemas constantly rained upon him by Pius.

Pope and King had a great deal in common, though there were aspects of Victor Emmanuel's life which could not be expected to appeal to the pontiff. They were nevertheless much the same kind of man, simple, honest and devout. The Pope, though hurling anathemas against the 'robber-king', wrote him gentle and polite private letters. In his turn, the excommunicate monarch always ended his letters with a request for the Pope's blessing! Pius could not logically give his blessing, but promised his prayers. This strange interchange continued for eight years, until one day it reached its climax with the mortal illness of Victor Emmanuel.

The Pope was asked to lift the ban of excommunication so that the King might receive the last consolations of the Church. Pius, or his advisers, agreed to do so if the King would sign a statement of submission and restitution to the Holy See. This Victor Emmanuel refused to do. The Pope, with tears in his eyes, sent his personal chaplain to the Quirinal with authority to absolve the King and give extreme unction if only the King would make a statement, even by word of mouth. The ministers refused to admit him to the King, perhaps afraid that Victor Emmanuel, who had been so reluctant to enter Rome, might weaken in his last moments.

'The wretches!' cried the Pope. 'They want him to die a heathen! He, the son and the father of a saint!'

He sent his prelate for the second time and again he was refused admittance. Eventually, though no one, I believe, knows how it happened, the King at his last gasp received the rites of the Church by the permission of the Pope, and no statement of restitution was asked. Within three weeks of the death of the first King of Italy, the last Pope-King followed him to the grave.

Having spoken of these men, the schoolmaster and I went to one of the cafés in the square and looked back at the Monument.

'I suppose it is rather a large tribute to the founder of a royal house that produced only four kings,' remarked my companion.

A dozen Vespas puttered past; a hundred motor cars covered us with their fumes.

'How I wish they had chosen Turin or Milan,' I said.

We crossed the road and entered the Palazzo di Venezia. In the superb *Sala del Mappamondo* the attendant nodded to a corner of the marble floor and said, 'His desk was over there!' 'He,' of course, was Mussolini. We walked to the windows and saw the balcony from which 'he' made speeches with outstretched arms and blazing eyes. It all appeared so remote and even Trajan's Column across the way was closer to one's sympathy.

§ 5

Among the pleasanter of the Roman street markets is that of the Campo de' Fiori, though the only flowers nowadays blossom on the clothes-lines of the surrounding tenements. It is a fruit and vegetable market with an outer fringe of old clothes. It stands in the heart of Renaissance Rome and beneath it lie the surroundings of Pompey's Theatre. The colossal Hercules, now in the Vatican Museum, was discovered a few yards away. It was an oracular statue and a small boy could climb inside it through an opening at the back of the head. The experiment was made in 1864, when a young mason squeezed himself into the statue in the presence of a number of eminent persons, 'and the sound of his voice,' wrote Lanciani, 'in answering the questions addressed to him, was really impressive and almost supernatural'.

All morning the careful housewives of the district move critically between the ramparts of tomatoes and aubergines in the Campo de' Fiori, pausing to taste a grape or to examine a bean, while the old red and ochre houses look down upon a typical street market of the Middle Ages. The Campo de' Fiori is the one living institution in Rome that matches the bell towers and the Cosmatic churches. The mediaeval note is also struck by a bronze monk with his cowl drawn over his head, who rises above the peaches and melons. The curious visitor who manages to fight his way through the vegetables to this statue will think it broad-minded of Rome to have perpetuated the memory of Giordano Bruno, who, for his heretical opinions, was in 1600 burned on this spot by the Inquisition. It is the nearest thing in Rome to a Protestant statue, and it is surprising to see that others commemorated on the plinth are Wycliffe and John Huss. The explanation is that after 1870 it was put up by an anti-clerical government, presumably to annoy the Vatican, and there it remains, on the site of the stake, where happily the only flames now are those of chillies and tomatoes.

During a visit to England Bruno lectured at Oxford, wrote an extravagant eulogy of Queen Elizabeth, met Sir Philip Sidney, and is said, by a curious and intriguing tradition, to have encountered Shakespeare in the printing-office of Thomas Vautrollier.

A few steps from the market and you enter a little piazza where two huge granite tubs spout water before the Farnese Palace, which some say is the finest of all the Renaissance palaces in Rome. It was built by Alessandro Farnese, who became Pope Paul III. The enormous oblong building, with its three rows of mathematically exact windows and a cornice designed by Michelangelo, was built during the reign of Henry VIII of England, which is the simplest way for an English visitor to place it in the right period, and to realize how late the Renaissance came to England; for nothing remotely like the Farnese Palace crossed the Channel until the reign of Charles I.

The courtyard is magnificent, and with some surprise I discovered in it the sarcophagus of Cecilia Metella. The doorkeeper, who spoke French, for the Palazzo Farnese is now the French Embassy, showed me his lodge and pointed out the thickness of the walls, and the steps leading to the barred windows for the use of archers or arquebusiers.

The usual question rose to my mind: what was here before and now lies underneath, sealed in this ancient soil? Everything in Rome stands upon something older. The builders of the sixteenth century discovered the answer when they came upon the remains of the barracks of the Red Charioteers—the *Factio Russata*—and one of the tessellated pavements has been preserved in a cellar.

This part of the Campus Martius was the region of the charioteers. The 'Blues' had their barracks on the site of the nearby English College, and the 'Greens' on what is now the Palazzo della Cancelleria. The race track known as the Trigarium, which was at the back, parallel with the Tiber, was the place where colts were broken in, harnessed between two trained horses in a *triga*. This part of the Campus must have been the resort of every tipster and bookmaker in ancient Rome.

If a magician waved his wand over any famous Roman palace and commanded the stones which compose it to fly back to their original buildings, there would be some curious scenes. The Farnese Palace would melt away to help fill the gap in the Colosseum, a part of it would come to rest on the Quirinal, where Aurelian's Temple of the Sun once stood, and piles of stone would descend into Trajan's Forum, the Baths of Diocletian and the Baths of Caracalla.

The innumerable palaces through which the visitor wanders in search of a picture or a ceiling leave him with a vivid impression of princely discomfort. They were built not only, as Veblen would have put it, as an example of conspicuous expenditure, but to house married sons, family dependents, and an army of servants. The system is a natural development of the mediaeval household—the 'family' as they called it in Rome—and it seemed to me that the atmosphere in many of the palaces suggests the thirteenth century rather than the fifteenth and the sixteenth in which they were built.

Marion Crawford, writing about seventy years ago in *Ave Roma Immortalis*, had some interesting things to say about life in a Roman palace.

The so-called 'noble floor' was reserved for the use of the head of the family and his wife. All the married sons with their wives and servants were lodged in other parts of the palace. The eldest son usually occupied the second floor, the second son the third, and the unmarried children had to put up with what was left. The low, rambling attic floor was occupied by the servants and often by the librarian, the chaplain and the steward. If there were a cardinal in the family, one of the many great reception rooms would be set aside as his throne room.

All the members of the family were expected to dine together at a huge table. 'Everything was managed through the steward,' wrote Marion Crawford, 'by a contract with the cook, who was bound to provide a certain number of dishes daily for the fixed meals, but nothing else—not so much as an egg or a slice of toast beyond that. This system still prevails in many households, and as it is to be expected that meals at unusual hours may sometimes be required, an elaborate system of accounts is kept by the steward and his clerks, and the smallest things ordered by any of the sons or daughters are charged against an allowance made them, while separate reckonings are kept for the daughters-in-law, for whom certain regular pin-money is provided out of their own dowries at the marriage settlement, all of which goes through the steward's hands. The same settlement, even in recent years, stipulated for a fixed number of dishes of meat daily—generally two, I believe—for a certain number of new gowns and other clothes, and for a great variety of details, besides the use of a carriage every day, to be harnessed not more than twice, that is, either in the morning or afternoon, or once in the daytime and once at night. Everything—a cup of tea, a glass of lemonade—if not mentioned in the marriage settlement, had to be paid for separately.

'The justice of such an arrangement—for it is just—is only equalled by its inconvenience, for it requires the machinery of an hotel, combined with an honesty not usual in hotels. Undoubtedly the whole system is directly descended from the practice of the ancients, which made every father of a family the absolute despot of his household, and made it impossible for a son to hold property or have any individual independence during his father's life. . . .'

The feelings of a young bride living in the palace of her husband's family were described by Vittoria Colonna, the late Duchess of Sermoneta, who had so many friends in England at the court of Edward VII. She married the eldest son of the Duke of Sermoneta in 1901, the first time a marriage had taken place between a Colonna and a Caetani since 1560.

'I always hated Palazzo Caetani with its gloom,' she wrote in *Things Past*. 'It is sad to think of the countless marriages in Italy that have turned out badly and unhappily owing to the old-fashioned custom of young wives having to live with their parents-in-law. . . . Palazzo Caetani is in itself a rather fine building, designed by Ammanati, one of Michelangelo's pupils, but spoilt by an extra storey built above its cornice by a practical but inartistic Caetani. Its darkness and melancholy are overwhelming. On the first floor, the so-called "piano nobile", where my parents-in-law lived, the electric light was in constant use at luncheon during the winter, and in several of the drawing-rooms it was necessary literally to grope one's way in the perpetual gloom.

'I remember the evening I arrived at Palazzo Caetani for the first time after my honeymoon at Frascati. Dusk was falling, dinner-time approaching, and there was no sign of life anywhere in my part of the house. I sat in the bedroom that had been allotted to me; my husband had been given one on another floor and so far off that I never really learned the quickest way to his room as there were several staircases and innumerable passages. My dear old English nurse, Sizy, sat near me. She was very ruffled at having left beautiful Palazzo Colonna with all its luxuries and comforts, and not at all disposed to make the best of things. Finally when it got quite dark, I suggested: "Suppose we rang the bell and asked the housemaid for some hot water?"

' "There is no bell, there is no housemaid, there is no hot water in this house," was Sizy's gloomy retort; and the funny part of it is that it was absolutely true. . . .

'None of my family-in-law ever dressed for dinner, and during that first winter, when we lived all together, I think I sat longer at the dining-room table than I ever have since in my life. A bell rang before meals to summon us all, but no one ever dreamed of moving towards the dining-room on hearing it, for the Caetanis merely considered it as a symptom that food might be expected before long. The story ran that the Duchess always said on hearing the luncheon bell: "That's nice; I still have time to go to the stables and see all the horses."

'And so it was the Caetani custom to drop in for meals at any old time, and the first arrival (which was always myself) was obliged to wait until the last had finished. I sometimes used to think my tired back would break in two. The Duchess used to come in one of the last, usually in a violet flannel dressing-gown and waving an enormous paper fan which seemed to me unnecessary as their rooms were bitterly cold. Each member of the family had a semi-circle of pickle bottles, patent medicines, sardine tins, etc., arranged round their plates, and these collections marked the places of each individual.

'The food was served by an enormously fat man called Girolamo, who wore an old frock coat of the Duke's, and, owing to an impediment in his speech, spoke a language that no one could understand. He was also a standing joke in the family, and the extraordinary silly things he did filled them with pure delight.

'The Duke had a special Bologna sausage, smelling strongly of garlic, near his place, and used to pare off thin slices that he presented in turn to members of the family as a great favour. I think he never really liked me after he discovered that I could not bear Bologna sausage. He was very clever and cultivated, and a most agreeable *causeur*; so were all his children, so the conversation at meals was often very pleasant and entertaining. Twice in the course of the winter the Duke appeared at dinner in evening dress, and this was a signal that he was going to call afterwards on the Queen Mother. On these occasions Girolamo invariably served him with a cup of extra strong coffee, with the usual remark: "If your Excellency is going to-night to visit Her Majesty, he will need something to keep him awake!"'

In delightful contrast to the stories of poison and assassination which cling to the Renaissance palaces, the writer notes that during the roller-skating craze of the early nineteen-hundreds 'the Roman palaces with their marble floors were very suitable to this, in fact in some houses we could pass from one drawing-room to another, all round the house without encountering any obstacles or anything but smooth surface all the way, and we used to go out to dinner taking our boots and skates in a bag. This amused Robert Hichens very much, and he described one of our skating parties in *The Fruitful Vine*.'

§ 6

When wandering about Rome, one comes now and then to a barrow full of old books set up in the shadow of a palace and surrounded by a few collectors, including, of course, the inevitable Franciscan, all seeking, though without much hope, for treasures. There is, alas, nothing in Rome like the Quays of Paris or the Charing Cross Road.

I often prowled round a number of trestle tables that were set up opposite the Palazzo della Cancelleria, but never found anything that quickened the heartbeat. I think the best find, which I refrained from buying, was the second edition, bound in full calf and in three volumes, of *Roderick Random*. It was spotless and well worth the ten shillings asked for it. I did, however, buy a book called *Six Months in Italy*, by George Stillman Hilliard, published in Boston in 1853, because I could not resist the author's description of the English in Rome at that time. It seems hardly possible that a national type can have changed so completely as the English appear to have done in the past century. The self-satisfied and arrogant individuals—our great or great-great grandfathers—as seen by this observant and detached American bear no resemblance to the men of today, but rather to the now obsolete caricature of 'John Bull' with his Union Jack waistcoat. After saying how unlike ancient Romans are the modern Italians, with which everyone must agree, Hilliard goes on to say, 'But the legitimate descendants of the old Romans, the true inheritors of their spirit, are still to be found in Rome; and in no inconsiderable numbers. In the morning they may be seen in Monaldini's reading-room poring over *The Times* or *Galignani*, galloping over the Campagna, driving about the streets and never looking to the right hand or the left, or gathering in groups in the Piazza di Spagna to hear the last news from home. In the afternoon they betake themselves to the Pincio, and for a certain season pace up and down its gravelled terrace with vigorous strides, their faces wearing a look of determined resolve, as if the constitution of their country, as well as their own, would suffer if they lost their daily walk.... They stalk over the land as if it were their own. There is something downright and uncompromising in their air. They have the natural language of command, and their bearing flows from the proud consciousness of undisputed power. . . .

'They, like the Romans, are haughty to the proud and for-bearing towards the weak. They force the mood of peace upon nations that cannot afford to waste their strength in unprofitable war. They are law-makers, road-makers, and bridge-makers. They are penetrated by the instinct of social order, and have the organ of political constructiveness. . . . An Englishman in his heart of hearts, regards emotion or enthusiasm as feminine weaknesses, unworthy of manhood. A fine dog or horse calls forth from him more energetic admiration than the most beautiful landscape or picture. He marches through a gallery with resolute strides—his countenance expanding as the end draws near. Five minutes' despatch to a Raphael: four a Titian or Correggio; and two or three are enough for less illustrious names. . . .'

Mr Hilliard concluded his eulogy of the English with these words.

'The English are proud of their own country, and for that, surely, no man can blame them. They are proud of its history, of its literature, of its constitution; and, especially, of the rank it holds and the power it wields at the present time. To this national pride they have a fair right. A new sense of the greatness of England is gathered from travelling on the Continent; for let an Englishman go where he will, the might and majesty of his country seem to be hanging over him like an unseen shield. Let but a hand of violence be laid upon an English subject and the great British lion, which lies couchant in Downing Street, begins to utter menacing growls and shake his invincible locks. An English man-of-war seems to be always within one day's sail of anywhere. Let political agitation break out in any port on the globe, if there be even a roll of English broadcloth or a pound of English tea to be endangered thereby, within forty-eight hours an English steamer or frigate is pretty sure to drop anchor in the harbour, with an air which seems to say, "Here I am: does any-body want anything of me?"'

I closed the book. I began to find Mr Hilliard painful reading.

§ 7

Such were the proud English of only a century ago, and their descendants, as they gaze from the windows of a motor coach and wonder how much is still intact of the beggarly allowance granted to them as a favour by the Treasury, may well sigh for the old days.

English travel to Rome has gone through several interesting phases, of which mass travel by motor coach is the latest, and perhaps the most popular. Apart from religious pilgrimage, which was the same in all ages, at the end of the Middle Ages Englishmen went to Rome and Italy to absorb the new learning, and while the first wave of scholars, all Balliol men, were book collectors, the second wave, still from Oxford, went to learn and returned to teach. By the time of Henry VIII Italy was full of Englishmen, some of whom had gone there, as William Thomas slyly notes, 'under the pretence of study', for foreign travel had now become the mark of 'a compleat Person'. It was also the only school for life at court, whence all blessings flowed. English ambassadors maintained a kind of preparatory school for future diplomats, and young men were sent abroad with a tutor who, it was hoped, would guide them into the straight and narrow paths.

When these young men returned to the old half-timbered mansions of England, where life went on much as it had done in Plantagenet days, they roused not only the natural pessimism with which old people view the young, but also a patriotic contempt for foreign ways; and possibly there was also some commercial jealousy on the part of old-fashioned hosiers, tailors and weavers, when they saw the superior stockings and clothes in which the wanderers returned. Even Henry VIII had to be content with stockings cut from cloth until a pair of good Italian hose came his way, and Elizabeth was delighted with the scented gloves brought to her from Italy.

No one was able to express more humorously the effect upon the stay-at-home Englishman of the mincing manners of the 'compleat Person' than Gabriel Harvey, whose 'little apeish hat' has immortalized the headgear of Edward de Vere, Earl of

Oxford; and quite as good was Thomas Nash's description of the 'affectate traveller'. 'You shall see a dapper Jacke,' he wrote, 'but hath beene but over at Deepe (Dieppe) wring his face round about, as a man would stir a mustard-pot, and talke English through the teeth, like . . . Monsieur Mingo de Mousetrap.'

With the Reformation, English travellers deserted Rome and converged upon Venice. The Inquisition was feared in Rome, and so also were the Jesuits, who were accredited with the ambition to lure young Englishmen back to the old faith, which could be quite dangerous for them when they returned home. Indeed at one period passports were issued with the proviso that the traveller must not visit Rome. When Charles I married Henrietta Maria, and his conversion was hoped for, the situation became easier; but it soon deteriorated, and Milton, when he reflected upon his Italian travels, said that in Rome fidelity to Protestant principles required some courage.

For a brief time during the reign of Charles II, when France replaced Italy in the affection of the court circle, French airs and graces, and French dance steps, were brought home as travellers of the preceeding centuries had returned with black doublets and scented gloves. Soon, however, Italy called again and the phrase 'The Grand Tour' found its way into the language. Richard Lassels was the first to use it in 1670, in the preface to a book of travel hints.

There then began a flood of books and guides designed for those who could afford to make a Continental journey. Many of them— an interesting indication of the seventeenth century interest in painting—stress the importance of 'limning' and of packing painting and drawing materials, just as a modern traveller packs his camera. There is a woodcut in Sandys' *Travells* which shows a Jacobean traveller earnestly sketching Avernus while his friend, booted and spurred, with hand on sword, stands by and points out features of the landscape, no doubt offering advice.

Travellers have always been curious, otherwise they would never have left home, but now for the first time one notices the prying or inquisitive traveller. According to Misson, whose *New Voyage to Italy* was printed in 1695, every traveller should take with him a piece of pack thread fifty fathoms long and divided into feet, so that he could measure the height of buildings: but this is nothing compared with the dour German instructions of Count Leopold Berchtold in 1789, who, in addition to sketching landscapes and costumes, and also machinery and any ingenious instrument, advised travellers to learn to play a German flute in their spare time to keep them out of mischief. He prepared a list of silly questions to improve the traveller's knowledge of the country, such as, 'Which are the favourite herbs of the sheep of this country?', and 'Are there many instances of people having been bit by mad animals?' 'Which food has been experienced to be most portable and most nourishing for keeping a distressed ship's crew from starving?' Everyone was advised to carry a bottle of vinegar, a bottle of the best French brandy, some spirit of Salmiac against fits, and some Hoffman's Drops. Upon arrival at an inn, it was advisable to air the room by throwing some of the vinegar upon a red hot shovel. At night the traveller should look under the bed and pile the furniture against the door. He advised the purchase of a pocket door-bolt.

Berchtold would scarcely be worth notice were he not an indication of a new type of traveller, a nervous and suspicious individual, who was venturing abroad not for knowledge and the improvement of his character, or for the service of his country, like the Tudors and the Stuarts, but anxious for his own safety and comfort. It is a far cry indeed from Count Berchtold's old maids peeping under their beds at night and dear Tom Coryat, too poor to hire a mule, tramping across Europe as gay as a lark in the time of James I, and returning home to hang up his shoes in the parish church.

The English travelling-coach of the nineteenth century was a marvellous piece of work, in which the owner could sleep and carry with him a house full of objects. Experiences in Italy from 1792 to 1798 inspired Marianne Starke to write a book which, while it may have helped some, must have appalled others and have deterred them from leaving home. She outlined an expedition on a scale which in these days would be considered sufficient for the conquest of Everest. The ideal coach should be specially made for mountain country, should have two drag-staffs for hills, axle trees of iron, special springs, and a chest full of spare parts. The traveller should take beds, leather blankets, carpets, cutlery, not forgetting a silver teapot and a kettle, spices, and, if he liked porridge for breakfast, oatmeal. He should also take a medicine chest, paying particular attention to a rhubarb grater, some dental forceps, Dr James's powders, castor-oil, opium and laudanum (which were the aspirin of the eighteenth and nineteenth centuries), spirits of lavender, peppermint, basilicum, and magnesia. In order to defeat the cold marble floors, he should take double-soled shoes and long drawers. Miss Starke forgot nothing, and her admirers must have set out ready for anything.

The Grand Tour now brought every type of Englishman to Rome. Many came to escape the grey skies of England; but the classical scholar persisted, and so did the ordinary educated Englishman who longed to visit the places known to him since his schooldays. Then there was the dilettante, the picture fancier, and the architectural peer, the first of whom was Lord Burlington, who himself measured all the Palladian buildings. Under the influence of Italian skies, and the sights and sounds of Italy, those latecomers to the Renaissance sometimes fell into a state of enchantment and went to school again, learning to be musicians, artists and architects. Smollett mentioned 'a boy of seventy-two ... actually travelling through Italy for improvement', and Peter Beckford knew an old Irishman 'turned of eighty', who was finishing his education in Rome in 1788.

It was all part of the redesigning of England, the changing of the English home into that Georgian interior which for grace and beauty has never been surpassed. Rome and its temples, the egg and dart moulding of fallen cornices, the grotesques of the Vatican, were in time all reflected upon the walls and ceilings, and in the beautiful pine mantelpieces, of English drawing-rooms. With the nineteenth century the travellers included the whole of of the robust English middle-classes. It was an American, Washington Irving, who described the travelling-coach of the Popkins family as 'an epitome of England; a little morsel of the old Island rolling about the world' with 'the ruddy faces gaping from the windows' and 'the dickeys loaded with well-dressed servants beef-fed and bluff; looking down from their heights with contempt on all the world around; profoundly ignorant of the country and the people, and devoutly certain that everything not English must be wrong.'

Smollett and Samuel Sharpe threw a dash of cold water on the exaggerated passion for Italy, yet it was a grand enthusiasm, the like of which we shall never know again.

Behind the travel literature of the eighteenth and nineteenth centuries, one sees a slow and quiet England where war never interfered with fox-hunting and life appeared fixed and secure. The people observed by Washington Irving and Hilliard drank their port beneath classical ceilings, and the hounds met on frosty mornings before Palladian porches. In visiting Rome, even those who could not remember a line of Horace or Virgil were in a sense at home. Many a faked Venus, shivering in unkempt parkland, and many a rustic temple, speak of their enthusiasm; and even today, those who have been ruthlessly educated to be chemists and physicists, and to hold down important posts in commercial combines, descend from their coaches and gaze around upon the Roman scene, so dear to their ancestors, conscious may be that there is something there to be understood and perhaps even loved.

§ 8

Among recent tenants of the Keats house at the bottom of the Spanish Steps was Dr Axel Munthe, the author of *The Story of San Michele*, who had his consulting rooms there when he was practising in Rome. In 1820, when Keats and his devoted Severn were tenants, the house was kept by a Signora Petri, who let out rooms and provided meals, one of which Keats threw out of the window! It was a cheap lodging and practically nothing is left of the rooms Keats knew, except maybe the ceilings.

As I climbed two flights of dark stairs, I had vivid glimpses through an occasional window of the sun-struck Spanish Steps and those sitting upon them, and I came at last to a heavy, English-looking door. It might have come from Oxford or Cambridge, or the Inner Temple. The Keats-Shelley Memorial Association has assembled within one of the best collections in existence of books on the poets and their contemporaries. It is a fine library, and also a fine-looking one, whose calf and morocco bindings took the eye of Henry James. I was shown the little corner room overlooking the Piazza di Spagna where poor Keats died, and I saw his pathetic, emaciated death mask, pathetic because of a faint smile which was not present during the last melancholy months of his life. Peace and serenity came to him on the other side.

I was surprised to be told by the loyal curator, Signora Signorelli Cacciatore, for this house seems to inspire devotion, that while hundreds visited the Keats House before the last war, thousands now come. She told me the story of the adventures of the Keats House during the war, which is an exciting one. The moment she realized that Italy was to be dragged into the war on Germany's side, she packed up the chief treasures in two boxes and sent them to the Monastery of Monte Cassino, where the archivist, Don Mauro Inguanez, concealed them in his cell. When the Allies landed in Italy, the Germans ordered the monks to leave, and many of their treasures fell into the eager hands of the Hermann Goering division. The Keats relics would also have done so had Don Mauro not sent them back to Rome as his own luggage. To the astonishment of the curator, they arrived one night in a German lorry and with an armed guard provided by the looters themselves.

An anxious time followed. Germans who tried to enter the house were told that it was shut up and empty. On June 4, 1944, the Germans left Rome by one gate as the Allies entered by another. The Signora stood at the window and watched this happening. It was a calm moonlit night. The last Germans had gone; the last bursts of machine gun fire were over. The silence was unearthly as even the usual sound of *La Barcaccia* was stilled, for the conduits had been bombed and, like all the fountains of Rome, it was dry. Suddenly a voice was heard calling from one of the windows in the Piazza di Spagna that the Allies were coming! She heard the rumble of approaching tanks. Then two files of armed figures passed silently in the moonlight. People ventured out of their houses and some flashed torches in the faces of the soldiers, who smiled and passed on into the darkness. Then an order was given and a halt was made. The Piazza was crowded. There in the moonlight the soldiers slept: on the pavements, in the dried-up fountain, on the Spanish Steps. For a moment it seemed to Signora Cacciatore that all these men were dead, victims of a silent battle fought in the Piazza.

'On the next day, at six o'clock in the morning,' said the Signora, 'the first Allied visitor knocked on the door. It was a Mr A. C. Sedgwick, the *New York Times* correspondent with the American Fifth Army, and with him was Captain Morgan, a British Public Relations Officer. "Everything all right?" asked Mr Sedgwick. In proof that it was, the windows were opened for the first time in four years.'

I thought this a touching little story and wished war had more of these happy endings. That an Englishman and an American should have been the first to arrive together at this shrine of the English language was pleasantly symbolic, and the moment was not lost upon the faithful Italian guardian of the Keats House.

Many visitors go, as I did, from the Keats House to the Protestant Cemetery, near the Gate of St Paul, where the poet is buried. This must be the most beautiful cemetery in the world and is certainly the best tended. It is administered by a committee of ambassadors and is fortunate in having as its superintendent Commendatore Marcello Piermattei, who is a walking dictionary of international biography. The cypress trees cast their long shadows upon the most extraordinary collection of exiles ever assembled in one place. Every few yards, as you glance at the headstones on the closely packed tombs, a name recalls some memory to you.

Keats and his devoted Severn lie near together; the ashes of Shelley are interred near those of his strange, romantic friend, Trelawny, who snatched the poet's heart from the flames of his funeral pyre at Viareggio. The unexpected name of R. M.

Ballantyne came to me like a memory of schooldays. I remem-bered the time so long ago when *Coral Island* was a gateway of enchantment, and I wondered how many modern boys have ever heard of it. Signor Piermattei told me that Ballantyne came to Rome, a sick man, in 1893, and died the year after.

Every few yards were the names of old friends and acquain-tances: Story and his wife, the American friends of the Brownings, John Gibson, sculptor, once so famous; those industrious writers, William and Mary Howitt, who settled in Rome and devoted themselves to animal welfare and eucalyptus trees; Goethe's only son, August; John Addington Symonds; and many another.

We came to the memorial to pretty Rosa Bathurst, the young beauty described so well by Cecil Roberts in *The Remarkable Young Man*, whose tragic death in 1824 plunged the foreign colony into gloom. She was riding with some friends along a narrow track above the Tiber when her horse slipped and fell with her into the flooded river. In an instant both horse and rider were swept away, and poor Rosa's body disappeared. It was an extraordinary coincidence that fifteen years previously her father, Benjamin Bathurst, had vanished even more mysteriously while acting as envoy to the court of Vienna. He was returning to England with important despatches, but vanished on the road between Berlin and Hamburg and was never heard of again.

We came to the grave I was most anxious to see, that of Charles Andrew Mills, of the Villa Mills, who entertained so many visitors on the Palatine during the first half of the last century. Though he appears in innumerable diaries and travel books, not one writer has left any account of him or his origin. He has gone down to history as an 'eccentric Scot', although he was a Scot only on his mother's side, and his eccentricity is doubtful if it rests merely on the transformation of the Villa Spada on the Palatine into a fashionable Gothic residence. Mills was, I suspect, a snob, and perhaps one of those expatriate Britons who achieved abroad a social distinction they may not have enjoyed at home. Neverthe-less he seems to have been a kindly and generous host, and Lady Blessington thought him 'amiable'. His interest is simply that he was the last inhabitant of the Palatine Hill. In his improbable

Gothic villa decorated everywhere with medallions representing the rose, the thistle, and the shamrock, and approached by gate-posts upon which were sculptured thistles, he entertained his guests in the ruins of Domitian's palace. Some visitors thought the villa and its flower beds had introduced a touch of suburbia to the Palatine, and perhaps they did. Mills has been variously and wrongly identified as Sir Charles Mills, the banker, and as the Mills who helped to found the Garrick Club.*

His grave is in Shelley's Section of the cemetery, number seventeen in the twelfth row, and the books of the cemetery contain the following notice: 'Charles Andreas Mills Esq. Inglese di anni 86 mori il 3 Ottobre 1846.' Unfortunately the grave is on the list of those which are not to be renewed, for no member of the family has ever paid for the concession of the plot or the care of the plain travertine plate which records the name of the last man to give a dinner party on the Palatine.

Only a few yards from the Protestant Cemetery are the graves of some four hundred British soldiers who died in or around Rome during the last war. Their relatives may think of them at rest in an English garden of green turf and flowers, and in the shade of trees within a few paces of the Gate of St Paul. While I was there, I saw the sight that always wrings the heart, of parents slowly passing along the line of geometrical crosses, seeking the graves of their sons.

The most striking feature of the scene is an isolated hill which rises immediately behind the British war cemetery to the height of over a hundred feet. It is as gaunt as a slag heap, and a cross has been erected on the summit. This is an artificial hill made of pottery, the largest collection of Roman pottery in the world. In ancient times the sherds from the neighbouring docks were piled there century after century, and though the docks have vanished, this curious hill remains and is evidently indestructible. The *amphora* was the standard measure, even of grain, in ancient times, and grain was never shipped in bulk, because of the danger of the cargo shifting from side to side of the ship. Among the imports which arrived in *amphorae* were oil, wax, wine, pitch,

* See Appendix, page 417

honey, olives and grain. Whenever an *amphora* was broken in transit, or during unloading, it was thrown on this space, which had been set apart by the magistrates.

I climbed all over the hill, whose name is Monte Testaccio—Mount Potsherd—and I thought it one of the most curious and fascinating relics in Rome. Vegetation can obtain no foothold, and at every upward step I dislodged a shower of pottery, and when I thrust a stick into the side of the hill I disturbed and pulled out fragments of pots and the handles of *amphorae* which had been buried and hidden for centuries. The great mass of this pottery came, I believe, from Mauretania, which is now North Africa, and from Baetica, which is Andalusia, in Spain. Some of the potters stamped the handles of the *amphorae* with their initials, and in scrambling about I dislodged two or three of these. The discovery aroused my fervour, and I went hunting about until my pockets bulged with potters' stamps. Two small boys who were playing on the hill thought it might be greater fun to assist me, and in fifteen minutes we had assembled such a large pile that I begged them to seek no more.

Monte Testaccio shares with the Catacombs the distinction of being the only memory in Rome of the ordinary life of common people. One looks in amazement at this vast mountain of broken pottery, seeing in imagination the beautiful ships moving across the Mediterranean with their cargoes of grain and honey. The vast pile speaks of grain warehouses and markets, of slaves out shopping and housewives with their baskets. Maybe somewhere in the incredible mound is a pot whose contents found their way to the table of Lucullus; perhaps there is still hiding in the interior a portion of a jar whose Spanish olives may have been eaten by Augustus, or nibbled by Horace.

At the foot of the mound all kinds of cellars and wine shops have been excavated in the pottery. Some of them go quite a distance into the hill, whose peculiar insulation keeps wine cool and at an even temperature all the year round.

§ 9

It was a perfect day for the Gardens of the Villa d'Este at Tivoli, which I had never seen. Rome sweltered in the airless heat and I thought it an ideal moment for what the Romans call a *scampagnata*.

The train sped out across the Campagna towards the Sabine Mountains, some thirty miles away, and the only people with me in the compartment were a young bearded French artist and his wife. They were travelling through Italy with bicycles, pausing for a day to two when he felt like painting or sketching, then moving on. Their method was the admirable one of taking the train from place to place and using each new town as a centre from which to bicycle into the surrounding country. The young man was arrogant and rather rude to his pretty young wife, who did not seem to mind. She clearly looked upon him as a genius, and, like a true artist, he imposed upon her. He had modelled himself on the hirsute Latin Quarter of the nineteenth century and she, with a fringe on her forehead and her almond-shaped eyes, might have sipped Pernod with Manet. I do not know enough about modern art to say whether the sketches produced from the bulging portfolio were good, but I did after a little difficulty recognize the Casino Borghese, the Pincio, and the temple of Aesculapius in the Borghese Gardens. I may have been looking at the work of some future Van Gogh, but I rather doubt it.

They both loved the Italians, though they excepted the Romans, whom they considered grasping and unsympathetic. The girl was entirely wrapped up in her touchy and acid husband and would never venture an opinion without first looking to him for approval. I thought she had a good deal to learn and was piling up trouble for the future. In the meantime the antique landscape with its farms like old fortresses, its olive groves and its cattle, had lifted towards the hills; and we were soon at Tivoli. My young friends immediately festooned their bicycles with their belongings and vanished lovingly down the road.

It is extraordinary how the air in summer alters after an hour's journey from Rome, and even at an altitude, like that of Tivoli, of only about seven hundred feet above the sea. It makes the ancient Roman passion for the country villa comprehensible and explains the constant summer wanderings of Pliny, Horace, Maecenas, and other old friends from the banks of the Tiber to the hills. I walked on through the little town and came to the famous cascades where the river Anio takes a tremendous leap into the valley below. And glancing up I saw in the distance, high on the edge of a hill, the pretty little circular temple of the Sybil, wearing its low roof like a hat on a tanagra figure. I suppose of all the relics of antiquity this is the one most frequently reproduced in the English countryside by our forebears. Like the Colosseum, it is something one has always known, yet it was a surprise to see it standing up there, looking so exactly like an old aquatint.

The entrance to the Villa d'Este was damp and decayed, and unlike what I had imagined it would be: but stepping on a terrace and looking down, I saw plumes of water shooting up above the heads of tall dark cypresses. I descended from this terrace into the sheerest fantasy. It was an extravaganza of falling water; of rising water; of water thundering up into snowy Alps under tremendous pressure; of water whispering and tinkling as it finds its way through moss and fern; of water lazily curving from the mouths of urns, and even, in some surely Freudian moment, from the breasts of sphinxes.

I came upon dark avenues flanked by colossal cypresses, nourished for centuries by the perpetual flood, where spouts of water arched from ancient masonry and gurgled away to a lower level, to be used again in some new fantasy. The old Arab extravagance of the water staircase, whose balustrades slide with rushing streams, which I seem to remember in the Gardens of the Generalife in Granada, added to the impression that I was wandering in the dream perhaps of a Bedouin or of someone from a parched land.

The creator of this water circus was Pirro Ligorio, the architect of that perfect jewel of garden design, the Casino of Pius IV in the Vatican Gardens. The man who paid for the Gardens, and who inspired them, was Cardinal Ippolito d'Este, the son of Lucrezia Borgia and Alfonso d'Este, Lord of Ferrara, whom she married, as her third husband, at the age of twenty-two.

It must occur to everyone who has sauntered about the streets of Rome that the return of water to the city after centuries of drought was one of the most spectacular events in its history. Like the Caesars, the Renaissance Popes drew rivers and lakes into Rome to transform them not into baths, but into public fountains. The Villa d'Este was only one of many similar manifestations of this rediscovery of water. Every villa of the Renaissance had its waterworks, and, reading the accounts of seventeenth century travellers, when the pure joy of making fountains had degenerated into baroque water tricks and jokes, one has the impression that it was hardly possible to visit any garden without getting drenched.

I looked carefully for water jokes in the Villa d'Este, but could find none: perhaps, after all this time, they are out of action, like the hydraulic organ. The hidden spring that released a jet of water into the face of the visitor was a jest that appealed to caliph, emperor, king and pope. No despot was able to resist the pleasure of seeing his vizier drenched. The sound of the schoolboy laughter of royal persons seems still to haunt the avenues of the Alcázar at Seville, the red hill of Granada, Versailles, and even that narrow passage at the top of Whitehall known as Spring Gardens; for the ancient jest spread everywhere.

'While the ladies are absorbed in looking at the fishes disporting themselves,' wrote Montaigne, 'you let go some spring: immediately the water spouts up from all these pipes in minute strong jets to a man's height, and fills the petticoats and thighs of the ladies with this refreshing coolness.' This was at Augsburg, but he found much the same thing at Tivoli. Like myself, Evelyn didnot discover any water jokes at Tivoli, and unfortunately Francis Mortoft, who was always getting soused in Italy, and was a perfect victim for the water joke, did not keep his Tivoli diary up-to-date.

These jokes expressed a curiously oriental sense of humour. If they were known, as I am sure they were, in the ancient world, they must have come to the west from Baghdad or Samarkand. It is not easy, however, to imagine the Romans roaring with laughter at someone with a wet toga, neither can the encrusted Byzantines have considered it amusing to be unexpectedly drenched. The gardeners of the Renaissance, however, rediscovered many other old garden devices. I was amused to come across the owl and the birds, which were not working, alas. I had never seen them before, but had read about them in the *Pneumatics* of Hero of Alexandria, who packs a book with water tricks and tells you how to make them.

The owl and the birds is quite a simple device. All that is necessary is an airtight cistern with an opening for the water to pour into from a wall fountain. Protruding from the cistern is a hollow pipe shaped like the twig of a tree, on which birds of painted wood or bronze are seated. As the air is expelled by the water, it whistles through the hollow pipe with a warbling sound like that of bird song. When the water reaches a certain height, it is siphoned into a receptacle under the cistern, which is attached to a revolving spindle on which sits the figure of an owl. As this receptacle fills, the weight of the water works a pulley which revolves the spindle, bringing the owl face to face with the birds, who fall silent, all the air having been expelled, as if startled by the appearance of the owl.

This delightful object was in working order when John Evelyn visited Tivoli in 1645, but he says that when the owl turned towards the birds, they did not become silent, but changed their notes.

As I walked about the gardens of the Villa d'Este I thought of the Renaissance gardeners as urchins delightedly dabbling in water. During heat waves in New York one sees photographs of children splashing about in streams of water played on them from fire hoses, and something of the same childlike joy in water is expressed by the fountains of Rome and of the Renaissance villas, and particularly, of course, by the Tivoli fountains.

The most interesting person associated with the Villa d'Este was Liszt, whose rippling, cascading *Fountains of the Villa d'Este* almost recreates them in the imagination. The roar of the cascades and the treble notes of the water spouts must have sung their way into his mind as he sat in the upper rooms of the villa, where he lived for years after he had been quietly ordained in order to escape a woman who was determined to marry him. While the black coat of an abbé was admirable protective colouring which saved him from the extreme penalties of his philandering, it did not put a complete stop to his adventures. And here in these melancholy shades, among the avenues of laurel and ilex, we may imagine him, a priestly, silver-haired figure, listening to the ceaseless symphony of the water.

§ 10

Horace mentions Tivoli—the ancient Tibur—as the heavenly spot in which he hoped to end his days, and his Sabine farm was not far off. Its now excavated site was so much visited in the last century that the local peasants believed Horace to be a distinguished Englishman. Every time the poet mentions Tibur it is with a caress. It is 'dew-fed Tibur'; 'breezy Tibur'; 'leisurely Tibur'; and so on, and others thought the same. All around upon the slopes of the Sabine Hills stood the villas of wealthy Romans. It is an attractive and haunted countryside, full of woods, streams, and stony slopes on which the ancient, twisted olive trees shiver and silver their leaves in the slightest wind. Even today the ploughman must often turn up a green coin or uncover a tessellated pavement.

I went down from the town to the Villa of Hadrian, and I was enthralled. Here the master of the Roman world came 'according to the custom of happy, rich people' to 'spend the last days of his life in peaceful pomp', and to devote his time to painting, music, poetry and literature.

Who could fail to be affected by this scene, and by the knowledge that Hadrian's dream of retirement was fated to end in a painful illness which no doctor could cure? It was from his villa that he went to Baiae to write the famous poem to his soul, and to die.

There are a hundred and eighty acres of Hadrian's Villa, and I must have tramped over most of them in the course of the afternoon, trying to imagine what this grand imperial estate looked like in the old days. It was surely the greatest piece of architectural

self-indulgence ever attempted by one man, and in comparison
with it the Villa d'Este and the efforts of all our eighteenth century
dilettante peers are games of nursery bricks. It was the emperor's
idea to bring together replicas of world-famous buildings which
had impressed him, so that in his retirement he could remember
the days of his imperial tours. It was much the same sentiment
that caused an eighteenth century nobleman to build a Tivoli
temple in his park.

It is impossible now to do more than climb about the foundations of the Lyceum, the Academy, the Prytaneum, the Stoa
Poikile and other famous reproductions, and to try, alas without
much hope, to reconstruct them in imagination. The replica of
the Egyptian sanctuary of Canopus must have been an extraordinary affair. In order to make it, a channel some six hundred
feet long was cut in the rock and a stream diverted into it to represent the canal which once linked the temple of Serapis with the
Nile. There were small swimming-pools and large ones, enormous
domed libraries, and a sunbathing beach whose sands were
artificially heated in the winter. In the centre of what must have
looked like a splendid international exhibition of architecture
stood the imperial palace, the residence of the court, and nearby
were the barracks of the Praetorian Guard.

Of all the strange and fascinating ruins I saw, the one which
most attracted me was a circular island dotted with the remains of
marble rooms, known, for some strange reason, as the maritime
theatre, which it could not have been. It is surrounded by a high
wall to ensure complete privacy, and the moat round the island
was crossed by a bridge on rollers which had the effect of a draw-
bridge. Once the bridge had been removed, no one could reach
the island unless he swam to it. A pleasing theory is that this was
the studio of Hadrian, who would retire there to read, write and
paint.

Hundreds of famous statues have been dug up from the villa
and are now scattered all over the world. Some are in Rome, some
in London and Berlin, others are in Dresden, Stockholm and
Leningrad: and there may be more to be discovered. In a secluded
part of the ruins I saw a light railway and men stripped to the

waist who were digging and carting away the earth in trucks. The man in charge, from whom I hoped to hear of some newly discovered treasure, would tell me nothing. Though polite, he had no desire to share with me whatever secrets the Villa of Hadrian might be about to reveal.

I took the evening train back to Rome, drowsy with fatigue and longing some day to return to Tivoli. Like a tune one cannot get out of one's head, my ears retained a steady roar and thunder of water, the voices of the white plumes of the fountains of the Villa d'Este.

§ 11

The *scirocco*, blowing all day, had filled Rome with the hot, uneasy smell of Africa. Nerves were short as they are during the Cape south-easter, and men popping about on Vespas seemed fit targets for one's exasperation. The marble in the Forum was too hot to sit on; the restaurants were encircled by nauseating whiffs of ravioli, and the asphalt of the Corso had melted into soft treacle. During the siesta I lay on my bed watching the incandescent stripes as they palpitated against the slats of the shutters, dreading the moment when I would have to go out into the airless streets again. But when I did so, something marvellous had happened: a soft, gentle wind, the *ponentino*, in which I fancied I could smell the sea, was blowing through Rome, and life was bearable again.

It was the night I had bought a ticket for *Aïda* in the Baths of Caracalla. I was driven there in a taxi by an Italian who had learnt his English behind barbed wire, like so many others during the last war. He told me he had just returned from Scotland, where he had been driving a Cadillac full of rich Americans. He loved Scotland: it had rained incessantly! Everything in Scotland was excessively *bello* or *bella*; and I thought how odd it was to be driving through this warm Roman night, past the Colosseum, with an Italian who was in ecstasies about Dunfermline and the Links o' Forth.

Half the public transport in Rome was collected round the ruins of the Baths, while the greatest crowd since the Goths had cut the aqueducts converged on them from all directions. The ruins loomed up into the night in cold detachment, disassociating themselves from the bright little buffets in their shadows, where crowds fought for sausage rolls, *pizze*, ice cream and cold drinks before the opera began.

From my seat in a segment of a gigantic semicircle I looked down towards a stage built up between two broken arches of the *calidarium*. These ruined masses of brick rose dark and tragic. They were like something imagined by Edgar Allan Poe, or like one of Piranesi's prison etchings. The old ruin, it seemed to me, was reluctant to be forced back into life. It had finished with people for ever. It had earned oblivion with bats and owls, and an occasional poet. It did not object to Shelley, but Verdi was just a little too much! The contrast between the dead giant and our bright expectant faces was a strange sight.

Then the lights went up, and I saw an Egyptian temple of stupendous proportions, and so far away. Surely human voices, even those of Italian tenors and sopranos, could not be heard across such a void? But they were. The orchestra was superb and so were the singers. The pageant was a triumph. A whole army marched on the stage, and as the famous march crashed out chariots drawn by circus horses, with ostrich plumes nodding on their heads, whirled onto the stage, culminating in the arrival of Rhadames himself in a magnificent quadriga. I was glad to have seen a real quadriga; and in Rome!

The priestesses performed their solemn measure above the tomb; down below Rhadames and Aïda sobbed their farewells. Then the lights were extinguished and we saw the ruins lying in enormous broken outlines against the stars.

There were no taxis and I set off to walk. The clocks were striking twelve when I reached the Colosseum. There was no one about and I had the monster to myself. For the first time it seemed pathetic, mouldering there in the night, tier upon tier, all the cruelty drained out of it at last. Time, as the Italians say, is such a gentleman.

§ 12

Rome is fond of floodlighting her monuments so that obelisks, palaces, the Colosseum, the Forum, all take on a hard, unwinking ghostliness as darkness falls. It is a theatrical illusion that can easily become tiresome. There must be many like myself who prefer their ruins by moonlight. The Trevi in limelight, with a noisy crowd in the foreground and the flashes of street photographers popping every few seconds, is not the happiest of memories, neither I think is the Forum improved when its few upright columns are lit.

There is, however, one place in Rome which floodlighting touches with sheer enchantment every Saturday night. It is the Piazza del Campidoglio on the Capitol. As you mount the steps which form one side of the square and see the three buildings which form the rest of it, and Marcus Aurelius rides towards you from the centre of the piazza, a bluish light reveals columns and pilasters, and white statues on roof tops: and you feel that you have stepped upon the stage of some superlative Palladian theatre. At any moment, with twittering cries and laughter, a crowd in Longhi masks might come running and scurrying round a corner to vanish with a whirl of black gowns and a glint of red heels; or it seems as though you see before you a dream of the Renaissance, idealized and perfect, washed clean of its sins.

It was a hot night when I first stood in this magic light. I thought perhaps the spirit of Rome was asleep there, while water dripped in this artificial moonlight. Rome and water and silence. On either side of the square the two museums blazed with light as if for a ball or a reception. The blinds were up, the windows were opened in the heat, and I stood in the piazza, beside Marcus Aurelius, looking up at golden ceilings and glowing frescoes in one building, while in the one opposite marble fauns and centaurs appeared to be about to turn and play their pipes.

I passed into the courtyard of the Palazzo dei Conservatori and saw something I had been vainly seeking all over Rome. It is the largest surviving fragment of the triumphal arch of white marble which Claudius erected, on what is now the Corso, to celebrate his invasion of Britain in A.D. 43. Even fairly recent books say it is let into the garden wall of the Barberini Palace, but only the scar left by its removal is to be seen there. I saw it now with the added thrill of discovery. The arch had a curious history. It was lost until the Renaissance, when a cluster of slums were pulled down and it was found hiding within them, perfectly preserved, its inscriptions and its sculptures intact. It was demolished, of course, and a hundred and thirty-six cartloads of the purest Luna marble were taken from it; and every time you visit the transept of St John Lateran, you are walking on the Arch of Claudius.

I recognized the fragment like an old friend, for not only did I know the inscription by heart, but in the days when I used to collect coins, the *aureus* of heavy, greasy gold which showed the arch, and was minted by Claudius to celebrate his conquest, was a great favourite of mine. And here, at last, was a portion of the original! There was less of it than I had expected, for it has been hewn in two so that half the inscription is missing, but the letters BRIT remain, the first four letters of Britannia.

While I was enjoying that thrill of historical association which is the charm of Rome, a party of English tourists came into the courtyard, led by a guide who pointed out all sorts of uninteresting things and took them past Rome's earliest reference to Britain without a word. I would like to have called them back and to have drawn their attention to the stone, which records the capture of Caractacus, and to ask them to imagine, as I have done so often upon the banks of the Medway and the Thames, that fantastic moment in our history when Claudius came marching through Kent with the Praetorian Guard and a corps of war elephants.

St Peter and St Paul were alive when this inscription was carved. Possibly the mason who formed those beautiful letters had put on his best toga, if he were a freeborn Roman, on the day of the triumph and had stood in the Forum to see Claudius pass with a Lord Mayor's Show of British huts and Celtic villagers, for we were not yet fair-haired 'angels'; and that day the whole of Rome must have been talking of druids, pearls, gold, tin, and the mysterious island which had now come within the confines of civilization.

Posterity has never ceased to smile at Claudius, but I can forgive much if a man is fundamentally kind, and I have the same affectionate feeling for him which one has for some eccentric don who amuses and irritates one with his peculiarities. He was really the least warlike of the Caesars, a stammering, weak pedant who had been laughed at by everyone as a boy, and pushed about by his relatives, who always expected him to do the wrong thing in public. Yet he came of a family of soldiers, and as his weak eyes were raised from his books he must often have been thinking, like many another of his kind, of great and daring deeds, but never dreaming that one day he would be Caesar. He was only sixteen days in Britain. He went there with his elephants as soon as he received a signal from his general to say that the enemy was under control; for even Caesar could not ask the Senate for a triumph unless he had been in action, or at least in the war area. And his pedantry even appeared on his arch! Scholars who have managed to piece together the missing words from fragments of the inscription have found it to be written in archaic Latin, the genitives ending not in *ae* but in *ai*.

I entered the Palazzo dei Conservatori, which, in compensation for the exasperating Roman habit of closing museums in the afternoon, was open on Saturday night; and here I found myself in a series of princely rooms, one after the other, like jewel boxes in the light of sconces under their gilt and coffered ceilings. Tremendous baroque battles were being fought on the frescoed walls; beautiful gilt chairs and console tables stood about; and no one else was there except the attendants, who rose and bowed politely as if I were a Roman prince wandering around his palace in the evening.

This is the way to see a museum in Rome, to move slowly from room to room, with the windows open to the magic night, drawn here and there to whatever pleases you. I met a hundred old friends whom I had always known, but had never met in the marble until this evening. I saw the Esquiline Venus, white, straight, and so young. And I stood gazing at an even more beautiful statue, one of the most exquisite in Rome, of a mysterious girl leaning on a wall and watching something with great attention. She is covered completely with the folds of her *stola*, which she has drawn up to her neck, and she is so full of life that I expected her to sigh suddenly and turn reluctantly away. Her hair is tied back, exposing her ears, she is bending slightly forward as she leans on her right elbow, and I could see the line of her arm beneath the marble folds of drapery. She is said to be the Muse Polymnia, one of the daughters of Zeus, and the Muse of sacred songs and the inventor of the lyre—a pagan St Cecilia: but I suspect that she was really the girl the artist loved, and everyone who sees her must love her too.

I crossed the Piazza to go to the Capitoline Museum opposite. The floodlit dream of the Renaissance was as perfect as ever, still waiting for the crowd of revellers and for music. Just beneath the arch of the Museum, in a little courtyard to himself, I saw the old villain Marforio, the famous partner in repartee of Pasquino, and one of the few ancient statues that was never buried. He is a large, portly man with the wavy hair and beard which the ancients gave to symbolic rivers, and he leans, as if at a banquet, holding a small vase from which pours a thin spout of water. It may have been the way the light was falling, but I thought him rather sinister. He has personality and I can understand how he has survived: he would be a bold man who would dare to use a hammer on him.

Upstairs, in room after room full of marble fauns, prancing centaurs, and the most wicked young Pans, I met again many an old friend. There was the Dying Gaul with his Royal Air Force moustache, who reminded me of young men one used to see in the nineteen-twenties at the Ritz or the Berkeley.

Then came the Capitoline Venus. The story is that someone anxious to preserve her from the Christians who might have sent her to the lime kilns as a pagan goddess, carefully walled her up in a hiding-place where she spent the whole of the Renaissance, emerging completely undamaged in the eighteenth century. She is one of the most beautiful of all the statues of Venus, though it is evident that the waist was not admired in ancient Rome and was a creation of the corsetted Middle Ages. When Prince Prospero Colonna was Mayor of Rome during the visit of Kaiser Wilhelm II in the early years of this century, a grand reception was held in the Campidoglio and afterwards the royal guest was conducted round the museums. The newspapers noted the interest shown by the visiting monarch in the world-famous masterpiece. What really happened was that as the Mayor of Rome and the Kaiser approached the Capitoline Venus, Prince Colonna said, 'Your Majesty, may I present my official wife?' The late Duchess of Sermoneta tells this story in her autobiography, *Things Past*.

The great number of Roman portrait busts in these galleries remind one again how closely the Victorians resembled the Romans in their appearance. There are Roman faces in the Capitoline Museum which might be those of mid-Victorian Birmingham manufacturers or temperance reformers; there are also among them Victorian statesmen, soldiers, and churchmen. Why the Roman type, which has now vanished from Rome, should have accidentally cropped up in England a century ago, I do not know, nor can I offer a guess. Having had the classics beaten into one with a birch rod can hardly be an explanation.

Like the Vatican Galleries, the Capitoline Museum is a good place to study the faces of the Caesars. Julius has the most sensitive face of all; it is the mobile face of an actor. Augustus has the saddest and the most beautiful face, Titus the most self-indulgent, and Nero the least reliable. Tiberius was not an evil-looking man and there is not a trace in his appearance of the enormities attributed to him. In some of his portraits he has the witty, malicious little mouth that I associate with some Irishmen. Caligula was clearly a spoilt and unpleasant young man; but Claudius, so often defamed, was solemn and dignified, with a thoughtful and intelligent face. The deterioration in Nero must have been appalling. He was a good-looking young man, but by the time of his suicide at the age of thirty-one he had the fat jowl and flabby neck of a debauchee of sixty.

The export of marble and bronze emperors must have been a thriving business in Rome, and the imperial image was sent out by the State to towns and cities all over the Empire, just as photographs of the reigning monarch are sent to British Embassies today. Evidently a high degree of fidelity was expected, even in places as far away as the shores of the Black Sea, from which Arrian, the historian, when governor of Trapezus, wrote to Hadrian.

'Your statue here is beautifully placed with the hand pointing out to sea. But it is not a bit like you. Please send me one from Rome to replace it.' He also asked if he could have a Hermes five feet high, and a statue of Philesius, four feet high.

One visualizes warehouses near the docks full of emperors and gods ready to be despatched to all parts of the Roman world.

As I passed between the ranks of noble Romans, I reflected that the history of shaving is an interesting subject. The first great man to shave every day was Alexander the Great, and though he set the fashion in the Hellenistic world, Rome did not copy him. The Romans of the Republic were all bearded, and we have the immortal picture of the old senators awaiting the Gauls, seated in their chairs in the Forum, silent and motionless, until one barbarian had the insolence to pull a beard to find out whether its owner was alive, when, at the insult, the old man rose and slew him. It was at least a century and a half after Alexander when the first cleanshaven faces begin to appear on the Roman coinage. The man who set the fashion was the Philhellene Scipio Aemilianus, who was born about 185 B.C., and was the first Roman who insisted on being shaved every day. Who can say how a fashion begins? The foremost men of Rome copied him and the emblem of man's wisdom and authority vanished under uncomfortable-looking bronze razors. Sulla was cleanshaven, and to imagine Julius Caesar with a beard is as unthinkable as Shakespeare or Walter Raleigh without one. All the Caesars were cleanshaven for more than a century, until Hadrian grew a beard, possibly to conceal a scar. Then followed the curled and probably scented beards of Antoninus Pius and Marcus Aurelius.

No one shaved himself, a habit which seems to have come down to many modern Italians. The rich man kept his own barber and others went to the barbers' shops, which were as fruitful a source of scandal and gossip as the fashionable women's hairdressing-saloons today. But it cost money and time to be well barbered and the plebs still grew their beards, as Martial notes more than once when he writes about 'hairy-faced farmers' and 'filthy beards', and mentions a certain Linus who had a beard as stiff as that of a Cinyphian billy-goat.

With such pleasant thoughts as these I wandered round this perfect gallery of ancient sculpture. Though I have haunted museums all my life and have suffered as much as anyone from those leaden-footed tramps down endless and unyielding marble corridors, I have never known a more friendly or a more attractive museum than the Capitoline. If anyone finds himself in Rome on a Saturday night when the Capitol is floodlit, he should go there and gather memories of Rome which will remain for ever among the perfect experiences of life.

CHAPTER SEVEN

*The Quirinal Palace – Pauline Bonaparte and her American
sister-in-law – the price of a Cardinal's hat – the Piazza Navona –
the Pantheon – the Hospital of S. Spirito*

§ 1

The time came when I decided to live in another part of
Rome. I think it was Seneca who remarked rather optimistically that every change is a delight, and Washington Irving went even further when he said that there is a certain
relief in change, even though it be for the worse; oddly enough,
there is some truth in this, for one plunges into change always
hoping for the best. Rome is now so overcrowded in summer that
most people are only too thankful to stay where they happen to
be: but by this time I was feeling a strong migratory restlessness.

My first attempts at house-hunting were a daily frustration.
Every inch of Rome's accommodation was, it seemed, booked up
for weeks ahead. I was almost resigned to failure when one morning, while walking along the broad Whitehall of Rome, the Via
Venti Settembre, I noticed the name-plate of a pensione simply
because it seemed out of place amid all the ministries and official
buildings, and on the spur of the moment I went up to the top
floor in a large mahogany lift. To my amazement I was given a
choice of rooms in an empty Swiss pensione! The place remained
a mystery to me until I left. It was like something in a novel about
the secret service, and I wondered whether I had inadvertently
given the password when I first rang the bell.

It was ready for thirty or forty guests who never came. Their
beds were ready; their places were set at table; yet I never saw
anyone except the maidservant who cooked my breakfast and
made the bed. The silence of the place, which in any other city
might have been uncanny and even rather sinister, was in Rome

too perfect to be believed. I walked as in a dream through the large flat with its empty rooms, but any attempt on my part to discover why this admirable place was empty in an overcrowded city was a sign for the servant to take refuge in what seemed to me stubborn and even hostile silence.

The building was full of varied activity that drained away in the evening and left it deserted. There were offices, private flats, doctors' reception rooms, and one enormous room whose doors were always wide open to let out the smell of new paint. Upon the floor of this room sat ten dark little girls sewing an immense scarlet carpet. Decorators moved in and added white chairs with scarlet cushions to match the carpet. It was the showroom of a fashionable *couturier*.

Here was indeed another Rome. In my old quarters, as soon as dusk fell my bedroom walls would be tinted with neon lights, the noise increased and the street seemed to have been waiting all day for the evening. Now at about six o'clock there was a clatter of chattering typists and working-girls upon the marble stairs, like evening starlings as they rushed for homeward 'buses. Outside in the Via Venti Settembre the sentries and doorkeepers saluted as ministerial cars swung out of the courtyards of the War Office and the gigantic Ministry of Finance; there was a military band as the guard was changed at the Quirinal Palace at the corner: then dusk would come and the darkness with its exquisite silence, until only a few policemen would be left standing under the archways, waiting no doubt for that mysterious moment in the night when they armed themselves with Sten guns. In the morning back came the chattering clerks and typists; the sentries would salute incoming ministers; and down the street strolled the most impressive figures in Rome, the young giants of the old Royal Horse Guards, now the Presidential Guard, on their way to the Palace, wearing brass helmets from which hung plumes of black horse-hair.

My local fountain was no longer Bernini's beautiful water-worn Triton, but the Acqua Felice, or Fountain of Moses, which, and I think unjustly, is the least admired fountain in Rome. Even those who flash past in coaches are told the story that Prospero Bresciano, the sculptor of the oddly squat and unattractive Moses, wilfully and against the advice of his friends, carved the figure directly from the travertine without making a model, and worked from a huge block lying horizontally in his studio. The unfortunate man had made no allowance for the height at which the figure would be seen, and consequently when it was unveiled and was seen to be out of proportion, the critical Roman crowd gave such a hoot of derision that Bresciano became hopelessly melancholic and at last grieved to death. The fountain is nevertheless a fine one and must have looked even better before the tall buildings and overhead cables enclosed it. With the exception of the lions in the Court of the Lions in the Alhambra, in Granada, the four amiable creatures which spout the Acqua Felice are the most amusing and friendly lions I know. I became quite attached to them, and I am sure that they never wished to eat a Christian, or do anyone a bad turn, but were always content to sit there primly whistling spouts of water from the distant Alban Hills.

It is said that when this water eventually reached Rome, brought there by Pope Sixtus V, his sister, hoping to please him, took him a cup of it. The Pope, who disliked scenes of this nature, refused to touch it, saying that it had no taste, in which, so Romans tell me, he was right. It is one of Rome's non-vintage waters. This ability to taste water and to be critical and excited about it is something which Romans share with the Spaniards. 'Do you have good drinking-water?'—which would scarcely be considered the happiest opening gambit with strangers in England— never fails to rouse Romans and Spaniards; indeed, when in doubt you can always safely talk about water, just as in England you can always criticize the climate.

§ 2

The Via Venti Settembre begins and ends with memories of Napoleon. His sister Pauline lived in the Villa Bonaparte, near the Porta Pia, and at the other end of the street is Monte Cavallo and the Quirinal Palace, the scene of Napoleon's attempt to bully and subdue the Papacy. Mrs Eaton, who saw the Quirinal in 1822, when it was still a papal residence, unkindly called it 'one of the largest and ugliest buildings extant'; but in a city where architectural masterpieces stand at every other corner, I like the low, unpretentious lines of the Quirinal and also its colour, which is that of dried orange peel. The mighty Sixtus V, who made it his residence, was born a shepherd boy, and it may have been the shepherd in him which caused him to enclose such a large tract of the Quirinal Hill. Maderna laid it out in endless and ingenious formality; and standing among the box hedges and trees it is strange to reflect that beneath the garden runs the long Quirinal tunnel, full of stale air and misty with oil and petrol fumes. Twenty-two popes have died in the Quirinal Palace and most of the conclaves of three centuries were held in it. When Victor Emmanuel II seized the palace in 1871, the attics were found to be choked with the wooden partitions and other carpentry used on those occasions to make the 'cells' of the Sacred College.

Napoleon's heavy hand fell for the first time upon Rome when French armies wearing the revolutionary tricolour entered the city in February, 1798, and the fickle Roman crowd, setting up the old cry of 'Freedom', demanded a republic. On the night of February 20 two men found their way to the Pope's apartments in the Quirinal; they were General Cervoni and an officer named Haller, a son of the Swiss botanist. Pius VI was eighty-two, frail and ill. They demanded his renunciation of temporal power. He refused. The Fisherman's Ring was pulled from his finger and he was hustled out of the palace into a carriage and out of Rome. He died in France the following year.

Five years later, when the gentle Pius VII was Pope, a messenger from Napoleon arrived at the Quirinal, asking him to officiate at the Emperor's coronation. An agnostic himself, Napoleon firmly believed in religion for others, and had restored the Church to France. The Pope consulted the Sacred College and fifteen of the twenty Cardinals advised him to accept the invitation. Accordingly, on November 2, 1804, he left Rome with a suite of six Cardinals and travelled across France 'through the midst of a kneeling people', as he expressed it.

Napoleon had erected palisades on the twists of the Alpine

passes so that the Pope should be in no danger, and when the Holy Father arrived at Fontainebleau he found that his rooms in the palace had been fitted up as a replica of those in the Quirinal. A few days before the coronation Josephine, who had been dreading the divorce that was already in Napoleon's mind, performed an act of feminine skill and cunning: she confessed to the Pope that she and Napoleon had not been married by the Church. Pius was appalled. He could have nothing to do with the coronation! Expecting a storm of rage when he faced the Emperor with this problem, Pius received instead a smile and a shrug. Napoleon ordered candles to be lit in the chapel of the palace and there and then he was married to Josephine by a Cardinal.

On the following December morning, grey and threatening, but with a gleam of sunlight as the hero approached, the Pope sat waiting in Notre Dame while a distant thud of guns told of Napoleon's arrival. The Pontiff, surrounded by his Cardinals, wore a cope of cloth of gold and a triple crown that sparkled with diamonds. Napoleon entered grasping a sceptre, wearing a laurel wreath of gold, and covered with a mantle of purple sewn with the golden bees which had been found in 1653 in the tomb of the Frankish king, Childeric. Madame Junot, who was within a few paces of the high altar, saw Napoleon several times check a yawn. When the Pope anointed him on his head and both hands, 'I fancied from the direction of his eyes,' she wrote, 'that he was thinking of wiping off the oil'. As the Pope was about to take the crown from the altar, Napoleon took it and placed it upon his own head. He then crowned Josephine, almost playfully, thought Madame Junot, as if he were trying on a new hat: 'he put it on, then took it off, and finally put it on again, as if to promise her she should wear it gracefully and lightly.'

The rift between France and the Holy See became complete five years later. Napoleon proclaimed the Papal States to be part of the French Empire, and Rome was to be a free imperial city with the Pope its bishop. Pius replied by excommunicating Napoleon, and the Emperor then ordered the arrest of the Pope. At two o'clock on the morning of July 6, 1809, French soldiers quietly over-powered the Papal Guard at the Quirinal while General Radet quickly made his way to the room where the Pope stood waiting with his Secretary of State, Cardinal Pacca. As Pius VI had done eleven years previously, Pius VII refused to renounce the temporal power, upon which the General forced him to descend the staircase to the piazza, where a coach was waiting.

It was a calm, starlit night, and Rome was asleep, unconscious of the drama that was being staged on the Quirinal. The Holy Father, his face wet with tears, solemnly extended his arms in blessing over the sleeping city, then took his seat in the coach with Cardinal Pacca. As the coach rattled out of Rome, the Pope realized that he had been hustled away without even his spectacles. He opened his purse. He had one *papetto*, which was about tenpence. The Cardinal of State had three *grossi*, which were worth sevenpence. There followed six years of terrible humiliations and trials, but at the end of that time Napoleon was in St Helena and Pius VII, then aged seventy-four and worn out with fighting the conqueror of Europe, returned to the Quirinal. He survived Napoleon by two years and, with a superb gesture of charity, welcomed Napoleon's mother, the wonderful Madame Mère, when she made her home in Rome after the battle of Waterloo. That amazing old woman is last seen against a background of old palaces, a sad figure in black who aroused the pity and admiration of all. She was a shrewd businesswoman, however, and was able to lend money to the Holy See at a lesser rate of interest than that charged by the banker Torlonia.

So one ponders in the Piazza del Quirinale . . . but there was a third escape. One night in November, 1848, a hackney coachman was ordered to wait at a rarely used door in the long palace wall. At length he heard someone on the other side opening the door with difficulty and two figures emerged, a servant carrying some baggage and a middle-aged priest, a muffler round his throat, and a shovel hat upon his head. The coachman must have thought it rather strange that when the servant opened the coach door, he dropped down on his knees as the priest entered. From inside the cab the servant kept on directing the driver by winding streets until they came to a dark and deserted quarter at the back of the Colosseum, where the travelling-carriage of the Bavarian

Minister, drawn by six horses, was waiting. In this way Pius IX fled in disguise from the revolutionary crowds who had assassinated his Prime Minister and his chief secretary, and were even then sniping at the Swiss Guard.

The major-domo had packed the Pope's three-cornered hat, his red slippers, his breviary, a change of linen, a bundle of private and confidential papers, and a little box full of gold papal medals. Meanwhile the pretence was kept up in the Quirinal that the Pope was still there. Lights were placed in his study, a prelate entered with documents, his chamberlain went in as if to read his breviary and the office for the day; the Pope's supper was carried in as usual; then it was stated that His Holiness had retired to rest, and the attendants and the Guard of Honour were dismissed for the night.

When the Pope's flight was known, a people's republic was proclaimed, but the Papal government was restored in two years' time by the French. By one of the ironies of history, it was Napoleon's nephew, Napoleon III, who invited the Pope to return. And Pius was still there twenty years later, older and sadder, when the army of Victor Emmanuel entered Rome on *Venti Settembre*, 1870. As the troops of united Italy poured into Rome some diplomats, anxious for the safety of the Pontiff, asked for an audience at the Vatican. The Pope told them that he did not think he had anything to fear, though he reflected that one of the generals had threatened to throw him in the Tiber.

'Only yesterday,' he said, 'I received a communication from the young gentlemen of the American College, begging, I should say demanding, permission to arm themselves and to constitute themselves the defenders of my person. Though there are few in Rome in whose hands I should feel more secure than in the hands of these young Americans, I declined their generous offer with thanks. . . . The poor old Pope has now no one on earth upon whom he can rely. Relief must come from heaven.'

This was so true that even diplomats were silent. In the whole world the only country to protest against the seizure of Rome and the end of that curious organization, the Papal States, was the Republic of Ecuador. The Quirinal Palace now became the King's palace and the Pope became the 'Prisoner of the Vatican'.

In the evening when the sun is setting behind St Peter's, the President's guard is marched out of the Quirinal to drum taps and shrill infantry trumpets. The two white marble horsemen tame their Greek steeds beneath a granite obelisk. A fat plume of water rises a little way in a fountain basin, and spills itself into a larger one beneath. This is the marble trough that once stood near the Temple of Castor and Pollux when the Forum was the 'Field of Cows'. You can see it in the engravings of Piranesi and Giuseppe Vasi and others of that time. So dusk comes to the Piazza del Quirinale, with its memories of Popes and Kings and the actions and reactions which are life.

§ 3

One of the guests at a luncheon party happened to mention that he had visited that beautiful mustard-coloured palace in a park, the Casino Borghese. He was asked if he had seen Canova's celebrated statue of Pauline Borghese reclining as Venus upon an Empire couch, one hand to her pretty head, the other delicately holding the apple of Paris.

He had; and he wondered whether, had she lived to-day, Napoleon's flighty sister would have been considered such a beauty. A young Italian argued that modern women have an infinitely higher standard of beauty than women born before the age of the cinema and cheap cosmetics, and drew a sad picture of Pauline passing unnoticed today among the crowds on the Lido. Perhaps there is some truth in this. Nowadays even the Gunning sisters might cross St James's Park without causing any comment.

The conversation then turned to Pauline and her peculiarities. She was twenty-three when she married, as her second husband, the dull but worthy Prince Borghese, who, though he covered her with the family diamonds, got little from her but contempt and tantrums. Someone mentioned her fantastic clothes and jewels, her habit of making footstools of her ladies-in-waiting, the huge negro who carried her to her bath; her use of illness as emotional blackmail, and, of course, the long procession of her lovers, the handsome hussars, artists, actors and musicians. The young man, who perhaps wished to impress us with his cynical knowledge of women, said that, like many another celebrated enchantress, Pauline cared little for love but only for herself. Though not a particularly original thought, someone asked him to elaborate it.

'It is so simple,' he said. 'A love affair was the only way she could prove to herself that her attractions were still as great as ever.'

'Or that she was still able to make other women jealous and unhappy,' put in an old man at the end of the table, whom I had imagined to have taken no interest in the conversation.

When we were leaving, I found myself descending the stairs with him.

'She was perfectly proportioned,' he remarked, 'but tiny,' and I realized that he was still thinking of Pauline Borghese. 'I'll tell you how I know. Many years ago I entered the Borghese vault in Santa Maria Maggiore. In that awesome spot, among all the dust, the tarnished metal and the tattered velvet, where the coffins of two Popes, Paul V and Clement VIII, lie with those of Cardinals, princes and princesses, I saw one coffin hardly larger than a child's. It had no name on it, for the family had grown to detest her. It was the coffin of Pauline Borghese.'

The next time I visited the Casino Borghese I paid closer attention to Canova's statue. One might have been in the presence of Pauline herself and the pose was one she adopted to the end of her life. Even in an age when nudity was fashionable, the statue was thought to be rather daring, except by Pauline. A woman friend once asked how she could have posed almost naked. 'Oh, there was a stove in the studio,' was her reply.

I thought the statue an unusual sidelight on the character of a vain and beautiful woman, and I doubt whether a similar wedding present has ever originated in the mind of a young wife; for such one might call it. Pauline sat for it at her own suggestion, soon after her marriage to Borghese, when she was still thrilled to find herself a wealthy princess. Canova, it seems, was at first reluctant to portray Napoleon's sister in such a pose, and tried to persuade her to be shown as Diana. This did not please her at all. She insisted on revealing herself as Venus.

How odd it is to come across the story that Prince Borghese was so shocked by his wife's statue that he kept it under lock and key, for nothing of the kind happened. It was Pauline herself in later life, long after the marriage had ceased to mean anything and when they were living apart, who, hearing that the prince had given permission for some friends to see the statue, wrote to him on January 22, 1818.

'I avail myself of this opportunity to ask you a favour; it is as follows: I know that you now and again give permission for my statue to be seen. I would like this not to happen any more—on account of the nakedness of the statue which borders on indecency. It was created only to afford you pleasure. As this is no longer the case, it is right that eyes should be withdrawn from it.'

Madame Junot, who was a gushing admirer of her own sex and was able to discover something attractive even in the repulsive Maria Luisa of Spain, thought Pauline irresistible, and says in her memoirs that Canova's statue was 'moulded from herself' and was an exact resemblance. 'It has been asserted that the artist corrected defects in the leg and bust,' she wrote. 'I have seen the legs of the princess, as all have who were moderately intimate with her—and I have observed no such defects.' There was, however, one, which Canova skilfully concealed, and about which Pauline was naturally sensitive: she had large ears with no rims to them.

She had one redeeming quality. It was absolute loyalty to her brother. She was the only woman who dared to make fun of Napoleon or who succeeded in beguiling him, and it is said that during the great days of the Empire, when all was triumph in the Tuileries, she once tried to improve his appearance.

'You are too obstinate about not wearing braces,' she said. 'Your trousers look as if they were falling off!' No other human being would have dared to speak to the Emperor like that, and he took her advice and went to Léger, the expensive tailor who made all Murat's extravagant uniforms. But Léger found him and his figure so difficult, and Napoleon such a reluctant payer, that he was relieved when the Emperor lost interest in his appearance, as he soon did. After the battle of Wagram a special messenger was sent by Napoleon to Pauline to tell her that he was safe. When the courier returned, Napoleon asked him:

'Did she give you a present?'

'No, sire.'

'I thought she wouldn't, the stingy little beast!' was Napoleon's brotherly comment. Yet when he was in need the 'stingy little beast' gave him all her jewels. She went to live with him on Elba, and when his travelling coach was captured at Waterloo her diamonds were discovered in a secret drawer. One wonders what became of them.

After the Napoleonic crash she saved enough to buy the Villa Bonaparte, which still stands near the Porta Pia, where she lived in state and drove out in a coach and four with postilions and outriders and two negro footmen mounted behind. This was the period in her life when enchanted British noblemen gathered round her, the most severely stricken being the dry and haughty Alexander Douglas, who became the tenth Duke of Hamilton. His wife, the handsome daughter of William Beckford, the author of *Vathek*, was with him in Rome at the time and cannot have seen the enslavement of her dignified husband with much pleasure; for it is said that Douglas sometimes helped Pauline to dress, and stood handing pins and ribbons to her maid, and was occasionally allowed the privilege of fitting the satin slippers to the beautiful little feet. In her will Pauline left him a gilt toilet cabinet and bequeathed to his wife two vases from her bedroom.

A note of comedy was struck when Douglas was summoned home to Scotland and left Pauline in the care of a reliable old family man, Lord Kensington, who the moment Douglas had departed fell so deeply in love with the princess that he became jealous of her doctor, and would have fought a duel with him had they been socially equal! But sad days were ahead. Napoleon's death shattered Pauline's nerves, while her vanity and pride were damaged beyond repair by her last lover, a young composer,

Giovanni Pacini. Flattered at first, the young man soon found her possessive, tiresome, and, alas, old. She also, the lifelong invalid, became eventually a truly sick woman. In her loneliness and in her everlasting need of money, she turned to her husband, Prince Borghese. This long-suffering man was by that time happily established in Florence. He was startled to receive letters containing such words as 'I want your love and your regard . . . my heart yearns for you'. He decided to fly from Italy, but Pauline pounced on him with Napoleonic speed, armed with a letter from the new Pope, Leo XII. The Holy Father recalled him to his duty as a good Catholic and a Roman prince and bade him take back his lawful wife: but it was for only three months. Pauline was dying of cancer. She faced death bravely and made her will with Napoleonic tidiness and exactitude, forgetting no one.

The most brilliant and beautiful member of the Bonaparte clan in Rome died at the age of forty-five. And what a clan it was! It is extraordinary how they all gravitated to Rome: Madame Mère, Napoleon's stately and careful mother, his brothers Lucien and Louis, his uncle, Cardinal Fesch, and later Hortense, the sprightly daughter of Josephine. Pius VII, though he had been bullied by Napoleon, magnanimously took the whole Bonaparte family under his kindly wing. He never forgot that Napoleon had restored Catholicism to France by the Concordat of 1801.

By far the most interesting of the Bonapartes was Madame Mère, who had hardly any French, and spoke the Corsican dialect of her youth. She was a stately old figure in black, and much respected in Rome, living carefully and saving every penny. Though old and almost blind at the time of Waterloo, she would have gone to St Helena at a moment's notice had she been allowed to do so. Instead, she embarked upon the strangest episode in her practical life. She fell into the hands of charlatans and became convinced that Napoleon had been miraculously transported from captivity. She survived him for sixteen years and died the year Queen Victoria ascended the throne.

The most unusual member of the family was a beautiful and witty young American woman, Elizabeth Patterson Bonaparte, who arrived in Rome from the States in 1821, with her son, Jerome Napoleon, aged fourteen. She was the repudiated wife of Napoleon's brother.

When Jerome was nineteen, and was serving with the French Navy in the West Indies, he found his way to the States. In Baltimore he met Elizabeth Patterson, the daughter of one of the richest men in New England. Patterson had emigrated from Ireland in 1766 and had made a great fortune in arms and ammunition during the American Revolution. Elizabeth, who was eighteen, fell in love with the young Frenchman and he with her. Patterson opposed the marriage, shrewdly scenting the opposition of Napoleon, but Elizabeth was a headstrong and ambitious girl and her father saw that opposition was futile. Warned by a sixth sense that Napoleon would try to break the marriage, he did what he could to make it as binding as possible. Though a Presbyterian, he arranged a Roman Catholic wedding, which was solemnized on Christmas Eve in 1803 by Archbishop Carrol of Baltimore, and attended by all the most prominent people in the state.

Then, as Patterson had foreseen, the storm broke. Napoleon was furious, for he had other plans for Jerome. He ordered his brother to return to France at once, and alone. Jerome disobeyed and did not return for two years. He then sailed in a ship owned by his father-in-law and accompanied by his wife. As soon as they reached Europe they found that orders had been issued everywhere that Elizabeth was not to land on French territory. While Jerome went alone to face Napoleon's anger, Elizabeth travelled to England, where her son, Jerome Napoleon, was born in Camberwell in 1805.

Unlike his brother, Lucien, who had also married against Napoleon's wishes but had resigned all part in the imperial scheme rather than give up his wife, Jerome weakly allowed himself to be dominated by the Emperor. As Pius VII refused to annul the marriage, a French Council of State issued a decree of divorce. Jerome was sent to sea and two years later was made King of Westphalia and married to Princess Catherine of Würtemberg. Napoleon gave Elizabeth Patterson an annual pension on condition that she remained in America and renounced the name of Bonaparte, which she did. When Napoleon was sent to St

Helena, she felt that the agreement was at an end, and obtained a divorce from Jerome by a special act of the Maryland legislature before setting off for Europe.

The arrival of the attractive and witty young American Bonaparte, with her strange history and her handsome son, caused a great sensation, especially among members of the clan. It was Pauline Borghese who invited her American sister-in-law to Rome and introduced her and Jerome Napoleon to society. All the other Bonapartes were kind and affable, but, as Elizabeth soon realized, they were either hard up or spendthrifts and nothing material could be expected from them.

Elizabeth was a cynical and ambitious woman whose main interest in life was money and rank. She was a snob, but then most people were in the nineteenth century, and she detested America and Americans. In the course of her long stay in Europe—she spent the best part of twenty-five years there—she wrote innumerable letters to her father about money, rank, and her dislike of her own country.

'I hated and loathed a residence in Baltimore so much,' she wrote in one letter, 'that when I thought I was to spend my life there I tried to screw up courage to the point of committing suicide.'

American men were in her eyes insufferable.

'The men are all merchants; and commerce, although it may fill the purse, clogs the brain. Beyond their counting houses they possess not a single idea.' She also thought them simple where women were concerned.

'Women in all countries,' she wrote, 'have wonderful cunning in their intercourse with men; they succeed better in America because the men are a century behind them in knowledge of human nature. . . .'

As she circulated sedately in European society, she became more regal than royalty. Though she had been shamefully treated by Jerome, it was the great pride of her life that she had married Napoleon's brother. What a wonderful wife she would have made for Napoleon himself! With Elizabeth Patterson as empress, Waterloo might never have happened.

Her great ambition was a splendid European marriage for her son. Unfortunately for her, he returned to America alone and married a Baltimore girl. She received the news in Florence.

'When I first heard that my son could condescend to marry anyone in Baltimore, I nearly went mad,' she wrote to her father. 'I educated my son with the intention of his living in Europe. I always told him and you that he never should degrade himself by marrying an American.'

This blow was followed by another, almost as severe. Patterson died leaving her less than she had expected and revenged himself by the following words in his will. 'The conduct of my daughter, Betsey, has through life been so disobedient that in no instance has she ever consulted my opinions or feelings; indeed, she has caused me more anxiety and trouble than all my other children put together, and her folly and misconduct have occasioned me a train of expense that first and last has cost me much money.'

She returned to live in America at the age of forty-nine. She had become a notable miser, and lived in a series of boarding-houses in Baltimore as if she were penniless. She became a strange old character, who always carried a red umbrella and a carpet bag, and her room was stacked with travelling trunks full of the European fashions of the past. She often took out a ball dress given to her in the old days by Pauline Borghese, and she had carefully preserved her husband's wedding-coat. She loved to talk of her past triumphs, and once asked someone who had recently returned from Europe if 'she had not heard of her beauty on the Continent'. When she died at the age of ninety-four she left a fortune of a million and a half dollars. The mother of the Baltimore Bonapartes, who should by right have been a queen, died in 1879 leaving much of this wealth to two grandsons, Jerome Napoleon and Charles Joseph.

Jerome became a distinguished soldier and, resigning from the American army, served in France under his cousin, Napoleon III. He was present at Balaclava, Inkerman and Sedan, and was one of those who escorted the Empress Eugénie into exile in England. The younger brother, Charles Joseph Bonaparte, became Secretary of the Navy in Theodore Roosevelt's administration of 1905, and was later Attorney General of the United States.

The American Bonapartes became extinct in 1945 when a childless old gentleman, called, inevitably, Jerome Napoleon, tripped and fell over his wife's dog leash near Central Park in New York, and died from his injuries. But the family continues in the female line on the Continent, a thought which would have compensated Elizabeth Patterson for many a sad and angry moment.

Napoleon intended to make Rome his second capital and he dreamed of standing upon the Capitoline Hill like another Augustus. Though his armies occupied Rome, and though he had abducted one Pope and humiliated another, he never ventured to enter the scene he had reserved for his final triumph. His influence on Rome and Italy were so great that one looks round for some visible sign of it: but there is only the Piazza del Popolo and the Pincian Gardens, which his architects had transformed.

The thought of Rome seems always to have been in his mind. When Marie-Louise's son was born, he was proudly given the title of 'The King of Rome', which belonged of right to the Pope. This was the young man known to Bonapartists as Napoleon II, to others as the Duke of Reichstadt, and to romance as l'Aiglon, who died at the age of twenty-one.

Those who wish to draw near to these memories should go to the beautifully arranged Napoleonic Museum in the Palazzo Primoli, at the end of the Via Condotti. Here are to be seen the portraits and personal treasures of the Bonapartes, autographs, letters, regal robes and dinner services. There is a room devoted to the gay Pauline. I felt that the unfortunate and deeply wronged Elizabeth Patterson should have been represented by at least a photograph, for she survived into the days of the camera. One of the most touching relics is a little box of precious woods containing the milk teeth of l'Aiglon.

§ 4

More than most men, priests must be the despair of their tailors: those rusty cassocks and old hats, those broad-toed unpolished shoes! Possibly St Jerome's savage attack on fashionable fifth century priests with their curled and scented locks, walking on tip-toe lest they should soil their feet, may have had a chilling effect ever since on any latent Brummellism in the Church. Though, if anyone wishes to see how smart a priest could look, he should go to Gammarelli and the other ecclesiastical outfitters in the Piazza della Minerva, not far from the Pantheon.

This is the Savile Row of ecclesiastical Rome. The windows display a fine selection of sombre hats, an occasional mitre, birettas, little cloth-covered violet and red buttons, braids and piping of various colours, strong shoes that look as though they could inflict a mighty kick on the devil, and those beautifully made skull caps, white for the Pope, red for a Cardinal, purple for a bishop, and black for ordinary priests, known as a *zucchetto*. After the death of a Pope, Gammarelli has the privilege, while the Conclave is electing the new Pontiff, of making three white papal cassocks, one for a tall figure, one for a medium, and one for a small, so that no matter which member of the Sacred College is elected, he can be clothed immediately in a white *zimarra* and conducted to the portico above St Peter's to give his first papal blessing. The only occasion in recent history when Gammarelli was at fault was on the election of Benedict XV, who was so tiny that the smallest of the three cassocks was too large and had to be pinned up before he could appear in public. Up to 1566 the Pope wore red, but in that year Pius V, a Dominican, was elected, and continued to wear his white habit, and the Holy Father has worn white ever since. His hat and his *mozzetta*, which is a little fur-edged velvet cape, his stole and his shoes, are, however, still red.

I have always thought that the most romantic of all headgear is the red hat of a Cardinal. This remarkable object sails majestically through history and art. In Rome you see it, old and dusty, hanging, many-tasselled, from the arches of a titular church to which it has been bequeathed by its owner. I looked in vain for a red hat in the windows of these shops, and was told it is not an article which is kept in stock, but is made only to order. I was also told that Cardinals' hats are not what they once were. They are now merely symbols and are never worn: the crown has almost ceased to exist and the famous hat is nothing more than a wide, stiff brim from which hang fifteen tassels. Nevertheless, they cost £20 each. There is a story that Cardinals owe these hats to a woman, the Countess of Flanders, who at the Council of Lyons, in 1145, complained that she could not distinguish the Cardinals in their mitres from abbots and other great persons, for their distinctive dress had not yet developed. From the time of Boniface VIII, in 1297, the colour worn by Cardinals was royal purple, but in 1464 Paul II, who loved to surround himself with magnificence, put the Sacred College into scarlet, though Cardinals still wear purple in Lent and Advent, and during a Conclave. At such times you can tell a Cardinal from a Bishop only by his red *zucchetto* and red stockings. John Evelyn was told in Rome that the Jews used to wear red hats by order until one day a short-sighted Cardinal saluted one of them, thinking him a fellow member of the Sacred College, after which the Jews were made to wear yellow!

When discussing the dress of a Cardinal, the manner of the ecclesiastical outfitter becomes hushed and reverent, much as a military tailor must contemplate, even in these informal days, the full dress uniform of a field-marshal. Of all the members of the Roman Church, the Pope not excepted, a Cardinal is the most dressy and has the largest wardrobe. His everyday costume is a black soutane and short black cape edged with scarlet piping, scarlet cloth-covered buttons and scarlet buttonholes. With this he wears a scarlet sash and stock—which is the right name for that flash of colour beneath a clerical collar—and scarlet stockings. Out of doors he wears an ordinary priest's hat trimmed with red silk ribbon and with fifteen gold tassels. In formal dress a Cardinal wears a full cloak of scarlet silk over his black soutane, and on state occasions his soutane is scarlet, worn with a lace rochet and a short round cape called a *mantelle ta*, which opens for the arms.

He needs an even more sumptuous outfit for papal functions, corresponding to court dress. This is a scarlet soutane with a train, a lace rochet, and a large, circular scarlet silk cloak cut like the ancient Roman *paenula*, which is drawn up over the arms in front and spreads out behind into a long train called the *cappa magna*. This cape has a hood of scarlet silk (covered with ermine for warmth from October 25 to April 25), and in the days when the red hat was worn, it was put on over this hood, as seen in old portraits. The skull cap, the *biretta*, the stockings and gloves are all of scarlet.

Cardinals today are no longer millionaires, neither do they drive about in the heavy coaches drawn by black stallions which were such a notable feature of Roman streets a century or so ago; but they have the status of princes. In Roman society it is customary for a Cardinal to be met at the foot of the stairs by servants with lighted candles, who escort him to the reception rooms and wait to precede him, when he leaves, to his car. A Cardinal's dwelling, no matter how humble, is still his 'palace', and he is entitled to keep a throne there, but it must face the wall and may never be used except when the Pope is dead and before his successor has been elected. There are about ten days during an interregnum in which a Cardinal can turn his throne round and sit in it before he attends the Conclave.

The sacerdotal outfitter must be as well versed in the minutiae of church ceremonial and custom as those skilled gentlemen in Covent Garden who fit out peers, generals and ambassadors by the hundred for state functions, and whose voices may be heard lifted in pain and dismay from the fitting-rooms when some much decorated client mixes the order of his honours. The experts of the Piazza della Minerva know that Catholic bishops have worn a purple *biretta* only since 1869, when Pope Pius IX, going into St Peter's one day and seeing them with their black *birettas*, thought they should be distinguished from ordinary priests. They know how to dress a Monsignor di Mantelletta for the street, for a *Cappella Papale*, for society and for church, and how to turn out a Monsignor di Mantellone for the same occasions, and how the dress of the Canons of St Peter's, the Lateran and S. Maria

Maggiore differs from that of the other Roman chapters.

The tailor warmed to his work when he saw my interest in these unusual matters and confessed to me in a solemn whisper, and with head-shaking, that he was gravely worried by a slight change in the colour of the episcopal violet.

Nothing interested me more than the beautiful gloves worn by the Pope and the Cardinals at those portions of the mass—up to the *lavabo*—when they are seated and wearing a mitre. As in ancient and mediaeval times, the ring is worn outside the glove, upon the third finger. I was told that a special kind of glove is made for dead Popes and Cardinals. Nowadays a Pope is buried in red gloves and a Cardinal in violet, but this was not always so. When the tomb of Boniface VIII, who died in 1303, was opened, he was found to be wearing white silk gloves covered with pearls.

While we were discussing these matters a cleric entered with a fine Irish-American accent, a big, muscular Christian with the figure of a New York traffic cop. He said: 'Is my fitting ready?'— whereupon a man with a tape-measure over his shoulder, who had been lurking near a rampart of ecclesiastical serge, glided out and led him into a fitting-room. The cleric had recently been made a bishop and had to buy a completely new outfit.

Two young French seminarists entered to buy a collar. While they were waiting for it to be wrapped up, they admired a golden mitre which was being shown to me. I placed it in their hands and said:

'Well, there you are. You will each have one of your own some day!'

They blushed like Sandhurst cadets who had been given a vision of a field marshal's baton.

The Irish-American emerged, still in his old clothes, but already, I thought, looking a little prelatial.

Between the Pantheon and the Corso are three of the most resplendent churches in Rome. They are encrusted with splendour. Cherubs fly about, angels blow trumpets, the altars gleam with the blue of lapis lazuli and the green of malachite; and in two of them lie the bodies of two of the most remarkable people who have ever lived, a man and a woman. Under the altar of S. Maria sopra Minerva is an illuminated coffin in which lies, small and frail, the body of a Dominican nun wearing a crown and holding a silver olive branch. This is the body of St Catherine of Siena, who endured almost unbelievable austerities and died at the age of thirty-three, having played a great part in world politics. She it was who cajoled Gregory XI, persuading him to leave Avignon and restore the Holy See in Rome.

In the ornate splendour of the Gesù lie the bones of the Spanish soldier, S. Ignatius Loyola, who founded the Society of Jesus. His life, like that of St Catherine, is a record of incredible difficulties and hardships conquered by faith; and nowhere but in Rome could one stand within the space of a few yards at two such shrines. The third church is that of S. Ignazio, whose splendours are over-whelming.

How clearly the Christian phoenix rises from its pagan ashes in this part of Rome, and nowhere more gracefully, than in S. Agostino, where the Madonna of Birth presides like Juno Lucina over expectant mothers. The wall nearby is covered with quaint and touching little pictures painted by devotees to illustrate the various dangers and predicaments from which the Virgin had extricated them.

§ 5

The Roman piazza, whose ancestor was the Forum and whose children are the squares of Europe, is capable of great variety. A piazza can be a junction, like the Piazza dell' Esedra and the Piazza Venezia; it can also be a backwater hardly more than a slightly wider street, like the Piazza dei Santi Apostoli, or the tiny Piazza Mattei, which nevertheless holds the most enchanting fountain in Rome—the Fountain of the Tortoises—or it can be a little local exchange where men are always discussing employment and suchlike things, as they do in the Piazza della Rotonda, opposite the Pantheon.

Those which linger in my memory are the Piazza di Spagna, with its ochre houses and its sweep of steps; the Piazza dell' Esedra with the gaunt pink ruins of the Baths of Diocletian in the background; the Piazza Colonna with its cafés and the surging Corso; the Piazza Barberini, with the Triton sitting so calmly in a traffic roundabout; and the Piazza del Popolo, in which you take your life in your hands whenever you leave the pavement. Neither the Piazza del Campidoglio nor that of St Peter's comes within the normal category.

Of all the piazze in Rome the one which gave me the greatest pleasure was the Piazza Navona, near the Pantheon, in the old Campus Martius. It is a long, narrow piazza whose shape corresponds to that of the stadium of Domitian which once stood there, and I do not know of a more striking illustration of the process which has continued throughout Roman history of the transformation of the old into the new. The piazza still looks like a Roman racecourse. When a taxi rushes from a side street and encircles the piazza, it is repeating on the same ground the course of ancient chariots, and even the *spina* of the stadium is represented today by the three groups of statuesque fountains in the centre.

In the cellars of the houses are to be seen the well-preserved foundations of the seats and corridors of the stadium, and the most accessible are those beneath the church of St Agnes. A priest took me down into an ancient Roman brothel, which is the strange shrine preserved in this church: it is the place where St Agnes was flung naked, and where her hair covered her and she received a miraculous garment of light. The three or four rooms covered with frescoes, unfortunately now peeling from the walls with damp, clearly show the *fornix*, or arch, of the old stadium.

The chief features of the piazza are the uninhibited fountains by Bernini and his pupils. The Fountain of the Rivers is fascinating, and though I admired the vigorous figures, I thought there was a faint touch of absurdity about the Nile, with its shrouded head, for its source was then a mystery, the horse plunging out of the cavern, the lion slinking down to drink; and the heavy obelisk resting, apparently, on nothing: but I returned time after time to enjoy them and the splash of water which had come underground from the Trevi and was on its way, with typical Roman wastefulness where water is concerned, to the Tiber.

In the eyes of Pope Urban VIII Bernini could do no wrong. At that time there were two other artists in the same happy situation: Velazquez in Spain, who was steadily painting the ever more upward mustachios of Philip IV, and Van Dyck in London, whose studio at Blackfriars was so frequently visited by Charles I. Though Bernini in his long life of over eighty years served eight Popes and filled Rome with his exuberant genius, no one gave him greater admiration and encouragement than Urban VIII, and he, of course, knew only Bernini's earlier works, the Barberini Palace, the Triton, and the baldacchino in St Peter's. It is recorded that after his election Urban VIII summoned Bernini and said: 'It is your great good luck to see Barberini pope; but we are even luckier that Bernini lives at the time of our pontificate.' The Pope loved to watch the artist at work, and someone entering Bernini's studio one day was astonished to see the Pontiff quietly holding a mirror while Bernini made a self-portrait.

After Urban's death Bernini's hasty Neapolitan tongue, and his rivals, brought him into disfavour with Innocent X, whose sister-in-law, the avaricious Donna Olimpia Pamphili, tried to wear the tiara. The only thing to do was to make friends with that terrifying woman. The house in which he succeeded in doing this, and in which she lived, occupies a corner of the piazza, a dark and solemn building, the Palazzo Pamphili. Prevented by disfavour from erecting the obelisk and designing the fountains in the piazza, Bernini was persuaded to design and make a model in silver, which Donna Olimpia placed skilfully in a room through which the Pope would pass one evening. Innocent was fascinated by the model and would consider no other artist's designs.

Innocent X was seventy-two at the time of his election, a gentle and compassionate man, but completely dominated by his widowed sister-in-law. The Vatican grew shrill with feminine disputes from which the poor Pope tried to hide himself, and the Pamphili Palace became the place where most decisions were made. As Innocent X lay dying, in the only shirt he possessed, and covered with a torn blanket, his sister-in-law slipped into the room and drew from beneath the bed two boxes of money which the Pope had managed to keep concealed from her. Innocent died alone, deserted by his enriched family. When asked to provide for his burial, Donna Olimpia said she was a poor widow and could not afford to do so. The body was taken to St Peter's and placed in a room where the masons kept their tools: a workman, out of pity, lit a candle beside it, and, as the place was full of rats, someone was paid to watch for two or three nights. Eventually a compassionate canon, whom Innocent had once dismissed, spent five crowns on the Pope's funeral. It is difficult to believe this sad story as you look at the portrait of Innocent X by Velazquez in the Palazzo Doria, or at his memorial in the church of St Agnes, erected a hundred years later.

The portrait was painted in 1649, when Velazquez was in Rome buying antique statues for Philip IV of Spain. Many believe it to be one of the three or four best portraits ever painted, and Joshua Reynolds considered it the finest portrait in Rome. I have often stood before it in the long corridor of the Doria palace, full of Louis XIV gilt settees and tables, and wondered if Innocent X may not have been rather a Jekyll and Hyde. As Velazquez saw him, this Pope was not a man to be bullied and pilfered by any woman; he looks shrewd and implacable, and not an attractive personality. Yet in the same palace is Bernini's bust, and here we see a kind and gentle dreamer, a man who would seek peace and give away his last farthing to avoid a scene. Which is the real Innocent X? Bernini knew him better than Velazquez, yet one must remember that Bernini had every reason to flatter the Pope, whereas Velazquez had none. I doubt whether two great artists have ever interpreted a man so differently, and it is a pity that most visitors to the Palazzo Doria leave after having seen the portrait and do not look for the bust.

During the pontificate of Innocent X there began in the Piazza Navona those curious water festivals which lasted until 1867. On Sundays during the great heat of July and August the pipes carrying away the fountain water were closed, and the fountains were allowed to overflow until the square was deep in water. Parties were given in the houses round about, bands were engaged to play, and the aristocracy in their gilded coaches drove slowly through the water. Among those who enjoyed this festival were the Old Pretender and Maria Clementina, who were known in Rome as James III and Queen Clementina of England. On one occasion in 1727 someone, happening to glance up at a balcony, saw Bonnie Prince Charlie, then a child of seven, excitedly throwing coins into the water for the street urchins. At the first stroke of the Ave Maria bell the coaches would disappear and the square was drained.

The Piazza Navona has known every kind of public entertainment: in Roman times there were chariot racing and athletic sports; in the Middle Ages there were tournaments and bull-fights; and in the eighteenth century there was the Festa di Agosto. Today its annual excitement is the Befana, a corruption of the word Epiphany, which is held in January. The Romans visualize Befana as an elderly fairy, a gruff old woman like a female Santa Claus, who gives toys, especially noisy ones such as trumpets and drums, to children. Like most public festivals, it is not, I am told, what it used to be; still, for a few days every year the piazza is bright with coloured balloons and eager, excited children.

Whenever I visited the Piazza Navona, I would contemplate the fountains and eat an ice in the *Gelateria* where the best ices in Rome are to be found, and would then look into the Palazzo Braschi, at the corner near the Pamphili Palace. This is now the Museum of Rome and is full of interesting things, particularly old pictures of the city and the Papal Court. There are also casts from the Cosmati tombs of Edward the Confessor and Henry III from Westminster Abbey. On the ground floor are coaches of the railway train made in Paris for Pius IX in 1858. The guardian will tell you that 'Pio Nono' was the first Holy Father to trust himself to this form of locomotion, and he proudly opens the doors so that you may enter the train. The coaches are quite fantastic, the art of the eighteenth century applied to steam locomotion. They consist of a saloon, a throne room, and a chapel. Doors of mirror glass admit to a papal couch upholstered in red satin. Most visitors are so dazzled by the rococo splendours that they are blind to the irony: that the first papal railway coach should belong to the first 'Prisoner of the Vatican'.

In a picture gallery upstairs I found a portrait of a black and white cat. This lordly and imposing creature prowled the marble halls of some seventeenth century palace and is here seen enthroned upon a tasselled cushion, wearing a broad collar to which bells are attached. Pinned to a curtain behind the cat is a little poem which says that a great and beautiful lady once kissed the cat and bade him keep his heart and mouth pure, and to remember her kiss. No one knows who the lady was. Let us hope she was not the countess in the old Roman story who, after her widowhood, doted on a cat and had a chicken cooked every day for him. One day she left home for a friend's villa in the Campagna, and during her absence the servants decided to eat the chicken themselves and place the bones in the usual place. The countess was surprised, when she returned, to notice that the cat did not run to welcome her, but sat looking the other way, deeply offended.

'What's the matter with the cat? Hasn't he had his chicken?' asked the countess.

'Yes, Signora Contessa,' answered the servants, 'see, the bones are on the floor where he always leaves them.'

The countess could not deny this, and shortly after went up to bed. The cat followed, for he slept on her bed. That night the cat suffocated and killed the countess.

Romans explain this story by saying that a cat is intelligent, but selfish and cruel. He reasoned that if his mistress had not gone out and left him to the mercy of the servants, he would not have been so badly treated. Therefore she was to blame and must die. Dogs are faithful, say the Romans, and cats are traitors. I am sure, however, that there is no need to say that the loyalty of English and Siamese cats has never been questioned! Perhaps every country gets the cats it deserves.

Before leaving the Braschi Palace I paused in the gateway to remember an undemocratic scene that occurred during the pontificate of Pius VI. The usual excitable Roman mob, trying to blame Napoleon's preparations to invade Italy on the Pope, attacked the palace of his nephew, the Duke of Braschi-Onesti, and called for his blood. Suddenly the gates were flung open and the Duke stood there, holding a dog-whip in each hand. Footmen appeared with baskets of gold which they cast into the crowd. While the yelling ceased and the crowd began to scramble for the coins, the Duke strolled about hitting right and left with his whips. Having demonstrated how to deal with a Roman mob, he walked back to the palace and the gates were shut.

§ 6

At the back of the Palazzo Braschi is the battered fragment of a marble group which once represented Menelaus supporting Patroclus, and has been known for centuries as Pasquino. During the Renaissance witty and sometimes libellous puns and comments would be found attached to this statue, and were answered by the statue of Marforio, who reclines so plumply on the Capitol. Some popes resented these pasquinades—so called from a tailor named Pasquino who was believed to be the originator—and rewards were offered to those who had composed them. The bait was rarely taken, but on one occasion a guileless punster went to claim the reward, but was unable to carry it away, for both his hands were cut off. Journalism was a dangerous occupation in Renaissance Rome.

A typical pasquinade was one which commented on the great number of English visitors who crowded the Sixtine Chapel so that Romans could not find room there. It began with a question from Pasquino.

'Where are you going brother, with your black dress and sword?' In the morning the reply was found on Marforio.

'I am going to the Sixtine Chapel to hear the Miserere.' Pasquino then remarked,

'You will go in vain. The Swiss Guard will turn you out, and the Pope's *camerieri* will send you about your business.' Marforio retorted,

'There is no danger, brother: I am certain to get in: *I turned heretic yesterday.*'

A road runs from the Pasquino statue across the Piazza Navona and by a side street into the Piazza S. Eustachio, where Marion Crawford remembered one of the old taverns of Rome, the *Falcon*. It was famous in winter for boar's head served with a sweet sauce and pine nuts, and for baked porcupine and other dishes now as extinct as the *Falcon* itself: but the *Orso*, one of Rome's mediaeval inns, in which Dante is said to have stayed, still exists beside the Tiber. It is now a fashionable restaurant where waiters in evening-dress pass beneath Gothic chandeliers and the barman knows that bourbon has nothing to do with the French monarchy.

A few steps more and you are in the busy little piazza in front of the Pantheon. You leave its light and noise and enter a hushed and windowless circle of masonry, and you look up instinctively to see where the light is coming from. In the centre of the coffered roof is a circle of sky, and at noon the sun thrusts a shaft of golden light into this inverted bowl, which travels slowly up the walls so that those on duty in the church must always know what time of day it is by this odd sundial. Nearly everyone who has visited the Pantheon mentions the strange effect of the clouds moving across this circle of sky, though I never saw this. One day, however, happening to be passing by during a sudden shower of rain, I went inside and saw a funnel of grey raindrops glistening and hurrying down, a silvery moving cobweb against the gloom of the building. The water is carried away into a channel made by Agrippa, which drained this part of the Campus Martius. J. H. Middleton said that in his time water was sometimes pushed backwards during floods and sprang up in the centre of the floor with the effect of a fountain. The sight of snow in the Pantheon must be even stranger, and perhaps this may have suggested to the poetic imagination of the Middle Ages the custom of showering down white rose-petals at Pentecost, while the Pope officiated, as a symbol of the descent of the Holy Spirit.

Like Smollett and President de Brosses, I was at first dis-appointed by the Pantheon, but after two or three visits I realized that it is the greatest of the architectural relics which have remained to us from ancient Rome. Imagine the dome of St Peter's on ground level: the Pantheon is slightly larger. It was cast in concrete in one piece, and I wonder whether our age of steel and concrete could reproduce such a work. We see the building now stripped of its glories: the veneers of precious marbles which once covered its walls have gone, and also the gilt tiles from the roof. As the Romans did not use gold leaf, but pure gold laid on in plates, the Pantheon must have looked like a golden mountain. What the Goths left of this splendour was taken in 663 by the Emperor Constans to adorn Constantinople, but he was slain at Syracuse on his way home and the tiles of the Pantheon were lost. The ceiling of the noble porch was so rich in bronze that Urban VIII was able to cast eighty guns from it, which he mounted on the bastions of S. Angelo, but the story that he also had enough for Bernini's great baldacchino with the twisted columns in St Peter's is not correct. Perhaps a few thousand pounds of the Pantheon bronze went into it, but most of the metal came from Venice.

While I was in the Pantheon one day, I noticed a woman enter with a bunch of carnations, which, after encircling the building and pausing at the tombs of kings and artists, she left at the tomb of Raphael. The great master, whose working life was only about sixteen years, died from fever at the age of thirty-seven and was followed to his grave by the whole of Rome. His unfinished *Transfiguration* was carried in the procession like a banner.

Raphael's love for a baker's daughter sends thousands of visitors every year to the Barberini Palace to look at the supposed portrait of *La Fornarina*. When Raphael was dying, the poor girl was driven weeping from her lover's death bed, for the messengers bearing the Pope's last blessing refused to enter until she had left; and she had the mortification of knowing that Raphael himself had asked to be buried near the remains of his fiancée, Maria Bibbiena.

When Goethe was in Rome a skull said to be that of Raphael was in the Academy of St Luke. The poet was greatly impressed by it and said that the noble bone structure was that 'wherein a beautiful soul might freely dwell': but the beautiful soul was certainly not that of Raphael. On September 14, 1833, a strange and macabre scene was witnessed in the Pantheon when a committee of churchmen and artists opened the tomb of Raphael. There they found the skull and bones of the artist, lying in a deposit of Tiber mud. They were on view in a glass case for some days and were finally reburied.

The bronze doors of the Pantheon, which somehow escaped the despoiler, were once covered with plates of beaten gold. You may spend days in the Forum trying to imagine what Rome was like in the days of its imperial greatness, but the Pantheon remains the only visible evidence, and is the only mighty building with roof and doors intact which has survived the storms and perils of eighteen centuries.

§ 7

The Piazza Santi Apostoli, off the Corso, is hardly a Piazza at all, but merely a narrow street. It contains the Church of the Apostles as well as two of Rome's largest palaces, the Palazzo Colonna and the Palazzo Odescalchi, which loom up like liners in dry dock. Deep beneath the street are the remains of the Scotland Yard of Imperial Rome, a place of columned halls, statues of gods and emperors, waiting-rooms, offices, and the quarters of the commander-in-chief of the seven main barracks of the *Vigiles*. The narrow end of this street is occupied by a dull little palace which no one would notice unless his attention were drawn to it. It has been converted into business offices and among them I noticed a pensione St George, which made me wonder whether there are still English Jacobites who like to stay in the building where the Old Chevalier died and where Bonnie Prince Charlie and Henry, Duke of York, were born; for this is the Palazzo Muti.

For seventy years this building was the headquarters of 'The King over the Water', and now in its shabby condition it could not be a more appropriate memorial to the sad fortunes of the exiled Stuarts. No Englishman can surely pass it without a thought of the lives fretted away there, of the futile plots and schemes, and of the spies who gleefully reported every event that occurred in those old rooms where typists now thump their machines and cooks prepare the dishes that smell so strongly on the ground floor.

I crossed the road and entered the Church of the Apostles, whose antiquity has been overwhelmed by baroque plaster. I found the priest in the sacristy and spoke to him of the Stuarts, but he knew nothing about them. Anxious not to disappoint me, however, he took me into the nave and pointed to a marble urn on a column which contains the heart of Clementina Sobieski.

She was sixteen when she arrived in Rome to marry James Stuart, the Old Chevalier, who was thirty-one. She was a pretty little thing with a tip-tilted nose, blue eyes, and light brown hair that fell almost to her heels. When she was a small girl she had played at being Queen of England, and she arrived in Rome full of excitement, happily unaware that she was fated to play this game, but never to win it, for the rest of her life. Her grandfather, the great John Sobieski, had beaten the Turks at the gates of Vienna and liberated Hungary from the Ottoman yoke. A part of her trousseau was a strange relic of this event. It was a state four-poster bed whose hangings were made of the curtain which had surrounded the standard of Mahomet. It was embroidered with Arabic texts in turquoises and pearls on a gold ground. The framework of the bed was silver, gilt and chiselled. She had also three huge rubies which had been found in the harem tent of the Grand Vizier Amurath. The arrival in Rome of this Arabian Nights bed was not stranger than that of Clementina herself.

On her way from Poland she had been kidnapped by the Emperor, who was in alliance with England, and locked in the Castle of Innsbruck, with the object, of course, of preventing a marriage designed to provide a Catholic heir to the English throne. Four gallant Irish officers pledged themselves to James to rescue his bride. They rode to Innsbruck through April storms of rain and sleet. The scheme was that a young woman was to be smuggled into the castle to take her place in Clementina's bed, while the princess slipped out to join her rescuers. It was a pitch dark night and snowing hard. The castle guards had gone indoors; the streets were deserted. As Charles Wogan, the leader of the rescue party, waited at midnight, he saw approaching him through the storm a young girl in a hooded cloak, slipping in the slush and walking slowly, head down, burdened with two parcels. In one Clementina had packed three chemises, a petticoat lined with ermine, a bodice and some handkerchiefs; in the other, wrapped in brown cloth, were the Crown Jewels of England, which had been sent to her by James as a betrothal gift.

Wogan took her to an inn, where the other rescuers were waiting. In a room lit by one candle the four men knelt and kissed her hand. They had bought a special coach with double springs for the journey over the mountains. They had ropes and also a leather cushion in case Clementina might have to abandon the coach and ride pillion. No sooner had they set off than the princess missed the Crown Jewels, which she had left in the inn. One of the men, O'Toole, rode back and found them lying behind a door.

The journey over the Brenner Pass in the snow was appalling. Twice the coach broke down, and once it was nearly flung over a precipice, but fortunately the blinds were drawn and the princess did not know. Eventually the axles gave way, and Clementina slowly crossed the Austrian frontier into safety in a cart. After five days they reached Bologna, where she was married to James by proxy. When they arrived in Rome James knighted all four Irishmen, and the Pope made Charles Wogan a Roman senator.

James was delighted with his pretty young wife, and she was anxious only to please him. Among notably inaccurate definitions of character drawn during a honeymoon must be placed the jesting letter in which James wondered whether his dear little bride even had a will of her own. He was to find out!

Rome found her charming and the first six years of their married life were perfect. Charles Edward (Bonnie Prince Charlie) was born in 1720; his brother, Henry, who became Cardinal Duke of York, was born five years later. Then the strain of the impecunious court, the dissensions and squabbles, the preoccupation of her always melancholy husband, and the presence of Protestant members of the household, whom James kept for political reasons, with the approval of the Pope, got on Clementina's nerves, for she was said to be more Catholic than the Pope himself. In a moment of hysterical anger she fled from the Palazzo Muti and took refuge with the nuns of S. Cecilia, in the Via Vittoria, a building which is now the celebrated S. Cecilia Academy of Music. Here she stayed obstinately for two years.

Cardinal after Cardinal, and even the Pope himself, pleaded vainly with her to return to the Palazzo Muti, for her action damaged the character of her long-suffering and saintly husband, and James was traduced from one end of Europe to the other as a wicked man whose evil ways had driven his poor young wife into a convent. It was excellent anti-Jacobite propaganda. Then, as suddenly as she had fled, she returned, and James received her with joy and affection: but she was a changed woman. Her life was now devoted to religion. When she died at the age of thirty-five, James and his two sons were heartbroken.

Clementina's fair colouring was transferred to Bonnie Prince Charlie, whose Polish blood transformed him into the earlier northern type of Stuart. The swarthiness of the later Stuarts began only with the children of Henrietta Maria, and the darkest of them all was the Old Pretender, the son of Mary of Modena, the 'Blackbird' of Jacobite song. James remained a sorrowful widower until his death thirty-one years later, spending hours on his knees at his wife's tomb.

The next mistress of the Muti Palace was the young wife of Charles Edward, who, at the time of his marriage at the age of fifty-two, was no longer recognizable as the brave lad who had set the heather alight. He was now well advanced in dissipation, but pulled himself together for a time when his pretty nineteen-year-old bride, Princess Louise of Stolberg, came gaily into Rome in company with handsome young Thomas Coke of Norfolk, whom she had met during her journey. The gossips rumoured, of course, that they had fallen in love on the way. However, they parted and never met again.

Louise delighted the Romans, who called her 'The Queen of Hearts', and even her brother-in-law, the Cardinal, found her charming. For a brief moment it seemed that the life of Charles

Edward might have taken a turn for the better, but he was too old to change, and his tragic portrait by Batoni, in the National Portrait Gallery in London, tells the story better than words. In five years' time, when living in Florence, Louise met Count Alfieri, the Italian poet, and they fell in love. He was a handsome, rather Byronic character who not long before had fought a duel in Hyde Park with an injured husband, and the plight of this beautiful young woman of twenty-four, chained to a jealous drunkard, roused his chivalry and love. One night, on St Andrew's Eve, always a difficult time for Bonnie Prince Charlie, he burst into her room and, accusing her of infidelity, tried to strangle her. Louise fled to a convent and appealed for help to her brother-in-law, the Cardinal, who arranged for her to go to Rome and take refuge in the same convent of S. Cecilia which had sheltered his mother.

Alfieri followed her to Rome, where the guileless Cardinal, the only person in Rome who believed the attachment to be platonic, took her from the convent and settled her in the magnificent Palazzo della Cancelleria, one of the grandest palaces in Rome. Alfieri lived not far off in a villa on the site of the present opera house. Here he wrote plays and poems and rode out with Louise into the country; and life seemed perfect. Alfieri was presented to the Pope, Louise was protected by the Cardinal, and so, to the amusement of Rome, the love affair proceeded evidently under the highest auspices! These happy days continued for two years, and during this time Alfieri wrote fourteen of his tragedies. Roman society approved of the love affair, and the Countess and the Poet were welcomed everywhere. One of the great moments of their life was the first performance of Alfieri's *Antigone* in the Palazzo di Spagna, when Roman aristocracy sat in candlelight watching the play, in which Alfieri acted, and afterwards flunkeys in the yellow and red of Spain served ices in cups of spun sugar. These days were to end abruptly.

Charles Edward was reported to be dying and was given the last rites. On what he believed to be his death-bed, he confessed his sins, and did not try to excuse himself, but he told the truth about the Countess and Alfieri and the provocation he had received from them. The innocent Cardinal of York was horrified. He was also outraged to think that an illicit love affair had been carried on, apparently with his approval, for two years! Driving back to Rome, he went at once to the Pope, who must have been equally innocent, for he also was shocked and readily issued a ban forbidding Alfieri to live in Rome. Thus, to the regret and sorrow of Roman society, the lovers were parted.

Alfieri went to England to buy horses, which, after literature and Louise, were his passion. The Countess soon left Rome for Alsace, where Alfieri joined her. They were driven out of France by the Revolution, and eventually settled in Florence. They were never parted again until Alfieri's death twenty years later.

But the Palazzo Muti had not seen the end of the Stuarts. Charles Edward recovered, and gave the old palace its last and most fortunate mistress, his illegitimate daughter, Charlotte Stuart. For years he had done his best to forget her and had once repulsed her with cruelty; but now in his old age, sick and worn out with disappointment, he turned to her and she came gladly. He had met her mother in Scotland during the '45. Her name was Clementina Walkinshaw, and after the Rebellion she had shared Charles' wandering life on the Continent, passing as his wife under such names as Mr and Mrs Johnson, or Thomson. They used to quarrel violently and often made distressing scenes in public, until one day Clementina fled, taking their child with her.

Charlotte was thirty-one when she joined her father. As he looked at her, he saw a female version of himself as he had been in the 'bonny' days: the same straight nose, tall figure and chestnut hair. For once the spies and gossips did not sneer or smile as the competent Charlotte introduced order and sanity into her father's life.

He was now an invalid and she nursed him with love and devotion. He could not bear her out of his sight. 'If goodness of heart were sufficient for the conquest of a throne,' wrote a contemporary, 'his daughter would occupy it immediately, for she is goodness personified; such goodness as comes not of duty but rises from the heart, which clothes itself with grace, conquers hearts and compels veneration.' The first act of Charles was to make her legitimate by deed and to give her the title of Duchess of Albany.

Under her care Charles became himself again. When he was feeling well enough, father and daughter went out together. They would be seen driving about Rome in a coach with servants in the royal livery of Great Britain, and with the monogram CR on the door under the royal crown: but usually he rested or dozed in the Muti Palace, sometimes wandering back in his mind to the Highlands of Scotland, and once, hearing the tune 'Lochaber no more', he burst into tears. But old and finished as he was, he kept a box under his bed with twelve thousand sequins in it, just in case he should be called back to the throne of his ancestors.

So the last two years of his life were spent in dignity and peace. At the end of January, 1788, Bonnie Prince Charlie, whose name will ring for ever in the songs of Scotland, died in the arms of the Master of Nairne. Loyal men who had devoted their lives to a lost cause stood round his bed, and his noble daughter soothed his last moments. There was no sound in the palace but the voices of Franciscan brothers saying the office for the dead.

Sad to relate, Charlotte, Duchess of Albany, survived her father by only a year and eight months. Her horse stumbled and fell with her at Bologna, and she died from her injuries.

As one looks at the shabby old Muti Palace today, one last memory comes to mind. Twenty-three years had passed since Charles Edward died. It was the year 1811. A plump little woman of fifty-nine stood looking up at the building, in company with a gouty man of forty-five. We may well wonder what was passing in the woman's mind, for she was Louise, Countess of Albany, the wife of Charles Edward. This was the palace to which she had come as a gay young bride thirty-nine years ago: but who was her lame friend? He was not her poet, Alfieri, who had been dead for eight years. His death at the age of fifty-four had been a shock to her, for their romance had been a happy one in spite of

Alfieri's frightful tempers, which often made her cry, and despite his loathing for the French, and for Napoleon in particular.

The man of 1811 was the French painter François-Xavier Fabre, whose portraits of Louise and Alfieri are still admired in the French Room of the Uffizi Gallery in Florence. Like Louise, he was a devout admirer of the Poet, and it seemed natural that after his death they should spend their lives together. Gossip, of course, said the usual things. During the Roman visit the two friends descended together into the crypt of St Peter's, where Louise stood beside the grave of her husband, his brother and their father. What did she think, as she stood there? Her diary contains no comment. Having seen Rome, they returned by easy stages to the Casa Alfieri, which faces the Arno at Florence.

Though Louise never became Queen of England, she was certainly Queen of Florence for the last thirteen years of her life. She used to sit in a large room facing the river, visited by everyone, and beloved and admired by all. All trace of her be-witching beauty had vanished in a German squareness of face and figure. She sat with an imperious air, dowdy and old-fashioned, with a *fichu à la Marie Antoinette* drawn across her bosom, proudly presiding over the memory of her Poet. It was, however, as the widow of the 'Young Pretender' that she interested her English visitors. One day when the news of the death of George III arrived in Florence, a silly woman, hoping to curry favour with the old Countess, cried dramatically, 'Princess, I announce the death of the Usurper!' Louise looked at her blankly and asked sharply: 'What usurper?'

When she died at the age of seventy-one, she left all her Alfieriana to Fabre: and the visitor to the old town of Montpellier, in France, which was Fabre's native place, will find it beauti-fully arranged and cared for in the Musée Fabre. Nothing would have infuriated Alfieri more than to think of his books and manu-scripts in that hateful land!

Visiting the Palazzo Muti again, I saw a memorial plaque tucked away in a dark passage, stating that Henry, Cardinal Duke of York had lived there, in whom the royal house of Stuart ended. How strange there should be no mention of his father or his brother.

§ 8

After Charles Edward's death the Cardinal Duke of York proclaimed himself Henry IX of England. He issued a pathetic medal upon which he styled himself 'King by the grace of God but not by the will of man', though no one except his servants, a few Irishmen, and those wishing to curry favour, ever addressed him as 'Your Majesty'. The Vatican did not recognize him as Henry IX, and outside his own palace he remained 'His Serene Highness, Henry Benedict Mary Clement, Cardinal Duke of York'.

He was the most attractive member of his family. He spoke English with a strong accent and was hurt and puzzled when he failed to make himself understood. He enjoyed great wealth until the Napoleonic struggles of the Holy See left him destitute, when, with great delicacy, George III persuaded him to accept a pension of £4,000 a year.

Frascati was the scene of his greatest happiness. Here indeed he was a king. As a young and wealthy cardinal bishop, he lavished money on his see until it was said want and poverty had been abolished. He lived in great state, entertained lavishly and was accessible to all, and his travelling carriage drawn by superb horses was a familiar sight on the road to Rome, galloping at top speed.

I wondered if any memories of the last Stuart might still linger in Frascati, and I motored out there one morning. At the end of fourteen miles I was in the glorious Alban Hills, mounting steadily towards a compact, biscuit-coloured town that stood in the clear Italian morning, looking from its heights across the Campagna to Rome. I could see the city far off in a faint autumn mist from which rose the domes of churches, touched by the sun.

Frascati had been the headquarters of Field-Marshal Kesselring, and the town had to be bombed by the Allies in 1943–1944. There were still many unhappy gaps in its buildings and other signs of war damage, but life was flowing strongly through the streets of what to many is the most attractive of the *Castelli Romani*. All the people I met radiated the famous Italian charm, which is absent in the overcrowded city of Rome, where men are busy and harassed.

The huge baroque cathedral had been damaged by a bomb, but one memorial had come through without a scratch: the long inscription bearing the royal arms of England which Henry had erected to the memory of his brother, who was first buried at Frascati before his body was removed to the Stuart vault in St Peter's. Nor far away I came to the site of an old building in which the Stuart Cardinal had established a library. It had been damaged during the war and now, rebuilt, was a conglomeration of flats, offices and shops. Going inside, I was surprised and pleased to find that the *Biblioteca Eboracense* still exists, and though the shelves are empty a bust of Henry still gazes down upon the scene. The caretaker told me that the books had been taken to the Vatican for safety and had not yet been returned.

The most interesting of all the Stuart associations is the strange old castle-like palace. When Henry took possession, it was in such a bad state of repair that once during a banquet he and his guests fell through the floor into the coach house beneath. The Cardinal, more fortunate than many of his guests, was gently deposited upon the roof of a coach. The ancient flight of narrow and picturesque steps leading down to the palace is known as the *Via Duca di York*.

While wandering about the town, which is famous for its white wine, I noticed several dungeon-like wine shops cut into the rock. I descended the steps of one and found myself in a scene that would not have surprised Cervantes. A few lamps and candles illuminated a cave hewn in the tufa, where several long tables of thick unplaned wood, black with age, stood in the gloom. At one of them a cheerful group of drinkers sat with flagons of Frascati before them. The pungent smell of wine came up from the vaults, and the laughter ceased as I descended the steps. The scene was as old as the world, and I was reminded of some picaresque novel or play: the no doubt estimable citizens of Frascati assembled there looked to me like a gang of robbers celebrating a coup.

Nothing could have been more courteous than my reception. Spilt wine was mopped up from an ancient plank of chestnut, an old bench was dusted, and I was offered a seat with a bow and a flourish. It took me but a few moments to discover that I had blundered into a social event. This was the last drink of the season before the *cantina* closed for the vintage, and it would not open again until the new wine had been pressed.

I remarked that wine in Frascati was an entirely different thing from the same wine in Rome.

'Ah,' said an old man who had not shaved since last Sunday, 'but those thieving Romans never give you true Frascati. It is Frascati and water! *Salute* . . . my lord!'

I loved that title! I had been called '*dottore*' in ruins, and '*professore*' in museums, but in this pungent cellar in Frascati I was listening to the last polite echo of the eighteenth century.

The proprietor of the *cantina* told me that he owned two hectares, about five acres, of white grapes, and his outrageous cheerfulness and his generosity, for he kept filling every flagon, was due to the excellent harvest he was about to gather on October 20. The grapes were trodden by foot, and he invited me to go and watch the treading. No wine of his, he said, would ever be pressed by machinery, which crushed the pips and made the wine bitter. I was astonished that five acres of vines could keep the *cantina* in wine for a year and still leave some to be sent to Rome.

He took me down into the vaults, more than ever like a catacomb, where about forty great tuns lined a rock tunnel. He said the temperature even in August never varied by more than one degree.

When we returned to the cellar, a lean old man standing in a beam of light that came from the street was peering into the gloom, crying in a loud voice, '*Olive dolci!*' He came down and we gave him a glass of wine to toast the new vintage and bought from him delicious green olives in brine. More people arrived and I made my escape. The proprietor accompanied me to the street level, repeating his invitation to the wine treading.

On the way out of Frascati is a terrace overlooking the Campagna to the west. I watched the sunset flare and burn over Rome. The whole Campagna turned into a purple sea in which the city of domes floated like a mirage.

I returned at that magic moment when the streets were filled with pink light.

§ 9

The Mausoleum of Augustus stands near the Tiber and is one of those miserable ruins which refuses to disintegrate. It has been a stronghold, a bull-ring, a circus, and a concert hall. Now it is a locked-up ruin where lame cats seek refuge from small boys. The ashes of five Caesars once reposed there: Augustus, Tiberius, Caligula, Claudius, and Nerva, as well as two Empresses, Livia and Agrippina, and other members of the royal family. No one knows what happened to the ashes, but it is not difficult to guess: the urn which contained the ashes of Agrippina was used as a grain measure in the Middle Ages.

The emperors were cremated a few paces away, near the church of S. Carlo al Corso, and I think that perhaps of all the ceremonies of ancient Rome, an imperial funeral might have surprised us most. The custom of the *conclamatio*, still observed when a Pope dies, is a direct survival of Roman practice. The moment an emperor was proclaimed dead, the whole of Rome stopped work and went into mourning. To the sound of melancholy horns and the wailing of women with unbound hair, the solemn funeral pomp wound its way to the Campus Martius, accompanied by those extraordinary objects, the wax ancestors, which were the proud possession of every aristocratic Roman family. These masks were kept in cupboards in Roman palaces and were valued much as ancestral portraits are by us. It was a joke in imperial times that a 'new man' had no ancestors, or only imaginary ones, just as in days when aristocracy was important, fun was made of a wealthy man who bought his ancestors in the auction room. This long procession of life-like wax masks, worn by members of the imperial family and by men chosen for their resemblance to the ancestors, would march before the bier on which lay the body of the emperor, clothed in purple. Members of the family, slaves freed under the emperor's will, with shaven heads and wearing caps of freedom, the Senate, members of the aristocracy, lictors with lowered fasces, and the Praetorian Guard, all had their place in the procession. In a silence broken only by the wailing of the mourners, the body was lifted to the pyre in the Ostrinum, or burning-place. On top of the pyre was an eagle in a cage. As the waxen ancestors grouped themselves round the pyre, a man with averted eyes applied a torch to the wood, and at the same moment the door of the cage was opened and the eagle flew up out of the smoke, symbolic of the emperor's soul winging its way to the other world.

On the banks of the Tiber a hideous concrete structure now stands near the site of the Ostrinum, but inside is to be seen one of the greatest glories of Rome, the *Ara Pacis Augustae*. This is the famous altar voted to Augustus by the Senate in 13 B.C., on his triumphant return from Spain and Gaul, when the great Augustan peace settled upon the Empire. Until recent years this large structure existed only in fragments in a dozen different collections, and a great portion lay beneath the Palazzo Fiano, in the Corso, whose foundations were actually built on its marble steps. How all these detached fragments were brought together, and the other parts dug out from beneath the palace, is one of the great romances of excavation; and when the Fascists come up for judgment perhaps the reconstruction of the Altar of Peace will cancel out their graceless Via della Conciliazione.

The first attempt to dig beneath the Palazzo Fiano was made in 1903 and wonderful objects were found, but water flooded the excavations and the stability of the palace above was endangered. In 1937 Mussolini's government took up the work in the sumptuous and aggressive manner which seems possible only to a dictatorship. First the underground water was frozen, then an elaborate steel construction took the weight of the palace and freed the marble steps of the altar.

Nine steps now lead up to a square courtyard open to the sky and enclosed by tall walls covered inside and out with splendid carving and decoration, and in the centre a further flight of steps leads to the altar. A frieze of life-sized figures runs round the walls, showing a grave and solemn assembly of men and women

walking in procession to the consecration of the altar; and among
them we see Augustus himself, his toga drawn over his head;
his successor Tiberius, Livia, the wife of Augustus, and his
daughter Julia. These beautiful portraits were made during
the lifetime of these persons by the finest sculptor of the day. It
is astonishing to see how little damaged are those portions which
have been lying for centuries under the Corso: saved from barbarians and Barberini, they confront us with all the startling
freshness of their resurrection.

§ 10

At dusk a stranger in the Via di Monserrato, finding his way
nervously from lamp to lamp, is relieved to reach even such a
dubious looking haven as the Campo de' Fiori. When darkness
falls the old streets of Rome sink back into a former existence and
fill with a stealthy vitality. Ancient palaces stand in the narrow
ways like masked conspirators, and the network of stout iron
grilles which masks their lower windows brings thoughts of
knavery and prisons; the forms of men ahead, slipping into
archways or side turnings, rouse in the mind the fears that such
streets seem designed to provoke. Happily, sometimes from an
upper storey floats down the reassuring voice of Bing Crosby,
saying that love is all.

At the corner of the Via di Monserrato is the English College
and its church, dedicated to St Thomas of Canterbury. The old
Palace, in which young Englishmen are now trained to be priests,
is a surprising contrast to its surroundings. All within is in good
English order. The Italian hall and the sweep of marble steps, the
reception room to the left, are Italian baroque, yet in some
strange way converted to England by centuries of English living
and English ideas and voices, and the presence of generations of
young men from English homes. When you meet Fathers Brown,
Jones and Robinson radiating that jolly, manly piety which is
characteristic of English Catholicism (as if, given the opportunity,
they would have taught St Augustine to play rugby), you
understand the stray whiffs of Stonyhurst which blow through the

corridors. One is not at all surprised to learn that Cardinal Hinsley inaugurated the swimming-pool by taking a header into it, surely the only recorded instance of a member of the Sacred College in a bathing-suit!

The land round about was in ancient times occupied by the training-stables of the charioteers. The famous 'Reds' were established on the site of the Palazzo Farnese, the 'Greens' on that of the Palazzo della Cancelleria, and the 'Blues' on that of the English College. A beautiful faun was discovered when the present building was being erected in 1682, and also part of a shrine to the god Silvanus, which had been dedicated in A.D. 90 by a charioteer named Thallus. In this part of Rome, however, it is easier to imagine mediaeval robbers and Renaissance assassins than the earlier tipsters and students of form who used formerly to haunt the place and peep over the wall to watch chariots practising in the Trigarium.

The old Scola Saxonum near St Peter's had long ceased to exist when Boniface VIII proclaimed the Jubilee of 1300, and consequently English pilgrims were cast upon the cupidity of Roman innkeepers. When the next Jubilee of 1350 took place, the stories of pillage and extortion no doubt decided an English rosary seller, John Shepherd, and his wife Alice, to turn their modest house into an English hostel. In the superb and beautifully kept library on an upper floor of the College, a great hall lined from floor to ceiling with sheepskin, vellum, and full calf, are preserved the original documents of the hospice and, later, the College. A thriving colony of English tradesmen existed in Rome during the reign of Edward III, and in 1362 a group of them bought the hostel from John and Alice, but retained them to manage it. We read the names of John, another rosary seller; William Chandeler, formerly of York; John White, merchant and citizen of London; Peter Paul Baker, a Roman citizen; John the goldsmith; John Gaylot, an English merchant; and John Ely, a serjeant-at-arms to the Pope.

For three centuries every Englishman who visited Rome stayed in the Via di Monserrato, and the unfortunate were entertained there as well as the mighty. An entry which interested me records the arrival in 1489 of two young Englishmen who were studying Greek in Italy, William Lily and Thomas Linacre. Lily was to become the first High Master of St Paul's School, and Linacre became the most distinguished physician of his time. Both were, with Grocyn, the first teachers of Greek in England and, like all the first Humanists, Oxford men. It is pleasant to think of these young Englishmen in their belted gowns and felt *birettas* walking the streets of Rome in the time of Innocent VIII. They may have mingled with the crowds who saw that fantastic procession in 1489 when the brother of the Sultan Bajazet made a solemn entry into Rome, escorted by Cardinals and sitting, with a veil over his face, upon a white horse provided by the Pope.

This young man had fled from his brother, the Sultan, and had taken refuge with the Knights of St John. When the Sultan offered a large annual sum if the Prince were kept in captivity, something like an auction sale for such a remunerative guest took place among the courts of Europe. The Pope, however, topped all bids with a cardinal's hat for the Grand Master, and so the Turkish Prince was sent to Rome. Lily and Linacre, like everyone else in Rome that year, would have heard that although the etiquette of the Papal Court was carefully explained to the young man, he refused to kiss the Pope's foot and stood haughtily, wearing his turban, at last consenting to give the Pontiff a reluctant kiss on the right shoulder. For six years the head of Christendom and the brother of his deadliest foe held their courts in the Vatican, then in the following reign of Alexander VI, the Borgia, the Prince died, it was rumoured of a certain 'white powder'.

Linacre returned to England and became tutor to Prince Arthur, the brother of Henry VIII, and after Arthur's death he was Henry's doctor. Another of his patients was Cardinal Wolsey. In his old age this great scholar was asked to give a little girl of five her first lesson in Latin: she was Mary Tudor. No doubt Linacre had similar Italian institutions in mind when he founded the College of Physicians, where a copy of a portrait of him may be seen. Another fine portrait hangs in the Rector's room in the Via di Monserrato.

In the reign of Elizabeth the whole character of the hospice changed. It then became a refuge for those Englishmen who preferred exile to Protestantism. Cardinal Allen, who founded Douai, organized the English College as a seminary where young priests were trained who, at the risk of their lives, were sent to England to administer the sacraments. The busy Father Parsons shuttled about from the Via di Monserrato to the Escorial and the English College at Valladolid, anxious to see the old faith restored, even at the point of a Toledo blade.

Forty-four young English priests from the College were caught and executed, among them Edmund Campion and Robert Southwell. It became the custom, before they left for England, to say goodbye to St Philip Neri, who lived opposite the College at S. Girolamo. The old saint always embraced them and spoke the words which the Church addresses to the Holy Innocents—*Salvete flores martyrum*. There is a fine stained glass window in the Catholic Cathedral at Shrewsbury which shows St Philip blessing the young priests and greeting them in the streets of Rome.

It was an exciting and terrible moment in English history: the time of priests' holes, spies, secret masses, arrests, the rack and the gallows. Not one of the important exiles, least of all Father Parsons, seemed to realize that times had changed since they had left their native land and, as Archbishop Mathew says, 'in the case of a foreign invasion every Catholic would in fact support the English Government without regard to its religious feeling'.

While the College produced forty-four martyrs, it also produced one of the most infamous spies of the time, a man who helped to bring Mary Stuart to her death. Even Titus Oates, I think, takes second place to Gilbert Gifford. This young man pretended to be an ardent Catholic, but was really spying for Francis Walsingham. With his background of Douai and the English College in Rome, he was accepted by unsuspecting English Catholics, and all their secrets were reported by him to the secret service. He wormed his way into the confidence of Mary, Queen of Scots, when she was imprisoned in Chartley Hall, Staffordshire, and, making a great pretence of secrecy, smuggled her letters through in oiled silk introduced into a barrel of Burton ale, after having first copied them for Walsingham. Incoming letters to the Queen were brought to her the same way. It has been said, but never proved, that Gifford was behind Babington's plot to murder Elizabeth; at any rate he was the carrier of Babington's letter to Mary and of her incriminating reply to Babington which, whether or not forged or doctored in some way by Gifford or Walsingham, was the final act of her tragedy. In the same year that Mary Stuart died, Gifford was ordained a priest. Six years later, his sins having found him out, this Judas died in a Paris prison.

Upon a table in the library I saw an exquisite little birdcage made of silver and gilded wood in the form of a baroque shrine. It is one of the dove cages used in 1935 at the canonization of St John Fisher and St Thomas More. It took me back to the scene in St Peter's about twenty years ago, when Andrea Bobola, John Leonardi, and Salvatore da Horta were canonized. During the Mass of Canonization I heard the sound of birds chirping, and the cooing of doves, and saw a procession of monks and men in black court dress walk up the nave of St Peter's carrying little gilded cages, also small silver and gold barrels of wine and loaves of bread on a golden tray. There was silence in the church except for the cooing of the doves, as the Postulants, or advocates for the new saints, knelt before the Pope's chair and made their offerings. Three times the cages full of bright chirpings were held up to the Pope, once for each of the three new saints, and the Pope leaned forward and blessed the birds as they put their heads on one side and gazed up into the blaze of light. There is no moment in any ceremony more beautiful than this, a relic of the offerings of bread and wine made in the primitive Church, the birds symbolic of the purity and celestial nature of the sacrifice.

The recent records of the College, that is to say since the seventeenth century, contain the names of many distinguished Englishmen welcomed there as guests, including many non-Catholics. Milton was there on October 30, 1638, when he dined in the refectory with the students. Six years later John Evelyn dined 'and afterwards saw an Italian comedy acted by the alumni before the Cardinals'; again, the following year he dined at the College and this time saw an English play. How interesting it is that the College should have retained its histrionic traditions; for I heard that the alumni were at that moment rehearsing *HMS Pinafore*.

We went into the chapel dedicated to Thomas à Becket, which is a recent building but contains older tombs and memorials, including that of Cardinal Bainbridge, Archbishop of York, who, said rumour, was poisoned by his cook in 1514. He is said to have had a foul temper, though he looks saintly and tranquil enough now. Another memorial in this church is a treasure for any collector of epitaphs. It records the death in 1778 of Martha Swinburne.

'She spoke English, French and Italian, and has made some progress in the Latin tongue; knew the English and Roman histories, arithmetic and geography; sang the most difficult music at sight with one of the finest voices in the world, was a great proficient on the harpsichord, wrote well, and danced many sorts of dances with strength and elegance. Her face was beautiful and majestic, her body a perfect model, and all her motions graceful.'

And this prodigy was only nine years of age! Her father was a Swinburne of Capheaton, in Northumberland, the family which produced Algernon Charles Swinburne, and he was the author of one of the first travel books about Spain. Poor prodigious little Martha was the first child of a large family, and it is to be hoped that the parental grief preserved on the walls of the chapel in Rome was softened by the arrival in due course of five daughters and four sons. One of Swinburne's sons became a page to Marie-Antoinette, one of his daughters married Paul Benfield, who had made a fortune in India and lost it, and Swinburne himself died of sunstroke in Trinidad.

Here also rests at last that stormy busybody, Father Parsons, the Jesuit who galloped about Europe in the sixteenth century with a finger in every Catholic pie, the author of countless pamphlets, a prince of propaganda, an Armada enthusiast, and one who knew everything except that the England of Elizabeth was not that of Mary.

§ 11

In the Via Giulia, near the English College, I came to an old palace with a painted façade, the Palazzo Ricci-Paracciani. Stepping into the courtyard to admire the building, I came on a strange scene. Workmen were busy mixing concrete and stacking bricks, while in a corner, surrounded by their hods and buckets, with her back to the wall, a queenly and life-size marble lady sat quietly reading. At first I thought she was the young Victoria. She was of that period, her hair parted down the centre, demure and regal, and glancing at the open book upon her knees, I saw that she was reading Dante's *Commedia*.

In these days, when palaces are split up into flats, life-sized marble ladies, even though as handsome and charming as this one, are a problem; so she was seated, I hoped temporarily, in the courtyard. While I was standing there, a man crossing the courtyard noticed my interest in the statue and paused. He told me that he was the owner of the palace and the statue, but beyond the fact that the lady had been an Englishwoman, he could tell me nothing. He said that he would gladly consult some family papers and write to me, and in a few days' time I received a letter from the Marchese Giulio Ricci-Paracciani.

The lady's name was Emily Rowles, of Camden Place, Chislehurst, in Kent, and her father was Henry Rowles, a prosperous builder, a magistrate, and chairman of the Globe Fire Insurance Society. He fell into debt and committed suicide. Before this tragedy, Emily met Prince Louis Napoleon, and of the many ladies whom the susceptible prince might have married, she, for a time, appeared the most likely. Their romance ended, however, with Napoleon's marriage to Eugénie, and shortly afterwards Emily Rowles went to Italy, where she eventually became the wife of an immensely rich Roman, the Marchese Giampietro Campana. Unhappily her husband was to repeat the misfortunes of her father, and fall into financial difficulties. His vast wealth vanished and as a great number of people were involved in the crash, he was sentenced to twenty years' forced labour. In her despair, Emily Rowles appealed to her old admirer, now Napoleon III. Through his intercession the Marchese's sentence was commuted to banishment, and after some years in prison he retired to Naples, where he devoted himself to spiritualism and eventually died in poverty. Emily was helped by Napoleon, who gave her a pension and also bought a great number of her husband's art treasures, which are now in the Louvre. It was during the period of her husband's trial, when she had nothing, that Emily borrowed seven thousand francs from her friend, the Marchesa Rosy Ricci-Paracciani, and, unable to repay her, gave her the beautiful marble statue of herself.

It is curious that after Sedan, and his deposition, Napoleon III remembered Camden Place, Chislehurst, where he had known Emily Rowles and her family during his youthful years in England. This was the house to which he and the Empress Eugénie now turned in their trouble, and where they went to live with their son, the Prince Imperial. Emily Rowles, who died in 1876, lived to see the Emperor whom she might have married established in her old home in Kent.

I hope that if there continues to be no room for her in the Palazzo Ricci-Paracciani, that the Museum of Rome will rescue her from the draughty courtyard, for the poor girl knew enough ill winds in her life, and she deserves a place among the nineteenth century memories of Rome.

§ 12

Wishing to be near to St Peter's, I decided to leave my pensione in the Via Venti Settembre and to look for somewhere to stay on the other side of the Tiber. I was fortunate in finding a room in a convent. This room, so white and clinical, contained only a bed, a wardrobe, a chair and a table. Above the table was a crucifix with a spray of last Easter's palm behind it, and above the bed was a richly coloured picture which showed the Blessed Virgin mounted upon a cloud and holding the orb of the earth.

I had never stayed in a convent before, though I have lived in a great number of monasteries: with Dominicans and Trappists; with Carmelites in Palestine and Franciscans in Spain; with Greeks on Mount Athos and in Sinai; and with Copts by the Red Sea. Of convents I knew nothing, and I was therefore at first rather doubtful about smoking. I did, however, timidly smoke a cigarette with a greater feeling of guilt than I have known since I was a boy and was delighted to see, some hours later, an ash tray upon the scene of my crime: the Church tactful and wise as ever!

After dark, when the vigorous children of this fecund locality had been driven to rest, the silence was blissful. The first night I lay in bed and listened to an owl hooting on the Janiculum Hill. How the Romans feared and abhorred this bird. Once when an owl hooted on the Capitol a reward was offered for it, and Rome had to be purified. It was caught by a bird-catcher, solemnly burnt, and its ashes scattered in the Tiber as if it had been a male-factor. Strange that in Athens the owl was revered and associated with Pallas Athene while in Rome it was, as Pliny called it, 'the monster of the night'.

After so much fearful mechanical noise, I lay listening to the screeching of the owl as if to the sweetest music. It is a curious thing that for no reason whatsoever, so far as one can see, certain moments in life are chosen by the subconscious for preservation. It is annoying that many important happenings which one would dearly like to remember vanish from the memory, while others of a most trivial nature are shot with immortal radiance. I knew that in days to come I should probably forget many notable things about Rome, but that this moment, as I lay in bed listening to an owl on the Janiculum, would be fixed for ever in my mind.

The convent was a small one in which American nuns kept a day school and accepted a few recommended guests. The only others at that time were a priest and a lively young American.

I was now so near St Peter's that during the day I could see the gesticulating and pointing visitors round the dome identifying the landmarks and tracing the green line of the shrunken Tiber as it flowed on through the summer heat. At night sparks of orange light tipped the masts of the Vatican Radio, and in between them, when there was no moon, the dome was rather a presence than a shape as it obliterated a million stars.

It was a curious and interesting region in which I now found myself. Only a few years ago it must have been on the edge of the city, but suburban houses and a few blocks of flats had straggled up the hill to stand, as if appalled, by the long ravines and sand-pits which lie on the western slope of the Janiculum. This rarely-seen side of the hill had a casual back-garden look about it, very different from the side everyone knows, where Garibaldi rides his horse among the flower beds.

The young American with whom I shared a table at meals was seeing the world before settling down in a family business in the States. In London he had deserted a conducted party which had not come up to his notion of ideal travelling companions. He had been disillusioned by Paris, and was now in ecstasies over Rome. He reminded me of a young milord of the eighteenth century, or perhaps the seventeenth, who was making the Grand Tour before settling down to his inheritance.

Another American arrived in a day or so with an exhausted wife and two tired infants. He was an officer with the American Army in Germany, and told me that he had motored across the Brenner Pass into Italy to spend one day in Rome! As the fretful children tearfully turned away their heads the moment a spoonful of food neared their mouths, and the weary wife pursed her lips and sighed inwardly, the husband asked me with an engaging smile: 'I guess we could see quite a bit of Rome in a day?'

Of the nuns I saw only brief glimpses as they flitted into church from a side door. They lived in a part of the convent with *Clausura* written above the door, and their only emissary was a little Italian sister with a charming American accent. She made the beds, swept the floors, polished everything, waited at table and, for all I knew, cooked the food. If her name were not Martha, it ought to have been, for Martha is the patron saint of good housewives and is shown in art with a soup ladle in one hand and often accompanied by a dragon. St Martha had vanquished the creature with holy water and having done so, resourcefully ticd it up with her girdle and probably taught it to wash-up and run errands!

'Do you think, sister, that I could have a latchkey tonight?' I asked her.

'Why, sure,' she replied and immediately produced one from the folds of her habit.

That was the night I came back late across a deserted Piazza di San Pietro. There was not a soul about. The lamps shone upon an empty space where the obelisk pointed to the stars. The two fountains were in full play in the darkness, with no one to admire them, and I caught a whip of their spray as I crossed the piazza. The closed cathedral rose up, immense and portentous in the night. I thought of the *Pietà* of Michelangelo arising there in a vast, empty darkness, lit only by the eighty-nine sanctuary lamps which burn night and day around the tomb of St Peter.

CHAPTER EIGHT

St Peter's in the early morning – the history of the Vatican Hill – the tomb of St Peter – the Roman cemetery under the church – S. Spirito in Sassia – Saxon pilgrims to Rome – the Janiculum Hill

§ 1

The word 'Rome' recalls a hundred bright pictures: the Trinità dei Monti, its feet in flowers; the Sacra Via, with the Arch of Titus against the sky; the haunted ilex avenues of the Villa Medici; the toy castle skyline of the Aurelian Wall; the cool roar of the Trevi; and the pink circle of the Castel S. Angelo on a still summer morning. Everyone who has been to Rome carries away such pictures. The glossy-haired women buying vegetables in the Campo de' Fiori; seminarists admiring a golden mitre in the window of an ecclesiastical outfitter's in the Piazza della Minerva; Verdi's horns and trumpets rising into the warm darkness as Aïda and her lover die amid the shadows of the Baths of Caracalla; and the Angelus sounding through the rosy mist of the streets at evening.

I would add to my own memories the Piazza di San Pietro at dawn. The lamps of the four candelabra around the obelisk are still burning in the greyness and there is a glow of artificial light under the encircling colonnade; in the background the church waits, immense and mountainous, for the first touch of the rising sun. It comes in a flash from the direction of the Tiber. The cross above the dome turns gold, the light floods down over the great church and the Vatican Palace, and the rich Roman colours of sienna and umber come back into the day.

It is an important moment in the Roman morning. As the doors of St Peter's open, men appear with brooms and besoms

317

to sweep the marble prairie of the porch, and at the same time many black figures are to be seen hurrying across the piazza, each one carrying a small suitcase or bag. These are priests from every part of the world, who happen to be visiting Rome. It is their privilege to say mass in St Peter's, and the altars are booked up for weeks, sometimes months, ahead. So in the first sunlight of the morning the priests carry up the sweep of steps the little bags containing their cassocks and from seven in the morning until noon every day the church echoes to variously pronounced Latin: mass after mass, and often no congregation save maybe a couple of passers-by.

The rising sun continues to shine upon the main entrance of St Peter's as if it were a Greek temple to Apollo. I wondered whether the priests noticed this, and if many of them knew how grieved was Pope Leo the Great in 460 about this problem of the rising sun. Having mounted the great flight of steps to the basilica, the early Christians 'turn round and bend themselves to the rising sun, and, with bowed heads incline their bodies in honour of the splendid orb,' wrote Leo the Great. 'We greatly grieve at this,' he added, 'done partly through the vice of ignorance, partly in a spirit of paganism.' All the churches built by Constantine the Great faced the east, notably the Church of the Holy Sepulchre in Jerusalem: some, like St Paul's-Without-the-Walls have been reorientated, but St Peter's still faces the rising sun.

§ 2

It might not be inappropriate to call the Piazza di San Pietro a Christian Colosseum. It is a vast architectural circle consecrated, however, not to death, but to life everlasting. There have never been two such immense stone circles in history, and Bernini may have been influenced by the Colosseum, and also by the vanished porticoes of ancient Rome, for the colonnades of St Peter's are the only place in Rome today that can be compared to the long covered walks which were such a wonderful feature of imperial Rome: places where the populace might shelter from the wind in winter and the sun in summer. These colonnades were in their turn derived from the long arcades of the Hellenistic world which had impressed Augustus when he was campaigning against Antony and Cleopatra. The Street Called Straight, in Damascus, was one of them; the Canopic Way, in Alexandria, was another, and a fine provincial copy of it can still be seen striding across the desert at Palmyra. It seemed to me natural and pleasing to link this up as I sat, as I did so often, at the base of Bernini's high columns, watching the life of the piazza.

Gazing down upon the impressive amphitheatre from the top of the colonnade are the statues of a hundred and forty saints. The sight of so many statues brings to mind the thought that there can be no similar open space in the world so free of pigeons; indeed there is not even one to pick up the oats from the nose-bags of the carriage horses. I suspect that there must be a grim and stealthy story of ravished nests behind this absence of nodding birds and the sudden thunderclap of wings.

Among the hundred and forty saints are, of course, most of the best known in the Calendar, but there are others which are not so well-known. There are twenty-five women among the seventy statues on the right, but only eight out of seventy on the opposite arm. Number five on the right as you enter the piazza is St Thecla, so well known in the Greek Orthodox Church, who followed St Paul all over Asia Minor disguised as a boy. St Rose of Lima is on the left colonnade, and she cannot long have been raised to the altars of the church when Bernini placed her on his colonnade. I noticed the statue of St Genesius, a Roman actor, who was making fun of Christianity on the stage when he became suddenly converted and refused to continue with the play. He is the patron saint of comedians and on those rare occasions when he is represented in art, he is shown wearing a cap and bells.

When Bernini designed the columns he thought that the baroque coaches of cardinals and princes would drive up and down beneath them, for the central aisle of the three into which the columns are divided is wide enough for coaches to pass each other, and the side aisles were for people on foot.

Though the site has been covered with masonry for so many

centuries, there are indications even now of the original slope of the Vatican Hill. It is highest on the north, where the Vatican Palace lies, and slopes to the south.

I wondered if St Peter ever came this way during his ministry in Rome and whether he saw the Vatican cemetery in which he was fated to be buried, and the Vatican Hill on which his church was to be built. He may have done so on some happy spring day before the shadow of Nero's hatred fell across the infant church. The Vatican Hill was not, of course, one of the Seven Hills of Rome: it lay outside the city wall and on the west bank of the Tiber. It was a lonely country district of clay pits and vineyards. The pottery was excellent, but the Vatican wine was said to have been the worst in Rome. 'If you want to drink something sour, drink Vatican,' wrote Martial, and Cicero also spoke of its poor quality. No doubt St Peter would have heard stories of the derivation of the curious word, Vatican: that it came from *vates* or *vaticinator*, a seer or prophet, for in remote times it was one of the places chosen by Numa Pompilius to reveal the communications from his spirit-wife Egeria.

St Peter would certainly have known of the Temple of Cybele, the Great Mother of the Gods, on the Vatican Hill, the Phrygian deity whose worshippers were baptized in bull's blood, to the pain and horror of Christians, who saw in such rites, and in those of Mithras, a horrible parody of their own sacraments. The Temple of Cybele was famous, and as far off as France and Germany inscriptions have been found in which priests of the Great Mother claimed that their ritual was the same as that practised on the Vatican.

In ancient times the road which led from the Tiber to the Vatican was called the Via Cornelia, and, like all the roads out of Rome, it was bordered by tombs. This road was also noted for the neighbouring gardens planted by Agrippina the Elder, the mother of Caligula, and part of the estate was bordered by the cemetery. Sporting young emperors like Caligula and Nero were in the habit of going to a racecourse which existed in the gardens to practise driving four-horse racing chariots, and so near was the hillside cemetery to the circus that when the crazy young

Emperor Heliogabalus wished to enlarge the course in order to accommodate elephants harnessed to chariots, some of the wayside graves had to be demolished. The rising ground to the north was covered with family tombs and it seems likely that anyone on this part of the hill must have been able to look down and see what was happening in the arena.

Those who happened to be in the cemetery on a night in A.D. 65, when Nero inaugurated the first Christian persecution, would have seen the ghastly sight described by Tacitus. Christians covered with the skins of wild animals were torn to pieces by ravenous hunting-dogs; others smeared with tar were burnt at the stake; some were crucified; and while this fearful scene was in progress Nero, dressed as a charioteer, ran races round a course lighted by the burning martyrs. Two years later St Peter was crucified on this same spot. The tradition in Rome has always been that he died *inter duas metas* (between the two pyramidal goal-posts) in the *spina*, or middle of the course. It has always been believed that he died at the foot of the obelisk which now stands in the centre of the piazza, to which it was removed in 1586. Its original position was to the south of the church, in the little courtyard a few yards from the Campo Santo, where a stone in the pavement marks the place. Thus those who claimed St Peter's body for burial had only a little way to carry it up the slope of the hill behind the circus. It is the tradition of the Church that a memorial was erected over the grave almost immediately and remained there, so that every Christian in Rome knew of it. When Constantine the Great built the first St Peter's, it was to enshrine this memorial, and the Church was built on the difficult hillside slope in order that the shrine might occupy the place of honour in the chord of the apse.

It might be thought that Rome had no more secrets to reveal, but this is not so. During the last war Vatican archaeologists investigated the tomb of St Peter and found what human eyes had not seen since the age of Constantine: the street of pagan tombs beneath the Church.

§ 3

During the past sixteen centuries traces of the Vatican cemetery have been seen under St Peter's on several occasions. The first time was when the old church was pulled down during the Renaissance and the present St Peter's was built, and again in 1626 during the construction of the foundations for Bernini's massive canopy above the high altar. In that year architects were digging all round the central area where the Apostle's tomb was believed to be, and the Pope, Urban VIII, was asked to decide whether an investigation should be carried out to see if the tomb were intact. There were two points of view: some were anxious to discover if the tomb of St Peter had been sacked by the Saracens in 846, and others had a superstitious fear of disturbing the Apostle's bones. Two or three unexpected deaths among the excavators seemed to support the fears of those who were quoting the letter which Gregory the Great had written eight centuries before, saying that calamities would attend any who ventured to move sacred relics. Though Urban VIII may not have been among the superstitious, he nevertheless decided against an investigation, and gave three chief reasons: if the Apostle's tomb were not discovered, doubt might be cast upon the existence of the body of St Peter in Rome; that the actual body might not be recognized among the great number of early popes buried round him; and that, owing to the great age of the tomb and the bones, some damage might accidentally be done. The excavators were therefore forbidden to penetrate beneath the High Altar and had to confine their work to the foundations for the bronze canopy.

Urban's fear that the tomb of St Peter might not be found must surely consign to the realm of wishful thinking the story, strangely repeated by many distinguished writers, that it had been seen by chance during the pontificate of Clement VIII—only twenty-eight years before. The story is that during the course of some alterations in the crypt, in the spring of 1594, a pavement gave way and through the hole was seen the tomb of St Peter, with the golden cross of Constantine, which weighed a hundred and fifty pounds, still lying upon it as it had been placed there in the fourth century. Clement VIII is said to have visited the scene at once with Cardinals Bellarmine, Antoniano and Sfondrato, and to have seen the Apostle's grave by the light of a torch: he was so moved by the sight that he ordered the tomb to be instantly sealed up. It is an attractive story, but had it been true Urban VIII would have known about it, for the Vatican still contained many who were alive at the time the incident is said to have occurred.

Such was the archaeological background of the tomb of St Peter when Pope Pius XI died in 1939, having expressed a wish to be buried near the tomb of St Pius X in the overcrowded crypt. Immediately the *Sanpietrini*, the hereditary workmen who for centuries have maintained the structure of St Peter's, set about exploring the crypt for a suitable position for his tomb. In the course of their probings traces again became visible of the pagan cemetery upon which St Peter's is built, and again a Pope was asked to decide whether the excavations should be continued. Pius XII made the courageous decision to carry on with the examination as long as the structure of the church was not endangered. So for ten years, which included the whole period of the Second World War, architects, archaeologists, and about ten members of the *Sanpietrini*, worked in the greatestsecrecy below the nave and the High Altar of St Peter's. The official report was issued in Italian in 1951, and the only scholarly account of the excavations in English is *The Shrine of St Peter*, by Professor Jocelyn Toynbee and Professor Ward Perkins, Director of the British School in Rome. This book, which is well illustrated, is indispensable to anyone who wishes to understand what has happened underneath St Peter's and the new problems presented by the discoveries.

Was St Peter's tomb discovered, is the first question which the reader will ask. The answer is yes: but it was not the tomb as Constantine theGreat left it. It had been rifled in ancient times, possibly by the Saracens, and all traces of the bronze coffin and the gold cross mentioned in early accounts of the burial have vanished. In the tomb cavity was discovered the headless skeleton of a human being of advanced age. Was this the skeleton of St Peter? No one knows. The cautious Vatican archaeologists have had the bones for several years, yet no statement has been issued about them.

What then is the result of the Vatican excavations? A street of beautifully decorated Roman tombs has been discovered, running beneath the nave, a street hidden and unseen since Constantine's workmen built the first church on top of it sixteen centuries ago. Under the High Altar of the present church an ancient shrine was discovered whose existence was the reason why the first church was built. On the plaster of the walls near this shrine pilgrims in Roman times had written their names, and one wrote an invocation to St Peter. Perhaps only a careful archaeologist would hesitate to recognize this shrine as the tomb of the Apostle.

The excavations have, however, demolished a belief held for a long time and in destroying it have posed a difficult problem. For a great number of years it has been thought that the south wall of St Peter's was built upon the north wall of Nero's Circus, and that the Vatican obelisk, which used to stand at the south-east corner of the church, marked the centre of the *spina*, where the chariots turned. When the excavators went down to the foundation wall of the church on the west side, where they confidently expected to find it resting on the masonry of the first century circus, they discovered that the wall was Constantinian in date, down to virgin soil. Therefore it seems that the Circus of Nero cannot have been where it was believed to have been, neither can the Vatican obelisk have occupied the central *spina*. No one knows what the explanation is. Perhaps the circus was further to the south: perhaps there is a second obelisk which has not yet been discovered. If excavations were made where the existing obelisk once stood, and which is marked with a black stone on the pavement to the south-east of the church, some clue to the mystery might be found.

The excavations under St Peter's were difficult and delicate: at times picks and spades could not be used and the *Sanpietrini* had to use their fingers. The foundations of the church, which were discovered to be inadequate, have been reinforced so that St Peter's is now stronger than ever. The whole street of tombs under the church has been preserved and is lit by electricity. It is possible to walk about it and to enter the tombs, as in some street in Pompeii or Herculaneum. It is, in my opinion, the most wonderful sight in Rome and it is a pity that it can never be shown to large numbers of the public: the space is too confined and the frescoes and wall paintings might easily be damaged. However, scholars and other interested persons who write to the office of the *Reverenda Fabbrica di San Pietro* may be admitted, but no group of more than eight people is allowed into the excavations. The crypt above is, however, open to the public, and if the electric light happens to be switched on in the street of tombs below, wonderful glimpses may be seen through the iron floor gratings.

§ 4

Sharp upon the stroke of ten I was at the side entrance to St Peter's, where a guide was waiting to take me down into the excavations under the crypt. He opened a fireproof door and led the way down a flight of steps. We passed beneath the church and the crypt, emerging into a strange and unforgettable scene which stood stark and cold in the light of unshaded electric bulbs. We were standing in a Roman street. The iron sky above was formed of girders. Tombs, one after the other, stood behind a continuous façade of beautiful red Roman brick which was pierced every few yards by massive travertine doorways and by windows, some decorated with egg and dart moulding. A road about five feet wide separated one row of buildings from those opposite.

Everything was covered with dust as if the centuries had fallen in white ash.

These tombs consisted of one room or, at the most, two. They were beautifully designed to look like the houses of the living, and the rooms were brightly decorated; there was nothing sad or gloomy about them. Some were painted in brilliant Pompeian red, and the walls and ceilings were bright with cupids, birds and flowers. They were little sitting-rooms for the soul. Some of the tombs were furnished with niches for cinerary urns, some with shelves for sarcophagi. I glanced up at the roof-line of the street, once in the open air of the hillside and now untouched by sun or rain for sixteen hundred years: and I thought of the people thirty feet or so above, who were at that moment walking upon the polished pavements of St Peter's, unaware of this strange scene below.

'Where are we in relation to the church above?' I asked.

'We are in the centre of the nave,' replied the guide, 'and about half-way up the church.'

He walked to the east end of the street, where our way was barred by a wall.

'This is the end of our excavations to the east,' said the guide. 'The tombs continue, no doubt, under the church towards the main doors, as they do to the west, but in order to excavate it would be necessary to underpin the basilica. I can't help wondering what still remains hidden there!'

The portion of the street which has been uncovered is about two hundred feet long and contains twenty-seven family tombs, some of them facing each other like a double row of houses. The inscriptions mention the names of a hundred and five people, sixty-seven men and boys, and thirty-eight women and girls. They are the tombs of wealthy middle-class Romans, most of whom lived between A.D. 125 and 300. There is evidence that some of the tombs had been bought and decorated during the lifetime of those buried in them, while others were probably built by speculators and sold already decorated.

Though I had read everything I could find about the excavations and had seen many photographs, I was astonished by the size of the area revealed and by the number of tombs to be seen.

'Come, let us visit some of the most interesting tombs,' said the guide. 'To begin with, here is the tomb of Gaius Popilius Heracla.' Above the door, inscribed in clear Roman lettering upon a marble slab let into the wall, was an extract of nineteen lines from the Will of the dead man. It read:

'From the testament, written on three leaves, of Popilius Heracla. Gaius Popilius Heracla to his heirs, greeting. I ask you, my heirs, I order you, and I rely upon your good faith, to build me a tomb on the Vatican Hill near the Circus, next to the tomb of Ulpius Narcissus, at a cost of 6,000 sesterces. For this purpose Novia Trophime will pay 3,000 sesterces and her co-heir 3,000. I wish my remains to be placed there and also those of my wife, Fadia Maxima, when her time comes to join me. I charge my freedmen and freedwomen with the right and duty of maintaining cult at that tomb. This applies also both to those whom I shall free by my will and to those whom I leave to be freed on certain conditions; and the same likewise applies to the freedmen and freedwomen of Novia Trophime and to all the descendants of the persons above mentioned. They are to enjoy the right of free access to the tomb for the purpose of making sacrifices there.'

'Look at those words,' said the guide, '*in Vatic ad circum*! You can perhaps imagine with what delight and amazement the excavators held their lamps to this inscription and read a contemporary reference to the Vatican and the Circus of Nero.'

It is a moment whose wonder will always remain. When the words were carved there was no St Peter's, but there was a man who wished to be buried next to his old friend in the cemetery near the imperial circus, with no idea that he was asking to be buried in the most hallowed spot in a Europe not yet born.

The white stucco walls of the next tomb were gaily painted with bands of Pompeian red and yellow, and that shade of ochre which is still the predominant colour in Rome today. It was the tomb of a woman named Fannia Redempta. Plump little red deer on tall spindle legs faced each other shyly on the walls, birds with red bodies and blue wings were seen in flight, there was a peacock, emblem of immortality, flowers and urns. My guide pointed to a sarcophagus on a shelf high up on a wall.

'The body of Fannia Redempta is still there,' he said.

A few lines of inscription say that she was thirteen when she married Aurelius Hermes and that after thirty-three years of happy married life she died, 'aged forty-six years, five months and seven days'.

327

We crossed the road and entered the family tomb of the Marcii. Against walls of Pompeian red we saw a superb sarcophagus deeply carved with whirling maenads playing pipes, a naked Dionysius, a graceful satyr holding a child and, in the strangest contrast, the sculptured faces of those buried there: Quintus Marcius Hermes and his wife, Marcia Thrasonis. He had a shrewd face with a little stubble beard, and might have been a money-lender; she looked a patient, middle-aged woman with slightly pinched-in cheeks.

We entered most of the tombs on our way to the place beneath the papal altar where St Peter was buried. In some tombs the workmen of Constantine had sliced off the elaborate coffered vaulting at ceiling level, but the damage looked as recent as though the demolition men had knocked off for a mid-day break. They were reverent workmen, and had carefully stacked the stray bones in safe places where they would be preserved, before they filled in the tombs. I wondered whether the great number of empty urn niches suggests a possible explanation to a question which the guide was unable to answer. How did Constantine pacify public opinion, which must have resented most bitterly this violation of a cemetery? Did he, I wondered, build a new cemetery to which those families still in existence removed the remains of their relatives? The act of *violatio sepulchri* committed by Constantine, an act the Church abhorred for centuries, seems to require an explanation.

A most unusual tomb is thought to have belonged to an Egyptian resident in Rome, but his mummy was not found in it. Striding stiffly forward upon the red wall is the god Horus, the only Egyptian god, I believe, ever pictured in an Italian tomb. A beautiful tomb is 'the tomb of the Quadriga', whose pavement shows in black mosaic a galloping four-horse chariot. My thoughts turned at once to the Circus of Nero and I wondered if this tomb were that of an imperial charioteer. Unfortunately no name has survived. We entered the tomb of the Tulii family, and I saw in a niche a graceful yellow alabaster vase still full of ashes. The tomb had belonged to a tax collector in Belgium, who had lived in the first century.

We entered the tomb of a consul designate, whose daughter, Ostoria Chelidon, was seen for a moment, before she fell into dust, lying in her coffin in a purple robe covered with a veil of gold. In another tomb we saw a mosaic which depicted Christ as a sun god in his chariot, and almost beneath the High Altar was the grave of a cheerful pagan named Flavius Agricola. This was discovered in 1626 during the excavations for the foundations of Bernini's canopy, and fortunately the epitaph was copied before it was lost or thrown into the Tiber. These are the words:

Tiber is my native place, Flavius Agricola my name, yes, I'm the one you see reclining here, just as I did all the years of my life fate granted me, taking good care of my little self and never going short of wine. Primitiva, my darling wife, passed away before me, a Flavian too, chaste worshipper of Isis, attentive to my needs, and graced by every beauty. Thirty blissful years we spent together; for my comfort she left me the fruit of her body, Aurelius Primitivus, to tend my house (or tomb?) with dutiful affection; and so, herself released from care, she has kept a dwelling-place for me for aye. Friends who read this, do my bidding. Mix the wine, drink deep, wreathed with flowers, and do not refuse pretty girls the sweets of love. When death comes, earth and fire devour everything.

Could anything more astonishing be imagined underneath the papal altar of St Peter's?

We now approached that sacred place which was enshrined by Constantine when he built his church upon a lonely hillside, a place so holy that rather than disturb a stone of it, or transfer it to a more reasonable site, he cut into the side of the hill at the cost of immense labour and built up a vast platform on the lower slope, leaving this sacred spot as the central feature of his building. This is the place venerated since the time of Nero as the burial place of St Peter.

I found myself in a narrow passage whose floor was that of the road made by the feet of Christians on their way up the hill to the shrine centuries before St Peter's was built. Ancient walls rose on all sides and I knew I was as close as a man can be to the burial place of the Apostle.

The world was well content to believe that Constantine, having enclosed the body of St Peter in a bronze sarcophagus, had protected it with masonry: 'at the head five feet; at the foot five feet; on the right side five feet; on the left five feet; below five feet; above five feet; so did he close Blessed Peter's body and hide it away.' Nothing could be more circumstantial than this account, probably written in the sixth century and based on contemporary evidence. As succeeding ages always accepted this account, the excavators had every right to expect that even if they did not discover St Peter's bones intact in the bronze coffin, they would at least find the place where the coffin had been buried, possibly with evidence that it had been sacked for the gold it contained.

Nothing like this was found, however. Instead the excavators discovered something startlingly unexpected. This was the remains of the small pillared shrine which had once stood isolated above the pavement of the first St Peter's, in the place where, later, the High Altar was to be built. It was the ancient shrine, the 'trophy', or 'memorial', of the Apostle mentioned by early writers as standing for all to see on the Vatican Hill before the church was built. There was an aperture in the upper part into which pilgrims placed their heads when they prayed, and a hole in the lower portion into which they let down handkerchiefs and other small objects to be sanctified by contact with the Apostle's tomb.

What remains of the shrine is badly damaged, for in their greed and haste the robbers evidently broke up everything in a violent attempt to get at the gold and silver. All evidence points to the Saracens of 846, who occupied and sacked St Peter's for a week, 'committing unspeakable iniquities' and carrying off even the altar. It has been estimated that in St Peter's and St Paul's Without the Saracens must have looted about three tons of gold and thirty tons of silver, and perhaps, as their ships could carry no more, they were only too ready to leave Rome with their almost fabulous booty. So the treasures of St Peter's, and all the exquisite objects with which piety had enriched the tomb for five centuries, were in all likelihood carried off by these pirates, whose ships sank in a gale off the coast of Sicily.

The bones which may be those of St Peter were found in a recess near the shrine. The rumour in the Vatican is that after they had been examined they were taken to the Pope's apartments, and then passed into the possession of archaeologists. All that is known about them is that they are said to be the bones of an elderly and physically powerful human being, presumably a male, and that the skull is missing. 'It seems strange,' say the authors of *The Shrine of St Peter*, 'that no authoritative medical analysis of these bones has been published either in the official Report or during the four years that have elapsed since that work appeared.'

'Our journey into the past is over,' remarked the guide. 'I think you will say that we have seen one of the most wonderful sights in Rome.'

From the edge of the piazza I looked at St Peter's, thinking that in future I should always see in imagination that dark street under the nave and the tombs of those who had lived in the Apostolic world.

§ 5

A young American priest who was staying at the convent told me that he intended to put his name down for an altar in St Peter's and say mass there one morning.

'I guess it wouldn't be possible for a humble guy like me to get an altar like that of St Pius X, which is booked up for weeks,' he said, 'but maybe I could get another one.'

'If I might suggest it,' I said, 'try and get the altar of Gregory the Great. He sent St Augustine to England and there couldn't be a more appropriate altar for an English-speaking Catholic.'

That evening he passed me in the hall and called out:

'That was a dandy idea of yours! I've got St Gregory the Great for seven o'clock.'

I walked down to St Peter's shortly after six the following morning. The piazza was hushed and empty. The lamps round the obelisk were still alight. Priests of all nationalities, were hurrying across the piazza and striding up the steps to say mass at the various altars. The church was still dark. A *sanpietrino* with a pair of scissors and a flask of oil was attending to the lamps round the Confession; others were throwing sawdust on the pavement and sweeping it up, the ancient Roman method of cleaning marble floors, which is mentioned by Juvenal and Martial. St Peter's was deeply impressive in that grey morning light. The church looked larger than ever without its crowds; there was a golden glow of candlelight from an altar where a mass had begun, and the glass coffin in which St Pius X lies, with a mask over his face, was brightly lit.

The Sacristy of St Peter's is the size of an ordinary church, and few laymen ever see it in the early morning, when it is one of the most impressive sights in Rome. An official sits at a desk with the altar book and checks the names of priests as they arrive to say mass at the altar which they have selected. Some altars were booked from seven until noon for a month and more. Priests, silently saying the prescribed prayers, were vesting themselves, while others waited. No sooner had one priest returned, having said his mass, than another, preceded by his altar boy, left for the now vacant altar. In a room at one side of the Sacristy was a pool of acolytes where a sharp eye was kept on proceedings. I do not know if there is a group word for acolytes, but perhaps a 'whisper' or 'scuffle' would not be inappropriate! The difference between the bearing of the priests and their young servers was notable. It was a morning routine for the boys, but the priests were dedicated to an experience which they would never forget: the morning they said mass in St Peter's. I watched the bustling little boys with their cruets and bells, followed by the grave, devout men, as they crossed the great sweep of marble pavement to the appointed altar.

My young American said mass at the altar of St Gregory and I was the only member of his congregation. I thought of the great man whose bones lie beneath the altar: of St Augustine tramping the roads of Kent, of Gregory's letters of advice, telling him what to do about heathen temples and how to handle difficult marriage problems, just the kind of answers a bishop today might give to a missionary in Africa.

After I had rejoined my American in the Sacristy, we went off together to the café-bar which so strangely exists in St Peter's. It is for the use of priests and closes at noon when masses cease and the last celebrant may break his fast. We were enveloped by the cheerful smell of coffee from a hissing urn behind a bar whose shelves displayed a noble array of drink, including even the formidable Yugoslav *sljivovica*. A cheerful matron gave us coffee and rolls, which we ate silently under the benevolent gaze of St Pius X.

As we walked round the church afterwards, I saw the Penitentiaries of St Peter's sitting in their confessional boxes in the south transept, hearing confessions in eight languages. The language spoken was written in bold letters above each box. Only in St Peter's and the patriarchal basilicas in Rome will you see the curious custom of touching people on the head or shoulders with a long rod, called a *bacchetta,* which each confessor holds. When not in use these rods protrude like aerials from the confessional boxes.

Every now and then a man or woman would suddenly kneel, and the confessor, without interrupting the revelations that were being whispered to him, would grasp the rod and tap the penitent on the head. This act of humility and the profession of faith which it carries with it is rewarded by special indulgences.

Selecting the box with 'English' written over it, I spoke to the priest inside and asked the origin of the custom. He turned to me a smooth, plump Irish face.

'This is the way of it,' he said. 'In the bad old days of pagan Rome a slave was given a token beating, an accolade, when he was granted his freedom. The custom has continued in the Church, which gives you a tap on the head as a sign that ye belong to the free company of Christian men.'

'County Cork?' I asked.

'And how on earth did ye know that?' he exclaimed.

We were interrupted by a woman who slipped into the confessional with her little burden of sins; soon she would emerge without it, looking much happier.

We continued our walk and the American priest asked what impressed me most in St Peter's. I told him that it was not its size, but its continuity. There is nothing else in the world like it. The seed of faith, love and reverence planted on this hillside in the days of pagan Rome had grown into this colossal shrine, and the size of St Peter's, the fact that you scarcely know where to look or what to look for, disguises its function: that it is really a shrine, the trophy of Anacletus grown and developed beyond the imagination of its originators. Not only is it the shrine of St Peter; it is also the shrine of his reputed chair, or episcopal throne, which is locked up near Bernini's gilt tribune at the western end of the church. The shrine also preserves and glorifies four great relics: the handkerchief of St Veronica, the head of St Andrew, a large piece of the True Cross, and the Holy Lance.

When my friend had gone, I went over to look at the beautiful *Pietà* of Michelangelo. He made it when he was twenty-four. A few steps away is the Dome of St Peter's, which he designed when he was seventy-two and whose erection he supervised until he died at the age of ninety. Here within a few paces are the beginning and the end of a life of genius.

The *Pietà* is the only work among all his mighty achievements which Michelangelo ever signed. The words 'Michelangelo Buonarotti, Florentine, Maker' are to be seen on the girdle of the Madonna. As I looked at the exhaustion of the Saviour's body, just taken from the Cross and lying across His Mother's knees, I thought of Gethsemane, the Trial, the Scourging and the Crucifixion. In this figure the artist has told in marble the last chapters of the Gospel. The expression of the Madonna as she gazes down at the dead body of Christ shows that she is in the presence of a sorrow too great for tears.

Few people notice the twisted columns in the pier balconies and the gynaecological sculpture round the baldacchino. If you stand under the dome and look up at the galleries in the piers upholding it, you will see in each gallery twisted white columns of purest marble, shaped like old-fashioned sticks of barley-sugar. Of the countless wonderful objects in St Peter's, they are the most historically interesting for they go back to Constantine himself.

Six of these columns were sent by the Emperor, it is said from Greece, when old St Peter's was being bui'', to uphold the canopy over the tomb. They were probably the first twisted columns of the kind ever seen, 'and placed as they were,' writes Professor Ward Perkins, 'they were bound to attract the attention and to excite the admiration of every visitor to St Peter's. They were copied intermittently throughout the Middle Ages.' An echo of them is to be seen in London in the twisted columns round the tomb of Edward the Confessor in the Abbey.

Six more identical columns arrived in the time of Gregory the Great, who altered the shrine of St Peter and used them, in conjunction with the original six columns, to make a screen in front of the shrine. When the old church was pulled down the precious columns were saved (only one of the twelve is missing), and Bernini copied them in bronze so that his gigantic baldacchino, with its twisted columns and its open-work structure, is a mighty version of the original canopy.*

Quite the most fantastic decoration in St Peter's was in some unaccountable moment placed by Bernini on the plinths of the four columns. The story is that a niece of Urban VIII promised to give the columns as a thank-offering if she were safely delivered of a child. The plinths have four sides and on nine of them are seen a female face which is said to portray the months of pregnancy, and the tenth represents a bouncing infant.

I was interested to learn that buried among the Popes in St Peter's—and a tablet in the Sacristy gives the names of a hundred and forty-three, including thirty-five saints—there should be five women. One of them, Matilda of Tuscany, who died in 1115, left her dominions to the Church and founded the temporal power of the Holy See. There are three exiled queens: Charlotte of Cyprus, who in 1461 arrived destitute in Rome, having been driven from her throne by an illegitimate brother and robbed by pirates on the way; Christina of Sweden, the daughter of Gustavus Adolphus, who abdicated in 1654 and became a Roman

* An early echo are the two columns of the porch of the University Church of S. Mary the Virgin, Oxford, erected 1637, only four years after Bernini's canopy.

Catholic; and Clementina Sobieski, the wife of the Old Chevalier and mother of Bonnie Prince Charlie. The fifth woman is Agnes Colonna, wife of Onorato Caetani, a hero of Lepanto and Governor of Rome during the pontificate of Gregory XIII. There was a sixth woman, Goya's acid-looking Maria Luisa of Spain, a Napoleonic refugee, whose bones were later removed to the royal vaults of the Escorial.

§ 6

After a morning spent in the Vatican Galleries, one of the stiffest walks in Europe, nothing delighted me more than to seek out one of the many inexpensive little restaurants which cluster on the frontier of the Vatican State. There was one in particular that pleased me. Behind the stuffy little dining-room was a court-yard where wooden tables and chairs were grouped beneath an immense and ancient vine.

It is one of my drawbacks as a traveller in Italy that I do not care for spaghetti, neither am I fond of fettuccine, and I cannot be persuaded to eat this popular dish, even when served with a golden spoon and a song and a dance, as it is in one Roman restaurant. Indeed the Italian appetite for *pasta* is astonishing, and I have sometimes wondered if it has come down the ages from the corn-fed Roman populace, for in spite of Lucullus and his like, the ordinary ancient Roman was practically a vegetarian and his staple food was wheat. Tacitus mentions soldiers who 'forced, for want of grain and vegetables, to subsist altogether on animal food, began to sink under their fatigue'; and Caesar more than once admired the fortitude of his legionaries who lived on a meat ration when corn was not to be had. The ancient Romans also had a prejudice against butter, which was a barbarian food and when rancid was used by such people as the Burgundians as a hair-dressing, and it may not be entirely accidental that to this day you have to ask for butter in a Roman restaurant. It is never put on the table as a matter of course, as in other countries.

To watch an Italian faced by a gigantic mass of spaghetti is always to me an interesting spectacle. The way he crouches over it, combs it up into the air and winds it round his fork before letting it fall into his mouth and biting off the fringe, rouses the awe of less expert eaters. No wonder the fork is said to be an Italian invention!

There are, however, a great number of other foods to eat in Rome. I liked *fichi con prosciutto*, a delicious dish composed of fresh green figs and Parma ham, an admirable though unlikely combination. Another dish I enjoyed was *Saltimbocca alla Romana*: a slice of ham, with a fresh sage leaf on it, is placed on a thin piece of veal the same size, and this is rolled up and fastened with a toothpick, then fried in butter. And nothing could be better than the fruit in Rome, and the green salads and vegetables of the *cucina Romana*. The red and green sweet peppers, *peperoni alla provinciale*, are excellent, and also the artichokes fried crisply in oil, *carciofi alla Giudea*.

It was in my little restaurant that I first saw *gineproni*, which made me so angry that I walked out and lunched at the restaurant opposite. *Gineproni* are thrushes sold by the dozen, their little bodies bedraggled and their feathers torn and bloody. They fatten on the juniper berries and, I was told, have a flavour of gin. They are considered a great delicacy and are as deplorable a sight as the *beccaficos* of Cyprus, the pickled blackcaps which have grown fat in the fig trees. The sight of the thrushes and other small birds hanging in bunches in the street markets explains the absence of bird song in Italy.

About this time of year, the end of summer, the shops and iceboxes of restaurants become filled with mushrooms of the most startling shape, size and colour. The Italian name *funghi* is itself rather alarming, the extra 'h' giving the word a horribly sinister look. Some of these monstrous growths, green and speckled, or red and angry, were lightheartedly consumed by customers, and though I am normally an adventurous eater, I could never bring myself to the point of ordering them. To me they were visible proof of the statement of Suetonius that Claudius was poisoned by *funghi*.

My restaurant was delightfully situated. Just around the corner were the golden-brown colonnades, the two fountains, and St

Peter's. To have a chair to sit on and a vine to sit under, so near St Peter's, seemed to me a wonderful thing. The fatigue of visiting the Vatican Galleries and the Library were easily assuaged at any time by a carafe of Frascati, a plate of minestrone, and a piece of Gorgonzola cheese.

In the evening the character of my restaurant would change. The people who dined there were different from those who had lunched there. The American woman who had lost her handbag, the visiting priest, the band of tourists chattering in French, German or English, were no longer to be seen. Neither was the persistent young man with the cameos, who always arrived half-way through lunch, rapidly summed up everyone and, like a polite shadow, approached any man who was having luncheon with a girl. With his eyes fixed firmly on her, he would open a leather-bound box full of cameos in trays. He could tell at once whether he was going to sell one, and if the girl was not interested he was quickly off to another table. It was astonishing to see how many he sold, and it was amusing to see how they were bought. An Englishman or an American, after a little half-hearted attempt at price reduction, would pay the sum demanded, no doubt in order not to appear close-fisted in the eyes of his lady: but the Italians had no such inhibitions. An Italian swain whose girl wanted a cameo would fight the man lira by lira. He would shrug his shoulders, turn away, become contemptuous, disparage the cameo, toss it about among the crumbled bread as if it were dirt, until one began to feel sorry for the cameo man, though he was really enjoying every moment of it. Like an expert swordsman who encounters a worthy opponent and feels admiration for him, even though he is pressing him hard, the man's dark eyes would fill with respect as he was steadily beaten down. At last, with a heartrending cry of 'You will ruin me!' he would part with the cameo and take what I suppose was a good profit. At least he was all smiles again immediately the deed was done, and approached the next victim with the same technique.

In the evening the cameo man was replaced by a man with a guitar. He was a thin, villainous-looking fellow who did not shave every day and had heavy-lidded, insolent eyes. A film-casting agency would have grouped him as a 'foreign gangster', but the type is several centuries old and the gang to which he belonged had haunted the Rome of the Borgias.

He would stroll in under the vine leaves and gaze round with his heavy eyes. The place was now full of local people, families, characters, and wits, and he knew most of them. Families, their napkins tucked into their chins, would be crouched over their plates of spaghetti, friends would be sharing a large flask of *vino bianco*, and the odd characters who haunted this place, and who probably lived nearby and worked in the Vatican, would be dawdling over their meal.

Selecting someone, the man would thrum his guitar for a moment before breaking into song. He was a man with a ready wit, and some of his songs were evidently malicious, for I once saw a stout Roman highly incensed, though his friends were delighted. Generally he was greeted with roars of approval.

Among all these dark people there was one man who came there as often as I did. He was big and jolly and stood out among the Italians because of his blond hair and moustache, and the fact that he liked beer better than wine. I discovered that he was a sergeant-major in the Swiss Guard.

Another habitué with whom I occasionally shared a carafe of wine was a man responsible for the cleaning and maintenance of the fountains in the piazza. He told me that the fountain on the right as you face St Peter's is older by sixty years than its companion. Gazing through the falling water, you can see the Borghese arms of Paul V, a crowned eagle above a dragon, while the fountain on the left bears the Altieri arms of Clement X, an inverted pyramid of six stars. The piazza must have looked strange with only one fountain, and Clement X, who was apparently always conscious that something was missing, must be given the credit for adding the final symmetrical touch. I told my friend that, having studied the fountains, I thought the more recent one looked older than the original, and he explained that the north wind, the *tramontana*, has a habit of sweeping round it and the cold blown spray has worn the stone, whereas, though so near, its companion is sheltered from the gusts. He also told me that the water which is tossed up in the Piazza di San Pietro comes from Lake Bracciano, forty miles from Rome. It arrives on the Janiculum and, after circulating through the Vatican Gardens and appearing in various papal fountains, makes its final superb appearance in the piazza before vanishing into the Tiber.

'Do you have any trouble with the fountains?' I asked him.

'Oh yes,' he replied. 'We have eels!'

Great numbers of eels, he said, breed in Lake Bracciano and at a certain time of year millions of minute fry are carried to Rome in the pipes and clog the fountains. It was his duty to shut off the water and clear the pipes of them. Some years it was worse than others, and how disappointed the visitors always were when the jets suddenly wavered and stopped. Without the fountains the Piazza was somehow lifeless and incomplete.

The Swiss sergeant-major, a jolly and likeable person, knew a great deal about the history of his corps. He told me that it is now believed that Raphael, and not Michelangelo, designed the slashed uniform, though neither of them originated it. It is a survival of the slashed, ripped-up or 'blistered' fashion which spread all over Europe when the Swiss defeated the Duke of Burgundy in 1476. After the battle the ragged *Landsknechten* tore down the silk pavilions and patched their torn doublets and hose with them, arriving home with one leg yellow, the other green, half a tunic white and the other half blue. At first people laughed at this crazy costume of rags and tatters, then it began to spread to the aristocracy until hardly an article of attire was not slashed to show some rich and brilliant colour beneath. It was probably in an attempt to make the Swiss mercenaries a little less chromatic that Julius II asked Michelangelo, or Raphael, to design the famous uniform of red, yellow and blue.

The only time the Swiss Guard has been called on to die for the Pope was during the Bourbon sack of Rome in 1527, when all except about twelve fell in the Piazza, with their backs to St Peter's, valiantly defending the Vatican against impossible odds.

The full strength of the Swiss Guard is a hundred and twenty, and they are recruited from the four Catholic cantons of Switzerland, Unterwalden, Lucerne, Uri and Schwyz. Recruits must be bachelors between eighteen and twenty-five years of age, at least five feet eleven inches tall, of good character and, of course, Catholics. Before he joins the corps, the recruit must have undergone at least his preliminary training in the Swiss Army. The colonel, lieutenant-colonel, major, captain, and two lieutenants, must all be Swiss army officers.

He told me that a Swiss Guard receives a pension after ten years' service, and this is paid in Swiss francs. Drill is very important and one of the first things the recruit must learn is how to handle an eight-foot halberd and how to sink gracefully on the right knee with the halberd held perpendicularly in the right hand, in the motions of the papal salute. I asked the sergeant if service in the Swiss Guard ran in families, and he said that this was so. Few of the men, he told me, learn Italian, and usually form a little foreign colony of their own. When off duty they put on plain clothes and wander into Rome, indistinguishable from any tourist, and these men, the most photographed in the world, sometimes take cameras with them!

There was some excitement in the restaurant one evening when a hen that had been roosting in the vine trellis lost its balance and fell in a state of panic into someone's spaghetti. There was an exciting chase and the bird was captured, to appear one day, I suppose, as *pollo in padella*. No by-laws prohibit the keeping of hens within a few yards of St Peter's, or, if they exist, they are not obeyed. This is characteristic of Rome, which has grown so fast but has left behind many a rustic nook; and it seemed to me remarkable to think that the successors of St Peter must sometimes be awakened in the morning by the crowing of a cock.

§ 7

Of all the places in Rome none holds more surprising memories for an Englishman than the Hospital of S. Spirito, near St Peter's. It is a huge Renaissance building on the west bank of the Tiber, between the Ponte Vittorio Emanuele and the Ponte di Ferro. The gates beneath the arcaded porch are often open on summer afternoons and, glancing inside, you see a vast ward with its rows of white beds at pavement level: and upon the wall facing the Tiber is the name of the street, Lungotevere in Sassia. The word Sassia is a corruption of Saxia, which comes down the ages from the time in the eighth century when pious Anglo-Saxon kings founded a hospice on the site, which grew into Rome's first English colony.

It was known as the *Schola Anglorum* or the *Burgus Saxonum*; and this word *burgus*, which comes from the Saxon *burh*, is still preserved all over this district in its Italian form of *Borgo*. Practically every street leading from the Castle of S. Angelo to the Vatican is a *Borgo*. There is the Borgo Pio, the Borgo S. Angelo, the Borgo S. Spirito, the Borgo Vittorio, the Borgo Angelico, and others; and immediately you leave this closely packed area every street suddenly becomes an Italian *via* again. The Borgo is a relic of the days when the region round old St Peter's was a cluster of Teutonic boroughs established by the piety of the newly converted northern barbarians.

The first of these 'Peterboroughs' was that of the English. It rambled over the site of the Hospital of S. Spirito almost to the steps of St Peter's, and there, century after century, lived a resident population of Anglo-Saxons, churchmen, pilgrims, and visiting kings and queens who had travelled across Europe to lay their gifts and say their prayers at the tomb of St Peter. The *Schola,* or Guild, or Fraternity, of the Saxons took up arms on more than one occasion to defend the church. When the Saracens landed in 846 the only people who had the courage to put up a fight were the English, the Franks, and the Frisians of the Borgo. Unhappily their bravery was in vain: the Borgo was fired, St Peter's was sacked, and the sight of the burning ruins was said to have killed Pope Sergius II.

As I followed the long wall of the Hospital down the Borgo S. Spirito, where it stretches almost to the Piazza, I noticed a curious turntable or 'wheel' let into it, like those still in use in convents of enclosed nuns. It is now disused and covered by an openwork grille. This is a relic of the time when, after having been repeatedly sacked and burnt, the *Schola Saxonum* was turned into a foundling hospital by Innocent III in 1204. The present building was erected by Sixtus IV in the fifteenth century, still as a foundling hospital, and it accepted *trovatelli* until recent times. The turntable in the wall held a crib in which the infants were placed. A bell was rung and, while the depositor slipped away unseen, someone inside revolved the wheel and removed the baby. Augustus Hare, writing in 1887, when foundlings were still received there, says that close to the turntable was a second grille without any apparent purpose: but it was, he explains, a peep-hole for the use of those who thought of adopting a child, and 'by looking through the second grille, they can see the child, and discover if it is *simpatica*, and, if not, they can go away and leave it'.

It is the Anglo-Saxon memories which haunt one in these streets. And what far-off ghosts they are, from perhaps the least known chapter in our history, a time when fifty years could slip by as if in a sea fog which blows aside sometimes to show a battlefield, a famine, a deserted Roman city, or swineherds building a fire on a tessellated pavement, then closing in for another half century, and parting again to reveal, in a burst of sunlight, Benedictine monks from the Caelian Hill preaching under oak trees to bearded kings and their flaxen-haired queens. No period in our history carries such a morning freshness with it. Bishop Lightfoot, reviewing the history of his diocese, said that its Saxon beginning gleamed like a 'golden age of saintliness, such as England would never see again', the most attractive, and in its spirituality the most splendid, in the annals of his church. It was an age of saints and scholars, and an unofficial Celtic wind blew from Iona over the monasteries which soon rose in forest clearings and beside the river, the first little outposts of Rome's new empire.

Aldhelm playing his harp on the bridge at Malmesbury on market day and, like Orpheus, leading the spellbound peasants to mass before they went on to their bargaining; Bede, when nearly blind, preaching to an empty church in which, when he had ended, an invisible congregation of angels thundered 'Amen'; Caedmon singing like a morning star among the munching cows in their byre; the holy nun, Leoba, falling asleep as her novices read the Gospels to her and, while fast asleep, correcting any slip or error; an embassy travelling to Rome with a gift for the tomb of St Gregory, in gratitude for having received Christ from him: these are immortal pictures of a magic England that, alas, was to fade, before the Norman Conquest, in sloth, self-indulgence and irregularity. While it lasted, it was England's most poetic age, and perhaps no man of our time has caught its feeling better than G. K. Chesterton in his *Ballad of the White Horse*.

> *Stiff, strange and quaintly coloured*
> *As the broidery of Bayeux*
> *The England of that dawn remains,*
> *And this of Alfred and the Danes*
> *Seems like the tales a whole tribe feigns*
> *Too English to be true.*

It is so strange to stand in a street in Rome and to know that beneath you, ten, twenty, thirty feet maybe, you would come to the level trodden by Saxon sandals, and that sealed in the darkness may lie some fibula of Saxon silver, some broken cup from which a Saxon mouth had drunk, some Saxon penny brought to Rome from Wessex, Mercia or Northumbria ages ago.

It does not somehow seem surprising that British chieftains like Caractacus should have gazed upon the splendours of Rome in the imperial age, but it is amazing to think that the eyes of Saxon Christians should have looked upon Rome while the streets were still full of bronze statues and the palaces of the Caesars were still habitable. This was the Rome that Benedict Biscop saw when he left Northumbria, a young man, in 653, and journeyed across Merovingian Gaul in the time of the *rois fainéants* on his way to the tomb of St Peter. He is the first recorded English visitor, but there may have been others who have left no trace. He was soon joined in Rome by another pilgrim, one also destined to inscribe his name in letters of gold upon the history of the North of England, St Wilfrid, that haughty thegn turned monk. Those two young men from England looked upon an astonishing sight. They saw the Pantheon still covered with its golden tiles, for Constans II had not yet stolen them; they saw St Peter's shining with the bronze gilt tiles from the temple of Venus and Rome, which Heraclius had given to Pope Honorius I only twenty-four years previously; they saw more than three hundred bronze statues still standing in the grass-grown streets and fora, which within the next ten years were to be torn from their plinths by Constans II and carried off to Syracuse. And when they mounted the Palatine Hill, as these Saxons must have done, they saw the imperial palaces, which were still kept up although no one lived there. From time to time the Byzantine Exarch would visit Rome from Ravenna and would stay at the imperial palace; Heraclius also stayed there when he went to Rome in 629; and Constans II, the last Byzantine Emperor to visit Rome, lived there in 663. Perhaps the most astonishing thought of all is that Benedict and Wilfrid may have met men who had spoken to Gregory the Great, whose death had taken place only forty-nine years before. Rome was only just recovering from the agonies of the Gothic Wars when these Saxon visitors arrived, and both Benedict and Wilfrid were to continue to visit the city until they were old men: Benedict to collect books, vestments and ikons for his monasteries at Wearmouth and Jarrow, and Wilfrid to lay his disputes and troubles before the Pope. As they explored that sad, ruined city, though to them a mighty and glorious one, where Byzantine St Peter's glittered in mosaics and shone with golden candelabra, they may have met many fellow countrymen, and the first wooden houses of the Saxon *burh* may already have been grouping themselves around the basilica.

Our practical ancestors were impressed by St Peter's function, which they interpreted literally, as the Doorkeeper of Heaven. It seemed to them only commonsense to remain on the right side of the saint who held the keys. 'If Peter is the doorkeeper,' said King Oswiu of Northumbria, 'I will in all things obey his decrees, lest when I come to the gates of the kingdom of heaven, there be none to open them.' Naturally, churches dedicated to the doorkeeper sprang up all over Saxon England. London, or rather Westminster, had its own St Peter's in the Abbey Church, which had been actually visited, approved and consecrated by the Apostle himself. The story is that one Sunday night, while Edric, a fisherman, was casting his nets for salmon in the Thames, he heard a hail from what is now the Lambeth bank. He found a stranger, and by his voice and dress a foreigner, asking to be ferried over to the new church, which was ready to be consecrated by Mellitus, Bishop of London. No sooner had the stranger stepped ashore on Thorney Island and entered the church, than the awe-struck Edric saw the building pulsating with light, while choirs of angels descended and ascended, bearing lighted candles. Returning to the boat, the stranger asked for something to eat. Edric confessed sadly that he had caught nothing that day and had nothing to offer. The stranger, who had been a fisherman himself, was sympathetic. He said that he was St Peter and that he had come to consecrate his own church. He commanded Edric to cast his nets again and promised him salmon on one condition: that he never again fished on a Sunday!

Many a Saxon, hearing this delightful story, must have cancelled a journey to Rome. Why face the perils of the long road across Gaul and the Alps to pray at the Apostle's tomb when upon the banks of the Thames stood a church which Peter himself had sanctified? It seems that perhaps St Peter's visit to London may even have been an attempt to stop pilgrimages to Rome, which had reached proportions that dismayed many a churchman of the time. St Boniface, writing to Cuthbert of Canterbury about 743, pointed out that all pilgrims were not pure of heart and that the journey to Rome was sometimes fatal to female chastity. 'There are very few cities in Lombardy, in France or Gaul,' he wrote, 'in which there is not an adulteress or prostitute of the English nation, which is a scandal, and the disgrace of the whole church.'

Nothing, however, could deter the Saxons from making the journey, and it became the custom for kings to abdicate and go to Rome to end their lives and be buried near St Peter in preparation for the rush on Judgment Day. The first to do so was Caedwalla of Wessex, who arrived in Rome in 694 and was baptized by Pope Sergius I, and given the venerated name of Peter: but within a few days, while still *in albis*, the white baptismal garments worn in those days by the newly baptized for a week, he fell sick and died, and was buried in the portico of the popes. Offa of Essex and Coenred of Mercia arrived together in 709, and were followed sixteen years later by Ina of Wessex and his wife, Aethelburga.

She was evidently a forceful woman who did not like to leave anything to the imagination. It is said that in order to convince her husband of the futility of earthly splendour she once filled the royal hall with filth and refuse and placed a sow with her litter in the king's bed. Some believe that Ina and Aethelburga may have been the founders of the *Schola Saxonum*, or possibly they may have rebuilt and enlarged it.

Before the days of Charlemagne these English visitors to Rome were tramping and riding across France, where, in contrast to England, the municipal structure of the Roman world still remained intact. These English men and women from an island where Roman cities stood ruined and desolate must have been surprised to see the red-tiled cities of Gaul flourishing under their bishops. They have left brief, business-like accounts of their routes, but what would one not give for a description of the people encountered upon the roads, the monasteries and the towns, the food, and the conversation at night around the fire in monastery or *xenodochium*. Alas, of such things the earliest pilgrims tell us nothing.

The *Schola Saxonum* was soon copied by other nations. The desire to lie near St Peter was by no means confined to England. The *Schola* of the Langobards followed, founded by Queen Ansa about 770, and its last relics lingered until the seventeenth century, when they were swept away to make room for Bernini's colonnade. Then came the *Schola Francorum*, founded by Charlemagne about 797, and this, wonderful to relate, still exists inside the Arco delle Campane entrance to the Vatican City. There is a representation of Charlemagne outside the building, with an inscription which states that he was its founder. It is now the Teutonic College, and I fancied that the German priests and students whom I met there were rather reluctant to admit that their foundation was so much junior to the Anglo-Saxon *burh* that once stood nearby on the site of the Hospital of S. Spirito!

Of all the Saxon visitors to Rome, the most interesting was Alfred the Great, who was sent to Rome at the age of about five, in the year 853. Pope Leo IV made the child the centre of a ceremony which would seem to have been more fitted for a nursery than St Peter's. The little boy was solemnly girded with a sword and invested with the tunic of a Roman consul, surely the most precocious consul in history! No one knows why the child was subjected to this dignity; maybe it was a compliment to his devout father and the kingdom of Wessex. Hardly had Alfred returned to England than his pious father, Aethelwulf, distracted by the Viking raids, decided to visit Rome, perhaps to ask at the tomb of the Apostle whether it was really true, as they said in England, that 'God and his saints slept'. So Alfred, now seven, again took the long road with the King and his thegns and a great chest full of presents for St Peter. It is an interesting sidelight on the resources of England at this troubled time that among Aethelwulf's gifts were a crown of pure gold weighing four pounds, two gold vases, a gold-mounted sword, two golden images, and a silver-gilt candelabrum, perhaps intended to replace the candelabra of Constantine stolen by the Saracens only nine years before. Alfred and his father must have listened to many a tale of this terrible time told by those Saxons who had fought the Saracens and had seen the Borgo in flames. It is recorded that Aethelwulf rebuilt and restored the Saxon quarter and either reaffirmed the hearth tax formerly imposed on English homes for the upkeep of the colony, or may have himself originated the tax which became known as Peter's Pence.

So one stands in this city of spectres, and in this ghostly Borgo S. Spirito, trying to visualize the cluster and huddle of thatched buildings which once stood here, sheltering our remote countrymen, and maintained at first by an annual chest of silver collected in the homesteads of England. In those fair morning days before the milk of piety had turned sour with time, it was a happy thought that every fireside in English hall and cottage was helping to light the candles round the tomb of St Peter: but when the gift became a tax, and the centuries followed each other, there was no outcry when in 1534 Peter's Pence was abolished by Henry VIII. One of the mysteries of Roman archaeology is that though English silver was sent to Rome for nearly eight hundred years, so few coins have been discovered. A hoard of Peter's Pence was found in the last century, oddly enough in the House of the Vestal

Virgins, and they are the Saxon coins which are now on view in the Museo Nazionale Romano in the Baths of Diocletian. Some believe that the absence of English coins is due to the fact that the annual levy was melted down and went into the Papal treasury as bullion.

These are a few of the memories of the Borgo S. Spirito, and I am sure that English visitors, who rarely go there, would be as fascinated by it as I was. Later pilgrims from Britain were Canute, who was in Rome in 1026, and Macbeth, in 1050, who threw his money to the poor, perhaps in an attempt to atone for Duncan's murder.

Though even earlier than the first English pilgrims to Rome, this beautiful wayfarer's poem by Gildas, written about 600, the first British travel document, has caught the spirit of the time and indeed of all time.

> *In health may I and all of my companions*
> *Safely arrive with no harm or injury—*
> *May my boat be safe in the waves of the ocean,*
> *My horses safe on the highways of the earth,*
> *Our money safe as we carry it with us*
> *To pay due heed to our poor necessities.*
> *May our enemies fail to do harm to us,*
> *However evil the counsels which inspire them,*
> *In the eternal name of Christ our Master,*
> *May my roads all lie plain before me,*
> *Whether I climb the rugged heights of mountains,*
> *Or descend the hollow depths of valleys,*
> *Or trudge the lengthy roads of open country,*
> *Or struggle through the thickets of dense forest:*
> *May I walk always in straight ways and shining*
> *To longed-for places. . . .*

§ 8

One morning I had the pleasure of looking over the hospital with the enthusiastic secretary, Signor Pietro de Angelis, the author of many books about it and its long history. He opened a safe and showed me a few corroded Saxon coins, too defaced to identify, all that could be seen and felt of England's long association with this part of Rome. He had every Saxon visitor at his finger ends, and how odd it was to hear someone refer to 'Alfredo Magno'!

The number of children abandoned in mediaeval and Renaissance Rome was enormous, and the usual method was to leave them, like Moses in the bulrushes, on the banks of the Tiber. Here they would be found by fishermen who sometimes even caught the infants in their nets. When the wheel was installed in the hospital wall, it superseded the Tiber as a means of disposing of the children.

'An army of foster mothers was organized and disciplined by an official known as the Master of Wet Nurses,' said Signor de Angelis, 'and at feeding time a flautist played to them, possibly the earliest known instance of musical therapy. It must have been an impressive sight!'

The board room is decorated with a series of fascinating frescoes. Pope Innocent III is seen seated upon his throne, wearing his tiara, and lifting both hands in dismay as a page holds up to him a naked infant, which he grasps by the foot. In the background stands a Tiber fisherman leaning on an oar and holding a net in which sit two other naked babies. Another picture shows the Pope asleep in bed (still wearing his tiara), while an angel hovers inside the huge four-poster and tells him to found a hospital for the abandoned infants. In a third picture the Pope is seen mounted upon a white mule, and accompanied by Cardinals, watching the building of the hospital.

We passed into the next room, which was one of the most beautiful early eighteenth century libraries I have ever seen. The walls were covered to the ceiling with books, mostly of the sixteenth and seventeenth centuries, bound in calf, vellum and pigskin. This was the library of the distinguished anatomist, Giovanni Lancisi, the author of a classic book on the structure of the heart. Among the treasures of the hospital is the *Liber Fraternitatis* in which are over a thousand autographs of popes, kings, queens, cardinals and others who have been interested in the work of the Institution. The two most interesting English signatures are those of Henry VII and John Colet, founder of St Paul's School, London.

The secretary opened a curious little door in an alcove. We entered a cell that was fitted with a window. Signor de Angelis unfastened it and asked me to look out. To my surprise, I found myself, rather as if looking down the nave of a cathedral from the roof, surveying the whole length of the immense Sixtine Ward, which passers-by can sometimes partially see from the road if the gates under the porch happen to be open. After five centuries this ward is still in use. The organ, which was installed in 1546, is still there and can be played. I saw the nurses busying about among the numerous beds—there are a hundred in the women's ward and a similar number in the men's.

'This window was put in by Monsignor Virgilio Spada in 1633 when he was Grand Master of the Hospital,' said Signor de Angelis. 'It was his way of keeping the staff up to the mark! He slept in this room and if he heard a cry in the night, or some sick person asking for help, he would watch through the window to make certain that the sufferers were quickly attended to. As the nurses and doctors could not see when he was watching—and he had the reputation of being a very keen watcher—they felt that the eyes of the Grand Master were always upon them!'

A story like this is a welcome change from the horrific accounts of medical callousness in ages past.

§ 9

For at least two centuries every visitor to Rome has admired the sunset from the Pincian Hill, but few people ever watch the wonderful sunrise from the Janiculum. One morning, awakening earlier than usual, I let myself out of the convent quietly and walked down the hill to St Peter's, where the dawn had not yet vanquished the lamplight. It is worth while to renounce an hour or two in bed to see the Piazza di San Pietro without a single human soul in it, and the only movement that of the two fountains, and the only sound the rhythm of falling water.

It is a short and pleasant walk from the colonnade to the ridge of the Janiculum, where I watched the light grow stronger every minute. On one side of the hill is St Peter's and on the other the Tiber and Rome. The lamps were now sparks burning in a cold greyness. It was deliciously cool up there among the flowers and the trees. Rome lay beneath me, a large silent blur in which I could distinguish only the Victor Emmanuel Monument, and a tower and a cupola here and there. Turning around, I saw that St Peter's had now detached itself from the sky and loomed up, ready to catch the first light of the rising sun. Rome lay in beautiful, blessed silence. In hundreds of garages the cars and Vespas stood motionless. In that exquisite moment, while the motorists of Rome were horizontal, I looked down upon the city, grateful for this blissful peace.

As I stood watching, facing the dim, incoherent mass of roofs and domes, the light grew stronger every second, and buildings, churches, towers and cupolas emerged clearly from the morning greyness, taking on individuality as colour flooded back into them, all the reds, browns and yellows of Rome; and the next instant the sun was shining in a cloudless sky. This was more wonderful than any sunset, this sight of Rome's new morning. All at once the roofs and domes were glinting and scintillating, the white Brescian marble of the Victor Emmanuel Monument sparkled like an iceberg, and I could see next to it the campanile of the Capitol. Away to the left I recognized the dome of the Pantheon, the trees of the Pincio and the Borghese Gardens, the towers of the Trinità dei Monti, and behind the Victor Emmanuel Monument the twin domes and the tower of S. Maria Maggiore. Far off to the west I could see a line of blue hills where Tivoli lay among its olives and its vines, and more hills in the distance where Albano and Nemi, still and windless, would be catching the first sunlight. I crossed the road and glancing down in the direction of St Peter's,

I saw the cross upon the dome bright in the rising sun, while the long shadow of the obelisk pointed to the church.

On the highest ridge of the Janiculum, looking down on Rome, Garibaldi rides a superb bronze horse: he is a regal looking Garibaldi, and the horse must have come from the royal stables. A little lower down the ridge Anita Garibaldi is riding an entirely different kind of animal, a wild and terrified mustang which is doing its best to bolt. And Anita is not only riding, but she is also holding an infant and at the same time firing a pistol. The contrast between her agitation and evident peril, and the statuesque placidity of her devoted husband only a few yards off, is perturbing. One feels that if Garibaldi only knew what was happening to his beloved companion so near at hand, he would be off his processional charger in an instant and rushing to the rescue.

Anita's difficulties depict that moment in her adventurous life when she escaped from her captors with her infant and gunned her way to freedom through a forest. The intrepid Anita was a born guerrilla fighter who by chance plunged into the life of camps and ambuscades for which she was so well fitted. Garibaldi's courtship of his wife must be the most laconic in history. He first saw her as he gazed shoreward from the deck of a ship off the coast of Brazil. 'I wanted someone to love me, and that immediately,' he related. From the deck of his steamer he spied 'some pretty girls occupied in domestic work. One of them attracted my attention above the rest. There was nothing for it but to go ashore; and I immediately directed my steps towards the house upon which my gaze had been so long fixed.' He went up to Anita and said, 'Maiden, thou shalt be mine', and, oddly enough, she was.

Another interesting character whom I was surprised to encounter on the Janiculum that morning was John Whitehead Peard, 'Garibaldi's Englishman', a bearded Cornish giant from Fowey who helped to unite Italy. Though other Englishmen did quite as much, if not more, than Peard, this huge sharpshooter caught the imagination of the Italians. His company were armed with a new weapon, a revolver rifle, which the American inventor, Samuel Colt, had sent to Garibaldi as an experiment, but these were said to have leaked at the breeches and to have scorched Peard's men badly. Peard's most amusing exploit was to be mistaken for Garibaldi. Entering a town with his men one day, he was hailed by the excited populace as the liberator. As it happened to be strategically advantageous for Garibaldi to be reported in that particular neighbourhood, Peard gravely accepted the situation, but it rapidly got out of hand. A Te Deum was sung in his honour, the town was illuminated, deputations appeared, troops had to be reviewed, and the dismayed Englishman, having committed himself, was obliged to face a number of embarrassing situations from which he was only released by the arrival of the hero himself!

As I walked down the Janiculum, I had another look at Anita Garibaldi on her plunging horse, and I thought of the number of bronze and marble horses there are in Rome. The most important is the famous horse which Marcus Aurelius rides without stirrups on the Capitol. The bronze still retains traces of gilding, and the legend is that when all the gold has returned, the forelock will turn into a singing bird and at the sound the world will end! There are the two splendid white marble horses which accompany Castor and Pollux at the top of the steps to the Capitol and, from the same stud maybe, the two huge prancing horses beneath the obelisk on the Quirinal, about which the pilgrims of the Middle Ages made up so many stories. There is the magnificent gilded cavalry charger ridden by Victor Emmanuel on the Monument, and, tucked away to the left as you enter St Peter's, a fine plunging horse by Bernini on whose back Constantine the Great is seated.

I went down to my little café in the Via della Conciliazione and, as usual, the bread had not yet arrived. The waiter flipped a table with a napkin and said that it was going to be hot again. While he was watering the orange trees in tubs, the boy rode up on a bicycle with the bread; and a tourist, stepping dangerously into the road, faced St Peter's and took the first photograph of the day.

CHAPTER NINE

A visit to the Vatican – The Vatican State – the Pope's motor car and 'chariots' – Vatican Radio – the Pope's Garden – an exquisite summerhouse – a forgotten relic of the Stuarts

§ 1

The biscuit-coloured palace of the Vatican, its blinds drawn, its windows shining in the morning sun, lifts itself above Bernini's colonnade at odd and unexpected angles. The old palace seems to drowse in the sun. An ardent Lutheran, gazing up, might fancy sly Jesuits flitting along the dim corridors, though the visitor who has been there knows there is only a bored attendant and the filtered light on Raphael's frescoes; while the ardent Catholic gazes up at the maze of buildings, wondering where the Holy Father lives.

Marion Crawford, writing in 1898, noted that every tourist as he crossed the Piazza looked up at the Vatican, doubtless wondering what goes on there. He described an itinerant vendor of photographs shaking yards of views out of gaudy red bindings, very much as Leporello unrolls the list of Don Giovanni's conquests, and 'points out the corner windows of the second storey, and informs the visitor that "Sua Santità" inhabits these rooms, and promptly offers photographs of any other interior part of the Vatican but that.'

Everything is the same today, the Piazza, the Vatican, the tourist, the persistent peddler with his yards of tinted *Ricordo di Roma*, save for one important difference: since Marion Crawford wrote *Ave Roma Immortalis*, the Pope has moved from the luxurious second floor of the Apostolic Palace into the attic.

No one now thinks it strange that the Pope should live in what used to be the servants' bedrooms of his palace, and few are those who think of the astounding changes which in less than a century have removed the Pontiff from the gilded salons of the Quirinal to the attics of the Vatican. What were regarded as misfortunes at the time have, however, proved to be blessings: the temporal kingdom of the Popes has vanished, but the Holy Father's realm has been extended into the minds and consciences of some four hundred million people in all parts of the world.

The Pope's window on the top floor of the Apostolic Palace is now better known than most of the sights in Rome. How the ghosts of Borgia and Medici, of Aldobrandini and Borghese, which surely haunt the corridors of the Vatican, must gaze in astonishment at the simplicity of the Pope's attic bedroom and the frugal room where he eats alone while, we are told, two canaries are let loose from their cage to fly about and settle on his arm or shoulder.

The reign of simplicity was inaugurated by St Pius X, who broke through Vatican etiquette when he showed no desire, upon being elected Pope in 1903, to leave the humble room which had been assigned to him for the Conclave. Stories are still told of his humility and simplicity. When the Vatican authorities realized that he would never consent to descend to the papal apartments on the second floor, they altered for him the top floor which has since been occupied by every succeeding Pope.

When I was crossing the Piazza one morning, I noticed a little group of men gathered at the end of the colonnade on the left, and a second glance proved them to be plain clothes policemen. There were also a number of uniformed police lingering in gateways and waiting unobtrusively on the road beyond the colonnade. I realized what was happening: the Pope was about to return to Rome from Castel Gandolfo for a conference or a meeting of some sort. So I waited to see him cross from Italy into the Vatican City.

The effect of Bernini's columns is to surround the Piazza di San Pietro with a dense forest, and so vast is the encircled plain that hardly a soul, save those drawn by chance to this remote corner of the wood, guessed what was happening. If the slightest rumour had spread from us, the excited crowds would have trooped over in their hundreds.

Suddenly a man in a blue lounge suit flung away a cigar and became an important police official. Everyone saluted him. The uniformed police lined the roadway, and the plain clothes men grouped themselves round the locked iron gate that leads up into the Vatican City, past the Teutonic College and the Campo Santo. An American girl with fair hair, accompanied by an older woman, invaded the scene. She walked up to the important police official and asked him what was going on. The official smiled upon the lovely foreigner and explained that the Pope was coming, and he even found a place for her in front of everyone else.

While I was thinking how right women are to take advantage of this power which vanishes so quickly, there was a tremendous roar of motor-cycles and twenty young men in blue uniforms, wearing crash helmets and mounted on powerful machines, wheeled to the side of the road at what I took to be the frontier, while three black touring cars went on unescorted across the invisible frontier into the Vatican State.

The Pope was alone in the second car. He was wearing his usual white soutane and a shovel hat of dark red. I had an impression of a thin pale face, two large black eyes behind gold-rimmed glasses, a thin hand tracing the sign of the cross; then the car passed the iron gateway, which had been opened by Swiss Guards who dropped on one knee as the car swept in and up the hill past the Campo Santo.

One of the few people who dropped to their knees when the Pope passed was, surprisingly enough, the American girl. Now she stood there with her eyes shining. 'My!' she said to her companion, 'wasn't that just too wonderful? He saw me! Did you see, he gave me a special benediction—all to myself?'

The mounted motor cyclists eased their crash helmets and lifted their goggles; the police official cast a lingering glance after the fair American and went off, no doubt to report officially that the Italian State had, in accordance with the Lateran Treaty, safely conducted the successor of St Peter across Italian territory.

§ 2

The first time I called upon an official at the Vatican I was over-whelmed, as I am sure many are, by the historical associations of such a visit. There is no other example of such continuity as the Papal Curia. For sixteen centuries it has been seated either at the Lateran Palace, at Avignon, or at the Vatican: the Papacy has had only three addresses since the age of Constantine the Great! 'The Papacy,' in Thomas Hobbes' famous sentence, 'is not other than the Ghost of the deceased Roman Empire, sitting crowned upon the grave thereof.' The statement, of course, is extreme and needs to be qualified, though many have noted not only the similarity of the structure of the Latin Church to that of the Roman Empire, but also its use of many imperial terms: diocese, prefecture, vicariate, consistory, and so forth; and when the Pope appoints a representa-tive he is called a 'legate', as he would have been in the days of Julius Caesar. One of the Papacy's most remarkable annexations, to my mind, is the title of 'Pontifex Maximus'.

All over Rome, on architrave and on fountain, to say nothing of Paul V's inscription across St Peter's, you see those words, often abbreviated, as on a Roman coin, to *Pont.Max.*, which can be puzzling to some visitors. I once heard a shrill and unashamed female voice ring out above the roar of the Trevi with, 'Whom do you suppose this Max was—this Pont Max whose name is every-where?' Pontifex means a bridge-builder and the title of Pontifex Maximus was given to the high priest in ancient Rome because of certain ceremonies which were performed to propitiate the spirits of the Tiber, to compensate them for the building, in remote times, of Rome's first wooden bridge. Julius Caesar was the Pontifex Maximus at the time of his murder. It seems that this pagan title was transferred to the Pope as early as the time of Leo I, in 440, and Longfellow, in *The Golden Legend*, says:

> *Well has the name of Pontifex*
> *Unto the Church's head, as the chief builder*
> *And architect of the invisible bridge*
> *That leads from earth to heaven.*

The Pontifex Maximus was never a high priest devoted to any particular god, but rather the regulator of the Roman state religion, therefore when Christianity replaced paganism, it is likely that the title fell naturally to the Pope. Though stone-cutters have used the title mercilessly, and no inscription on tomb, fountain or building in Rome would be complete without 'Pont Max', the Popes do not apply the title to themselves. The title they have used on Bulls since the time of Gregory the Great, and still use today, is *Servus servorum Dei*—Servant of the servants of God.

With these thoughts, I approached the palace of the Pope. The entrance is the Bronze Door beneath the colonnade on the right. Here I found the Swiss Guard under a senior NCO, no longer merely picturesque but keenly interested in everyone who approached. Here is the place, if anywhere, where those giving their names as Attila or Luther would present themselves, or where anyone anxious to convert the Pope would appear. Fantastic as it may seem, this occurred more than once during the eighteenth century. The most determined missionary was a Scotch minister who had convinced himself that the 'whore of Babylon' in *Revelations* was the Pope, and that it was his duty to go to Rome and win him over to Presbyterianism. He managed to get near the Pope during a ceremony in St Peter's and, approaching, cried in a loud voice: 'O thou beast of nature with seven heads and ten horns! thou mother of harlots, arrayed in purple and scarlet, and decked with gold and precious stones and pearls! throw away the golden cup of abominations, and the filthiness of thy fornication!'

The Swiss Guard took charge of him, and he would have been sent to the galleys but for the intervention of Clement XIV, who seems to have been less shocked than anybody. The Pope paid his passage home to Scotland and remarked that he was 'obliged to him for his good intentions and for undertaking such a long journey with a view to do good'.

Naturally the Swiss Guard at the Bronze Door are always on the look-out for possible missionaries, and they watch like angry wasps as you mount the steps, but, having put you down as harm-

less, transform themselves into gay Swiss *lepidoptera* and wave you
on to a reception room at the right of the entrance. Here are two
elderly laymen in black, sitting at a desk with telephones. They
ring up the person with whom you have an appointment and tell
him of your arrival, then they instruct you where to go. There are
no forms to fill in, no messenger boy to follow; instead you have
the rather startling experience of finding yourself at large in the
Vatican.

In my experience the receptionist was more helpful than any I
have encountered in the brusque realms of British bureaucracy.
Having asked to see an Australian monsignor whom I had known
years before, the receptionist told me that he was no longer at the
Vatican, but had been made a bishop and was somewhere in
Africa. Seeing that I was at a loss, he kindly suggested that I
might like to see his successor; and so I found myself crossing the
enormous courtyard of St Damasus in the blinding sunlight,
watched from afar by the only other human being on the landscape, a papal gendarme. I thought how different it was to be not
a sightseer, but that historical character: someone with business
at the Vatican!

I heard a car change gear as it came uphill and appeared suddenly through the arch of the Cortile del Pappagallo (whose parrot
was it, I wondered . . .), to emerge and draw up at the doorway of the Apostolic Palace at the right. Ahead of me rose the
glassed-in loggia whose drawn blinds protected the frescoes of
Raphael. Water was dripping somewhere into a wall fountain,
no doubt from the same underground streams drained and piped
by St Damasus, who was Pope in 366, to supply the baptismal
font in the first St Peter's.

The gendarme lifted a white cotton glove to a Napoleonic hat
in salute and waved me towards a doorway. Here I was ushered
into a lift in which were standing two young monsignori hardly
out of college. Just as the attendant was about to close the lift door,
a Cardinal attended by his secretary strode into the building, and
as he entered the lift the two monsignori flattened themselves
into the background just as two subalterns might have done in
the War Office if the lift had been unexpectedly invaded by the

Chief of the Imperial General Staff.

The Cardinal's buttons and buttonholes were of red silk, and so was his sash. He strode out of the lift, his secretary scuttling after like an earnest black rabbit, beneath his arm one of those bulging briefcases which are such an impressive feature of business life on the Continent. An attendant was waiting for me. He took me along a corridor and motioned me to a bench. I had now lost all sense of direction. I was like someone who had been led with bandaged eyes into a fortress, and I was burning with curiosity to know where I was. Would it be outraging the etiquette of sixteen centuries if I ventured to tip-toe forward and peep through the blinds I decided to risk it. I saw that I was high up above the portico of St Peter's, and at a right angle to it, almost on a level with the gigantic saints. I could see people walking about the roof and gazing down to the piazza below. In the back ground rose the dome, and round its gallery clustered more visitors looking down on Rome and the Tiber, and to the Alban Hills beyond.

I slipped back to my bench just in time. The attendant, silently appearing, made that curious Italian sign of beckoning, which is nothing like the lifted English forefinger, but is a furtive almost sinister movement of the fingers of the right hand as if scratching the head of a large, invisible dog. I followed him and met a young English monsignor who had recently arrived from Japan.

§ 3

There is no income tax in the Vatican State, no customs duty, and no currency control. When I went to cash some travellers' cheques in the ultra-modern marble Vatican bank, I was told most courteously by the cashier that I would receive a slightly better rate in Rome, but I was so interested in this bank, whose chief customers were bishops and monsignori, that I was glad to forego a few lire. While I was waiting for my passport to be checked, an aged nun joined the queue and, fumbling in her black garments, produced a cheque book and drew what I supposed were the necessary housekeeping funds for her convent. Like everything in the Vatican, the bank works smoothly, silently and efficiently.

No one knows how rich the Vatican is. It is the only state in the world that never publishes an annual budget, and those who deal with its finances are answerable to no one but the Pope. It is, however, no secret that to compensate the Papacy for the loss of its temporal power, seven hundred and fifty million lire in cash, and a billion lire in five per cent state bonds, were handed over by the Italian State on the signing of the Lateran Treaty in 1929. Therefore the Vatican should be a good deal more solvent than most states in this modern world, also it has no national debt stretching its horrible tentacles out to unborn generations.

Among the Vatican's chief sources of income is 'Peter's Pence', the contribution for the upkeep of St Peter's tomb, which originated in Anglo-Saxon England. This is now contributed by Roman Catholic communities all over the world. The beautiful stamps so frequently issued by the Vatican are another source of income. Hardly a visitor comes to Rome who does not make a point of sending home a card with a Vatican stamp on it, posted in one of the blue Vatican post-boxes, and I was told that a fair average income from stamps is about £15,000 a year.

The Pope is the last of the world's absolute monarchs, and is his own treasurer and answerable to no one. As the owner of every bit of property he could, if he wished, give away millions and bankrupt the Holy See, which Benedict XV nearly did. His generosity was apparently devastating. 'He kept huge sums of money in a drawer of his desk and disposed of them personally for the creation of Catholic schools, convents, missionary settlements, and the like,' writes C. M. Cianfarra in *The War and the Vatican*. 'A bishop who intended to ask the Pope to finance a project for the building of a convent in Palestine was warned not to mention the subject because, on seeing the request for the audience, Benedict had remarked: "I am sure he is going to ask me for money to carry out his plan, and I don't have it."

'Therefore when he was received, the bishop talked of general subjects such as the condition of the Church in Palestine, the number of converts, etc., without even hinting at his project. Finally, as he was taking leave, Benedict said, "Well, what about your plan? I am sure that the estimate must be prohibitive."

' "It's about one hundred thousand lire, Your Holiness," stammered the embarrassed prelate.

' "In that case, We shall contribute," said the Pope. He opened a drawer and handed the surprised bishop a packet containing one hundred one-thousand-lire bills.'

It is perhaps no wonder that when Benedict XV died in 1922, Cardinal Gasparri, says Cianfarra, 'made an inventory and found that the Holy See was literally broke'.

There are about a thousand citizens of the Vatican State, which include quite a number of women, the wives and daughters of lay functionaries, and the German nuns who cook the Pope's food and attend to his housework. The majority of the citizens are not priests or ecclesiastics. There are the Swiss Guard, the pontifical gendarmerie, the Vatican firemen, the gardeners, and many others who live within the boundaries. All Cardinals in Rome are automatically Vatican citizens and so are Papal Nuncios when sent to foreign countries. These fortunate people are exempt from income tax and currency control, and they are entitled to buy all the necessities of life, and a number of its luxuries, at duty free prices at the Vatican store, which is known by the Latin term, *Annona*, a word that in ancient Rome signified the year's produce in corn, wine and fruit.

How pleasant it is that the old Papal States, which sprawled across the map of Italy until 1870, should have been distilled into this attractive little model state where there is no taxation, no poverty, no crime and no commerce; for Vatican citizens are forbidden to undertake any gainful occupations. I believe the last of the Vatican vineyards was pulled up some years ago when it was discovered that an enterprising gardener was making a fluid, no doubt as sour as that mentioned by Martial, which he called 'Pope's Wine'!

The main gate of the Vatican City is the Gate of S. Anna in the Via di Porta Angelica, where a Swiss Guard is always on duty to ask your business. A narrow road stretches uphill. On the right is the church of St Anna of the Palafrenieri, or Grooms, which is now the parish church of the Vatican City; on the left is a canteen where the hospitable Swiss Guards entertain their friends to something stronger than coffee, in a homely room decorated with frescoes which show their predecessors performing mighty deeds with sword and halberd.

A few paces up the hill and you come to the most delightful post-office in the world. It is a marble hall without a single advertisement. There is a marble table in the centre at which you can sit, generally in company with the inevitable Franciscan, and write a telegram or a cable. This central office handles the Pope's private mail and delivers to his secretary about a thousand letters every day, some from lunatics and eccentrics. When Benedict XV was very old, he received a letter from an excited lady who wrote that she had had a private message from God to say that Antichrist was already in the world and would reveal himself in a few years' time. It is said that the aged Pope handed the letter to his secretary with a smile, saying, 'Thank God, that will be the concern of my successor!'

The post-office is at the corner of the main street of the Vatican City, the Via della Tipografia. There is an excellent chemist's shop nearby, managed by the Fatebenefratelli, the 'Do Good' Brothers, who run the splendid hospital on the island in the Tiber, and opposite is the general store, which sells everything, including wine, spirits and tobacco, at prices which rival those of Andorra. The vegetables, milk and eggs come from the papal farm at Castel Gandolfo, and I looked with interest at the eggs, remembering the beautiful hen *palazzi* with their bright mosaic decoration.

Window dressing is regarded not as an art but as an offence in the Vatican City; the purchaser must not be tempted. The *Annona* is generally crowded, for it shuts every day at half-past eleven. While I was there I saw a Dominican buy a bottle of Benedictine, which seemed to me a charming transaction.

Nearby is the office of the *Osservatore Romano*, the Vatican evening paper, and not far off are the Polyglot Printing Works, which can set up and print a book in Coptic, Syriac, Hebrew and a dozen other unusual languages. Across the road is the Armoury of the Swiss Guard, where the steel helmets, the halberds, and the huge double-handed swords that are carried in pontifical processions, are precisely arranged and burnished; there also are the colours and drums of the corps. I was passing this building one day with a young seminarist from the English College.

'I remember,' he said, 'once going there to collect a suit of armour which the Swiss Guard was kind enough to lend us for a performance of *The House at Sly Corner*. They were awfully decent, but they refused to lend the helmet. It bore the arms of Pope Julius II, the regimental badge, and they considered it should not appear on a stage. Still, they lent us everything else!'

What a delightful and unexpected glimpse of domestic life in the Vatican!

Among the surprises of the Vatican City I shall always remember an imposing building with the words inscribed above the wide gates, *Raedis Pontificum Servandis*—For the keeping of the Papal chariots—otherwise the Papal Coach House. It is now a garage. The doors were open and in the entrance stood the Pope's black touring car—SCV1—an American car of special design with a glass roof and only one throne-like seat at the back. SCV, by the way, are the Vatican registration letters. The car was surrounded by a strong smell of disinfectant and, glancing inside, I saw that several bags of camphor had been placed on the floor.

There were two or three other cars of antique pattern which, though they could hardly be used nowadays, were kept in beautiful order and behind them was the enchanting sight of the Pope's chariots, among them the huge scarlet and gilt state coach which used to be drawn by six white horses. The footboard was a gilded carved group showing two well-nourished cherubs dancing forward with a tiara, as if that uneasy crown were something gay to be awarded as a prize at a fancy dress ball. From the roof rose eight gold pines. The coach is slung high from the ground on curved springs and must have rocked like a cradle. The doors open crisply and a little set of carpeted steps lets down and can be folded back into themselves. The Pope sat on a crimson and gilt throne, and opposite him sometimes sat two Cardinals. Near his right hand was a little box which might have contained a breviary or a snuff-box. The Pontiff must have been more easily seen and admired as this great vehicle swayed slowly along than he is today, even though his motor car has a glass roof.

The coach was used for the last time only two days before the famous *Venti Settembre*, in 1870, when Pius IX drove in state to perform his last public act as a temporal monarch. Some time before he had given permission to an English company to restore the old Marcian aqueduct and to reintroduce this ancient supply to Rome. This had been achieved on September 18, 1870, but the fountain at which the official inauguration took place no longer exists: it used to stand where the railway station is today. The Pope drove down from the Quirinal in the state coach, greeted everywhere by shouting crowds as '*Papa Re!*', and having drunk a cup of water and praised its purity, he thanked the magistrates for having given it his name—Marcia Pia. Two days later the troops of Victor Emmanuel entered Rome, and Pius IX became the first 'Prisoner of the Vatican'. Since that day, though the old coach is evidently as spry and springy as ever and could take the road tomorrow, the grooms, the postilions and the splendid white horses have all died and have had no successors.

On the walls round about hang the state saddlery, the red velvet saddles of the postilions and the outriders, the gold plumes of the horses and the embossed bridles and traces, the steel burnished, the gilding polished, the leather soaped and washed. I saw hanging the trappings of the Pope's white mule, which date from the days of the *Cavalcata*, when the newly elected Pope would ride through Rome and down the Sacra Via to take possession of the Lateran. One sees such things with wonder, and there rises in the mind a vision of splendour, pageantry and symbolism that will never again be seen in the world. The last pale vestiges of such magnificence are the great ceremonies in St Peter's and the coronations of the Kings and Queens of England. One cannot leave the Pope's chariots without recalling that day in 1769 when for the last time a Pope rode through Rome.

He was Clement XIV, who was elected Pope in May, 1764, a hale and hearty man of sixty-four, who decided to revive the pageantry of older days and ride in state from the Quirinal to the Lateran. The crowds were greedy and discontented. They were annoyed to discover that the fountains were still flowing with water and not with the wine they had hoped, and the fluttering among them of sixty-six thousand bread tickets, though a vivid enough commentary on the times, did not compensate them for the hard cash which they had expected to see flying through the air. The procession moved down from the Quirinal Hill to the Piazza dei SS. Apostoli, then to the Capitol, and along the Forum and up the Sacred Way to the Lateran Palace. First came horsemen in crimson velvet and gold lace, wearing brass helmets and carrying gilt lances, who cleared the way, and behind rode four Knights of the Guard, followed by the Grand Master of the Horse and the valets and mace-bearers of the Cardinals, wearing scarlet cloaks. Then, lest the Pope should become tired of riding, came his empty travelling litter, the *portantina*, covered with draperies of scarlet and gold, with ten white mules in the shafts attended by grooms in red coats with folded hoods. Four mounted trumpeters followed, heading a long line of chamberlains—there were some hundreds—all in scarlet; and then followed the heads of the princely houses, Odelscalchi, Albani, Giustiniani, Mattei, Altemps, Fiano, Caffarelli, Salviati, and Anguillara and others, attended by their pages and servants. Then came a detachment of the Swiss Guard in armour and steel helmets, carrying their great swords, followed by Prince Colonna, the Prince Assistant to the Papal Throne, in full armour, riding a Spanish stallion. Behind him, stretching in a long line, were church dignitaries and an Auditor of the Rota, carrying the Papal Cross, then more Swiss Guards and—the Pope.

There is in the British Museum a print which shows Clement XIV as he appeared to his subjects upon that memorable occasion, and an extraordinary spectacle he must have been. He did not ride the traditional mule, but a sprightly white palfrey which was bedizened with nodding tassels of crimson and housings of crimson and gold. A precious saddle-cloth, stiff with golden embroidery, hung to within a foot of the ground, but the saddle itself was concealed by a figure which at first sight looked like that of a portly old lady. The Pope wore flowing robes which were bunched up behind him on the horse's rump, and over them a lace rochet, a stole of gold bullion, and a red cape edged with white fur. The whole effect was topped by a huge shovel hat, which he wore over his skull cap. As he rode forward, administering the papal blessing, twenty-four pages walked beside him, dressed in cloth of silver, with white silk stockings and white plumes in their little round caps. The boys had been chosen for their birth and beauty and each one carried an object which the Pope might possibly need, and among them, most providentially as it turned out, was a spare hat; for, as Clement was passing the Arch of Septimius Severus, his palfrey reared and His Holiness was tumbled in the dust. He was uninjured and mounted again with a regal jest.

The second part of the procession, which was as gorgeous as the first, included the College of Cardinals, riding two by two in their scarlet, wearing caps instead of Cardinals' hats, and preceded by servants carrying their arms on gilt escutcheons. Among them was Henry Stuart, Cardinal of York.

All that remains of such splendour now hangs upon the walls of the papal garage, and it is typical of the Vatican that it is still fresh and clean. The *portantina* is not, however, kept in the coach house and I was unable to see it. The other litter, the *sedia gestatoria*, is, of course, well known and is in constant use today, but a third, the *talamo*, is not perhaps so familiar and has not been seen for some years. This word, which must surely be derived from *talaris*, a garment reaching to the ankles, is the name given to a curious structure invented I believe in the seventeenth century for Corpus Christi, when the Pope passed in procession through the streets adoring the Host. As it would have been impossible for anyone to have remained in a kneeling position for so long, the *talamo*, a low stool, was designed, on which the Pope sat while his robes were disposed round him in such a way that he appeared to be kneeling.

A hundred yards or so from the garage, against the mighty walls of the Museum, is the Vatican Fire Brigade, known by the interesting name of the *Vigiles*, which was that of the ancient Roman police force reorganized by Augustus and stationed by him in all the wards or regions of the city. The papal *Vigili* have a streamlined duty-room, with a telephone switchboard in touch with every corner of the Vatican.

'What is the number of the Pope's gold telephone?' I asked.

'Vatican City a hundred and one,' was the reply, 'but you would have some difficulty in speaking to the Holy Father!'

The fire-fighting equipment, to say nothing of the pumps, for winter floods are a great danger on Mons Vaticanus, could not be more efficient. Every afternoon when the Vatican Museum is closed, the *Vigili* patrol the endless galleries, peering into every corner. Once a year, on January 17, the feast day of St Anthony, whose temptations were so severe that they were like flames, and who is therefore the patron saint of firemen, the *Vigili* parade in full dress and attend mass at S. Anna; then at noon, in their decorated quarters, they receive a visit from the Cardinal Vicar of the Vatican City, who is welcomed by the sergeant-major. After the Cardinal has replied and departed, they sit down to a feast.

§ 4

At the highest point of the Vatican Gardens stands the Vatican Radio Station and the Pope's private walk. As this part of the hill has never been built over, or shaved off and lowered, like so many of the famous Seven Hills, it preserves its original height. The masts of the Vatican Radio are now one of the landmarks of Rome. Though they do not perhaps improve the landscape, one gets used to them, and at the convent I would look forward to their terminal sparkle at night, as cheerful and gay as the star on the wand of a fairy queen. The present station is the reconstructed summer palace built by Leo XIII on the highest ground in the gardens. It is now magnificent with many kinds of marble, and hums with electric vibrations. At the base of the dome are the words from *St Matthew* of Christ to His disciples: 'What I tell you in darkness, that speak ye in light; and what ye hear in the ear, that preach ye upon the housetops.'

I do not know of a more beautifully situated radio station, unless it is Radio Andorra on its Pyrenean mountain, whose insistent voice dominates the air over southern France and northern Spain. The immensely powerful Vatican Radio broadcasts on twenty-four short, and three medium, wave-lengths, and in every language. Its signal, the bells of St Peter's, followed by a voice saying '*Laudetur Jesus Christus*, this is Vatican Radio . . .' are known all over the world. The station was described to me as 'the Pope's spiritual power-house'.

The universality of the Roman Church is a commonplace of speech and writing, yet it is with astonishment that one sees proof of it so casually in the routine broadcast arrangements of this station: twice a day in Hungarian and Czech; twice a week in Bulgarian; three times a week in Ukrainian; four times a week in Slovene and Croat; once a week in Byelo-Russian; three times a week in Roumanian; and so on, with periodic broadcasts in all the oriental languages. The Jesuits are the wireless experts of the Vatican and are in charge of the station.

There is one activity of the Vatican Radio which is probably not well known; that is the routine broadcast of the Secretary of State to dignitaries of the Roman Church in all parts of the world. Every Cardinal, Papal Nuncio and Apostolic Delegate stationed in a foreign country has a radio set on which he receives signals from the Vatican. Certain times are appointed during which announcements and instructions may be heard, and it saves a great deal of time if a Cardinal in, for instance, South America, can listen at a given time and hear, 'We entirely approve of the suggestion contained in your letter of the seventh, but suggest . . . etc., etc.' I doubt if the world contains such a striking contrast within a few hundred yards as Vatican Radio and the *Raedis Pontificum Servandis.* . . .

The Vatican railway station, which is not far off, is built of white marble, like a rather distinguished branch of Barclay's Bank, and is the cleanest and most stately of stations, but it has never yet seen a passenger train! There is no ticket-office, no bookstall, no left-luggage office, indeed none of the things one associates with a station, but there is accommodation for choirs which have never yet sung a valedictory hymn to a departing pontiff. The station was built soon after the signing of the Lateran Treaty, and an extraordinary feature are the gigantic iron gates which cross the tracks and can be opened or closed in a minute by electricity.

So I returned downhill to that picturesque cluster of palaces which houses part of the Roman Curia. In various parts of Rome other buildings have been granted extraterritoriality and contain departments which cannot be accommodated within the overcrowded one hundred and eight acres of the tiny Vatican State.

Many to whom the Government of the Roman Catholic Church is a mystery are nevertheless aware that it is the oldest administration on earth, and some would say the wisest; certainly no other has had such an extensive experience of human nature. It is the unique continuous growth of centuries, and though it has been modernized on countless occasions, it still carries with it many a strange relic of the past. Unlike the governments of ordinary states, which think in terms of their years of office, the Vatican thinks in centuries. Time is not important; its policy is based on the belief that while the individual is mortal, the Church is eternal. That was the attitude which exasperated Napoleon. He might kidnap and bully a Pope, but he could not browbeat the Church.

'Do you know that I am capable of destroying your Church?' he once shouted at Cardinal Consalvi, the Secretary of State.

'Sire,' replied Consalvi, 'not even we priests have achieved that in eighteen centuries!'

The strangest thing about the Roman Curia is that when a Pope dies, the administration perishes with him. All departments of government become moribund until the new Pope revives them. As most Popes are old men on their election and their reigns are not often long, the frequent interregnums in past times, especially when the election of the new pontiff was delayed for months, sometimes for years, created periods of anarchy; but nowadays the Curia springs into life again in about two or three weeks. Until this happens, power is vested in the Cardinals.

The Pope is the last absolute monarch, and his advisers, or cabinet ministers, are provided by the College of Cardinals which, in theory, number seventy. Only a small proportion of these are Prefects, or heads of departments, and are known as Curia Cardinals. The Government consists of twelve departments called

Congregations, each headed by a Prefect, who is always a Cardinal. The Pope himself is prefect of three Congregations. These attend to every aspect of spiritual life. The legal machinery of the Vatican consists of three Tribunals: one looks after problems of conscience and sin, another is an appeal court, and the Holy Roman Rota resembles an ordinary law court, though its sittings are in camera. The judges sit in threes, and lay lawyers who have specialized in Canon Law are allowed to plead before it. All the marriage problems of the Roman Catholic world are heard before this court.

A group of six departments known as Offices is concerned with the mundane affairs of the Church. The most important of these is the Secretariat of State, and the most influential of the Pope's Ministers is the Cardinal Secretary of State, who is the only Cardinal living in the Apostolic Palace in daily personal touch with the Pope.

A most interesting branch of the Secretariat of State is the Secretariat of Briefs to Princes and Latin Letters. In the old days this department drew up communications in elegant Latin which the Pope sent to monarchs. As there are no monarchs today who would be able to make much of such correspondence, the Secretary of Briefs translates into Latin all the numerous pronouncements of the Holy See. The *Acta Apostolicae Sedis*, which is the official organ of the Holy See, is written entirely in Latin.

The chief Latinist of the Vatican is Monsignor Antonio Bacci, Papal Secretary for Briefs to Princes, who has founded a review called *Latinitas* which champions the use of Latin in ordinary life. I was shown a copy in which a football match was reported in Latin, and another which contained an advertisement for washing powder that perhaps even Cicero might have passed.

Latin is the language in which all lectures in the Gregorian University are given, and it is also often the only means of communication between seminarists of different nationalities. Wonderful scraps of colloquial Latin may be heard in the corridors of the Gregorian, and though Monsignor Bacci might not consider them pure enough for circulation to princes, as the author of a dictionary full of Latin words for modern use, he would at any rate not disapprove of them. His dictionary, which has gone into three editions, is called *Lexicon eorum vocabulorum quae difficilius Latine redduntur*. Among the Latin equivalents for modern words are:

Atom Bomb: Globus atomica vi displodens; pyrobolus atomicus.

Boy Scout: Puer explorator.

Sea-plane: Cymba volatilis.

Motor torpedo-boat: Aligera navis tranatantia missilia jactans.

Oil-field: Regio bituminosi olei dives (Olei incendiarii).

Radar: Radioelectricum instrumentum monitorum.

Safety-razor: Novacula ab inferendis vulneribus tuta.

Television: Imaginum transmissio per electricas undas.

Tea with milk and sugar: Theana potio saccharo lacteque condita.

Toothbrush: Peniculus dentarius.

Central heating: Calefacientis aquae ductus.

Spaghetti: Farina subacta et vermiculata.

Macaroni: Farina aqua subacta ac tubulata.

Many of the congregations, and the Secretariat of State, are internationally staffed. There is not an European language, and scarcely an oriental one, which is not spoken in the Vatican. The junior members of the ministries are drawn from every part of the world and you are just as likely to meet a Chinese monsignor in the corridors as an Englishman, a Spaniard, or an Italian.

The monsignori 'clock-in' at half-past eight in the morning, and leave at half-past one. They do not work in the afternoons, except upon special occasions. It is a strange sight to see priests and friars standing in a queue in the early morning, with books and briefcases under their arms, waiting to register at the same kind of fumed oak time-clock which you would find in any factory.

In addition to the Secretariat of State and other departments, the Vatican also houses that picturesque ancient organization, the Papal Court. This is divided into the Pontifical Chapel and the

Pontifical Family. The Chapel includes all the dignitaries who are to be seen during a great ceremony in St. Peter's: those figures with ruffs and swords and members of princely houses who often bear titles which tell of long obsolete duties; it includes also the Palatine and the Swiss Guard, the Pope's confessor, a Jesuit, his private chaplains, his physician, his surgeon, the *scopatori segreti*, the servants who attend the Pope, the *bussolanti*, the ushers, the bearers of the *sedia gestatoria*, and many others. On paper the Papal Household is enormous, but actually, and in the true meaning of the word, it resolves itself into a valet, two or three servants, and a few German nuns who cook the pontiff's frugal meals and clean his flat.

§ 5

The days I spent wandering idly about the Vatican Gardens were among my happiest in Rome. I listened with delight to bird song, which I had heard nowhere else. I thought the gardens exquisite. I found quiet places under the oaks and the horse chestnuts where even the dome of St Peter's was invisible, and where there were no sounds but that of a fountain and perhaps an old gardener wheeling his barrow or adjusting a water jet.

These gardens have been loved by a number of good and saintly men in the course of the past eighty years: Pius IX sometimes rode his white mule under the oak trees; Leo XIII, St Pius X, Benedict XV, Pius XI, and, of course, Pius XII, have all walked and prayed there. Though now no longer 'imprisoned' in this pleasant place, the Popes during their voluntary confinement gave the gardens a uniqueness which they still possess; and one cannot walk there or sit under the trees, or look at the fountains, some of them modest affairs which one might find in an ordinary garden and so unlike the tremendous papal fountains of Rome, without seeing in imagination the white figures of the 'captive' Popes moving in the shadow of old walls, their red shoes treading the lawns.

'I suppose I shall never be able to travel again,' Pius XI is said to have remarked sadly as he looked down for the first time as

Pope upon the Piazza di San Pietro; and no doubt in the days before 1929 the thought of never again setting foot outside the Vatican must have been a sad one for a man who had led an active life.

Pius XI is the only Pope who took a practical interest in the gardens and laid down some fifty miles of pipes connected with innumerable irrigators, so that now over thirty acres can be watered. The lawns must be the only grass in Rome that remains fresh and green until the end of summer.

The Vatican water, so well known to millions as it makes its final spring into the sunlight in the Piazza di San Pietro, was brought into the city in 1612 by Paul V, who repaired the underground aqueduct of Trajan. Romans will tell you that the Aqua Paola is not the best drinking-water, and that it also has the unpleasing reputation of turning marble black; still there is a great quantity of it, and every visitor to Rome knows to what a height it can be flung. Before it appears in public, it runs through the papal gardens and enlivens many a fountain there.

In the highest part of the gardens, next to a grove of horse chestnuts which strew the ground in autumn with glossy 'cobblers', the Pope walks every afternoon when he is in Rome. A special covered way has been made, divided by a wall built at such an angle that the Pope can walk on one side if the wind is blowing in winter, and on the other side in summer. This is the most strictly guarded spot in the Vatican Gardens.

About four o'clock in the afternoon the gendarme on duty in the court of St Damasus claps his hands in a discreet and reverent way, as a sign to his companion on the opposite side of the courtyard to do the same; and so the signal passes through the gardens and every policeman knows that the Pope is about to step into his car and be driven to the walk. As the car approaches, each gendarme drops on one knee and salutes. The Pope strides briskly up and down for an hour or so, rarely lifting his eyes from the pages of a book. Near the walk is a replica of the Grotto at Lourdes, which was presented to Leo XIII by French Catholics, and a blue-gowned statue of the Blessed Virgin stands against the entrance, just as it does at the Grotto de Massabielle; and the water of Lourdes is represented by three jets and the invitation '*Allez boire à la Fontaine et vous laver*', and the date 1858.

I noticed a few empty cages on the way to the Pope's Walk, and these have from time to time housed animals given to the Pontiff. The last inhabitant was an eagle which was presented to Pius XI as a living reference to his mountaineering exploits when Cardinal Ratti. The bird died a few days after its master in 1939. A more appealing pet which was not kept in a cage was the favourite cat of Leo XII, an animal with which he shared his simple daily dish of *polenta*. This Pope also had an intelligent little dog, which, Cardinal Wiseman said, passed after Leo's death into the possession of Lady Shrewsbury. Another papal cat was owned by Pius IX. One can imagine the airs and graces these animals assumed in the Vatican when summoned by a papal flunkey, as this cat was, to take its place at table with the Holy Father, after which Pope and cat said goodbye and the animal was removed. Leo XIII, that distinguished looking Pope who lived to be over ninety and was the first of the apostolically austere modern Popes, kept a few deer, a couple of ostriches and a pelican. Now the only pets in the Vatican are the two canaries of Pius XII. As a lover of birds, the Pope must be happy to hear the morning and evening song in the gardens, and may perhaps contrast that cheerful sound with the silence of the birdless Italian countryside around Castel Gandolfo.

I came one day to what I think must be the most unusual of all views of the dome of St Peter's. Near the wall of Leo IV a formal garden has been made with box hedges, a central fishpond, and a whole series of archways of clipped ilex of a height and width to enable one exactly to frame the dome of St Peter's between them; a most surprising *coup d'oeil*, not unlike the one in the gate of the Knights of Malta, which uses the distant dome as the climax to a long avenue of trees. Here, of course, the dome seems almost on top of one, and when I saw it in its rustic arch, the afternoon sun was full upon it and the gallery above was black with visitors gazing down into the Vatican gardens.

I believe there are a few practical jokes in the gardens if you know where to look—jets which drench the visitor—but they are not working now. I think the last Pope to take an interest in them was jolly, childlike Pius IX, who, when in the mood, loved to drench his Cardinals.

I thought the most beautiful object in the gardens was the gay little summerhouse, or casino, made by Pirro Ligorio in 1560 for that mild, cultivated and entirely worldly Pope, Pius IV, who enjoyed an agreeable pontificate of six years. In England it was the age of Elizabeth I. The queen was twenty-seven and had been on the throne for only two years; it was the very year in which Rizzio's body went bumping down the back stairs of Holyrood; and in Rome, Pirro Ligorio was given permission to cart away from what is now the Piazza Navona as much of Domitian's stadium as he needed for the Pope's summerhouse.

The lovely building, which Lanciani called 'a perfect image of an ancient Roman country house', was built entirely of this old stone. It is a poetic composition whose charm, grace and dignity place it among the most elegant remains of the Renaissance. The paved garden is perfect: it is an oval space surrounded by stone seats like the lowest tier of a Greek theatre, and is backed by a low wall on which at intervals stand urns, each one planted with an aloe. The oval is broken only by two tall Renaissance gateways and by a classical garden house whose façade is an apricot-coloured frieze of figures in high relief.

I looked over the wall many times, enchanted by what I saw, but could never go inside, for the casino was always locked. One day, however, a gardener was sent with a key to let me in.

In the centre of the courtyard two cherubs ride dolphins on either side of a marble fountain, and two others flank the entrance, seated upon strange sea creatures which have the beaks of eagles, the webbed front legs of *hippocampi*, and the tails of fish. The fountain walls are covered with superb shell mosaics and among them, as if to accentuate the paganism of the whole design, is the many breasted figure of Diana of the Ephesians.

Amid the beauty and peace of this garden the only sound came from the jets of the fountain. The sunlight on the peach-coloured walls, the procession of classical figures with lutes and lyres, the heavy swags of fruit and flowers, all so untouched by the passing of four centuries, formed a scene I shall never forget. It was one to which, it seemed, the sophisticated Popes of the Renaissance might at any moment enter in their pride and splendour, with their red-polled Cardinals.

I returned several times to look over the garden wall, and I thought that this garden and the Fountain of the Tortoises in the Piazza Mattei were the two monuments of Renaissance Rome which most delighted me.

It was in this magic circle that Pius IV entertained his learned and artistic friends, and here he listened also to the counsel of his saintly nephew, Charles Borromeo. Pius VIII and Gregory XVI often gave audiences in the villa, but Leo XIII thought the site unhealthy and built himself another summerhouse on the highest part of the hill, now, as I have said, transformed into the Vatican Radio Station. As a guest of Pius IX, it must have been delightful, after having dined beneath the grotesques of the Vatican Library, to stroll across under the calm night sky to the little oval garden. 'Pio Nono' was the last Pope to hold a public dinner party and, having smiled benevolently upon his guests from the high table where he ate alone, he would walk over to the casino to join them for coffee.

§ 6

While I was strolling in the gardens one day with an officer of the Swiss Guard, we came to a series of old steps which lead to the famous Corridoio di Castello, the corridor which, since the Middle Ages, has stretched from the Vatican to the Castel S. Angelo. An NCO of the Swiss Guard has his quarters at the top of the steps, and I was told that it is the duty of the Guard to keep the keys of the corridor, along which it is still possible to pass secretly to the fortress.

'Naturally we hope that if the Holy Father ever asked for the keys, it would be for purely antiquarian reasons,' said the officer. 'And we always have them ready.'

An air of incredible age hangs about odd and unfrequented places such as this. They are never cleaned up for visitors, and remain just as the centuries have left them, like an old attic full of lumber which no one visits from one generation to another.

As we explored this queer, dusty bit of the Middle Ages, we came to the locked gate leading to the corridor, a place which has the attraction of a secret passage. The top is a machicolated walk and the corridor itself is a narrow, arched passage hardly wide enough for two people to walk abreast, and is roughly paved with brick and lit every few yards by windows let into the thick walls.

I thought of that terrible morning of May 6, 1527, when, aided by a fog that followed the sunrise, the armies of Charles V advanced to the attack on Rome. There were Lutheran Germans, Catholic Spaniards and Italians, but there was nothing to choose between them: they were all ruffian mercenaries who had been unpaid for months and thirsted for loot. As they stormed the Borgo, Clement VII, appalled by the fate his politics had brought upon Rome, was on his knees in St Peter's. At first he was resolved to dress in full pontificals and meet the enemy seated upon his throne, as Boniface VIII had waited for Sciarra Colonna two hundred years before: but as the cut-throats broke into the Hospital of S. Spirito, slaying all the patients to spread terror, and as the cries of the dying and the explosion of cannon were heard on the very steps of St Peter's, the Pope was persuaded to take flight along the covered corridor to S. Angelo. 'Had he stayed long enough to say three creeds,' wrote an eyewitness, 'he would have been taken.'

Wearing the enormous scarlet train of his *cappa del papa*, the distracted Pope was shown into the vaulted corridor and, to help him along, a Cardinal looped the train over his arm. Clement wept as he looked down through the windows of the passage and saw the fearful scenes in the street below and in the space before St Peter's, where the Swiss Guard was dying to a man.

The windows were so close together in the corridor that a Cardinal, afraid that the Pope might be recognized by arquebusiers from below, flung a cloak over his head and shoulders, and in that way Clement VII was smuggled into the castle. This was the celebrated occasion when, in the frantic press of refugees, one Cardinal was almost trampled to death, another was pushed through a window, and a third was hoisted up the ramparts in a basket, while a little earlier in the morning Benvenuto Cellini, aiming his arquebus through the morning mist, was one of the many who claimed to have shot the Constable of Bourbon.

Lanciani, writing fifty years ago, said that Roman mothers still sang fretful children to sleep with a lullaby which began with the words, *'Fatti la nanna, e passa via Barbone!'*—'The man with the long beard, Barbone, having usurped the name of Bourbon'—so persistent was the memory of those days of terror.

The pillage of Rome by twenty thousand Germans, fourteen thousand Italians, and six thousand Spaniards, lasted for eight days. Unspeakable barbarities were committed: Cardinals, their hands tied behind their backs, were dragged through the city and held for ransom, and one was carried in a coffin to the Capitol and would have been buried alive if someone had not paid for his release. 'The sacred precincts of St Peter's fared worse at the hands of the Catholic Spaniards and Lombards,' said Lanciani, 'than they had at the hands of the Saracens in 846. The Spaniards searched every tomb. They stripped the corpse of Julius II of its pontifical vestments; they gambled with their booty, and rested themselves by lying stretched out on the venerable altars; they used the chalices of marvellous mediaeval workmanship as drinking-cups, in company with profligate women; and they stabled their horses in the aisles of the sanctuary, preparing their litters with precious manuscripts collected by Pius II and Sixtus IV. . . . The busts of St Peter and of St Paul, the head of St Andrew, and that of John the Presbyter, were stolen respectively from their shrines in the Lateran, in the Vatican, and in the church of S. Silvestro in Capite. A German soldier hoisted on the point of his lance the spear which was believed to be the one with which Longinus had pierced the side of the Redeemer on the cross . . . the Veil, said to have belonged to St Veronica, and to bear the impression of the Saviour's features, was dragged from tavern to tavern among the jeerings and taunts of the drunken soldiery.'

The Germans were the most ferocious until drink came their way, when they lapsed into buffoonery and, mounted on mules and dressed in splendid copes and mitres, mimicked with drunken gravity the ceremonies of the Papal Court. The Spaniards excelled in cruelty and the Italians in inventiveness.

Ninety Swiss and four hundred Italians, with the Pope and thirteen Cardinals, were besieged in the castle. There were no provisions, and an occasional stew of ass meat was saved as a delicacy for the Pope. Some children who were found tying vegetables on strings for the hungry garrison to pull up were shot by the Spaniards, and a poor old woman who took a few leaves of salad for the Pope was hanged.

The unhappy pontiff upon whose head retribution for the worldly sins of the Papacy seem most unfairly to have descended, for Clement himself, though vacillating and untrustworthy, was not a bad man, wept and prayed and eventually capitulated. The jewels of the papal tiara, which Benvenuto Cellini had extracted and sewn into the Pope's garments, had to go to swell the enormous ransom. Several months later the Pope managed to leave Rome disguised as a market gardener. In the following year the final touch was placed upon his humiliation when he made friends with Charles V and placed the imperial crown upon his head. The Emperor is one of those men whom one always thinks of in his old age; perhaps Titian's portrait in the Prado is responsible for this. He was, however, an ugly, ill-formed young man of only thirty when his adroitness placed the Papacy in the hollow of his hand. Henry VIII of England, who was married to Charles's aunt, Catherine of Aragon, once thought of him as a feeble youth!

In the corridor to S. Angelo one feels, as one does in the Tower of London, that nothing cheerful could ever have happened there.

§ 7

Bewildered crowds speaking every language under the sun stride bravely through the Vatican museums from ten o'clock until two. As they do so, they cast hasty glances at a collection which could scarcely be examined in a lifetime. Nevertheless, it is a wonderful experience to pass along the endless corridors and to see, in no matter how perfunctory a manner, the great treasure house of the Renaissance Popes. One passes from Egyptian rooms to Etruscan, and from Greek to Roman, amazed by the richness of the ancient world.

Pope after Pope added to the collection, and a puritan Pope was a rare event, like the stern Adrian VI who, shocked by the paganism of Renaissance art, threatened to whitewash the Sixtine Chapel and fling the Laocoön into the Tiber.

Then there is the Pinacoteca, where silent crowds stand grouped all morning before Raphael's *Transfiguration*. The Renaissance was probably the most wonderful period for an artist that has ever been known. Rome never had any indigenous genius, and the wealth and taste of the papal court drew the great artists of Italy as to a promised land where fame and fortune awaited them.

I have often wondered, as I have walked through the Vatican galleries, how one explains the surge of genius during the Renaissance and how it was that a constant succession of great artists were at the service of the Popes. Unlike our own age, which is one of specialists, the whole of the world's knowledge could in those days be found on the shelves of one room, and it was true to say, as Pius II said of Nicholas IV, that what a scholar did not know was outside the range of human knowledge. The versatility of the great artists was astonishing: Leonardo da Vinci and his scientific experiments, Michelangelo turning his genius from sculpture to painting and architecture, Raphael giving advice about smoking chimneys to the Duke of Ferrara, and going off to paint a dead elephant at the request of Leo X, with no feeling that his art was being disparaged.

Many of the great artists were temperamental, dilatory, spendthrift and difficult to get on with, but they did not, I think, assume the airs and graces of a later time. They were essentially good workmen and were extraordinarily amenable to the wishes of their patrons, which explains many an indifferent old master.

When the beautiful and charming Isabella d'Este was decorating the four little rooms in the Reggia at Mantua, which may still be seen, she was in touch with a number of the best artists of the time, and though she wrote to them humbly, as if asking a favour when she requested a painting, she evidently considered even the most famous of them simply as an interior decorator.

Having failed to secure the services of Leonardo da Vinci, who was 'studying the course of rivers and the flight of birds', she was advised to try Filippino Lippi or Botticelli, but she preferred Perugino. Like most artists, he was in need of money and agreed to accept her commission. He then received from Isabella a detailed description of the picture she required, which was to be an allegory of the kind fashionable at that time on the battle between Love and Chastity. Her letter ended, 'you are forbidden to introduce anything of your own invention'. So poor Perugino, who painted exquisite Madonnas and saints, set to work obediently, and with no hard feelings, on a crowded canvas more suited to Carpaccio. He was continually spied upon by his anxious patron, who sent agents to his studio to report on the progress of the picture, and when Isabella learnt that, contrary to instructions, Perugino had depicted Venus naked, she briskly ordered him to clothe her, since 'if one single figure were altered, the whole meaning of the fable would be ruined'.

As one walks through the Vatican Gallery, noting what appear to be the extraordinary lapses of the old masters, one wonders how many other genuises of the Renaissance worked under similar conditions and were not allowed to introduce anything of their own invention.

A part of the Vatican museums which was always a joy to me, and gave me a feeling of light and happiness, was the gorgeous Library of Sixtus V. The great hall, encrusted everywhere like a reliquary, covered with airy grotesques, its ceilings an art gallery in themselves, is the only great library I know in which not a single book is visible. Like the classical libraries, of which it is a copy, the books were kept—for the library is no longer used—not upright as in modern times, but lying flat in beautifully designed and painted cupboards. A few special treasures are to be found in glass cases; and how surprising it is to come across the letters of Henry VIII to Anne Boleyn.

Beneath the stanze of Raphael I entered the Borgia Apartments, which I thought the most interesting of all the rooms on view in the Vatican. The moment I passed under a low marble door lintel and saw the rich rooms leading one into another, their gilded ceiling vaults framing the finest frescoes of Pinturicchio, I had the feeling that five centuries had melted away and that a bony hand was beckoning me into one of the window alcoves.

These beautiful rooms are jewel caskets which the Borgia Pope, Alexander VI, made for himself, in which he plotted and schemed for his children and in which he died. 'I am Pope and Vicar of Christ!' was his joyful cry when he had been elected, but, of course, he was not: he was merely a secular prince, an unscrupulous and greedy man whose misdeeds would hardly have been remembered by history had he occupied any throne but that of St Peter.

His son, the notorious Cesare, who haunted the streets at night, masked, and with his men-at-arms, was suspected of even more crimes than those he committed, and was a type of Italian gangster which is by no means extinct to-day. The notorious Lucrezia was a young woman with a weak face and beautiful hair, which she was perpetually washing, one suspects to maintain the famous gold. Glancing up at the frescoes I saw Alexander, Cesare and Lucrezia, beautifully painted by Pinturicchio. The portrait of the Borgia is marvellous. He kneels before the risen Christ, his fat, self-indulgent jowl, double chin and hooked beak in profile, his plump ringed hands held together in prayer; a handsome young soldier nearby is Cesare, and another young man in Roman dress is probably his brother, Giovanni, whom Cesare murdered in 1497. In another fresco Lucrezia is seen as St Catherine.

Most of Alexander's sins sprang from parental affection, and this unholy father, bad as he was, has come down to us clouded by something like the calumny which obscures the Caesars: but, as Bishop Creighton so truly said, it is difficult to judge the Borgias fairly without seeming to palliate iniquity.

I left the Borgia Apartments with the thought that I had seen few rooms so soaked in the atmosphere of a past time. Even in the Tower of London or Hampton Court one has the feeling that those who lived there have been long dead and have no further interest in the scenes of their earthly lives: but the Borgia rooms are haunted by uneasy spirits.

In the Sixtine Chapel I had an impression of exquisite blueness, the blue of the Virgin's mantle. Everyone was gazing upward at the ceiling. In a dozen languages the guides described how Michelangelo had spent four and a half years on his back upon the scaffolding, painting the ceiling, and ever afterwards had to hold a letter or a book above his head in order to read it. It would be easier to appreciate this sublime work lying on a couch with a pair of field glasses, and the guides carry little mirrors which they hand to their charges.

Michelangelo with his broken nose (broken in youth by the fiery Torrigiano) was the greatest as well as the most attractive character of the Renaissance: a sad, lonely genius, whose life was simple, whose faith was great, and whose works are like the language of another world. The day after he died in 1564—he was eighty-nine—a magistrate went to make an inventory in the house where the old man had lived alone for so many years. An iron bedstead covered with a quilt of kid-skins stood beneath a white linen canopy. Nearby was a cupboard of Michelangelo's clothes: a grey overcoat and a brown one lined with fox fur, a cape of Florentine cloth lined with satin, a satin blouse with red silk ribbons, two black hats, and nineteen shirts. The wine cellar contained a flask of vinegar and five jars of Trevi water, and in the stable stood a small chestnut pony. More than eight thousand gold ducats were found tied up in handkerchiefs or placed inside jugs and jars.

No one can leave Rome without taking away some memory of Michelangelo: the dome of St. Peter's, the Moses in S. Pietro in Vincoli, the *Pietà* in St Peter's, the church of S. Maria degli Angeli, and, perhaps above all, the heavenly blue of the Sixtine Chapel.

§ 8

The Library and the Archives of the Vatican are housed to the north of the Cortile di Belvedere, and were opened to the public in 1881. They are known only to scholars and students, and have inspired, and continue to inspire, countless learned books in every language in Europe. The chief librarian is a Cardinal who bears the resounding title, 'Librarian and Archivist of the Holy Roman Church'.

In a stillness like that of the British Museum Reading Room, the scholars and research workers sit at tables which run the length of a great hall whose walls are covered from floor to ceiling with books. The attendants move noiselessly, placing before the scholars manuscripts yellow with time, which can be deciphered only by those trained to do so. I noticed among the readers many members of religious orders in their habits, and spoke to a Dominican who is working on land tenure in eleventh century Ireland.

One of the librarians took me into the steel alcoves of the Archives and, opening a safe, placed in my hands a parchment heavy with red wax seals, each one with its signature. It was the petition sent by Henry VIII to the Pope, begging for the dissolution of his marriage with Catherine of Aragon. Though the document has been published, I was told that the names of all those who signed it have never been printed. From the moment when a King's Messenger left Whitehall with the petition and rode across Europe and handed it to the Papal Curia, it has been carefully filed away and is as fresh and new as the day it was drawn up more than four hundred years ago.

I then held the dossier of Galileo's trial; I was given a paper signed by Michelangelo; a document from Ferdinand and Isabel of Spain, with a gold seal the size of a saucer; a letter written by Benedetto Latini, the tutor of Dante; the Concordat between Napoleon and Pius VII; and an enormous parchment bearing three hundred and five signatures and seals, which was the Act of Abdication of Christina of Sweden. Then, almost as an afterthought, I was shown a Byzantine parchment signed in red ink by the first of the Palaeologi in the thirteenth century.

All these treasures were produced casually, just as a collector might show a few of his possessions to someone who was pressed for time. While I was looking at them, I noticed something I had never before seen in a great library. Every fifteen minutes the lights went out and had to be switched on again. When I asked why this was so, I was told that as scholars and others who are living in remote centuries are rather absent-minded and leave the lights on in the Archives, these are automatically switched off at regular intervals.

I was introduced to a professor who has made a special study of Papal Bulls. He told me that the Papal Chancery continued to use papyrus as a writing material long after the rest of Europe was using parchment. The use of papyrus went out only about 1022. In the old days Papal Bulls were bound with either a silk cord, to which the leaden seal, or *bulla*, was attached, or a cord of hemp. The silken Bulls were *litterae gratiosae* and the hempen ones were *litterae executoriae*, so that you could tell at a glance whether the Bull brought good or bad news. The silk Bulls were also attractively decorated with the Pope's full name, but the less pleasant ones bore only his initials, surrounded by an ominous black decoration.

Bulls were sometimes so stylized, and written in strange Gothic characters known as Lombard, without marks of punctuation, that it was necessary to send a transcription with them, and this script was only abolished by Leo XIII about sixty years ago.

Though everyone knows that the Pope takes a new name upon election, it is not so well known that he signs the originals of Bulls with his old Christian name, which is the only time he ever uses it again. It is, of course, never heard in the Vatican until he lies dead, when the Chamberlain approaches his bedside and softly calls him three times by the name he bore before he was Pope.

One of the most closely guarded rooms in the Vatican is that in the Chancery where the great seal, or *bulla*, is kept, with which all the acts of the Church are signed. Anyone found near it without a reasonable explanation might easily find himself excommunicated. It is a heavy metal stamp, several feet in height, worked by an arm, or lever, which gives an impression of the heads of St Peter and St Paul facing each other, and the name of the reigning Pope.

Gold seals, which were frequently used by monarchs in their communications with the Vatican, were rarely used by the Papal Chancery, though this did occasionally happen. The earliest example is the letter sent by Leo X granting Henry VIII the title of 'Defender of the Faith'.

§ 9

The fabric of St Peter's is maintained by a race of hereditary acrobats who have been employed on the task, father and son, for centuries and have earned the name of *Sanpietrini*. They are trained to be utterly careless of heights and, as they climb about the dome or swing in bosuns' cradles from column to column near the roof. I am told the spectacle is like that of a trapeze act without a net. The *Sanpietrini* dig the tombs of the Popes and, as I have said, a selected few were entrusted with the excavations beneath the high altar. In former times many of them lived with their families on the roof, and you may still see some of their houses there, near the post office in the shadow of the dome.

The head offices of the *Sanpietrini* are near the Sacristy, and one day when I went there I was surprised to be shown into a room whose two beautifully painted eighteenth century doors showed the royal arms of England under a Cardinal's hat. Of course they could have belonged to no one but the last of the Stuarts, but their presence in this office puzzled me until I was told that some years ago they were saved from an old house that was pulled down near the Sacristy and placed in their present position. This was the house occupied by the Cardinal Duke of York when he was made archpriest of St Peter's in 1751. I was pleased with this discovery. I had not thought it possible to find an unknown Stuart relic at this late date, as these attractive and symbolic doors can, I think, claim to be.

I had gone to the office to learn something about the illumination of the dome, which is the greatest feat of the *Sanpietrini* and is seen only at long intervals. Though the bells of St Peter's are now rung by electricity, the *Sanpietrini* shuddered when I asked if they ever lit the dome by turning on a switch. No true Roman, and certainly no member of the *Sanpietrini*, could bear the thought of St Peter's outlined in hard, cold electricity.

I was told that the custom of illuminating the basilica goes back to the time of Bernini, who designed the hanging trays to hold the flares between the columns of the colonnade, and the method of lighting has been handed down by tradition through the *San-*

pietrini and even the kind of tallow used is a special mixture for which they have the recipe.

In past times St Peter's was illuminated regularly twice a year, for Easter and for the feast of St Peter and St Paul. At Easter only flares were used, because of the uncertainty of the weather, but for the feast of St Peter and St Paul flares and *lanternoni* were used together, these being candles in foot-high paper shades.

It costs about a thousand pounds to illuminate St Peter's and three hundred and sixty men are required, divided into groups of two or three, each man responsible for several flares. As the clock is about to strike nine all the men are hiding in the darkness, ready at a signal to swarm down the ropes with their torches. At the first stroke of nine the signal is given by the chief of the *San-pietrini* who lights the flare on the summit of the cross and immediately the men fling themselves out into the darkness, touching off the flares and swarming over the dome like bees, until, as the clock finishes striking, the whole of the dome is outlined with flickering tongues of fire.

'What happens when a member of the *Sanpietrini* is too old to perform these acrobatics?' I asked.

'Then we retire, but to other tasks about the church. There are a hundred daily tasks to be done. You may see an old man sweeping the nave in the early morning. Ah, but when he was young what a *bella figura* he made upon the dome!'

These faithful attendants are like the guardian spirits of the church, and one wonders if perhaps the blood of those workmen who rebuilt St Peter's runs in their veins.

CHAPTER TEN

Rome in rain – a pilgrims' hostel – the Castel S. Angelo – Tras-tevere–the game of 'Morra'–how the Pallia are made–the island in the Tiber–an English Cardinal–goodbye to Rome

§ 1

I met a delightful young couple in St Peter's who spoke English with a faint and puzzling accent. When they asked me to tell them from what part of England they came I was defeated, but making a guess, said East Anglia. They laughed and confessed that they had never been to England; they were Danes.

They invited me to lunch with them in a pilgrims' hostel in which they were staying, within a few steps of St Peter's. It stood on the banks of the Tiber, facing the embankment, and only a few yards from that street sign which had delighted me from the moment I first set foot in Rome—Lungotevere in Sassia. The hostel was a large and beautiful Renaissance palace that, having come down in the world, appears in old guide books as a military academy. During Holy Year in 1950 it was turned into a hostel for pilgrims and has remained so ever since. A shallow flight of stairs made for long dead Cardinals mounts to vast apartments and anterooms which have been matchboarded into spartan dormitories where the pilgrims rest their weary bones. The room in which they write postcards and look at television still suggests toher scenes and another world. Several batteries of horse artillery could have performed a musical ride in the splendid courtyard.

My new friends did not live in the hostel, which was reserved for groups and bands of pilgrims, but in the garden, where a few self-contained rooms and bathrooms had been built for the use of individual travellers. This garden delighted me. It was full of gigantic trees, and was a wilderness of brambles and weeds where wandering hens laid their eggs in dead fountains buried in impenetrable shrubberies. Lying in the bushes were pieces of broken marble bearing half-effaced coats-of-arms. It was a queer and attractive place, and when I learned that my friends were returning to Denmark in a day or so, I went to the office and arranged to take over their room in the garden. So I made my fourth move in Rome, and found myself in quarters which, though as stark as a cell in a monastery, were in many ways the most congenial I had found.

I was completely free and could come and go as I liked; and I thought myself extremely fortunate. My room was imperceptibly cared for by pale and spectral young orphan girls in hideous black garments and thick woollen stockings, who performed their duties under the eyes of nuns.

The most surprising things about the hostel were the pilgrims themselves. The mediaeval conception of a pilgrim was a venerable man with a long beard, hastening before it was too late into the odour of sanctity; but in this hostel one had difficulty in finding anyone much over the age of twenty. They came from all countries and their faces shone with health and enthusiasm. Sometimes they trooped about with their village priests, and I thought them an encouraging glimpse of young Europe and an interesting aspect of the social revolution. Young people now climb alps, go to winter sports, visit the Riviera and Rome, and do many of the things once enjoyed only by the wealthy, with no luggage but a knapsack and practically no money. Since the Middle Ages there have never been so many people roving in bands or groups about the Continent, and I should like to think that this knowledge of other nations may lead to international understanding and a more peaceful world.

When I had moved into my garden room, I reflected that there is much to be said for changing one's background in a strange city. There is always a temptation to settle down in one place and try to make a temporary little home, and it should be resisted. A move is like a fresh start in life; you orientate yourself afresh and discover new aspects of the same city. The expensive Rome I had seen from the Via Veneto was different from the businesslike Rome of the Via Venti Settembre; and how different was the

Janiculum, where the nuns pursued their unhurried lives, from this bustling pilgrims' Rome, with its cameras, its maps, its nylon stockings drying on the high window ledges, its babel of different languages, and its air of constant arrival and departure. My village street now led in one direction to St Peter's and in the other to that marvellous part of Rome—Trastevere.

It was now, I realized almost with a shock, October; perhaps the most beautiful month of the year in Rome. The trees had changed into a hundred shades of red and gold. Sometimes an unearthly pearly light washed the city, sharp and clear like a spring morning on the Acropolis, and in the evening that curious pinkish flush in the streets, which lasts only from dusk to darkness, seemed to be accentuated. Masses of splendid fat grapes, black and white, filled the street stalls. They reminded me that Bacchic revels made respectable by church processions—a collaboration that would not have surprised Gregory the Great—were taking place in the wine towns of the *Castelli Romani*, where the grape harvest had now been gathered. Some pungent whiff of this Virgilian moment seemed to enter Rome in the morning with those odd-looking wine carts and their rows of little barrels, the driver sitting up beneath a huge ribbed umbrella, in shape like the shell of some shabby and discredited Aphrodite. They trundled into Trastevere and replenished the tavern cellars with more than usual jollity and it was often in my mind to go out to Frascati and look up my friends of the wine vaults who were, I supposed, now knee deep in the new vintage: but I never did so.

My introduction to the garden room was memorable for my first Roman thunderstorm. The afternoon had been more than usually hot and disagreeable and Trastevere smelt and felt like Tangiers in summer. Then in the small hours of the morning I awakened to hear thunder rolling overhead and to see every detail of my little room in flashes of blue light. Suddenly rain began to drum on the frail roof of my hut, and glancing through the window I saw a moving sheet of descending water pouring into the thirsty soil.

I stayed at the window while the lightning flashed and the thunder cracked; and the whole scene was lifted out of the ordinary for me because this was Rome. The ancient Romans believed that lightning by day was sent by Jupiter, but at night by an obscure deity named Summanus, who apparently took over from him after dark. They believed that a man killed by lightning when he was awake was always found with closed eyes, and one killed when asleep, with his eyes open. It was forbidden to place such bodies on the funeral pyre: they had to be laid in the earth. They also believed that the only mammal which was immune from death by lightning was the seal, and that was why, as Suetonius says, Augustus, who was terrified of lightning, always wore a sealskin vest.

Some of the flashes were so startling that I dropped the curtain at times and turned from the window, not surprised to remember how often Roman temples were struck by lightning and aware now why those superstitious people, who could never do any-thing without first peering at the liver of some wretched heifer, dreaded the thunderbolts of Jupiter.

The rain continued all the next day, and I thought that Rome looked incredibly shabby under a wet and cloudy sky. The colours of the buildings, which owe their beauty in sunlight to their uneven patination, now stood revealed in this grey wetness rather like the reveller who returns in fancy dress by daylight. Rain has an unbelievably dislocating effect upon the public services of Rome. This storm, which London would scarcely have noticed, stopped the trams and even interfered with the telephones! And the surprised expression on the faces of the Romans was amusing as they went to work with umbrellas and mackintoshes, or skidded along on their Vespas, as if some fearful natural calamity had struck the city. Even the hens in the garden appeared rather indignant, and female-like seemed to blame it all on the cock, who sat apart, bedraggled and with an angry yellow glint in his eye, hunched beneath a garden seat.

When the rain ceased, however, and the sky cleared, there followed days more beautiful than any I had known in Rome. The air was washed clean; the burning heat had gone; and there was an almost April-like freshness in the early mornings. Awaken-ing earlier than usual one day before the sun was up, I put on a dressing-gown, and in slippers crossed the road to the Tiber embankment and looked down on the river. It was running much faster now, and the pale, cloudy green was changing to brown, though there were still many islands of reeds and grass in the centre which had grown up during the low water of summer. It was quiet and lovely and Rome was not yet awake. The red circle of the Castel S. Angelo rose only three bridges away.

There was a movement far below, near the river. A poor old man and a woman, who had somehow survived the storm, perhaps beneath the arch of a bridge, crept out into the cold morning and urgently began to cut rushes as if the rising Tiber were about to steal even that from them. With arms full they hobbled back through the dripping grass; and I wondered if they would mend chairs with them or plait baskets.

The sun first struck the gold wings of St Michael on the summit of S. Angelo before flooding down upon the time-nibbled ramparts, then colour flooded back all over Rome and bells began to ring for early mass.

§ 2

From the Tiber embankment I often watched the changing lights and shadows on the Castel S. Angelo. Though so battered and mediaeval, it is still in its general outline the tomb of Hadrian.

In the last months of his life the Emperor, his body swollen by dropsy, went to die at Baiae on the sunny Bay of Naples. He suffered agonies and ordered his doctors and bribed his slaves to kill him. He found out the exact place beneath his heart where a quick stab would be fatal; but no one had the courage to take the life of the master of the world. Strangely enough, as he lay in his pain and humiliation, the story grew that he could perform miracles. There was a blind girl whose sight was restored after she had kissed his knees; there was a blind old man from Pannonia who came to him and was touched and healed. How ironical that such stories should have gathered about the death bed of a sick man who could not help himself.

As he lay in a villa overlooking the Bay, he composed those five lines which, more than anything ever penned in Latin, have tempted and eluded the skill of the translator—Hadrian's *Address to his Soul.*

> *Animula, vagula, blandula,*
> *Hospes comesque corporis,*
> *Quae nunc abibis in loca,*
> *Pallidula, rigida, nudula,*
> *Nec ut soles dabis jocos?*

A collection of a hundred and sixteen English versions of this wistful little stanza were collected in 1876 by David Johnston and published by the *Bath Chronicle*, a rare little book. Now, of course, many new versions have accumulated in the eighty years that have passed, for everyone who writes a book about Hadrian has an irresistible compulsion to tackle those five lines and give his own rendering.

Byron, when nineteen, attempted it, but added a line, which was not quite fair. He wrote:

> *Ah! gentle, fleeting wav'ring Sprite,*
> *Friend and associate of this clay*
> *To what unknown region borne*
> *Wilt thou, now, wing thy distant flight?*
> *No more, with wonted humour gay,*
> *But pallid, cheerless, and forlorn.*

Charles Merivale ventured on a more strictly accurate rendering:

> *Soul of mine, pretty one, flitting one,*
> *Guest and partner of my clay,*
> *Whither wilt thou hie away,*
> *Pallid one, rigid one, naked one,*
> *Never to play again, never to play?*

And recently I came across one which I liked, written by Thomas Spencer Jerome in *Roman Memories.*

Genial, little, vagrant sprite,
Long my body's friend and guest,
To what place is now thy flight?
Pallid, stark, and naked quite,
Stripped henceforth of joke and jest.

It was on July 10, in the year A.D. 138, that the 'genial, little, vagrant sprite' left the body of the great Hadrian and took its flight into the shades. The Emperor's ashes were kept at first in Cicero's villa at Puteoli, then brought to Rome to be placed in the mausoleum on the banks of the Tiber which the Emperor had started to build three years before his death.

The tomb must have looked rather like a gigantic wedding cake, a distant predecessor of the Victor Emmanuel Monument. It was a circle of white marble, with two tiers of columns surrounding it, beneath which stood more than sixty statues. Upon the top thousands of cypresses, the thin dark *cupressus pyramidalis* still found in Italian cemeteries, rose in a vast cone, and this hanging forest was drained by an ingenious system of shafts, and surplus water carried down through the building into the earth and the Tiber. Where the trees rose to a point it is believed there stood the giant bronze fir cone now in the *Giardino della Pigna* of the Vatican, though some think that on the summit was a golden chariot in which stood a statue of Hadrian, driving four horses.

The Emperor designed this strange building himself, and the effect must have been that of a new and original type of pyramid. As in the Pyramids, a long sloping ramp led up inside the tomb to the burial chamber in the heart of the building. All we see now is the immense brick core, for every scrap of marble has long since vanished.

In this mausoleum were deposited the ashes of Hadrian, Antoninus Pius, Marcus Aurelius, and Septimius Severus, an emperor who, like Hadrian, had known Britain well.

This mighty tomb succeeded the circular Mausoleum of Augustus on the opposite bank of the Tiber, which by the time of Hadrian was full of the ashes of the Caesars.

All these urn burials were safe and protected, century after century, until the Gothic raids on Rome in the fifth and sixth centuries. One of the most terrible and sacrilegious moments was when the barbarians forced the bronze gates of the imperial tombs and rushed inside to tear the urns from their niches and scatter the ashes of the Caesars in their search for gold.

I was surprised by the size of the Castel S. Angelo. To realize what a vast stronghold it is, you must become lost in the dark passages, find your way by winding staircases and come suddenly into glorious rooms covered as completely with bright 'grotesques' as the Vatican Library; you must emerge into unexpected courtyards stacked with stone cannon balls, pace the sentry walks, and see the embrasures where Cellini fired his bombards. The first object that caught my eye was the shaft of a Renaissance lift. It had been installed by Pope Leo X about 1513 to save the back-breaking climb to the papal apartments on the top floor. It was, of course, worked by man-power. Teams of men operating an intricate system of winches, brakes and pulleys, would crank the Pope and his Cardinals to the top, inch by inch. It is a pity that the lift itself has not survived; it was probably the most beautifully decorated lift that has ever been known.

The long sloping ramp, part of the original mausoleum, winds round and round, and eventually you come, in the very core of the building, to a place where the walls, once faced with marble, are of immense blocks of travertine, and here the urn of Hadrian was deposited. There is nothing there now, but on the wall nearby someone has had the touching thought of putting a tablet bearing the famous *Animula, vagula, blandula*.

I read these lines in the almost dark passage, thinking no longer of Popes and Anti-Popes, but of that more distant scene above the Bay of Naples where Hadrian lay dying. That the soul is a guest of the body and must someday leave and continue its mysterious journey, is the essence of his little verse, a sentiment which surely no Christian Father could condemn. It may be the thought of an agnostic, but not of an atheist, and it is impressive to encounter it here: the last question of a man who had examined all faiths, including Christianity, in his search for truth.

Upon the top floor, where apartments as glorious as any in the

Vatican are to be seen, I came to a surprising sight: the bathroom of Clement VII, who was besieged in the castle during the Sack of Rome in 1527. Who could have dreamed, reading accounts of the Sack and of the starving garrison, that the Pope had this glorious little bathroom, centrally heated with hot air circulating within hollow walls, where hot and cold water fell into a marble bath. Every inch of this perfect Roman room, floor, walls and ceiling, is a gay pirouette of painted stucco, and recalls the famous bath of Cardinal Bibbiena in the Vatican, which Raphael decorated with scenes considered so improper that the room was walled up for centuries.

Anyone who knows the Castel S. Angelo will, I think, agree with me that it is one of the most frightening buildings in the world. One does not need to be psychic, or even unduly sensitive or fanciful, to feel that agony and suffering still cling to the dark corridors. Mounting the stone steps in the dim light, it would not surprise one to hear a fearful scream, or opening a door to come upon some scene of murder or torture. There are beautiful rooms in which a man might sit listening to music, while a few yards off are dungeons; in at least one of the gayest rooms a trapdoor opens on an oubliette. Compared with S. Angelo, the Tower of London is almost a happy place.

I thought of those dreadful women of the tenth century, Theodora the Senatrix and her even more terrifying daughter Marozia, who made and unmade Popes and, says Gibbon, may have been responsible for that strange myth of the Middle Ages, Pope Joan. I remembered that great Pope, Gregory VII, who had to take refuge in S. Angelo from the fury of the Emperor Henry IV, whom he had humiliated at Canossa.

I saw the prison which Beatrice Cenci occupied before her execution. Though modern research has cast a new light on this tragedy, Shelley remains more powerful, and people prefer to think of her as the innocent victim of an unspeakably vile father whom she killed to save her honour.

She was executed on a September morning on a scaffold at the end of the bridge facing S. Angelo. As the beautiful head of Beatrice bowed to the headman's axe, romance and poetry claimed her for ever, and it is as *La bella Cenci* that she has continued to live in the memory of Rome and of the world.

Another ghost to be met at every turn in this castle is that of the Borgia Pope, Alexander VI. There is a record of him standing upon the ramparts one day in the Jubilee Year of 1500, watching his beloved daughter, Lucrezia, cross the Ponte S. Angelo on her way to the Lateran and the prescribed visit to the great basilicas. She rode a richly caparisoned jennet and her husband Don Alfonso rode on her right hand, a lady of her court on her left. Behind came the captain of the papal guard, Rodrigo Borgia, and an escort of two hundred nobles and their ladies.

As she crossed the bridge, the Pope, who may have been wicked but was certainly one of the most doting parents in history, watched her with eyes brimming with affection. Gold was the passion of his life, and he stayed watching until his golden-haired daughter was lost to sight.

How unexpected it was to discover in one of the grand papal apartments of the castle a large canvas representing 'The Entry of James III of England into Bologna'. There is a large classical archway; a crowd of people; travelling coaches in the background; in the foreground a woman pointing out the exiled Stuart to her children; and a Cardinal, who has doffed his red biretta before royalty, makes a welcoming gesture towards the archway. James wears a bell-bottomed wig, a blue silk coat, with the star and riband of the Garter, and he carries a walking-stick hooked over his arm. Among the little group of Jacobites in attendance is a striking young lad of about fourteen who must surely be Bonnie Prince Charlie. It is a pity that the picture is not dated. I imagine that it must have been commissioned in those days when James was given royal honours at the Papal Court and when it was believed that the Hanoverians might be displaced; until, as hope grew faint and died away, the picture, like others in one's own experience, migrated to the attic, in this instance the Castel S. Angelo.

The view from the top of the castle is one of the grandest in Rome. To the west is St Peter's and the long narrow corridor running from a bastion of the castle to the Vatican, and to the east is the whole of Rome, with the Tiber looping round the Campus Martius, a sight never to be forgotten.

§ 3

Someone introduced me to a priest who exactly fitted my idea of an eighteenth century abbé. He was charming, worldly, amusing, and obviously accustomed to moving in the best society. His hobby was miniature photography. This mutual interest drew us together, and it might have been disappointing to some, seeing us solemnly pacing beneath the trees, to know that we were discussing nothing of more importance than focal lengths and the virtues of thin emulsion developers.

I hope, should some Veblen be studying the social peculiarities of our time, that he will enter miniature photography under the heading of 'conspicuous expenditure'. When those small cameras were invented about thirty years ago, amateur photography was practically a suburban hobby; at any rate no one could claim that the possession of a camera was a social asset. The snob value of the costly camera may possibly date from the moment when the Duke of Windsor, as Prince of Wales, was not ashamed to be seen in public with one. Since then they have become more expensive and more popular, and their mechanical deficiencies have called into existence a great mass of attachments, such as the priest possessed, until the owner is faced with so many alternatives that by the time he has decided which instruments to use, the subject he desired to perpetuate has either vanished or is no longer worth a photograph. Bernard Shaw was one of the earliest miniature camera addicts and, referring to the reckless expenditure of film the small camera encourages, remarked that such machines are like the codfish that produces a million young in order that one may survive.

One evening, while I was writing in my garden room, there was an urgent tapping on the window, and the priest stood outside, a tripod in one hand and his suitcase of equipment in the other. His eyes shone with excitement.

'Come quickly!' he cried. 'There is not a moment to lose! The Castel Sant' Angelo is on fire!'

Without pausing to consider how this could have happened to the venerable and impregnable hulk, I ran out and together we raced across the garden and the courtyard to the Tiber embankment. There I saw the castle.

In honour of one of the innumerable congresses which are always meeting in Rome, it had been illuminated with flares. It was ringed about with hundreds of yellow spurts of fire. A blue floodlight was focused upon the figure of St Michael on the summit, and the scene, which was so mediaeval that I felt the fourteenth century had returned, was reflected in the Tiber. The countless flares cast a flickering reddish glow over the whole castle, which stood out against the dark sky, awesome, threatening, yet somehow at the same time gay. Fire, the devouring enemy of castles, had been tamed and domesticated and, like a circus tiger, was performing its pretty trick for the enjoyment of Rome.

The priest was enthusiastic. Should he use a five or a nine centimetre lens? What exposure should he give? Above all, was he in the right place? Though he had all night to take his photographs, he acted as though the illuminations might be extinquished at any moment. Deciding that we were on the wrong side of the river, he rushed off across the bridge and erected his tripod on the opposite bank. And he was right. The view was even more magnificent. One could imagine that some mediaeval Pope and the Holy Roman Emperor were feasting together in this gala fortress during a rare moment of friendship and agreement.

Hours later I returned to look at S. Angelo. The oil flares were still burning, yet here and there a dark gap showed where one had expired.

§ 4

I was sitting in a café in Trastevere, which was much like any other café in Rome except that the habitués perhaps gave one a swifter, keener summing up as they glanced for a moment from their absorbing affairs.

'If you want to buy gold or diamonds, or if you had lost anything and wished to give a reward and no questions asked, this is where you would come,' said my companion.

'Gold and diamonds—here?'

'Yes; and they say, with what truth I don't know, that all the streets round about are honeycombed with passages into which everything of value stolen in Rome finds its way.'

I now fancied that I observed something slightly sinister in the glossy-haired young Borgias round the *espresso* machine. A superb fifteenth century assassin slipped a *gettone* in the bar telephone and began to speak coaxingly, pleadingly, gesticulating all the time with his free hand. He bowed and swayed as he spoke, and moved to and fro to the length of the telephone cord, and once, catching the eye of a friend, he suddenly and cynically winked. Then he dropped the telephone and rejoined his companions with one of those diffident Roman shrugs. I thought that possibly somewhere in Rome a flattered woman had just replaced the receiver too.

What incredible airs and graces these young Italians put on in public. This, I suppose, is *far figura*, which the dictionary defines as 'To have a striking appearance; to look well'. It goes deeper than that, however, and has a profound spiritual significance. To cut a good figure, to have *panache*, to preserve one's 'face', are necessary to the self-respect of the Italian, and to reduce him in his own estimation is to earn his eternal enmity. The swashbucklers and bravos of the Renaissance must have been great exponents of *far figura*: one senses it in the portraits of the time: the insolent eyes, the negligently held glove, the ringed hand on the hilt of a sword. In Trastevere *far figura* is as important as being Roman. One might think it peculiar that anyone should wish to claim relationship with the populace of old Rome, the most crafty, fickle and disgraceful mob in history, yet the Trasteverini do so all day long. Actually, I believe their origin is Corsican. One hears the self-satisfied *noialtri* all over Rome, but nowhere more frequently than in Trastevere. It means 'people like us' and has the same complacent significance as the Spanish *nos otros*. I once asked a friend who lives in Rome what he thought a group of unusually engrossed men were talking about, and he replied, 'Of themselves and Rome, but, first, of themselves!' Pass close to any group at a café table and listen for those words, *noialtri* and *i Romani*, and you will not be disappointed. The Romans in general, and the Trasteverini in particular, appear to find themselves of perpetual interest.

It was while I was leaving this café with my Italian acquaintance that we met the spitfire. She was a bold, sturdy young girl who kept pace with us, and said to her friend, in a voice intended for us:

'Pah, these foreigners! They come to Rome and look at the palaces, but why don't they come and look at the filthy hole I have to live in!'

'Quickly, tell her we'd like to see it!' I whispered.

Rather reluctantly, afraid of cutting a *brutta figura* I suppose, my friend overtook her and did as I suggested. Finding herself addressed courteously in Italian, she was deflated. Her eyes slowly travelled in contempt from our feet to our eyes, then uttering a Trasteverine insult, which even my friend could not understand, she looked for a moment as though she were about to fly at us. Instead, she shrugged her shoulders and walked haughtily away; and I pitied the man who ever tried to argue with her or to get the better of her.

Trastevere is not, however, composed entirely of bravos and spitfires. Humanly speaking, it is the most interesting region in Rome. It is a small, outward bulge of land in a loop of the Tiber, which corresponds to the Campus Martius a little higher up on the opposite bank. Its one wide main road is surrounded by a network of streets and alleys throbbing with life and vitality. There are lanes where the washing hangs from house to house and where the intimate garments of the district are flown like pennants. Here may be seen the last vestige of that Papal Rome which our ancestors knew two hundred years ago. As so often in Rome, one feels that the faces are not modern, but those to be seen in the art galleries. They are the people in the background; the minor gentry, the grooms, the postilions, the porters, the men-at-arms.

If Trastevere were to dress in mediaeval costume once a year, as Siena does, it would provide one of the most remarkable spectacles in Europe.

Though the noisy Vespa is here, as everywhere, there are also the more human sounds of Martial's Rome. In a thousand little workshops, some in cellars and basements, men work at a multitude of varied tasks, and are never too busy to spare a moment for the man next door. I met a venerable inventor of a machine for grinding car parts who, mistaking my mild interest for mechanical enthusiasm, drew me into his dark cavern and explained the process in the greatest detail. 'And they send me work even from Milan!' he said proudly. A factory which once made snuff for the Popes is still busily at work in Trastevere, and you can see hundreds of little Carmens there, making powerful looking cigars and cigarettes. Not far off I saw girls turning out thousands of cartridge cases. In what was once a garden, a potter was firing his kilns, while in a shed nearby were hundreds of pots and plates wet from the potter's wheel, and no doubt made of that same Vatican clay mentioned in antiquity.

A gay and festive air is given to Trastevere by shops full of *confetti*, the sugared almonds given away at weddings and sometimes strewn, as the ancients strewed nuts, before the happy pair. There are bowls everywhere of not only the usual pink and white almonds, but also green, red, and pale blue. The Trasteverini are inclined to marry among themselves and when a wedding takes place a family will cheerfully run into debt in order to launch a son or a daughter sumptuously into married life.

In the last century Augustus Hare said that murder, though a less common crime in the Rome of his day than in England, was more frequent in Trastevere than elsewhere, which he attributed to the 'extreme excitement which the Trasteverini display in the pursuit of their national games, especially that of Morra'.

This game is now forbidden by law, but I have seen it played many a time. It is simply the art of guessing how many fingers you and your opponent have held up, and it is, of course, the *micare digitis* of ancient Rome: but to turn a corner suddenly and see a circle of men or youths playing *morra* is to imagine that some violent street auction is in progress. It happens quickly, the shouting is loud and the gesticulation magnificent; then, at the sight of a stranger, the game stops and sometimes the players vanish round the corner.

One of the finest sights in Trastevere is the Piazza S. Calisto, where an old fountain casts up a tuft of water in front of the Church of S. Maria in Trastevere, the first church, it is believed, ever to be dedicated to the Blessed Virgin. To one side, and occupying an angle of the square, is the old palace of S. Calisto, which technically is not in Rome at all, but in the Vatican City. It is one of several buildings belonging to the Holy See which were granted extraterritoriality by the Lateran Treaty.

I thought the front of the Church of S. Maria, gleaming with mosaics, a wonderful memory in miniature of the first St Peter's. Once you had crossed the enormous atrium of Constantine's church, the building that faced you must have looked much like this. Indeed should anyone wish to imagine what the first St Peter's was like, let him study the atrium of S. Clemente, the exterior of S. Maria in Trastevere, and the interior of St Paul's Without.

I came to a dusty piazza and a gay little fruit market. There was an exquisite girl selling grapes. I walked up to buy some, and immediately a hundred angry voices shouted at me and menacing men advanced on all sides. I glanced round, bewildered, when I noticed with dismay that I had walked into a scene that was being filmed! This sort of thing is liable to happen to anyone in Rome. Palaces, bridges, street markets, are all at some time or another film sets. Two or three vans drive up; electricians arrange their lights; the camera men set up their tripods and cameras; actors move casually into the scene; and Rome does not always stop to watch. I apologized to the director and, feeling rather foolish, for my appearance had stopped the film, I took refuge in an archway. Beyond it I saw a scene of peace and beauty, the courtyard of the Church of S. Cecilia in Trastevere.

Three Franciscan friars were talking together on the edge of a marble fountain. Behind rose a tall, exquisitely shaped Roman cantharus of white marble, which must have come from some ancient baths, and from its graceful mouth rose a thin jet of water, while another fell from the body of the vase into a marble basin. In the background was the porch of the church, upheld on columns of African marble. One of the brothers was resident in Rome and the other two were pilgrims; and all three were Belgians. They had just come from the nearby church of S. Francesco a Ripa, which stands on the site of the monastery where St Francis stayed in 1219, when he came to Rome to ask the Pope's consent for his new order. The friars could speak of nothing else, and what was more wonderful than anything—they had prayed in the cell of St Francis.

Maderna's famous figure of St Cecilia is beneath the altar of the church and shows her as she was seen by those who opened her tomb in the catacombs in the sixteenth century. It was the reproduction of this statue which I had seen in the Catacomb of St Calixtus. Underneath the church I saw the Roman vapour bath in which the saint was locked by her persecutors. The lead water pipes are still embedded in Roman masonry.

Near the church door is the tomb of an Englishman, Cardinal Adam Easton of Hertford. He had been titular Cardinal of the church of S. Cecilia during the reign of Richard II, and he died in 1397. I stood fascinated by this link between Trastevere and the clean little county town in England, and when I had the time I went to the admirable library of the British School in Rome to find out how Adam Easton came to die so far from home. It was a strange and violent story.

When the Popes returned to Rome from Avignon the Sacred College was composed almost entirely of Frenchmen, and the King of France hoped to retain the Papacy in his pocket. Gregory XI, who had returned to Rome with the help of St Catherine of Siena, died in 1378. As the Cardinals met to elect his successor, a bloodthirsty Roman mob shouted for a Roman, and not a Frenchman, and to enforce its demands even thrust spears up through the floorboards of the room where the Conclave was sitting. The startled Cardinals elected a Neapolitan, Bartholomew Prignano, Archbishop of Bari, who, they hoped, might prove an obedient sheep. Instead, Urban VI, as he chose to be called, turned into a tiger and began his reforms by reforming his Cardinals. He was rude, violent and extremely tactless, and some Catholic historians have even considered him a bit mad: but I do not think he was, for reasons I shall give in a moment.

Hating the Pope they had chosen, most of the Cardinals fled from Rome and elected an Anti-Pope, Clement VII; a guerrilla war then began between Urban and Clement in which the whole of Europe took sides. France, of course, sided with Clement, and England with Urban.

Those Cardinals who had not been able to escape, among them Adam Easton of Hertford, were taken about by Urban as his prisoners, and for the only time in history the Pope stood alone without a single Cardinal. At one time, when he was besieged in a castle, the angry Pontiff would appear regularly at a window two or three times a day with bell, book and candle, to lay down a barrage of excommunication on his foes. He then put to death all the Cardinals charged with plotting against his life, with the exception of Adam Easton, who was spared at the request of Richard II. Urban then created an entirely new Sacred College.

The reason why I believe Urban VI was sane is that all through these fearful times St Catherine of Siena sheltered him with her saintly wings and stood by him. They present a strange picture: the violent and ferocious old Pope hurling his anathemas about like guided missiles, and the Saint always telling him to curb his temper and to be mild and gentle! And when he had got the better of his enemies and was able to return to Rome, this terrible old man took off his shoes and entered St Peter's barefoot. That was a side of Urban which perhaps few saw except St Catherine. She was in Rome, just before her death, when the usual Roman mob was persuaded to storm the Vatican. The Pope ordered the gates to be flung open, while he sat waiting on his throne, his chest bared for their daggers. When they saw him, the mob dropped their weapons and fell on their knees. If Urban's conduct were 'akin to lunacy', as Monsignor Baudrillard has said, at least no one can say that he lacked moral and physical courage.

The Englishman from Hertford survived the Pope for eight years. The manner of his escape was interesting. He smuggled a letter out of prison—*De sua calamitate*—to Benedictines in England. They went to Richard II, who pleaded successfully for his life. Before releasing him, however, Urban stripped him of his rank and Easton went out to hide himself as a poor monk for eight years until, with the death of Urban and the election of Boniface IX, he was restored to his dignities. I reflected, as I stood by the tomb in Trastevere, that it held the bones of an English scholar who had lived his life before the good Duke Humphrey and the Balliol men were born, who are always regarded as the first English scholars of the Renaissance.

§ 5

The pallia which the Pope sends to new archbishops and metropolitans have been woven for centuries by nuns in Trastevere. I found that their convent actually adjoins the church of S. Cecilia. The building is old and vast and I was told that it had once held a large and wealthy Benedictine community, but now only thirteen nuns live there in great poverty.

Every year on January 21, the feast day of St Agnes, two lambs are carried to the altar of the church of St Agnes, on the Via Nomentana, during the singing of the Agnus Dei.* They lie in little wicker baskets, decorated with blue ribbons. After the Pope has solemnly blessed them, they are sent to Trastevere to be cared for by the nuns until Maundy Thursday, when they are shorn, and from their wool about twelve pallia are made every year.

These are narrow bands of white wool three fingers wide, decorated with six black crosses. They are worn round the neck and over a chasuble in such a way that one strip falls in front and one behind, both sides resembling in shape the letter Y.

In early days this most ancient of vestments was worn only by the Pope, and even today he alone may wear it on all occasions. It is infinitely older than the papal tiara, and the moment when the Pope is invested with the pallium at his coronation is the most

---

* They are blessed by the Abbot-General of the Canons Regular of the Lateran, after which they are taken to the Vatican for the Papal blessing before they are delivered to the nuns.

solemn in the ceremony; perhaps one might compare it with the unction of a lay coronation. 'Receive the pallium,' are the words used as it is placed in position, 'to the glory of God, and of the most glorious Virgin, His Mother, and of the blessed Apostles, St Peter and St Paul, and of the Holy Roman Church'. As the strip of lambswool descends upon the shoulders of the Pope, he becomes the shepherd of Christ's flock; at least that is the meaning which later ages gave to this investment.

The early popes gave the pallium to bishops as an honour; Gregory the Great sent the first pallium to be bestowed in England to St Augustine in Canterbury. Nowadays it is uncanonical for a newly appointed archbishop to exercise his function until he has received the pallium, and having received it he can wear it only on specially solemn occasions; and it is always buried with him.

Having woven the new pallia, the nuns of Trastevere hand them over not, as one would imagine, to the Vatican, but to the subdeacons of the Lateran—for such is the rigidity of Christian tradition—who hand them to the subdeacons of St Peter's, who hand them to the canons, who place them in a golden casket beneath the high altar of St Peter's, immediately above the traditional tomb of the Apostle. So several beautiful and venerable ideas and customs are mingled in this act. One thinks of the Lamb of God and of the Good Shepherd bearing the sheep upon His shoulders; one thinks, too, of the mediaeval pilgrim letting down cloths and rosaries to be sanctified by contact with the tomb of St Peter.

§ 6

Trastevere is connected with the Rome of the Seven Hills by several bridges and—food. It is the fashion to cross the bridges and to dine late in Trastevere, as late as in Spain, at one or other of the little restaurants where, in my experience, the food and cooking are twice as good as anywhere else in Rome, and much less expensive.

I felt that I had achieved a more than casual status when I could

find my way about Trastevere alone at night. I admit the first
time I was lost there I was a little startled by the intricate alleys,
sometimes with hardly any light except a spark burning at a
street shrine, but I comforted myself with the thought that few
modern assassins and robbers wear masks as they used to do in the
fifteenth century. I have dreaded masks since I was a child, and to
meet a man in a mask on a dark night in Trastevere would be my
idea of chilling horror. It is extraordinary, reading the lives of the
Borgias, to note how frequently men went masked at night in
Rome; people apparently thought nothing of it. They referred to
these strollers rather dreadfully as 'masks'. It was a 'mask' who was
seen talking to the Duke of Gandia on the night he was murdered; Cesare Borgia was often a 'mask'. These 'masks' gave the
last touch of panic to an age of elegant crime.

Feeling as I do about masks, it took some courage to approach
a figure who had all the qualities of a 'mask' as he stood in the
darkness, and to ask in indifferent Italian the way to the Viale
Trastevere: but the response of this possible 'mask' cured for ever
my fear of the dark lanes. He became immediately a voluble
Trasteverino in shirt sleeves, who had been captured in the
Western Desert, who knew a number of English nouns and a
whole verse of *Sarie Marais*, and he cheerfully accompanied me
through the labyrinth to the bright lights.

I had two favourite restaurants. One was almost next to the
Porta Settimiana and claimed to be the home of Raphael's mistress, La Fornarina. I always chose a table beneath a vine trellis
that covered a small garden. It was cool at night and delightful to
sit there and compose a simple Italian meal from the long type-
written menu. The cooking was excellent and was done not far off
to a chorus of cheerful voices and the clattering of plates. People
from the other side of the Tiber began to arrive at about ten
o'clock, and one might have been in Madrid. Fashionable-
looking young women were willing to be brought here by pillion
on a Vespa, and by eleven o'clock the streets round about were
full of these parked wasps. The musicians would arrive as soon as
the tables were occupied, a man with a guitar and a vocalist, who
played and sang, and, having passed round the hat, would go off to

the next restaurant on their beat. No Italian ever fails to give something to these often indifferent musicians, just as a beggar is never refused.

My other restaurant was one patronized almost entirely by Trasteverini, indeed I think the only foreigners I ever saw there were those I brought with me. The entrance to this place was separated from the street by a bead curtain through which one passed like Alice through the Looking-Glass, to find oneself in a series of rich and delicious kitchen smells. It was a restaurant noted for its fish soup, an Italian bouillabaisse, a rich fruit salad of the Mediterranean. There were prawns, shrimps, lobster and clams in it, codfish, bits of octopus and squid, and anything else that happened to be in the fish market that morning. It was a pleasing and satisfying dish, and you were not expected to eat anything else. They also composed an excellent *fritto misto di mare*, which was almost as good as the *zarzuela de mariscos* of Barcelona, the highest praise I can give.

By midnight the restaurant sounded like a cocktail party that has achieved that carefree moment when cigarettes are left to burn out on walnut and mahogany, and out of the great babel of voices could be distinguished the words *i Romani . . . noialtri . . . noialtri . . .* and *i Romani.* I once asked a man how long a pedigree was necessary before such words might be used, and he replied that seven generations born and bred in Trastevere made a man a genuine *Romano di Roma.* I was amused one evening to discover that an Italian friend, whom I had taken to this *trattoria,* understood only half of what was said to him. The Trasteverini are bilingual; they speak Italian like everybody else, but they prefer their own racy and ironic dialect.

My walk back at night took me past the lonely red tower of the once powerful Counts of Anguillara, and into the square where the statue of an elegant frock-coated and top-hatted figure stands in the lamplight above the taxis, and most surprisingly turns out to be the Chaucer-cum-Phil May of Trastevere, the dialect poet, Giuseppe Gioacchino Belli. He seems to have been the re-incarnation of Pasquino, and was the most fortunate of poets: marriage with a wealthy wife did not strangle his inspiration, but gave him the leisure to follow his bent, and also the fine top hat which has been immortalized with him.

One night I went into the best confetti shop in Trastevere and acquired several kilos of white, blue, pink, red, yellow and green sugared almonds. I bought a special box and had them carefully packed and addressed to a friend in England whose daughter was about to be married. Then I innocently faced the problem of sending a parcel out of Italy,

The angry sibyls in black who sit behind the grilles of Italian post-offices hissed at my parcel, then contemptuously dismissed me by attending to the man behind me in the queue; and it took me some time to discover, as I believed, that I was expected to take it to the central railway station. I wasted half-an-hour in queues there, to be told to go to the central post-office in the Piazza di S. Silvestro in Capite. Behind this building is a squalid room where all those who wish to send a parcel outside Italy, if it be only to Corsica or Sicily, are obliged to comply with outrageous bumbledom. First I had to buy for a hundred lire a declaration form to be completed in triplicate, stating that I was sending *confetti* to a friend, then I was passed to the Customs officers, who charged me a hundred and ten lire for another form and ripped open my carefully packed parcel. They passed it to another official, who was ready with brown paper, string and lead seals, and at last I was given the parcel and was entitled to have it weighed and stamped. I saw it vanish down a chute with the feeling that it might reappear at the door or come back to me through the window. Actually it arrived speedily in England.

The counter of the parcels office was strewn with old trousers, shirts, blouses and skirts, alarm clocks, children's toys, bunches of grapes, and all sorts of objects which people were sending to their friends and relatives. Even Italians were ignorant of the regulations and produced massive parcels sewn in sacking which had to be ripped open and re-sewn after examination.

A woman described to me the red tape in which she was entangled when she inherited a small legacy from a foreign country.

'For weeks I tramped from ministry to ministry,' she said,

'filling in forms, giving the names of my grandmother and my mother's maiden name, answering hundreds of questions, finding that I had used a form that did not bear the proper stamps, sitting in ante-rooms all over Rome, until one day I burst into tears and said to the officials, "I renounce it! Take it and do as you like with it! I never wish to hear anything about it again!" And I rushed from the building.'

§ 7

It was a lovely morning, with no wind and not a cloud in the sky, and it was my last morning in Rome. The air had that silk-like quality, as if filtered through crystal, which is surely the gift of Greece to Rome and comes after the first rains, etching domes, palaces and temples in unforgettable clarity. As I walked beside the Tiber, I saw the red bricks of Hadrian's tomb reflected in the yellow-green waters of the river and I could see the front of S. Spirito in Sassia, and, still more distant, the dome of St. Peter's.

The *giornelli,* or as some call them, the *girarelli*, were turning as usual, surely the laziest form of fishing ever devised. Protruding from boats moored to the bank are windmill-like nets which revolve in the current. Presumably the fisherman lurks within sight of these contraptions and if a fish is caught rushes out and pounces upon it before the *giornelli* returns it to the Tiber: but on the countless occasions when I have watched these nets I have seen them perpetually and optimistically turning, and always empty.

When I came to the Ponte Palatino I saw a man with a long bamboo rod, letting his line drift down towards the Cloaca Maxima, and, as I have always hoped to see a man catch a fish from a bridge, I lingered near him. It would have been wonderful to have seen a fish landed at this particular place which, as so many ancient writers have said, was where the best *lupi* were to be caught. Old books identify the *lupus* with the pike, but I think modern scholars believe it to be the shad. Nothing happened, and I became tired of waiting and crossed the bridge to look upstream.

Here I was faced by one of the most romantic sights in Rome, the little island in the Tiber. It is a small wedge of land in the centre of the river and it still looks like a ship, as it did in Roman times. It is crowded with buildings and might be a mediaeval castle sailing down the river. Though the island is moored to the banks by a bridge and is therefore easily accessible, I had never explored it; and this I now decided to do.

Of all places on earth which a medical man might care to visit, the Isola Tiberina is, I should say, the most inspiring. Nearly three centuries before Christ the island was sacred to Aesculapius, and a temple to the god of healing and a hospital for the sick stood there. Today the whole island is occupied by one of Rome's best hospitals, St John Calybit, tended by the Brothers of St John of God.

While I waited in the little central piazza, wondering which bell to ring, a motor ambulance came rushing along the embankment and turned across the bridge to the island, to draw up at the out-patients' department. Nearby was a large pharmacy where a great number of poor people were receiving medicines from the brothers, who looked like Benedictines in their thick black habits with a broad scapular and hood.

I was shown up to a room hung with portraits of the Hospitallers, the *Fate-bene-fratelli*—or the 'Do Good, Brothers', as they are popularly called. The founder of their institution, St John of God, was a Portuguese soldier who, when wounded in battle, determined to devote his life to God. Upon his recovery, in 1538, he gathered around him others, all laymen, who wished to help the poor and heal the sick. They maintained a hospital and a pharmacy where they gave medicines to the poor, as I had seen the Brothers doing that morning. Their curious name originated with an almsbox which they placed in the church on the island, with the words '*Fate bene, fratelli!*' written upon it.

The Prior entered the room with two brothers, one of whom was an Australian. They responded to my interest in the most friendly way and were delighted to show me the hospital. As we toured the bright wards and the modern operating theatres, they told me that fifty-one brothers from twelve different countries work in the hospital, which employs a large lay staff that includes thirty doctors, five dentists, two pharmacists, and a hundred and twenty others.

I thought how strange it was to come across X-ray rooms and laboratories in a group of buildings which, from the banks of the Tiber, suggests straw pallets and alchemists.

'We performed four thousand, six hundred major operations last year,' said the Prior, 'and treated a hundred and sixty-four thousand out-patients.'

One of the brothers, who is writing the early history of the island, took me down to water level to show me the staff and serpent of Aesculapius which can still be seen carved on what in Roman times represented the prow of a ship.

'It is an extraordinary story,' he said. 'About 291 B.C., when Rome was suffering from a pestilence, it was decided to send a delegation of priests and doctors to Epidaurus, in Greece, to seek help from Aesculapius in his famous temple. The answer was original. One of the snakes which were kept in this temple made its way to the ship in which the Romans had come and coiled itself up there. The delegation returned, rejoicing at such a great honour, and no sooner had the ship berthed in the Tiber than the snake slithered overboard and took refuge in the reeds of the Isola Tiberina. The Romans believed this to be a sign that Aesculapius wished a temple to be built there, which was done, and at the same time, in remembrance of the ship which had carried the snake to Rome, the island was given the form of a ship. In the centre rose an obelisk, which represented the mainmast.

'The temple became famous and sick people even from foreign countries visited it to consult the doctors and to drink the miraculous water which still exists in a well in the Church of St Bartholomew, which we will visit in a moment. Like the temple at Epidaurus, this Roman temple of Aesculapius became famous for its dream cures. Whether the patients were drugged with opium or some other narcotic that produced dreams, whether the visions were simply hallucinations, or whether one of the priests acted the part of Aesculapius and in the dim light spoke to the patients and effected a mental cure, or whether hypnotism entered into it, we cannot say. But these dream cures were famous here and in Greece, and it seems that the snakes played their part in the cures and were trained to flicker their tongues over any ailing part.

Dogs were also sacred to Aesculapius and were trained to lick the patients.

'That the island in the Tiber which used to be a hospital two hundred years before Christ is still a hospital today would, of course, be amazing in any other city but Rome. . . .'

We went up to the dark church of St Bartholomew, founded in 1100 by the Emperor Otho III. Ancient columns from a Roman temple uphold the roof; and we gazed down into the well whose waters were famous before the time of Christ. I wondered whether Rahere had been cured of his malaria upon the island of St Bartholomew, and whether the vision of the saint appeared to him in a place so famous for visions, bidding him found a church in London. It may well be that the origin of 'Bart's' is to be sought in the island of Aesculapius.

I told the brother I was sorry to have discovered this wonderful little island of healing on my last day in Rome. If only I had been familiar with it earlier, I should have returned many a time. And when I stood on the Tiber embankment and looked back at the island, I thought that in a world in which evil is striving for the mastery of the minds of men, it is with happiness and gratitude that one sees in places such as this how a good deed can grow and prosper through the centuries. To seek out good thoughts and to reverence them is the privilege of those who have lived for no matter how brief a time in the mother city of the western world.

The next morning, as the aeroplane rose into the air, I saw Rome for a moment, shining in the sunlight of another day. I looked down with gratitude upon the city where I had learnt many things: but one does not say goodbye to Rome.

Charles Andrew Mills
1760—1846

Towards the close of the seventeenth century a London goldsmith named Matthew Mills sailed from Gravesend for the West Indies.[1] He was to found, in the island of St Kitts, the family of prosperous planters to which Charles Andrew Mills belonged.

His grandfather, also a Matthew Mills, was killed in a duel fought at daybreak on a lonely beach on the island of St Kitts, on November 19, 1752. The son of the duellist, and the father of Charles Andrew, was Peter Matthew Mills, who died in 1792 leaving Charles Andrew (his third son) £10,000 and certain sugar plantations. Mills's mother was Catherine Hamilton, the descendant of Walter Hamilton, a soldier of fortune, who had arrived in the West Indies about 1690 with a privateering expedition. Hamilton claimed kinship with the Dukes of Hamilton, and found favour with Sir Timothy Thornhill, who made him captain and adjutant of the forces which he enlisted to resist the French, in 1713 Walter Hamilton was appointed Governor of the Leeward Islands, with the rank of Lt-General.[2]

Mills is frequently mentioned in the records of St Kitts as 'the Hon. Charles A. Mills', a prefix which denoted that he was a member of the Legislative Council. He was also well known in London, though what he was doing until the age of forty-six is a mystery which perhaps awaits solution in the old Colonial files of the Public Record Office and in the annals of St Kitts. The earliest reference to him known to me is in a letter which Keppel Craven wrote to Charles Kirkpatrick Sharpe in 1808.[3] 'I am expecting a visit from Mills on his way to the Western Ind,' wrote Craven, from which it is clear that Mills, then forty-six, was already well known to that group of aesthetes and amateur archaeologists—a group which included Edward Dodwell, the Greek traveller, and Sir William ('Topographical') Gell—with whom he was to spend his old age in Rome.

On the occasion mentioned by Craven, Mills was evidently returning to the 'Western Ind' to become Collector of Customs in Guadeloupe, then under British rule, a post he held from 1809–1817. At the end of that period he was dismissed under circumstances which seemed to him unjust. Two disgruntled letters from him are to be found in the Liverpool Papers in the British Museum,

[1] Oldmixon, John: *The British Empire in America.* 2nd Edition, 1741. Vol. II P. 295.
[2] French, George: *Answer to a Libel.* 1719.
[3] *Letters from, and to, Charles Kirkpatrick Sharpe.* 2 vols. 1888.

Vol LXXIX. These are the papers of Lord Liverpool, who was Prime Minister at the time. Mills wrote from 16 Queen Ann St, Marylebone, London, on September 11, 1817, to Charles Arbuthnot, one of the joint-secretaries of the Treasury.

'It is certainly a circumstance of some mortification that after near eight years service, during which period my best efforts have been employed to render myself useful, to find myself dismissed without recompense.

'I can only suppose that the Claimants for Treasury patronage are so numerous that it is impossible to meet the views of all. My dismissal would be rendered less painful if Lord Liverpool would be gracious enough to present me to the Prince Regent, and would do me the honour to recommend me as a Servant of the Public who has conducted himself with Integrity in the several situations he had held under Government.

'I should value the Honour of Knighthood as a Testimony of Approbation and it would ever be a gratifying Circumstance to me, to have this Proof of having merited his Lordship's Protection.'

Nearly a month passed and Mills, having had no reply from the Treasury sent a second letter to Charles Arbuthnot, dated October 6.

'My health requires a little Change of Scene, and I am induced to go to the Continent for a Short Time before I receive an Answer to the Request made to Lord Liverpool in my letter to you. I am induced to hope that His Lordship will not refuse this small Mark of Favour to a Person who has worked hard for eight years in an unwholesome Climate, and who waives his Claims of Remuneration, but who certainly wishes to evince to the World that he has served the Public faithfully.'

Mills arrived in Rome late in 1817. There is a curious story that he was accompanied by a young man who was supposed to be an adopted son. Dr Alfonso Bartoli, Director of the Palatine, to whom I owe this information, says that he remembers having seen a letter written by this mysterious young man, but it has now been lost. Shortly after Mills arrived in Rome, Caroline, Princess of Wales, the estranged wife of the Prince Regent (and afterwards Queen), came there in the course of her Continental travels. Sir William Gell was her chamberlain. Mills and Gell were old friends, and Mills began to attend the royal dinner table. If he still entertained any hopes of a knighthood, or any favour from the Prince Regent, this must have been the swiftest way to end them.

In 1820 both Mills and Gell were witnesses for the defence during Queen Caroline's trial for adultery before the House of Lords. Mills's evidence was crisp and to the point: he had dined many times at the royal table, but had never seen anything to criticize in the conduct of his hostess. The Windsor Archives, in which the proceedings of the trial are now lodged, contain a letter from Mills to the solicitor for the defence; it was another letter about the nonpayment of money. He pointed out that he had received only £58 16s for his expenses during the trial, instead of £108 11s. His letter was written from Paris on November 15, 1820.[1]

'It could not be your wish not to do what was proper,' he wrote, 'nor can it meet the views of Her Majesty that her Friends should not only be exposed to great inconvenience by their Detention, but also to pecuniary Embarrassment. The fact is that considerable extra expense will be incurred by my Journey being delayed. I must now travel in a covered Carriage which require more Horses, and everything is doubled while crossing the Mountains. . . . It is most repugnant to my Feelings to have a Correspondence of this nature forced upon me which perhaps in Delicacy ought to have been avoided.'

Back in Rome, Mills returned to the villa on the Palatine Hill whose possession, and the strange outward shape it took under his ownership, constitute his only claim to fame. In 1818 he had acquired this property jointly with Sir William Gell, but later became the sole owner. It was an old house which had stood for centuries above the ruins of Domitian's palace and was called the Villa Spada. Its chief feature was a small frescoed portico designed and painted by Raffaellino del Colle, showing Venus lacing her sandals, Jupiter pursuing Antiope in the form of a satyr, and other mythological scenes, which Mills employed Camuccini to restore in 1824.

Soon, however, the shades of Strawberry Hill and Fonthill Abbey were to cast their improbable shadows upon the Palatine Hill, and, perhaps under the guidance of a fashionable English architect who may have been wintering in Rome, the Villa Spada emerged as the Villa Mills, complete with pinnacles, battlements, casements and cloisters. Upon the spandrels of the pointed arches were medallions containing a rose, a thistle and a shamrock, and upon the gateposts two large sculptured thistles reigned alone. This has caused Mills to be termed 'an eccentric Scot', though his eccentricity was merely the architectural mode of the time and the thistles were probably a sign of pride in his mother's descent from Governor Hamilton of the Leeward Islands. Such was the strange Gothic building in which the last dinner parties were held upon the Caesarian mount.

Mills was not apparently a pleasant individual, indeed only Lady Blessington found him charming. He had a different effect upon Henry Fox, who dined with him and Dodwell in 1827 and described them as 'always particularly odious'. A few days later Fox dined with the Blessingtons, when the only other guest was Mills. 'Lady B. thought it distinguished to confess aloud,' he wrote, 'or rather to profess without provocation, her total unbelief in Christianity, to which Mills gave his simpering acquiescence.'[2]

[1] Windsor Archives. Papers re Trial of Queen Caroline. Box. 10. 10.
[2] Journal of the Hon. Henry Fox, edited by the Earl of Ilchester. 1923.

In the following year, 1828, Lady Blessington was walking in the garden of the Villa Mills, 'with our amiable friend the owner, Mr C. Mills,' when Napoleon's mother arrived and Lady Blessington was presented. Henry Fox was in Rome again in May, 1830, and found Mills and Gell a couple of querulous old bachelors whose friendship had evidently become threadbare. He went on a picnic with them to Veii and noted Mills's acid behaviour to Gell, and on the following morning he had breakfast with them in the Villa Mills when 'both snapped at each other, but Mills was quite the aggressor. They evidently have a strong dislike one for the other under the pretence of great regard'.

In 1842, when Mills was eighty-two years old, Harriet, Lady Granville asked him to rent the villa to her, but he declined to do so. Writing to the Duke of Devonshire, she described a morning on the Palatine and said that she had seen 'Mr Mills's garden, all full of roses, Cape jessamines and heliotropes, himself and Lady Charlotte Bury driving off from his door rather damaging the effect'.[1]

That, as far as I know, is the last glimpse of Charles Andrew Mills. He died four years later, on October 3, 1846, and was buried in the Protestant Cemetery. His tombstone gives his age as eighty-six, but the entry in the burial register of All Saints Church, Rome, signed by James Hutchinson, Chaplain to the British Residents in Rome, gives it as eighty-seven. The Villa Mills then came into the possession of Colonel Robert Smith and in 1856 it became a convent of the Order of the Visitation, when a new wing was added which is to-day the Palatine Museum. The Villa Mills itself was pulled down in 1926 and remains of the ancient palace beneath it were then excavated. There are two good photographs of the Villa Mills, before and after its demolition, in Margaret R. Scherer's charming book, *Marvels of Ancient Rome*. [1955.] The thistle gate-posts are illustrated in Lanciani's *New Tales of Old Rome*, page 325.

Mills made two wills, one in Paris on June 27, 1842, and the other in Rome. I have been unable to trace the Roman will, but a copy of the French one is in Somerset House. He left all his property, except that in Italy, to his niece, Catherine Amelia, Baroness Gallus de Glaubitz. The appraised value of the estate, as recorded in the Probate Act Book, 1847, was 'one thousand pounds, within the Province (of Canterbury)'.

I am indebted for many of the biographical details in this brief account of an elusive character to Mr S. W. Shelton, who drew my attention to the Liverpool Papers, and to Oliver's *Caribbeana*, to Mr E. O. Challenger of St Kitts, for information about the Mills and Hamilton families, and to Mr Chester L. Shaver, who kindly sent me a copy of the French will.

[1] *Letters of Harriet, Countess Granville.* 1894.

Bibliography

Barry, W., *The Papal Monarchy*

Bury, J. B., *The Invasion of Europe by the Barbarians*

Carcopino, J., *Daily Life in Ancient Rome*

Cesare, R. de, *The Last Days of Papal Rome*

Crawford, F. M., *O Roma Immortalis*

Creighton, M., *A History of the Papacy*

Dill, Samuel, *Roman Society in the Last Century of the Western Empire*

Fowler, W. Warde, *Social Life at Rome in the Age of Cicero*

Frazer, J. G., *The Fasti of Ovid*

Frothingham, A. L., *The Monuments of Christian Rome*

Gibbon, Edward, *The Decline and Fall of the Roman Empire*

Gregorovius, Ferdinand, *History of the City of Rome in the Middle Ages*

Hale, J. R., *The Italian Journal of Samuel Rogers*

Hare, Augustus, *Walks in Rome*

Hayward, F., *A History of the Popes*

Hutton, Edward, *Rome*

Kirby, P. F., *The Grand Tour in Italy*

Lanciani, Rudolfo, *Pagan and Christian Rome*, *New Tales of Old Rome*, *Ancient Rome*, *The Destruction of Ancient Rome*, *The Ruins and Excavations of Ancient Rome*

Lowrie, W., *Christian Art and Archaeology*

Lyall, A., *Rome Sweet Rome*

Northcote, J. S. and Brownlow, W. R., *Roma Sotterranea*

O'Flaherty, H. and Smith, J., *O Roma Felix*

Parks, G. B., *The English Traveller to Italy*

Richmond, I. A., *The City Wall of Imperial Rome*

Rodd, Rennell, *Rome of the Renaissance and To-day*

Rostovtzeff, M., *A History of the Ancient World*

Scherer, M. R., *Marvels of Ancient Rome*

Story, W. W., *Roba di Roma*

Toynbee, Jocelyn and Perkins, J. W., *The Shrine of St Peter*

Tuker, M. A. R. and Malleson, Hope, *Handbook to Christian and Ecclesiastical Rome*

Wiseman, H. N., *Recollections of the last four Popes*

GUIDE BOOKS

Baedeker, Karl, *Rome and Central Italy*, 1930

Muirhead, L. Russell, *Rome and Central Italy (Blue Guide)*, 1956

Nagel, *Rome and its Environs*, 1950

Index

For convenience of reference certain entries have been collected under headings in bold type. The headings are: Arches; Catacombs; Churches; Emperors; Forum; Fountains; Museums; Obelisks; Palaces; Piazze; Popes; Porta; Rome, ancient buildings and customs; Sacks of Rome; Saints; Vatican City; Via; Villa.